To: Sabi.

I trust you will find some useful information here on executive pay.

Best wishes,

Bill Oler

Understanding Executive Compensation & Governance

A Practical Guide
3rd Edition

Edited by Irving (Irv) S. Becker and William (Bill) M. Gerek
Korn Ferry Hay Group

About WorldatWork®
The Total Rewards Association

WorldatWork is a nonprofit human resources association and compensation authority for professionals and organizations focused on compensation, benefits and total rewards. It's our mission to empower professionals to become masters in their fields. We do so by providing thought leadership in total rewards disciplines from the world's most respected experts; ensuring access to timely, relevant content; and fostering an active community of total rewards practitioners and leaders.

WorldatWork and its affiliates provide comprehensive education, certification, research, advocacy and community to our members and the total rewards community. WorldatWork has more than 70,000 members and subscribers worldwide; more than 80% of Fortune 500 companies employ a WorldatWork member. Founded in 1955, WorldatWork has offices in Scottsdale, Ariz., and Washington, D.C., and is affiliated with more than 70 human resources associations around the world.

WorldatWork Society of Certified Professionals® is the certifying body for eight prestigious designations: the Certified Compensation Professional® (CCP®), Certified Benefits Professional® (CBP®), Global Remuneration Professional (GRP®), Work-Life Certified Professional® (WLCP®), Certified Sales Compensation Professional (CSCP)®, Certified Executive Compensation Professional (CECP)®, Advanced Certified Compensation Professional (ACCP)™ and Master Certified Compensation Professional (MCCP)™.

© 2016 Korn Ferry Hay Group

ISBN: Hard back: 978-1-57963-378-3
       E-book: 978-1-57963-379-0

Editor: Erin Ryan Goodnow
Design: Hanna Norris

WorldatWork.
The Total Rewards Association

www.worldatwork.org

Contents

PROLOGUE

This third edition of our book has been retitled *Understanding Executive Compensation & Governance: A Practical Guide* to reflect our expanded scope on critical topics that boards of directors must address. Our book is a reference guide for compensation committees and other board members, HR professionals, corporate management and other decision makers. Its purpose is to furnish readers with easy access to a wide range of executive compensation and board governance topics by providing insight on current best practices, design techniques and trends.

Understanding Executive Compensation & Governance is a hands-on, practical guide that we hope helps in the evaluation and refinement of executive compensation programs and board governance. A major challenge confronting boards and executive compensation professionals today is establishing a consistent and transparent connection between pay and value added. This must be done in an environment in which regulators, shareholders and even lawmakers carefully scrutinize all aspects of executive compensation, benefits and perquisites — especially the relationship between pay and performance. In addition, boards need to both evaluate top executive talent and the board itself, while also managing succession for the CEO and board members in an orderly and thorough process.

We believe companies are well-positioned to respond to current challenges. The Dodd-Frank Wall Street Reform and Consumer Protection

Act of 2010 (Dodd-Frank) and rulemaking by the U.S. Securities and Exchange Commission (SEC) have raised the bar on governance standards. The SEC and various stakeholders will continue advancing this process, so ensuring board and senior-executive accountability is as important as ever. The requirements of the say-on-pay provisions under Dodd-Frank and enhanced compensation disclosure have improved transparency of the programs and facilitated competitive analysis, thus providing a clearer idea of how companies think and operate. In addition, accounting rules allow flexibility in designing compensation programs that better reflect pay-for-performance principles. Compensation expense no longer dictates plan preference. This level playing field provides compensation committees with additional vehicles to use in designing executive pay programs that meet business strategy needs.

These issues are only some of the topics we address in this new edition. The following chapters are a compilation of articles by Korn Ferry Hay Group consultants from *The Executive Edition* series, supplemented by material written specifically for this volume. This is not a technical reference per se; in focusing on what works best, we have avoided presenting too much detail on tax, accounting and regulatory issues.

This book is targeted mainly to a U.S. audience; nonetheless, with its focus on design, we believe it is a useful resource for non-U.S. companies operating in a pay-for-performance environment. In this edition, we have updated and expanded previous chapters with new material as well as developing several new chapters. Notably, we added two new parts to the book on topics that we have captioned the CEO Life Cycle and the Board Life Cycle. These address the issues of compensation, evaluation and succession of CEOs and board members, respectively. Other new chapters cover executive pay in bankruptcy proceedings, retention awards, sign-on bonuses and compensating executives at portfolio companies of private equity firms, as well as litigation regarding executive and director compensation.

The chapters are grouped in five sections:

- "Part I: Executive Pay Design and Strategy" examines issues relating to overall executive compensation strategy and includes design issues relating to the basic components of pay — base salary, annual incentives, equity and non-equity long-term incentives — plus discussions of related topics, such as peer group selection, performance measurement, competitive benchmarking, stock ownership guidelines, executive benefits, equity retention and employment agreements.

- "Part II: Governance, Disclosure and Compensation Committee Initiatives" begins with a discussion of compensation committee governance followed by a chapter on the tools compensation committees use in overseeing executive compensation. We next discuss the basic principles affecting current executive compensation disclosure, followed by a chapter on the recent requirement to address potential risk in executive compensation programs.

- "Part III: The CEO Life Cycle" starts with a summary explaining the three core topics of CEO evaluation, succession and special compensation. Because much of the preceding chapters address executive compensation matters that are especially pertinent to CEOs, we devote a chapter to the often-neglected area of CEO evaluation and feedback before turning to the critical area of planning for CEO succession. Too often these topics are examined in isolation when a more effective approach is to consider them together. Finally, we discuss two special topics relating to CEO pay — compensation strategies related to various CEO transitions and CEO compensation when preparing for an IPO.

- "Part IV: The Board Life Cycle" identifies three core components of board evaluation, succession and pay, following a similar approach as was taken in Part III regarding CEOs. In today's governance climate, the duties and responsibilities of directors have expanded significantly; boards cannot fall behind in addressing the challenges and opportunities presented in a fast-changing business world.

- "Part V: Executive Compensation in Special Settings" addresses the compensation issues that arise in extraordinary situations, such as mergers and acquisitions, initial public offerings, bankruptcy, private equity portfolio companies, and other special situations. We also include a chapter on executive and board compensation in tax-exempt organizations. Finally, we end with a chapter on international compensation which addresses executive pay issues in ten major countries: Australia, Brazil, Canada, France, Germany, Italy, Mexico, the Netherlands, Singapore and the United Kingdom.

I would like to thank WorldatWork for publishing this third edition of our book and Korn Ferry for its ongoing support of our executive compensation and board initiatives. Korn Ferry acquired Hay Group in December 2015 and our executive and board compensation consulting team is now a part of Korn Ferry Hay Group. I also want to thank our clients who furnished insights in working together on executive pay and board projects.

Special thanks once again go to Bill Gerek, my co-editor. As the long-time editor of Hay Group's *The Executive Edition,* he has created a consistent theme and tone for our executive compensation and board publications over the years. Most of all, I would like to thank the consultants who have contributed their time, effort and intellectual capital to making this book possible.

— Irving (Irv) S. Becker
North American Leader —
Executive Pay & Governance

Major Executive Compensation Trends and Challenges

Say on Pay

Subject to certain exceptions, the 2010 Dodd-Frank Act requires publicly traded companies to seek an advisory vote of shareholders on executive pay at least once every three years. This extremely important development provided shareholders with a distinct voice in pay matters and armed proxy advisers with additional clout in influencing the proxy voting process. Having a true "pay-for-performance" executive compensation program has never been more important.

In addition, a purely legalistic approach to the Compensation Discussion and Analysis (CD&A) section of the annual proxy statement no longer suffices. Companies and compensation committees, out of necessity, must become effective communicators to furnish shareholders and others with clear, user-friendly explanations of the rationales behind their pay decisions. With this heightened scrutiny, there is a temptation to play it safe and develop pay programs similar to those of their peers. This would be a mistake; compensation strategies that work for both executive and shareholders must consider the unique situation and business strategy of each company.

Institutional Investors/Proxy

Say on pay has considerably augmented the ability of institutional investors and their proxy advisers to influence executive compensation. In addition to demanding that compensation committees establish a clear link between what management accomplished and the amount of pay delivered, advisers can recommend a "no" vote on say on pay. Further, shareholders can vote against compensation committee members if desired changes are not made without explanation of the committee's rationale.

Institutional investors continue to focus on performance metrics, thus complicating the work of compensation committees. They no longer simply look at dilution models and vote yes or no; they now use detailed financial formulas or "black box" approaches to determine pay-for-performance relationships and are active in criticizing companies that do not meet their guidelines. Some companies are focusing exclusively on financial metrics causing them to shy away from nonfinancial measures that are difficult to disclose and describe. This reliance on only financial metrics may not be in the best long-term interests of the shareholders.

Compensation Philosophy

An organization's executive pay programs should be based on a formal, written compensation philosophy closely tied to the primary business strategy. It should be reexamined annually along with other human resources programs, such as performance evaluation, communications and management succession.

Long-Term Incentives

Most companies today use some form of portfolio approach to long-term incentives (LTIs) in order to ensure the adaptability and resiliency of their LTI program. Performance-based plans, which include full-value plans with performance-based vesting and traditional stock options to which performance features have been added, have become the favored approach for LTIs and the largest portion of the LTI mix. Add in more disclosure to address the Dodd-Frank rulemaking and pressure from institutional shareholders to do a better job of linking pay to performance, and it is not difficult to understand the continued interest in performance-based equity plans. These plans can, however, be complicated to design and monitor, and they often increase the workload of compensation committees.

Compensation Committees

Dodd-Frank has raised the profile and responsibilities of compensation committees — much like Sarbanes-Oxley did for audit committees — which has resulted in increased scrutiny of their processes and decisions. Compensation committees are now more involved in the details of executive compensation planning and implementation, especially regarding long-term incentives.

With the proliferation of performance plans and the need to quantify and justify total pay, compensation committees must focus more on long-term performance drivers. Committee members need to spend more time ensuring they are choosing the right meaures, monitoring the metrics to assure they are driving the right executive behaviors, and adjusting them as appropriate.

Compensation committees are not as close as management to the operations of the business, often leading to concern about how performance is calibrated and not wanting to establish goals that are too easy or too difficult to meet. A frequently asked question is, "How do we know we have set the right targets?"

Internal Pay Equity

Because compensation committees continue to be frustrated in relying solely on external market data, internal pay equity analysis also is being considered. While many companies disclose that they use both internal and external pay factors, their approaches to establishing internal pay equity often suffer from shortcomings in methodology. Internal pay equity too often focuses solely on comparing pay levels without looking closely at what executives actually do in their jobs. This shortcoming likely will become more apparent as companies supplement the required disclosures under the final rules adopted by the SEC regarding the so-called CEO pay ratio. By going beyond job titles and pay ratios, companies can better judge what is unique about each executive position and determine pay levels that are defensible and fair. Even after this is accomplished, however, there is still the need to reconcile internal pay equity with external benchmarking.

Total Remuneration

Often, in focusing on the technical and motivational aspects of an annual or long-term incentive plan, a committee neglects to put the parts together and look at the total picture. The use of tally sheets was a useful initial step in this process. Other tools and approaches such as realized pay and realizable pay advanced the analytics available to compensation committees. We anticipate an increased focus on total remuneration, both in terms of total amounts actually or potentially delivered to executives and the role each element plays in achieving organizational goals. This far-reaching exercise needs to encompass extrinsic pay elements (salary, annual and long-term incentives, benefits and perquisites) as well as intrinsic elements (work culture, job satisfaction, work environment and development opportunities).

Volatility of Pay Outcomes

The current benchmarking practice is to look at pay levels and mix of pay against peers — what is the total compensation value against peers and what is the value of each element in the mix of compensation. This snap-shot approach is useful but only goes so far. It does not capture a true picture of pay value over time compared to peers. Many compensation committees would benefit from undertaking an analysis that projects current grant values into the future under a range of outcomes based on the level of incentive awards and performance scenarios. The resulting volatility score gives an extended and more accurate picture of the competitive landscape by identifying the effects of potential swings in the pay package. It is also a powerful tool in assessing risk in pay programs.

PART I

Executive Pay Design and Strategy

CHAPTER 1

Compensation Strategy

By Irv Becker and Craig Rowley

Creating an effective executive compensation strategy is a complex process — more so than ever before. On one hand, the strategy must incorporate and reflect important internal issues unique to the company: short- and long-term business objectives, accounting costs for the company, internal pay equity/positioning, industry market competitiveness, administrative processes and perceived value by executives. On the other hand, the strategy must be formulated to withstand external scrutiny from shareholders, regulators, institutional investors, proxy advisers, and the press, all of whom increasingly demand information not just on generic guiding principles, but on details of the rationale of specific program design elements as well.

Thus, a compensation strategy must consider many factors and elements if it is to fulfill its purpose of supporting organizational goals, reflecting actual business performance, paying competitively and rewarding executives for value provided. These objectives are valid regardless of the organization's size, industry or developmental stage.

A compensation strategy must be reviewed and revised as the company grows and matures. The need to update the strategy can come from inside the company, such as when a new business strategy is implemented, an acquisition takes effect or new talent must be recruited. The need for revision also can arise from outside the company through changes in compensation trends, tax and accounting rules, the performance of the overall economy and stock market, or increased demand for executive talent in the marketplace. Whatever its specifics, a compensation strategy must have senior executive and outside director buy-in and be accepted and understood by all parties.

This chapter:

- Relates compensation strategy to business strategy and discusses approaches for evaluating the current program, developing performance metrics and maximizing the effectiveness of various long-term incentive vehicles.

- Recommends that organizations look beyond simple pay multiples and consider factors such as job size and complexity in analyzing internal pay equity. The importance of incorporating internal and external pay equity considerations is stressed.

Providing a Strategic Guide for the Compensation Committee

The articulation of a formal executive compensation philosophy has taken on critical importance at public companies in the current executive pay environment of enhanced disclosure and shareholder say-on-pay voting. The need for compensation committees to clearly explain the rationale underlying the design of various pay components of the executive compensation program has grown due to heightened scrutiny by the business media, proxy advisory groups, U.S. Congress, regulators (especially the IRS and the SEC), and institutional shareholders, among others.

An organization's executive compensation philosophy must encompass much more than the unhelpful and overused phrases that "we target the market median" or "we pay for performance to attract, retain and motivate talent." The compensation philosophy should offer specific guidance for the compensation committee's numerous decisions concerning executive pay and be used to evaluate the effectiveness of the compensation program by identifying any potential shortcomings in existing plans. The compensation committee should view the philosophy as a tool to influence management's performance and reaffirm the business strategy, not simply as a perfunctory task to "check the box" on corporate governance compliance.

Surfacing Issues in Compensation Design

In addition to furnishing important information to outside parties, the actual exercise of developing a robust executive compensation philosophy offers the compensation committee an opportunity to learn whether its members are on the same page in the design of appropriate compensation programs. The process needs to consider members' views on target pay levels, mix of pay elements, the comparator peer group or relevant survey data (i.e., the market for talent), the value of various executive jobs, performance metrics and targets, and other pay design issues.

The development of a compensation philosophy also can provide needed insight on whether the senior executive team and the compensation committee view the pay program's strengths and areas for improvement in the same manner. Ideally, management needs to own the design of compensation programs, which are tools to implement the company's business strategy. In addition, due to management's tremendous personal stake (some may call this "enlightened self-interest") in the compensation arrangements, the compensation committee may discover that any proposed changes actually provoke a long-overdue dialogue with management on various design issues that have been on autopilot for some time. The compensation committee may use this interaction to signal to management the committee's ultimate stewardship of the executive compensation program, along with the importance of needed input from the management team.

Addressing Business Strategy

When compensation committee members and senior management work together as a design team to develop a comprehensive compensation philosophy, it is critical to start with the organization's business strategy. For example, each participant could be asked to explain, in up to three sentences, the annual and long-term strategies for creating shareholder value. These might include initiatives such as acquisition of competitors or complementary businesses, creation or acquisition of new service lines or products, an emphasis on international growth, divestitures of underperforming assets, privatization, positioning for a sale, or rapid organic growth.

Defining the meaning of "high performance" should be explored by the team of compensation committee members and senior management. Each person could outline what superior business and operational performance at the company should look like. These descriptions should include financial (e.g., earnings growth) and nonfinancial (e.g., customer satisfaction) metrics. Superior performance also can include qualitative measures, such as the creation of a succession plan or talent management program. The desired outcome is, in a subsequent step, to be able to define clear goals (threshold, target and maximum, where appropriate) for the variable pay plans that promote the agreed-upon business strategy.

Evaluating Current Executive Pay Programs

As noted, the development of a compensation philosophy should involve a candid exchange among the team members concerning the core strengths and possible weaknesses of the current executive compensation program. Ascertaining the program's strengths guards against detrimental changes, while a consensus on opportunities for improvement may surface needed modifications that can promote talent retention and improve financial performance.

To avoid addressing the elements of total direct compensation (TDC) — base salary, and short- and long-term incentive opportunities — in a haphazard or piecemeal fashion, the team members should agree upon an overall TDC competitive market position for executives for planned, budgeted or targeted company financial performance.

In other words, by salary grade or officer title, a competitive market position (e.g., 60th percentile) should be established for a typical competent executive when the organization performs at pre-established annual target levels that are expected (i.e., 50 to 60 percent achievable). This competitive position creates an overall framework by which the mix of the three elements of TDC can be "sized."

The approach can be viewed as establishing the size of the TDC "pie," which can then be sliced into three pieces that form TDC. Once this is accomplished for planned performance, the mix of pay elements can be addressed by answering the following questions:

- What is the desired base salary competitive position in the talent market?
- For variable compensation, what percent should be focused on short-term financial results, assuming target financial performance of the organization? What percent should be focused on long-term financial results?
- What percent of LTIs should be cash versus equity and performance-based versus nonperformance-based?

Performance Metrics

Once the TDC competitive position and mix of pay elements are established, the process can turn to the performance metrics of the variable pay program (which measures are discussed in more detail in Chapter 7). The dialogue should start with the development of a list of financial and/or operational metrics that drive company success and positively impact share price. Examples to consider could be earnings or revenue growth, expense control and profit margin. Next, macro financial performance indicators that outside analysts use to compare the organization to its competitors could be developed. Examples include return on capital, earnings per share and return on assets. Identifying these drivers may help establish both short- and long-term incentive plan performance metrics.

Agreement also should be reached concerning the minimum annual level of return on a shareholder's investment that warrants a financial payout to executives. This threshold return could be expressed as earnings growth or share price appreciation, and it should guide the development of performance plan goal setting that results in cash payouts and/or vesting of equity awards.

Finally, the method of evaluating financial and operational performance metrics should be established, which could include absolute internal financial targets, performance relative to industry peers, or performance relative to an index (e.g., S&P 500). Measuring performance relative to peers can motivate "best-in-class" performance during weak economic seasons; measuring performance relative to realistic internal goals promotes participants' engagement by focusing their attention on specific outcomes that they believe they can influence.

Long-Term Incentives

The compensation philosophy also should address the use of LTI vehicles (e.g., stock options, performance shares, time-vested restricted stock). Therefore, a conversation around the proper role(s) of LTIs in executive compensation programs can help with the compensation committee's selection of the appropriate instruments. Examples of the role of LTIs and potential vehicles are shown in Table 1-1.

TABLE 1-1

Examples of the Role of Long-Term Incentives and Potential Vehicles

Desired Role of LTI	Potential LTI Vehicle
Retain executive talent	Time-vested restricted stock
Encourage capital accumulation in rising market	Stock options
Encourage capital accumulation in flat or depressed market	Time-vested restricted stock
Drive company performance	Performance shares/units
Promote stock price appreciation	Stock options
Provide tax efficiency for the executive	Restricted stock units
Promote actual ownership	Time-vested restricted stock

Other Compensation Strategy Questions

Numerous other questions and procedures could be addressed by compensation committees and management that might affect the executive compensation philosophy and its effectiveness:

- What multiple of base salary should executives hold in stock?
- How can the philosophy be communicated so that all parties understand it and have buy-in toward the compensation program?

- To what degree should individual behavior and performance factor into base salary increases and the size of incentive awards each fiscal year?
- To what degree should public disclosure affect the design of the executive compensation program and levels of compensation?
- To what degree should the company be involved in the planning and funding of executive retirement?
- How should decisions concerning which benefits/perquisites to offer be made (e.g., employee feedback, best practices, peer-group prevalence, general industry prevalence)?
- How might the compensation philosophy affect shareholders' say-on-pay voting?

A compensation committee needs to take seriously its vital role in establishing a comprehensive philosophy that guides all aspects of executive compensation. The more that senior management can be engaged in this process, the more likely the total compensation program will increase perceived value to those executives, thereby increasing the likelihood of retaining talented executives and motivating them to performance that increases the organization's value.

Additionally, the compensation philosophy should be reviewed regularly to confirm that it aligns with current business strategy and responds to changing organizational and economic conditions, and that it continues to effectively aid executive pay decisions.

Building Internal Equity

Compensation committees increasingly are asking questions about what internal equity is and how to implement it as part of a well-designed executive compensation process and program. Major organizations have discussed internal equity in their proxy statements.

The concept of internal equity isn't new. However, the discussion of internal equity — which focuses on pay relationships between executives — has become carelessly oversimplified in many cases. Focusing only on pay relationships between executive roles without understanding how those roles differ can yield information that is not only meaningless, but potentially debilitating to the health of an executive compensation program.

Debates and discussions on internal equity typically define the term narrowly as the pay relationships between different positions at different levels in a single organization. This approach looks to understand whether executives in that organization are paid appropriately relative to each other rather than relative to the external market. However, the concept of internal equity also should examine pay differences as a function of organization structure, job size and incumbent performance. While some may consider internal equity to mean the relationship of the pay of the CEO to the next level of executive reporting to the CEO, that focus may be overly simplistic.

A Useful But Often Misunderstood Concept

The landscape for executive compensation has changed — and is changing. Shareholders and compensation committees have become proactive in challenging the externally focused, peer-group driven approach to benchmarking executive pay. Many have complained that an over-reliance on external market data from a peer group or survey has led to a "ratcheting" effect, where the same group of comparator organizations benchmarks against each other's pay levels, to find that what was a 75th percentile market positioning one year is a 50th percentile positioning just two years later.

Market comparisons encourage the lower-paying companies to accelerate their pay increases to meet the market. The result has been an ever-escalating executive pay structure that compensates on a mindset that an organization's executives need to be paid at least at the market median rather than on the actual demands of the role or its performance.

As a result, the need for a true internal equity-based approach — one that helps compensation committees understand the market but is driven by internal fairness — has never been more apparent.

The Problem With Multiples

In managing the concept of internal equity, companies have been encouraged by some commentators to use "pay multiples," or that one position that is targeted at roughly "x" times another position. For example, this concept is promoted by the suggestion that the CEO should be paid at a level that is no more than two times that of key executives reporting to the CEO. In building on this questionable approach, some companies use pay multiples to manage the internal equity among executives. This ensures that an employer's pay relationships are linked to each other rather than to the external market (which may lead to a greater, or in some cases smaller, multiple). While the internal fairness of executive pay is very important, a simplistic approach that does not consider other relevant factors is misguided.

The problem with a multiples approach is that top organization structures are not the same across a peer group and, as a result, not all executive roles at a given organizational level are equal in value. Some organizations have a narrow span of control, and possibly a COO is the top position reporting to the CEO. Another organization may operate as a holding company, with group heads reporting to the CEO. Still others may have a more integrated structure, with either vertical or horizontal integration of businesses.

In short, not all organizations — and, therefore, not all executive roles — are structured similarly. As such, a pay multiple that is appropriate for one employer may be entirely meaningless for another due to differences in structure. Even less useful are comparisons of CEO compensation to the compensation of a company's median employee under final SEC rules issued under section 953(b) of the Dodd-Frank Act. Differences among companies, their operations and their workforces make disclosures of such "CEO pay ratio" little more than blunt tools aimed at limiting CEO pay without regard to these differences in organizations, executive roles or, most notably, performance.

Further, an individual executive's pay is a function of the background of how the incumbent secured the job, as well as his/her sustained performance and potential. A CEO recruited from the outside by a company in a turnaround situation likely will be paid more than a newly appointed CEO in a more stable organization who is promoted from within.

TABLE 1-2

Company Example Assumptions

Dimensions/Company	A	B
Parent Company:		
Revenue	$5 billion	$5 billion
Countries (with assets)	40	5
Employees	12,000	5,000
Value added	High	Low
Complexity	High	Low
Group Head		
Revenue	$2 billion	$2 billion
Countries (with assets)	30	3
Employees	5,000	1,500
Value added	High	Low
Complexity	High	Low

Company A

The chairman of the board is the former CEO. The CEO was "homegrown" and came out of the group-head position a year ago. Currently, the incumbent is paid low relative to market references. The company has 12,000 employees in 40 countries, and key staff functions are decentralized. The relatively new group head (one of three) reports to the CEO, was a candidate for the CEO position and was managing a smaller group prior to the decision to fill the CEO position with the current incumbent. The group head is paid slightly above market for this position. The group head is accountable for five separate high value-added, high gross-margin industrial product businesses that are characterized by proprietary technologies and consultative relationships with customers. The group has 5,000 employees in 30 countries around the world. North America represents 40 percent, Europe 40 percent and Asia-Pacific 20 percent of assets, employees and revenue generation.

Company B

The CEO recently was recruited from the outside and given the chairman of the board responsibility, as well. Pay to recruit the best candidate is above market references. The company has experienced performance issues and the new CEO has a mandate to turn performance around. The company sells into 10 countries, with assets in five of these. All business operations are based in the Americas, and there are 5,000 employees. Key staff functions are highly centralized. The group head reports to the CEO. The incumbent was promoted up from the head of manufacturing position, and the former incumbent was given an early retirement package. The new incumbent is paid below market references. The group-head position (one of three) has responsibility for two commodity products manufactured in a single plant location. Raw material accounts for 75 percent of product value, and gross margins are relatively low. The group employs 1,500 employees in the United States, Canada and Mexico. It manufactures in the United States and exports 15 percent of its production to Canada and Mexico, where distribution centers and sales offices are located.

Consider two separate companies with "group head" positions accountable for $2 billion in revenue in a parent company with $5 billion in total revenue. In most surveys, both the CEO and the group head positions would be valued as the "same-sized" job in comparing the two organizations. Look at the facts in Table 1-2 more closely.

Using traditional market data, the CEOs of both companies would be priced as each heading a $5 billion international company. Both group heads would be priced the same as well, relative to group heads managing $2 billion in revenue. Using an approach based on job content, the first company's CEO position likely would have a higher market value than the second but, using traditional market pricing, both would have the same market value. The same is true for the group head position — the market value of the job in Company A would be higher than in Company B using a job content-based approach that recognizes complexity as well as size. As discussed here and amplified in Table 1-3, a job-content approach to defining job size would result in a difference in both job size as well as market value for these positions.

Job-Content Approach to Defining Job Size

Survey Level/Company	A	B
1	CEO	
2		CEO/COB
3		
4	Group head	
5		
6		Group head

TABLE 1-3

Incumbent pay would be driven by the situation and by incumbent background as well. In Company A, the ratio of the CEO's pay to that of the group head would be expected to be much smaller than in Company B. It would not make sense to say that the multiple should be two times in both companies. Further, the multiple would narrow in both companies if a COO position was established.

A More Balanced Approach

The answer is to look not only at job titles and the size of the organization, but also at the jobs themselves: How big and complex are they? What do they actually do? The key is to understand the size of each role. In addition, incumbent experience, performance and prior compensation history should be considered. "Job sizing" allows a more informed snapshot into the internal equity of pay practices. Simply put, it focuses on the design of each job and essentially looks to rank (or score) jobs based on their content and complexity. Chapter 3 includes a discussion of common work-valuing processes and explains how they can be used in making decisions on executive compensation.

External Benchmarking Still Matters

Taking an internal equity approach absolutely does not mean that a company should avoid incorporating external benchmarking into the process. However, the market should be viewed as a point of reference, not a mandate on precisely how a position should be paid. Before making a decision on pay, external market data should be balanced against the internal perspective.

Balancing internal equity with external benchmarking can be done in a variety of ways. In its simplest form, compensation committees can consider internal equity alongside external market competitiveness, balancing the need to pay executives at a certain level of competitiveness with the need to pay executives appropriately relative to other roles and incumbent factors. Pay levels for executives should be a function of:

- Organization structure
- Size and complexity of the job
- Incumbent experience and demonstrated performance
- Potential (will current pay keep other interested employers at bay?)
- Succession (can pay for increased responsibility be managed effectively?)
- Internal equity (will pay be viewed as fair, all factors considered?).

Managing All Factors

However it is done, integrating internal equity into the compensation benchmarking process will move compensation governance going forward, as it adds another important dimension to looking at executive pay.

That said, there is a danger in examining internal equity in a vacuum. Using only a blind application of a pay-multiple approach can lead to recruitment and retention issues for some executives, and overpayment for others. Neither of these outcomes should be acceptable to shareholders.

For these reasons, it is clear that both the relative size of an organization's executive jobs and the "going rate" matter. Using internal equity in pay decisions forces a company to account for how its executive roles are unique. Compensation committees that consider internal equity alongside external competitiveness are able to create an executive compensation program that balances fairness and competitiveness with what jobs actually do, and that helps ensure that compensation decisions are not at the mercy of the market, but make sense — all factors considered.

Implications

On the surface, defining a competitive pay level seems easy. Companies have embraced a free-market approach by paying their executives similar to other executives in a representative group of peer organizations. The size of the company — typically defined by revenue — is the most common approach to recognize company and job differences when determining a competitive compensation level.

However, relying solely on a market-based approach could provide a false sense of security. Although size is an important consideration, it does not adequately address the value that the job is adding to an organization. For example, even in organizations of similar size, not all CFO positions are created equally. Factors such as importance of international markets, type of ownership and capital structure greatly influence job complexity — hence the value that these jobs add to the organization. Some CFOs have accountability for other functions, such as information technology, administration, and strategic planning; others do not. These additional variables should be considered when determining an appropriate pay level, much the same as companies use a host of financial measures to evaluate investment alternatives.

CHAPTER 2

Peer Groups and Alternative Approaches to Benchmarking

By Cory Morrow

Increased disclosure requirements, shareholder activism, and media attention have reinforced a market-based approach for executive compensation analysis and design. Given the high level of scrutiny associated with executive compensation, devising an appropriate peer group is an important activity for the compensation committee. Directors are faced with publicly disclosing peer group companies, explaining the selection criteria used in developing the peer group, and defending the peer group's appropriateness for benchmarking compensation, performance analysis and pay program design.

In this environment, the development and use of a compensation peer group is a critical tool for assessing the competitiveness and appropriateness of the various elements of a company's compensation programs. Utilizing a properly constructed peer group can provide a valuable perspective on issues such as compensation levels, performance benchmarks, pay elements, and short- and long-term incentive plan design. In addition, in some cases, the peer group may be used in a relative total shareholder return (TSR)-based long-term incentive design. Each company needs an objective and systematic approach to constructing a peer group that best fits its unique organizational characteristics, one that goes beyond simply targeting executive pay levels and allows the committee to assess compensation in relation to the value delivered to the company and shareholders.

This chapter:

■ Introduces the sources from which companies can benchmark executive pay and describes factors used in the peer selection process. It also outlines an approach that results in a more comprehensive picture of competitor practices by supplementing proxy peer analysis with functional job information from a larger database of employers.

■ Discusses the need for a dual analysis that not only may target compensation at a percentile of market, but also uses business performance analysis to rank executives' annual and TDC against the company's performance relative to competitors.

■ Discusses the use of external performance comparisons in setting and validating performance measures across various time periods and, ultimately, how peer group analysis and market data can be used in setting executive compensation.

■ Examines an approach boards can use to go beyond benchmarking and explore the business case for CEO pay.

Proxy and Survey Comparison Groups

Companies generally have two alternatives for benchmarking executive pay: published survey data from third-party providers and company-selected proxy peer groups.

Survey databases are an excellent source for broad, robust data for almost any type of executive position. General market or all-industry databases provide the broadest scope of data for compensation comparisons. These databases are particularly appropriate for corporate and staff roles in which industry expertise is not necessarily required and executives can move fairly easily between industries. General market data may also be appropriate for organizations in niche industries or with few direct competitors of similar size. Alternatively, many surveys are available for specific industries. This allows benchmarking to markets that are more similar to the subject organization and still provides robust compensation data.

In terms of matching executives to a database, the most precise approach is to use job size/grading or possibly a multivariate analysis that also allows for considerations such as employee numbers and internationality. This methodology can be the best way of capturing the scale and complexity of a business while still using a wide set of comparators; however, the downside is a loss of transparency because data are summarized and presented in aggregate (i.e., there is no individual detail on each company's executives). Whether this level of sophistication is necessary depends on the organization's circumstances. In our experience, such an approach is the most appropriate for:

- Comparing roles below the C-suite level where job title matching alone can be extremely imprecise, particularly in today's complex matrix structures in which roles with the same title often have very different responsibilities
- Injecting some rigor in the process of assessing the appropriate effect of an organization change to pay levels
- Organizations that are the top or bottom of a comparator group where the data may represent outliers.

Best Practices in Proxy Peer Group Selection

SEC disclosure requirements (see Chapter 14) as well as increased activism by shareholder groups are leading compensation committees to take a closer look at the process for determining executive pay. One area receiving significant attention is the selection of an appropriate peer group for executive pay comparisons.

For benchmarking of named executive officers (i.e., CEO, CFO, and three other highest paid executives), developing a custom peer group of other publicly traded companies can be a solid source of competitive data. Not only is this a way to obtain compensation values, but it also can provide details on incentive program design, benefit and perquisite offerings, and other executive policies, such as severance and change-in-control agreements.

Comparator peer groups are used by compensation committees to inform executive compensation decisions, including the establishment of target levels for executive pay and the design of short- and long-term incentive compensation programs. A peer group used for compensation benchmarking should be constructed:

- **Specifically for the individual company.** Because each organization has unique characteristics, the comparator group must be custom-built for that particular entity.
- **Based on a set of sound design principles and criteria.** Beginning the peer group design with a set of principles helps ensure that the process is sustainable and objective. It also avoids a course that many shareholder activists suspect is too often followed — starting with the answer and working backward.

The most effective peer groups typically include 12 to 20 companies that represent the company's market for talent (where it looks to recruit executives and which organizations poach its talent). Fewer than 12 companies may not provide statistically significant results and can be skewed by outliers; more than 20 companies introduces the likelihood that the group has gone beyond true and relevant "peers."

In developing a compensation peer group, the focus should be on design principles that drive the success of the individual company and reflect its market for executive talent. Selection criteria for developing a peer group commonly include:

- **Organizational size.** Size is measured by revenue for most industries, but asset-based for some industries (particularly financial institutions). A general rule suggests peer companies should be between 0.5 times and 2 times the size of the subject organization. Although some companies look at market capitalization, use caution when considering this measure. Market capitalization typically is not the preferred measure of scale because it:
- **Can be volatile,** which should have a limited effect on pay.
- **Is aligned to (expected) profitability rather than scale.** Therefore, it can understate comparisons for companies in low-margin sectors and arguably inflate salary and annual incentive benchmarks for speculative enterprises.
- **Industry.** Use of industry classifications, such as Global Industry Classification Standard (GICS) codes, can help identify companies either narrowly in common sub-industries or more broadly in industry groups or sectors. The broader classifications may be more appropriate for companies that operate multiple lines

of business, or simply when there is an insufficient number of companies in the narrower classifications.

- **Business model/complexity.** Organizations may choose to screen companies or refine the groups by only selecting companies with similar business models. For example, a company that develops, produces and markets its product may choose to exclude companies in the same industry that only provide a related service but do not actually develop and produce a product.

- **Global versus domestic operations.** Companies that operate on a global basis with executives who have accountability for global results may exclude (or limit the number of) domestic-only companies and vice versa.

- **Regulatory environment.** For many companies (e.g., utilities), regulatory complexities play a significant role in executive responsibilities; in those situations, constructing a peer group with companies that have similar complexities would be appropriate.

- **Founder-headed or controlled businesses.** These types of executives often have compensation arrangements that differ from typical market practices and, therefore, it may be inappropriate to include these companies in a peer group (unless the subject company is a founder-led or controlled business, in which case it may actively seek to include these types of organizations).

Peer groups should be reviewed annually to ensure they remain relevant and continue to meet the aforementioned criteria. Companies often need to be removed due to mergers, acquisitions, going private, bankruptcy, regulatory changes and other developments.

Of course, these standards need to be adapted to the particular organization. For example, in some industries, the number of companies that truly could be considered peers is quite small. An independent U.S. corporation's most direct competitors may be relatively small divisions of much larger U.S. employers (or foreign-owned companies) that do not file proxy statements, or privately owned companies for which pay information is difficult to obtain. In this case, a design principle that requires selecting the corporation's closest business competitors would be inappropriate. In other instances, a company may compete for talent with much larger organizations, and it may be appropriate to include a limited number of such companies in the peer group. An alternative approach is to denominate the larger company as a peer, but exclude its pay levels from any summary statistics (e.g., they can be shown separately). (See "Suggested Attributes of a Peer Group.") By following these practices, a compensation committee will be able to develop a peer group of companies that provides valuable and representative data on market compensation practices.

Using Comparator Peer Groups in Shareholders' Best Interests

A compensation committee should use the peer group to compare compensation levels (how much) and design (forms of pay delivery). The "how much" analysis should be informed by title-match benchmarking (e.g., CEO, CFO) and compensation rank where sufficient title matching is not possible (e.g., second-highest paid officer). The levels should be viewed not only by total dollar amount, but also by the mix of fixed, variable and equity pay at the peer companies.

Given that a large percentage of executive pay is not in the form of guaranteed compensation, it is useful to examine a company's compensation structure in comparison to that of its peers. This may include a review of target incentive award opportunities, types of equity used and performance metrics selected.

The decision about the type of awards can be informed by current peer group and market practices, but primarily should be driven by assessing which award vehicles most closely align executive pay with the organization's strategic goals. In nearly all cases, an organization's pay should be informed by the market, but also tailored to its own unique circumstances.

Comparing Performance of Peer Group Companies

If a compensation committee only uses a peer group to assist with the establishment of top executive pay levels, its task is incomplete. To understand the overall benefit that executives provide to shareholders, the compensation committee should compare the company's performance with that of its peer group. This comparison allows

Suggested Attributes of a Peer Group

The development of an appropriate peer group involves a consideration of various factors, but should include at least the following four attributes:

Be Current

Markets are dynamic. As a result, a corporation that was an appropriate peer last year may have changed its focus, modified its line(s) of business, been acquired, experienced a dramatic change in performance or even gone out of business. For these and other reasons, a company may no longer truly be a peer. Similarly, the company itself may have changed, either by organically growing faster than its peers or through acquisition, divestiture, or by entering/exiting various markets. Accordingly, it requires effort to evaluate the companies included in the comparator group on an annual basis. In addition, it is essential to understand the peer companies being utilized by institutional shareholders to assess a company's pay-performance relationship. Where these data points are available, it is worth taking the effort to compare these peer groups to the one approved by the compensation committee.

Be Composed of a Representative Number of Companies

A base number of organizations is key for the validity of the summary statistical compensation data. Companies with a few direct competitors often focus on too narrow a group of potential organizations and may face difficulties establishing a valid peer group. Consequently, for purposes of compensation benchmarking, it may be necessary to loosen the rigidity of the selection process to create a sample size that is sufficiently robust to provide meaningful data from a statistical viewpoint.

Be Reasonable in Relationship to Peer Companies

More specifically, an appropriate peer should be reasonably related to the companies used in the performance graphic in the corporation's annual report, particularly to the industry line-of-business index. Because a large portion of executive pay is variable and often linked to corporate performance, best practices suggest that there should be commonality among the companies used to determine whether compensation is appropriate and those used to illustrate corporate performance.

For example, there may be a disconnect if the company's compensation peer group consists of companies in the Dow Jones Industrial Average Index — all household-name, large-capitalization corporations — while the company's performance graph contains relatively unknown, small capitalization companies. Also, shareholder interest groups compare key aspects of a company's program to business peers, especially when looking at share allocations.

Be Performance-Based

Frequently, comparisons are made on the basis of organizational size, not performance. The most useful size metric generally is company revenue. While there is a strong correlation (especially with base salary) between revenue size and pay (within the same industry), other variables may need to be considered.

the compensation committee to determine the degree of alignment of executive pay with actual business performance relative to the comparator peer group. Analyzing this pay-for-performance also serves the best interests of the company's shareholders. Results provide insight into the relationship between executive pay levels and company performance as well as whether pay is commensurate with the performance level achieved (i.e., where a company provides executive pay above median, does it consistently exceed peer group median performance?).

In exploring this question, compensation committees should look for a directional, as opposed to precise, relationship between pay and performance. It is unrealistic to expect a company that performs at the peer group's 40th percentile to have its executive compensation pegged precisely at the 40th percentile. However, if this company properly aligns its pay programs with performance considerations, shareholders should reasonably expect executives' compensation to be directionally equivalent to that of company performance and fall between the 25th and 50th percentiles of the peer group, particularly over the long run.

As shown in Figure 2-1, area B displays a pay-for-performance directional relationship; areas A and C do not. Concerns with the shaded areas include:

- In area A, executive compensation may be viewed as an excessive expenditure of the shareholders' assets because compensation rank is significantly higher than performance rank. In this case, the compensation committee may consider one or more of the following:
  - Freezing or slowing the growth of base salaries
  - Modifying the relationship between performance and payout
  - Revisiting the payout opportunities
  - Raising the performance metric targets
  - Changing the performance metrics
  - Modifying relative performance metrics that compare the company's performance against a peer group
  - Delving deeper into the cause of the apparent pay-for-performance disconnect.
- In area C, there may be a risk of losing talented executives because performance rank significantly exceeds compensation rank. In this situation, retention concerns may cause the compensation

committee to raise salaries, increase payout opportunities or review the performance metric targets.

FIGURE 2-1

Pay-for-Performance Relationship

A: High pay relative to performance

B: Directional pay for performance relationship

C: Low pay relative to performance

Executive Compensation — High / Median / Low

Company Performance — Low / Median / High

External Performance Comparison

A robust pay-for-performance analysis does not involve merely a comparison of a company's absolute business performance to its internal, committee-approved performance targets (absolute performance goals). It is possible for a company to repeatedly achieve or exceed its internal financial and nonfinancial goals, resulting in incentive awards paying out at or above target levels, but still fall behind the performance of its peer companies. A pay-for-performance analysis should analyze a company's performance relative to its peer group's performance.

Another benefit of a comparison of company performance relative to its peer group is that the compensation committee is able to validate the performance goals it establishes for its executive variable pay programs. The analysis can reveal whether the internal performance goals warrant the corresponding payouts when compared to the peer group's aggregate historical performance.

For example, an examination might reveal that the one-year earnings growth goal established by the compensation committee for target performance corresponds to the historical 25th percentile earnings growth of a comparator peer group. Such a discovery might prompt the compensation committee to increase the annual incentive plan's earnings growth target, lower the payout opportunities, or further explore the rationale behind how and why the performance objectives were set.

Performance Measure Selection

Once a comparator peer group has been approved by the compensation committee based on the agreed-upon criteria and principles, performance measures are selected and then weighted. Determining the proper number of performance measures requires a consideration of the company's circumstances. While multiple measures may enable a compensation committee to address various factors relevant to performance and limit any potential "gaming" of the outcomes that can occur when only one measure is used, too many measures may lose desired focus and prevent the program from being meaningful. Only in atypical situations have we seen well-crafted programs use more than four measures.

Performance Measurement Periods

Performance for the selected metrics might be evaluated for both one- and three-year (possibly up to five-year) performance periods for each company. Then, for example, each company's CEO cash compensation and total direct compensation can be ranked and plotted against its corresponding composite performance ranking.

Figure 2-2 shows an example of CEO cash compensation versus one-year company performance, with a ranking of one representing the best performance/highest compensation. As shown, Company Alpha has the best composite one-year performance ranking as well as the highest CEO cash compensation. However, Company Charlie, with the third-highest performance ranking, is next to last in cash compensation. Absent other retention, organizational and personal factors, Company Charlie may be at risk of losing its CEO to another company unless changes are made to the CEO's cash compensation or long-term incentive award program.

Although no analysis of executive pay relative to company performance will be all encompassing, the approach suggested can show whether a directional relationship exists between pay and performance. Given the increased corporate governance requirements and outside scrutiny of executive compensation, it is crucial that compensation committees make efforts to assure investors that they truly are overseeing an executive compensation program that aligns pay and performance.

Use of Peer Groups in Setting Compensation

Once a peer group is established and data have been collected, the work is not done. Compensation committees have a responsibility

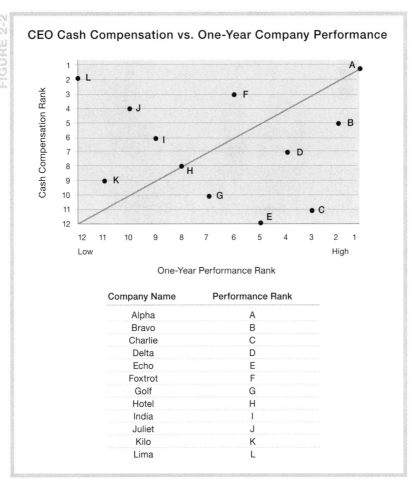

to apply their judgment in evaluating peer group data. For example, after selecting the suitable peer companies based on the aforementioned criteria, we may find that an organization's revenue is at the 30th percentile of the group. If this organization has a philosophy of paying at the median of its market, is it appropriate to target the median of its peer group? Perhaps the company should lower its target positioning to better match the size of its desired peer group. Similarly, if a company has been under-performing, it may be inappropriate to select only high-performing peer companies and target at the median of that group. Consideration needs to be given to these factors so that the compensation philosophy works in alignment with the peer group.

Market data will always have a role to play in setting executive pay. How else can the compensation committee be assured that pay is sufficient to attract and retain its key talent but not excessive? In any case, the approach chosen for benchmarking needs to be thoughtful and deliberate. This means selecting the right comparators, taking the context into account and looking at competitiveness in various performance scenarios. Ultimately, a compensation committee needs to rely on its business judgment while using benchmark data as one input, but not as an absolute answer.

Making the Business Case for CEO Pay

Peer group benchmarking has its place in deciding how and how much to pay a top executive, but it is only part of the decision-making process. To really make the most of the opportunities presented by CEO pay determinations, we suggest boards (and their compensation committees) take a broader view — and make the business case for CEO pay.

Building the Business Case

To start building the business case for executive reward, the board needs to ask questions like:
- What do we want to achieve as a business?
- How will our CEO pay design support that?
- How will we measure the return on our investment?

It sounds simple, but doing this is actually a fairly involved exercise — and one that's worth the time and effort. In addition to creating a context for a CEO's pay that makes sense to both the organization and outsiders, building a business case can help the board close the gap between the CEO and the day-to-day realities of the organization and make the board better equipped to address any challenges around "fairness."

Why There Is More to Life Than Just Benchmarking

Historically, the consensus has been that pay levels are the key to attracting, retaining and motivating the right chief executive. As a result, companies saw the data gleaned from peer group benchmarking as enough to justify decisions around pay. Many still do.

To get to "the" number, organizations would work out the size of the individual's job, benchmark it against similar organizations in the market, and find their target level (typically the median). And, historically, this basic approach has worked well enough.

But changes in the economy as well as added pressure from shareholders have affected the way we think about executive compensation, to expose the shortcomings of the traditional benchmarking process and put pressure on organizations to find new and better ways to reward their top people. The focus on capital returns, the desire for top-line growth and the pressure on profits forced many companies to reconsider not just what they pay, but also how they structure that pay. For example, we consider how organizations design their executive incentive plans and balance those factors against the other elements of the total package.

In our view, traditional peer group benchmarking is maligned for two main reasons:

1. The ratchet effect. Because CEOs are a relatively small and static pool, there isn't much to compare against. And as everyone in that pool seeks to be competitive, companies rarely want to pay below the 50th percentile — which drives pay levels up.

2. Getting in a muddle over the median. If you are car shopping, you don't buy a car just because it costs an average price for that make and model — you buy it because you think you're getting the best

quality car at the right price, all factors considered. It should be the same with setting and designing CEO pay. The median (or above) should not dictate what an organization pays — it's one data point of several factors to consider when making pay decisions. Too many organizations still see it as the "magic number," and it isn't.

Also, CEOs don't tend to leave to take other CEO roles. Now we start to see why peer group benchmarking — while a helpful reference point — isn't enough on its own to justify pay levels. The board must look at factors specific to the organization, its business and culture, and the person in the job (or the one the board is hoping to hire). For examples, see, "Building the Business Case for CEO Pay: Questions to Ask."

Fairness Is in the Eyes of the Beholder

The perception of fairness is understandably a factor in evaluating CEO pay, and the discussion has gone beyond the boardroom and entered the mainstream. This means that the number of people who have an opinion on how fair (or not) a CEO's pay is has grown exponentially. Boards need to take these views seriously when making decisions around pay.

A "moral compass of fairness" can illustrate these many perspectives. It starts with the classic benchmarking question: what is the size and scope of the job compared to peer organizations?

But then boards need to consider:

- What that person has done to deserve that pay
- What the shareholders think is fair, based on the outside world as they see it
- What individual board members think (e.g., "that's a lot more than I got when I was a CEO")
- How it appears to the rest of the organization: is it more of a pay gulf than a pay gap?

From there, the debate extends to the general public, which, thanks to increased disclosure, can now act as judge and jury. As potential customers, clients and shareholders, it matters what they think.

Finally, and at the heart of the issue, there's how the CEO views his/her pay package — and not just the magnitude. While the actual amount is important, the structure and design of the package can send very clear signals to the CEO about the company's expectations and how success will be measured.

Building the Business Case for CEO Pay: Questions to Ask	
The strategic case	What is it we want to achieve as a business? Is this person going to take our organization where it needs to go next? How will the way we propose to pay support our strategy?
The economic case	How much can we afford to pay? Does that mean we need to promote internally or can we hire externally? Who are our competitors for people and for business, and what do they pay? How will we measure our return on investment?
The personal case	Why is this the right person for the task? Are they going to be the right fit? How do their competencies match the task at hand? What do they think about the issue of pay, and will that affect their behavior — positively or negatively?
The political case	What is the desired message? What will the reaction be to this appointment among investors, other stakeholders and the general public? Could it affect our share price? How will this person deal with our stakeholders?

The company should consider:

- **Fairness at the top** — With the spotlight still on CEO pay, many organizations have started to talk about establishing "internal equity" (the perception that the organization pays people according to the relative size and difficulty of the job they do). But few are doing something about it.

    When we talk about internal equity, we don't mean using an arbitrary ratio to control the maximum amount a CEO can earn compared to some hypothetical "median" employee. That ratio might be interesting to the media, but it's typically meaningless to the business, because it doesn't, on the most basic level, take the structure, size and uniqueness of the CEO's job (or organization) into account.

- **Pay differentials between CEO and direct reports** — We do think that looking at the pay differentials between the chief executive and his/her direct reports, then evaluating the relative size and complexity of those roles, brings an important perspective to the CEO pay debate. It also makes sure that the people at the layer below feel appropriately rewarded for the work they do.

  At this next level, the market data tends to be a truer reflection of the market for talent, partly because the pool of people to compare against is much larger. And because those people are more likely to leave to become CEOs at other companies, benchmarking becomes a more useful (and justifiable) exercise than at the CEO level. By benchmarking pay for these jobs and comparing their size and complexity with the CEO's role, we can build internal equity considerations into a recommendation for how much the company pays the CEO compared to the layer below.

- **Use of findings on these differentials** — Sometimes, the recommendation might be that an organization close the gap between the two. Whether or not it decides to take us up on this advice depends on how it sees the role of the CEO. In some companies, a large gap reflects the fact that responsibility for delivering the business strategy sits solely on that person's head — though that can also be a red flag to investors, who question what would happen to the company if the CEO got hit by the proverbial bus.

■ **The impact of stakeholders** — Organizations have many stakeholders, and as our moral compass of fairness shows, they may all have different ideas about what constitutes appropriate pay for your CEO. Here are some of the factors to consider.

- **Who "owns" the organization?** — Is it privately held, publicly traded, government-controlled, or other type of organization? Each ownership model leads to a different kind of reward structure because different owners have different aims and different ways of rewarding a CEO who achieves them. A chief executive brought into a family-owned business, for example, probably wouldn't be a big shareholder because it's not in the family's interest to relinquish control. But a publicly traded company that wants to encourage a long-term view may require its CEO to build up a large number of shares to drive that view, and to reflect shareholders' interests. And the chief executive of a failing company, where the government has become a majority shareholder, might need to give up his or her annual bonus as a public display of belt-tightening.

- **What's its pay philosophy and culture?** — What a CEO is paid sets the tone for the culture of the organization — and these days, that information is likely to be in the public domain. It's important that a CEO's pay reflects the company's overall philosophy for paying its people, as well as the corporate culture, otherwise the gap is there for all to see. Employees and customers may vote with their feet and their wallets.

- **Is there a successor standing in the wings?** — A substantial majority of CEO jobs go to insiders. This has a big impact on pay, not just for the person who's eventually promoted into the post, but for the person in the role now.

    For example, if a company has three solid options for a successor, it doesn't need to pay its current CEO as much as if a replacement is hard to find. And when the time comes to appoint a successor, the internal candidate won't become twice as valuable overnight. But the board will need to adjust the executive's compensation package to reflect what it wants the new CEO to achieve, and the risk to which that exposes both them and the organization. While investors may balk at the inevitable premium needed to pay for an external candidate, they equally may need reassurance that a company "lifer" has the broad experience and understanding of the wider market needed for the business to thrive. In both scenarios, adjusting the design of the CEO's incentives, and the balance of base/variable pay in the package, can soothe shareholder concerns.

Pulling It All Together

So a board has done internal and external benchmarking and looked at all the other factors that might constrain or affect what the company can or should pay. Now it just needs to come up with a number, right? Not quite. What the board must do is to set both the levels and the structure of the package. And this can take many different shapes; there's no need to constrain the board's thinking to what's considered "normal."

Consider this example: Company A wants a chief executive who can keep the business stable for five years. So it says to its new CEO, we'll pay you $1 million a year for five years, guaranteed — but in five years you won't have a job. So after three years, we'll start looking for someone to replace you, and we expect your last year to be all about handing over the reins.

Meanwhile, Company B wants to grow rapidly. In five years, it aims to be snapping at the heels of the market-leaders in its industry. So it hires a CEO on a fixed annual salary of only $1, on the under-standing that if that person takes the business to new heights, he or she will receive a huge bonus.

Both packages have their merits, but for the one chosen to succeed, the CEO needs to perceive what is offered as being of equal value to a package with a different structure elsewhere. Getting to a package that both the CEO and the board or compensation committee can agree upon might involve time and trade-offs, but it's worth the invest-ment to make sure the CEO is not only happy, but understands what needs to happen in order for the incentives to pay out. Otherwise, he/she might perceive the package as being worth less than it is.

Final Cautions

It's clear that both the relative size of an organization's executive jobs and the "going rate" matter. Using internal equity in pay decisions forces a company to account for how its executive roles are unique and allows it to create an executive compensation program that balances fairness and competitiveness with what jobs actually do. So rather than being at the mercy of the market, its pay decisions make sense, all factors considered.

Boards need to be wary of exaggerating the importance of the indi-vidual in its calculations. The impact of an overpaid CEO on morale in an organization is potentially much greater than the impact on that person's pride of being paid below the median. Transferring too much power to the CEO puts the business in a vulnerable position, too. When designing a CEO pay package, a board must remember that at the end of the day, the organization should be stronger than the individual. If the CEO is stronger, the company is on dangerous ground — what happens if and when he/she leaves?

CHAPTER 3

Valuing Work and Establishing Base Salary

By Jim Bowers and Tom McMullen

As its name implies, base salary is the foundation for the other components of an executive compensation program. Every paycheck is a reminder of the link between the executive's efforts over the last pay period and how the organization perceives the value of those efforts.

Many organizations today determine base salary levels (and other elements of compensation) by benchmarking their job functions/ titles to external compensation surveys. However, these types of matches often provide limited value in determining how much a job is really worth to a specific organization as strategies and structures differ. The data provide information on what's paid in the market for comparable positions but do not reflect incumbent experience and performance.

This chapter:

- Reviews key terms in valuing executive jobs.
- Provides you with an understanding of common work-valuing processes in use today, and how they support executive compensation and talent management decisions.
- Discusses the importance of the base salary component in the total compensation equation. It defines the purpose of salary and its use as the starting point in determining the value of annual and long-term incentive awards as well as benefits programs, such as pension, long-term disability and paid time off.

■ Explains how executive pay can be affected by many factors, including company size and scope, industry, geography, desirability, supply/demand, executive negotiations, incumbent track record, and other factors.

Examining Markets and Jobs

First, a few basic definitions. "Market" is typically defined as economic activity where buyers and sellers are driven by the principles of supply and demand. "Job evaluation" is about determining how much the job (or role) is worth to the organization. "Market pricing" is about determining how much others in the labor market pay for the capability required to accomplish the objectives in a predefined job or role. "Valuing work" is the combination of these internal and external factors. The market for talent often is not clearly defined and certainly is not managed within a tight range.

Market pricing may have the outward appearance of being precise and defensible, but market data is typically a sample based on matching titles and basic functions without consideration for other relevant factors.

For example, let's look back at the two group head positions described in Table 1-2 of Chapter 1. Both are accountable for $2 billion in revenues and in most surveys would be matched to the same job and result in the same benchmark compensation levels. However, as we observed in Chapter 1, the two positions are clearly not worth the same in the market. The group head position at Company A has a much larger size job and should be compensated greater than the group head described for Company B, holding all other variables constant. Job evaluation enables a company to decode its organizational structure and incorporate all elements of job design to ensure it is making the most accurate job content matches to the market. Job evaluation-based market pricing would produce substantially different values for the above two positions, while market pricing without job evaluation would not. Job evaluation adds precision to market pricing.

The Role of Job Evaluation

Robust job evaluation methodologies can help sort out the value of jobs to the organization and directly link this to a market price. Job evaluation methodology makes market pricing easier and more precise as it enables pricing of all executive jobs, not just a sample of jobs. Job evaluations can be priced relative to specific jobs, functions, geographies, industries and organization size.

Many of the world's largest and most admired organizations use job evaluation to facilitate executive compensation decisions. Job evaluation works regardless of the compensation structure. It provides a company with better defensibility and rationale to support market-pricing processes as well as flexibility with managed control. Further, the process of job evaluation helps to clearly define job content in terms of the capability required, positions' accountabilities and performance standards.

The process of defining the price range of a job — its base salary range as well as short- and long-term incentive opportunities — combines the value of the job to the organization with the price of the job in the market. Once the value range is established, the actual price paid incorporates other factors, such as incumbent performance.

In its most basic form, job evaluation is a system for determining the size of a job relative to other jobs in the organization. Beyond that, it is used to derive a market value for jobs of similar size. Rather than simply benchmarking to a "job match," compensation data can be derived for a particular point value or range of point values.

Hay Group's job evaluation methodology was initially developed by Edward N. Hay in the early 1950s and has been refined over the years to accord with new learning and developments. It is comprised of three main factors: (1) know-how, (2) problem solving, and (3) accountability.

The three main factors can be represented by a simple model:

Input		Processing		Output
Know-How	→	Problem solving	→	Accountability

- For any given job there is a relationship among the three factors. The Output, or end results expected of the job (the accountability), demands a certain level of Input (know-how) and processing of this know-how (problem solving) to enable delivery. The criteria used are common compensable factors and have been proven to be compliant with government regulations around pay fairness.

Compensation Benchmarking and Job Evaluation

Compensation committees are certainly familiar with the process of compensation benchmarking from proxy statements, which starts with developing a peer group (as discussed in Chapter 2). Compensation data so obtained is then summarized by job match or pay rank. The approach has become a standard analysis performed on an annual basis to benchmark the competitiveness of executive pay versus peer group companies. Proxy data certainly provides the compensation committee with a great deal of information, as more detail is disclosed in proxy statements than ever before.

While proxy analysis is a great tool for benchmarking pay and has a level of transparency that market pay surveys do not, it falls short in several areas:

- Revenues alone do not adequately estimate compensation levels. Typical R-squared values for regressions of pay on revenue are 0.3 to 0.5, whereas R-squared values for pay on job evaluation scores are in the range of 0.6 to 0.8 (note: R-squared value of 0 indicates no relationship, R-squared value of 1.0 indicates a perfect relationship).

- Typically, only CEO and CFO positions can be accurately matched. When certain company job benchmarks do not exist in the peer group companies, executives are matched by their internal pay rank among the other named executive officers (NEOs). While this provides data on other similarly ranked executives, it fails to align with the job and complexity of the role.

- The approach fails to establish specific market rates for "combined" or "hybrid" roles (e.g., CFO who is also the chief information officer or accountable for a business unit). Further, a CFO role may differ depending on acquisition focus and need for more creative financing for growth. Proxy data does not provide sufficient insight on the internal organization structure and succession planning effects on pay.

- Job titles do not reflect the business strategy of the organization and how this impacts job size (e.g., low-cost, high-technology or high-customer focus).

- Many organizations develop a compensation philosophy whereby they target a given market percentile versus the proxy peer group — typically the market median. Paying at the median of the market is not always a sound strategy as other factors such as performance are not considered. When assessing pay, it is important to have a strong performance connection. Market values are merely a point of reference and should not be deemed a mandate.

In determining the value of executive jobs through the process of job evaluation, the following factors should be considered:

- **Industry** — the nature of the industry, unique industry challenges, and the degree of regulation have an impact on job complexity.

- **Revenues** — good predictor of job size within an industry and one of the key factors utilized in determining the level of executive accountability, but value added (revenues minus purchases) should also be considered.

- **Assets** — often utilized to determine executive accountability in financial services or insurance companies but also relevant for industrial companies.

- **Market capitalization and/or enterprise value** — sometimes considered, but only for named executives in the proxy. Use of these values reflect performance and are therefore used as judgment checks on revenue-driven comparator organizations rather than the primary metric.

- **Employee headcount** — an important measure, but an organization should be careful to use full-time equivalents; also location and reliance on technology can affect cost.

- **Governance** — clearly has impact on the top job (e.g., CEO vs. CEO/Chairman or the dual board structure existing in some countries).

- **Geographic scope of company** — adds complexity, and thus job size (e.g., just domestic operations vs. international operations).
- **Organization strategy/structure** — affects the relative value of positions below the CEO (i.e., NEOs).

Once these factors are utilized to develop job evaluation scores and resulting grades for the CEO and other executives, more precise market data can be collected that better reflect specific job accountabilities (vs. using only external market pricing). In addition, job evaluation has applications for managing executive talent beyond determining competitive compensation levels:

- Succession planning (job evaluation is linked to competencies and behaviors, executives can be assessed vs. what is required for their role and the next role)
- Linking executives to the organization strategy by describing their specific accountabilities and the nature of how they affect the accountabilities (e.g., developing a clear plan for implementing the strategy)
- Defining the impact of acquisitions, joint ventures, matrix organizational structures (e.g., the executives in an acquired company may not be compensated to the same degree as a stand-alone company).

One thing is clear: Pay data and resulting decisions should be based on more than either matching to the market or using internally driven job evaluation. We suggest a combination of internal value and external market pay as the key elements to determine the value of the executive role. An organization should know both; one approach without the other will yield an incomplete answer. All this information, research, and trial and error in developing the most effective approach to valuing work dictates that job content is the key — without understanding job content you cannot truly value work.

Base Salary: The Foundation of Total Compensation

Base salary is the least complex form of compensation, yet some would argue it is the most important when viewing pay via the broader workforce. For top executives, base salary typically is not the highest value of compensation, but it can have a significant bearing on the actual value of other pay components, which are often expressed as a percentage of base salary. Salary as a percentage of total compensation is even as low as below 10 percent for CEOs of large capitalization companies, but is also typically the highest salary in the company.

In addition to driving the value of other forms of compensation, salary is an important part of the attract-and-retain equation. It is not considered as strong in its ability to provide motivation to an executive; arguably, compensation is only motivational when it is at risk. Under this view, fixed compensation is not motivational. Psychologists generally have maintained that salary is a hygienic factor rather than a motivational one. That is, salary either satisfies or dissatisfies, but does not motivate or change behavior. For lower-level jobs, salary is much more important to meet basic needs (e.g., security, ability to provide basic needs for self and family). While these needs may be lessened for executives due to higher pay levels, security cannot be ignored as a psychological factor for executives, especially in today's market. At executive job levels, salary is often a way for executives to "keep score" relative to the perceived job worth when compared to others within and outside the organization.

The term salary dates back to the Roman Empire when Roman soldiers were paid in a valuable commodity — salt — that could be bartered for other goods and services. "Salary" actually means "salt money." Despite the importance of salary in history, its significance often is misunderstood and confused in the media with other forms of compensation. Sometimes total compensation (including base, annual incentives, and long term incentive grant values) is called "base salary." Of course, this is highly inaccurate, especially when CEO compensation may be 90 percent in the short- and long-term incentive categories.

With the current focus on executive pay, base salary may be viewed negatively by shareholders and other interest groups if it appears too high from some perspectives. One consideration in setting salary for a public company's CEO, as well as any of its other highest-paid executives subject to Internal Revenue Code (IRC) section 162(m), is that the tax law does not consider salary to be performance-based compensation exempt from a $1 million deduction limitation. Increasingly, public companies emphasize performance-based compensation to obtain better tax treatment but also to appease shareholder interest groups that provide recommendations on shareholder say-on-pay votes.

Relation to Market

As discussed previously, determining an executive's base salary typically is a function of the market and the value of the position and person in it to the organization. Most organizations measure the market for executives based on some combination of the nature of the job, organization size (revenues), industry sector and job size (job evaluation).

Employers often claim that they establish the market reference or midpoint of a salary range on the basis of market median of the relevant peer group. The vast majority of companies state that their pay philosophy is at market median; yet, as measured in compensation surveys, actual pay around median varies significantly — especially at executive levels. The typical salary range (+/-20 to 30 percent) around market reference produces a pay spectrum from about the 10th percentile to the 90th percentile of market for most executive positions. The actual pay variation around market reference is based on incumbent experience, performance, tenure in a given job as well as incumbent bargaining power.

Many companies maintain that base salary is largely paid for incumbent factors, including how one performs the job, and not just on achieved results. As such, competencies and behaviors are significant factors in determining the appropriate salary increase and resulting new salary. Incentives are more aligned with total organizational performance.

Managing Salary

Given the importance of base salary as referenced above, it would seem that salary should be managed more effectively and with greater differentiation than is typical. Some employers have an over-reliance on market movements and adjust executive base salaries fairly consistently and do not manage salaries to reflect the performance and value of the person and position to the organization. A more effective approach involves managing the market as a reference post rather than as a driver for how much an executive should earn in base salary. In addition, the actual base salary within the salary range should reflect demonstrated performance over time as opposed to pay for tenure within the company. Sometimes, but less frequently today with increased disclosure, executives get a higher percentage adjustment than other employees based on the premise that the top performers rise to the top. This is increasingly viewed as flawed logic, and the performance bar is raised the higher one is in the organization. Increasingly, base salary increases for executives match in percentage terms what other employees receive.

Managing salary is important because it is the foundation for other compensation programs and represents one of the largest fixed costs in managing an enterprise. At a market reference of $300,000, the typical market range from P10 to P90 is +/-$60,000 to $90,000. (See Table 3-1.) However, an incumbent paid at the maximum versus the minimum would find a total direct compensation difference of $360,000, assuming target short- and long-term incentives as a consistent percentage of base salary. This does not include the value difference in benefits (e.g., income replacement and retirement).

TABLE 3-1

Impact of Salary on Total Direct Compensation

Salary	STI %	STI $	TCC*	LTI %	LTI $	TDC**
$210	50%	$105	$315	50%	$105	$420
$300	50%	$150	$450	50%	$150	$600
$390	50%	$195	$585	50%	$195	$780

TCC* = total cash compensation (salary plus annual incentive pay)
TDC** = total direct compensation (TCC plus long-term incentive pay)

When organizations search for talent from the outside, potential recruits often focus on increasing their salary. But employers should exercise care not to distort internal pay relationships. Instead of paying more salary and affecting internal equity, signing bonuses and restricted stock can be helpful in both attracting and retaining top talent. It can be argued that salary is "forever." Two executives — one paid $210,000 and the other paid $390,000 for the same position — will generate quite different TDC costs over time. The difference over 10 years is roughly $4.9 million in TDC, assuming a 4-percent annual increase. Not small change.

One would hope that employees in the lower half of the salary range (0–50 percent) are continuing to grow in their capability related to the job — and may be newly promoted into the role. The top half of the range (50–100 percent) should represent above-market pay for consistent, high performers or newly hired executives who bring unique and proven skills and experiences to the job (for example, someone hired from a competitor who has been highly successful in a similar role).

The middle half of the range (25–75 percent) represents market pay for solidly performing executives who are competent in the core aspects of their role. Note that here tends to be an obsession with the midpoint of the salary range (100 percent of the market target or 50 percent of the penetration within the range). Sometimes market data may imply a level of precision in measuring the market that doesn't actually exist (a midpoint of $245,352 for example). While the development of a compensation structure is based on a significant amount of data and analysis, there is quite a bit of art to the process as well. Organizations often use the "compa-ratio" statistic (an executive's base salary divided by the midpoint of the salary range) to determine where someone's pay falls within the range. Over time, companies would like to have a positive correlation between performance and position in the salary range (top performers paid above market, solid performers paid around the market, marginal performers below market). In reality, though, employees are paid throughout the salary range and their pay at any point in time may or may not reflect their current level of performance.

Another core concept in executive base pay management is allocating salary increases relative to performance. First, organizations need to ensure that performance assessments translate into differentiated rewards. Many organizations spend an agonizing amount of effort to ensure that managers comply with some sort of a distribution curve of performance ratings. But what value is this if the highest performer still receives only marginally more rewards — whether in merit pay, incentive pay or options — than the average performer? The ratings are merely a means to an end. And the end game is higher compensation for the highest performance, not just a perfect distribution curve.

Other Elements of Managing Base Pay

There are several other practices when making executive base salary decisions. These include the following:

- **New Hires:** Senior leaders are faced with a wide range of candidates (both internally and externally) whose qualifications are at the minimum required for satisfactory performance to those who bring unique skills and experiences and can hit the ground running. Typically, most organizations try to hire employees below the market target (midpoint) for the job. This helps preserve internal equity (fairness) in the organization while giving newly hired executives the opportunity to earn merit increases as they develop in the role. However, sometimes it's necessary to bring in an executive at a higher salary than the market target. Decisions like that are usually driven by market demands for or by the exceptional qualifications of the executive. Also, it is typically more expensive to replace from the outside than to fill jobs internally, as a high performer in another company wants a significant premium in pay to justify switching employers.

- **Promotions:** A promotion is traditionally viewed as a move from one executive role to another of greater authority, impact, complexity, responsibility and income. As such, a "promotional increase" should be larger than a normal merit increase or annual cost of living increase. If promotions are implemented at the same time as the annual merit increase, many companies take into account dollars allocated for the employee's annual increases in the promotional increase amount. Most executive promotions involve jobs changes that are significant and typically are more than one grade apart or have a clear difference in market value; a promotional increase in the 7 to 15 percent range would be appropriate in most situations and in some cases greater than 15 percent if the new role requires a big stretch for the executive.

- **Demotions:** A demotion is usually based on performance or business circumstances (job elimination, etc.). Sometimes it's initiated by the employee (due to work-life issues). Many organizations are uncomfortable reducing an employee's salary in certain situations — especially in demotions due to business circumstances. While this may be understandable, it's critical that the organization keep clear records because a future jobholder should be properly placed in a salary range geared to the job, not relative to the previous jobholder's salary.

- **Lateral Transfers:** A lateral transfer is a move to a new role in the organization that's similar in scope and complexity to one's current role. Ordinarily, lateral moves result in the transfer of an executive to a new job within the same pay grade or same band with a similar market target. These moves may be employee-driven (for example, a personal desire to learn a new area of the business) or company-driven due to a re-organization, the need for executive development, or because a current executive has skills for which the company has critical needs. A lateral move is an opportunity for an employee to try something new, face new challenges, and add breadth to their work experience. While a lateral move may not automatically result in a pay increase — especially if it's driven by the employee's request — moving executives around is an investment in the organization's future. If the value of the development experience is obvious, then base pay increases may also be part of the equation.

- **Developmental Moves:** Developmental moves may be lateral or downward to new roles designed to expand the executive's capabilities while increasing their value to the organization. Developmental moves help executives prepare for larger roles in the company. These moves are crucial to increasing employees' skills and knowledge by enabling them to take on different challenges and learn new skills. Typically, executives receiving developmental moves are on a "fast track" and consistently rated as high performers. Most developmental moves don't require pay adjustments. However, based on the executive's potential, level of personal risk being taken, and the expectation of adding significant value in the short-term, an executive could be eligible for an increase.

- **Hot Skills/Geographic Pay Differentials:** Sometimes, established guidelines just won't work for a job. When pay guidelines are established for a headquarters in Chattanooga, for example, but an executive needs to live and work in Manhattan, the organization is faced with a geographic premium issue. This also can happen when the organization is faced with a hot skills issue, such as a "seller's market" for computer security executives with specific know-how. In these cases, many organizations simply add a figure — a "differential" — to the data they're using to determine salaries. Some organizations accommodate the special need by creating a distinct, time-bound "contract supplement."
- **Pay for Potential:** Sometimes it is necessary to protect against loss of mission-critical, high-potential talent by over-paying relative to market. Most employers limit personal pay grades or levels to those with the highest performance and potential, and use premium pay as a way to protect against regrettable turnover of key talent. Typically such personal pay decisions are limited to 10 percent or less of the executive population.

While many employees are unaware of all the perquisites, benefits and intangibles their companies offer, nearly everyone knows their own base salary. Every paycheck is a reminder to executives of the link between work and reward — and an opportunity for leaders to reinforce key messages about their organizations' strategies and decisions.

CHAPTER 4

Annual Incentive Pay

By Garry Teesdale and Brian Dresch

Annual incentives can best be defined as compensation tied to performance, measured relative to a performance standard and earned during a 12-month period. People often use "annual incentive" and "bonus" interchangeably when, in fact, they are two different things. An incentive focuses on motivating and rewarding desired behaviors and results based on planned metrics and defined results, while a bonus tends to be after the fact and discretionary.

Annual incentives, which originated at Bethlehem Steel in 1911, were for many years essentially profit-sharing vehicles to reward non-owner managers. By the 1960s and 1970s, these plans had evolved into a tool reinforcing the importance of a company's budget (i.e., target bonuses tied to budgeted earnings). In the late 1980s and early 1990s, organizations began to consider tying bonus awards to performance using a measure of value. Today, annual incentives in many forms are ubiquitous in U.S. and foreign companies.

It is important to remember that annual incentives are just that: annual. Companies often let their plans continue unchanged year after year without considering modifications in company goals or operations. Most often, companies revisit their annual incentive plans when a major corporate change is pending or occurs, such as a transaction (e.g., sale or acquisition) or restructuring (e.g., Chapter 11 bankruptcy), a new strategy or a new CEO. At this point, the old incentive model may no longer be appropriate, or a symbolic change may be required.

In other situations, companies may conclude that the current plan is not working — that there is a disconnect between the actual or perceived level of performance and payments received by employees. This can be the case during periods of economic turmoil when many companies struggle to determine annual incentive goals and payment levels. Another reason for change is when an organization realizes it is not in line with the market or has learned about an interesting new annual incentive approach that it wishes to examine.

In any of these situations, it is critical to have an annual incentive design that forges a strong link between performance and payout level. Without an effective design, the annual incentive plan simply becomes a bonus.

This chapter:

- Reviews how annual incentives can affect individual and team performance and discusses design considerations such as plan purpose and objectives, eligibility, funding, calculating awards and payout alternatives.

- Addresses the difficulties in administering and budgeting for an annual incentive plan and discusses the issues that arise in an economic downturn, including steps companies can take to maintain the efficacy of the plan while company performance remains below par.

- Describes some common pitfalls in annual incentive plan design and how to avoid them.

- Addresses the use of "umbrella plans" (for public companies) and how they may be used to assure the tax deductibility of payments under section 162(m) of the Internal Revenue Code (IRC).

The Design of Annual Incentives

Short-term variable compensation has become a critical component of most employers' total reward programs. Diverse perceptions exist regarding the use of variable pay. (See "Advantages and Disadvantages of Variable Pay Programs.") As the prevalence of annual incentive plans continues to grow, companies question whether they influence behavior or improve performance beyond what could be attained in their absence.

Design is the foundation of an effective annual incentive plan. To be effective, an annual incentive plan must increase the focus on performance by encouraging the delivery of specific goals and desired behaviors. Implementation also is critical — the programs communicate and reinforce messages around corporate aims and personal performance.

An effective plan also should link the cost of such compensation to affordability, align the amount and mix of pay with market norms, provide defensive support against accusations of excessive payments, and achieve favorable tax treatment.

Six critical questions should be considered in designing annual incentive plans:

- What is the plan's purpose?
- Who will participate?
- What should the objectives, measures and standards be?
- What should the level of opportunity be?
- How is the plan funded?
- What are the payout alternatives?

Advantages and Disadvantages of Variable Pay Programs

Advantages

- Reinforce desired employee performance and behaviors.
- Align individual goals and objectives with organizational goals and objectives.
- Create a strong alignment between productivity, costs, revenue and performance.
- Support a performance culture by differentiating the rewards paid to top performers versus average or below-average performers.
- Maintain competitiveness in the labor market.

Disadvantages

- May be difficult to administer given the difficulties in tracking and measuring performance.
- Require a variable cost structure, which is more difficult to budget than straight salary costs.
- Employees can develop an entitlement mentality if measures are not understood.
- Short-term incentives may encourage short-term vision.
- May discourage the right behaviors if improperly designed.

TABLE 4-1

Incentive Plan Design Issues

What a Company Says ...	What the Real Issue May Be ...
"Our annual incentive plan may not be aligned with typical market practice."	"We need comfort that our plan is 'normal.' Is there anything new we should know about?"
"I read an article about EVA-based (or RONA, sales, etc.) incentive plans — that's what we need."	"Our current performance measure(s) may not be the most effective."
"Our incentive plan is broken."	"The plan didn't pay out. The problem could be a design, target-setting or calibration problem — perhaps performance was poor."

Plan Purpose

Understanding why a company may need to alter or develop a new annual incentive plan is the first step. As design is a critical success factor, it is important for a company to understand the real issues behind its reasons. (See Table 4-1.)

Plan Participation

Eligibility in a variable pay plan depends on both the organizational compensation philosophy/strategy and several key decision factors:

- At what organizational level does the employee reside? How does that position affect organizational performance?
- Should employees who have poor performance ratings be eligible for participation?
- Does it matter if an employee is eligible for other variable pay plans?
- Is the employee full or part time? How does that affect the employee's contribution?
- When does eligibility begin?

FIGURE 4-1

Performance: Objectives, Measures and Targets

Performance Objectives

What are the organization's performance goals?
1. Increase profit?
2. Grow sales?
3. Reduce costs?
4. Improve quality?

Most companies with broad-based annual incentive plans provide awards to about 70 to 80 percent of the employee population. Companies use various criteria to establish annual incentive plan eligibility — typically one or two factors are used to determine eligibility. Position title/reporting relationship are the most common criteria used, followed by salary grade/band.

Plan Objectives, Measures and Standards

Performance measures play a key role in the design of variable compensation plans. Before a company determines performance measures, it first is essential to determine the intended goals and outcomes of accomplishments (objectives) and how the results will be measured (standards), as outlined in Figure 4-1.

When selecting the performance measures to use, a company first should examine the business strategy and determine how it wants to achieve the business results. The next step is to determine how individual and/or team contributors can affect those results and what performances are needed to achieve organizational goals.

There is no shortage of performance measures; finding the appropriate balance among corporate, business unit and individual metrics is an ongoing challenge for most organizations. Financial measures

Performance Measures

What measures and indicators do we use to measure progress against these goals?

1. EBITDA?
2. Market share?
3. Cost per unit?
4. Returns per unit?

Performance Targets

How do we set the necessary standard of achievement to get a bonus payment?

1. Budget?
2. Relative to peers?
3. Versus last year?
4. Absolute target?

can be placed into three basic categories: accounting, value-based and company value, as in Figure 4-2.

FIGURE 4-2

Three Categories of Financial Measures

	Accounting	Value-Based	Company Value
Measures	■ Earnings ■ EPS ■ ROE ■ ROA	■ EVA ■ Economic profit	■ Discounted cash flow ■ Net present value
Measurement Period	■ Distinct (results-based)	■ Distinct (results-based)	■ Forward-looking
Underlying Rules	■ GAAP ■ Lower of cost ■ Double entry ■ Industry rules ■ Revenue realization	■ Capital charge ■ Economic logic	■ Cash flows ■ Cost of capital

A majority of companies rely on two or more performance measures, often combining financial measures with some assessment of individual performance. The most common measures applied are revenue, operating income, business unit performance and individual performance.

An assessment of individual performance in determining participants' awards typically is based on formal assessment. Individual reviews and qualitative measures are used more frequently for individuals lower in the organization.

Opportunity Level

The level(s) at which an incentive plan measures and rewards performance can have a significant effect on its overall effectiveness. A company must determine at what level performance should be measured, as well as how it will differ by employee/group. For example, should support staff be held accountable for overall corporate performance? Or should the CEO's performance be measured against individual goals?

Once the proper levels of opportunity are defined, the next step is identifying the appropriate weighting. A company must determine how measures at each level should be combined to determine a final award and the degree of influence that discrete measures should have on the overall payout.

The measurement focus of incentive plans should be tailored to meet the organization's operating structure. To determine the appropriate balance, an organization should consider:

- Business unit profiles and growth prospects
- Amount of interaction and interdependency between business units and corporate
- Degree to which an executive can control key performance measures at various levels
- Management and corporate culture.

Award Calculation

After identifying the annual incentive plan measures, associated performance objectives and individual award opportunity, it is time to examine how to combine them. Specifically, think about the issues associated with performance measure weightings. While there are numerous possibilities, companies typically employ one of three approaches:

- **Additive.** Awards are calculated separately for each performance metric and added together to determine the incentive payout. Metrics are independent of each other; metrics with greater importance (i.e., organizational impact) are weighted more than less critical performance targets.
- **Multiplicative.** Award for performance on one metric is adjusted based on performance of another metric. Metrics are mathematically linked to reward for a balanced performance against both metrics.
- **Matrix.** Levels of performance on two measures from axes of the matrix. The annual incentive is determined by the intersection of performance level of each measure. Like the multiplicative approach, measures are mathematically linked to reward for balanced performance against both measures simultaneously.

Payout Range

A payout range — the award amounts provided to participants based on performance outcomes — can have a significant influence on behavior and compensation. The two critical components of any payout range are:

- **Threshold.** The level of performance below which no incentive award is provided.
- **Maximum.** The level of performance above which no additional incremental awards are earned.

It is common practice to set the range of performance targets relative to the company's business plan for the current year (e.g., target achievement equals 100 percent of plan). Thresholds and maximums are then developed around this target.

The payout range can be symmetrical or asymmetrical. A symmetrical range allows the threshold for payment at the same percentage below the target as the maximum is above it, whereas an asymmetrical payout range typically provides more upside potential to plan participants. (See Figure 4-3.)

An asymmetrical payout range usually is associated with a company's philosophy to reward proportionately more for performance that is above target and less for performance that falls below objectives. A critical consideration in determining appropriate leverage is the relative positioning of performance targets to industry norms.

If the performance targets are industry-leading, the plan could reflect higher-than-average opportunity with modest downside leverage and high upside leverage. Conversely, if the performance targets are within industry norms, high leverage may be appropriate on both sides of target.

The perceived odds of attaining goal levels are an important consideration when setting incentive plan goals. Participants must believe that at the onset of the performance period the goals have a reasonable likelihood of being achieved. If the goals are too stringent, the participants will discount them and virtually ignore the targets. If the goals are too easy, the plan will not drive stretch performance. From an employee motivation and incentive design perspective, Table 4-2 lays out a rule for the likelihood of attainment when setting performance goals.

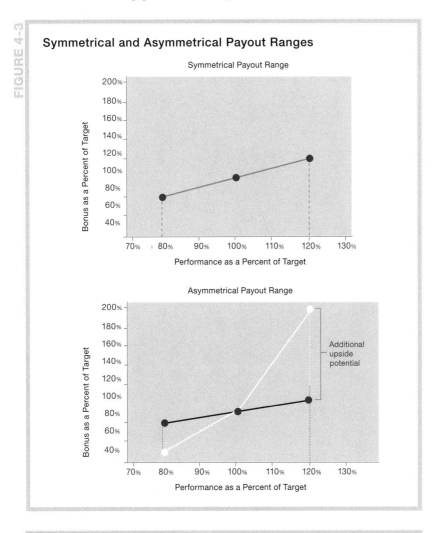

FIGURE 4-3

Symmetrical and Asymmetrical Payout Ranges

Symmetrical Payout Range

Asymmetrical Payout Range

TABLE 4-2

Attainment of Performance Levels

Performance Level	Odds of Attainment
Threshold	8 out of 10
Target	5 out of 10
Maximum (Stretch)	2 out of 10

Many companies establish a minimum or threshold level of performance that must be achieved to receive any payout under the incentive plan. "Circuit breakers" commonly are built into the funding of the incentive pool or serve as the threshold of performance for one of the plan measures. Some companies still allow incentives below the threshold under certain circumstances, at least partly negating the purpose of the threshold.

Not all threshold levels operate as circuit breakers. A company may set a threshold for measures that are mutually exclusive, thus allowing some portion of the bonus to be paid if performance exceeds threshold on one measure while falling short on the other(s).

Dealing with Economic Turmoil

Determining annual incentive plan goals and appropriate payout levels can be especially challenging during periods of economic turmoil. Management and compensation committees struggle with ways to maintain effective incentive plans while business plans and goals fall below normal or desired levels of performance. In many cases, normal objectives for maximizing short-term profit give way to improving cash flow and better positioning for future profitable growth. This often leaves employees feeling that they are working harder than ever with little hope of achieving established performance thresholds. On the other hand, management and compensation committees need to maintain fiscal responsibility and control compensation costs in line with reduced performance.

One way to address the situation is to widen normal performance ranges. For example, if threshold performance goals are normally set at 80 percent of planned performance, the threshold may be reduced to 50 percent of plan, often coupled with a corresponding reduction in the amount of threshold-level incentive payment (e.g., 25 percent of target payment rather than 50 percent of target payment). Some organizations go a step farther and provide enhanced incentive opportunities to drive performance past target and toward established maximum performance levels.

Another approach is to fund some level of an incentive payment pool for high-performing employees for improving the business or achieving specified strategic goals under a difficult set of circumstances even though current financial goals are not achieved. In the end, it is important to achieve a balance among annual profit, growth and performance, and setting goals with reasonable odds of attainment that drive employees to achieve desired results. At some companies, payments for achievement of short-term milestones or strategic goals are deferred in the form of restricted shares. In that way, the level or value of payment is linked to continued employment and the effect that short-term achievements have on future share value. However, once economic conditions start settling down, it is important for a company to return to a more normalized performance and goal-setting approach with an appropriate balance between short- and long-term compensation design.

Plan Funding

The way an organization funds incentives plays an important role in achieving a fair balance between the interests of shareholders and plan participants. Funding for cash-based incentive plans focuses on pools of money, whereas funding for equity-based plans focuses on pools of shares. There are two common approaches used to determine overall annual incentive plan funding:

- **Sum of targets.** The aggregate amount of awards to be paid under the plan is determined by adding the target awards of all participants. Companies usually then modify the pool resulting from the aggregate targets based on a formal schedule relating to performance.

- **Financial results-based formula.** A fund is established using a percentage of a financial measure (e.g., 3 percent of net income) or a percentage of a financial measure that exceeds a hurdle rate (e.g., 5 percent of net income in excess of an 8 percent return on equity).

The challenge with the sum of targets approach is, depending on the measures and the company's ability to correlate the different payout levels with performance, it does not necessarily link to the employer's ability to pay these incentives. Conversely, the financial results-based formula is relatively rigid on whether bonuses will be paid at the level earned. To address these challenges, the solution for many companies is a combination of both approaches.

For companies establishing a maximum pool, the most common method to express this is as a multiple or percentage of the target pool. It is not uncommon for a company to set an overall limit on the amount it will pay out in any one year. This limit sometimes is called a "stakeholder protection clause" because it protects stakeholders against possible windfall payments under the plan due to unforeseen events.

Payout Alternatives

In some cases, a company may want to provide senior managers with flexibility in choosing how they receive their incentive payout. There are two general types of incentive payout alternatives that employers most commonly offer to employees:

- **Deferral opportunities.** In addition to base salary, many companies allow participants to elect to defer receipt of all or a portion of their incentive awards/payments.
- **Cash-bonus exchange.** Companies also may allow employees to exchange a portion of their target or actual annual cash bonus for stock options and/or time-vested restricted stock.

If you're wondering why would a company offer these opportunities, and why would an employee take advantage of them, see Table 4-3.

Annual incentives are an important part of total compensation. Employees may not always see the link between base pay and organizational objectives, whereas variable pay provides visibility about how their actions affect the company and its achievement of goals. The plan design is critical for any annual incentive pay plan to be both effective and to align employee performance to organizational objectives.

TABLE 4-3

Employee and Company Benefits

Employee Benefits	Company Benefits
Tax effectiveness: Delays tax on the exchanged incentive value (until employee realizes value from equity award).	**Stock ownership:** Provides an additional opportunity for employees to increase their ownership levels.
Additional upside/wealth accumulation potential: While the exchange for equity-based compensation entails more risk than cash, it also provides significantly more upside potential.	**Tax/income statement effectiveness:** Improves cash flow for company in the short-term (though long-term EPS effects may be less beneficial).
Flexibility: Furnishes ability to customize pay, a growing market trend.	

Plan Design Pitfalls and How to Avoid Them

Based on our research and experience in the assessment of incentive programs, we identified three common traps to avoid when designing or deciding upon an incentive plan.

Pitfall 1: Pay and Performance Relationship — Is Your Performance Line Too Steep?

Does your incentive plan act as if it has an on/off switch? Over the past several years, has the plan either paid out at maximum or not paid out at all, while hardly ever paying out at target levels? If this sounds like your company's incentive plan, then the slope of the payout line might be too steep and deserve further investigation.

The following are typical outcomes when a line is too steep:

- **Payouts increase/decrease disproportionately with only incremental changes in performance.** While payouts from incentive plans commonly range from 0 percent to 200 percent of target payout, performance ranges are often much narrower. Accordingly, in a plan with a very steep performance line, an incremental change in performance leads to a disproportionate change in incentive payouts.

- **Lack of motivation.** Because the performance range is so narrow within a plan with a steep performance line, it often becomes apparent to executives early in the year whether or not the plan will pay out. Both outcomes (whether no payout or a maximum payout) can lead to less than optimal motivation.

- **Pay and performance relationship is out of whack.** Extremely steep payout lines can lead to outcomes that can under reward and over reward performance, almost never getting it right.

Compensation committees can consider the following actions:

- **Graph the payout line and test the upper and lower limits.** Once graphed, review the slope and test the appropriateness of payouts at the threshold level and the maximum level. Ask yourself if the relationship is reasonable and defensible. If it is apparent that the answer to this is "no," then you need to adjust (probably flatten the pay to performance relationship).
- **Consider typical odds of attainment** (See Table 4-2.) If your company is far off from this standard, is there a reason why? Look at your incentive plan payments over the past five to 10 years and determine if they align with customary chances of attainment. If your plan is not aligned, it may be because the slope is too steep.
- **Benchmark your payout line against industry and competitors.** Incentive plan information is widely available via compensation surveys and publicly disclosed information. Graph your lines and compare the slopes against competitors or industry. Understand the differences between your company's plan and the market to explain why there are differences.

Pitfall 2: Rigid Definitions of Performance That Don't Control for Unpredictable External Factors

The past few years have shown that setting meaningful goals in an uncertain economy can be very challenging, and that actual performance can be heavily affected by unpredictable external factors. Public companies in particular feel this pain, since making adjustments to goals in the middle of a performance cycle can void the income tax deductibility of certain incentive payments under a shareholder-approved plan. We discuss this later in the chapter.

Typical outcomes of this pitfall include an inability or unwillingness to adjust measured performance or to exercise negative discretion in determining payouts can have a potentially damaging effect on incentive alignment. Without such judgment, earned pay can reflect an outdated understanding of an environment that disregards both windfalls and constraints under which performance was achieved. Controlling the impact of positive and negative external factors is an important element of plan design to ensure that a company is incentivizing the maximum contribution to "core" performance and rewarding associated outcomes. When persistently negative factors are allowed to materially influence plan payouts, retention issues are likely to arise.

The ability to control the impact of external factors on incentive plan goals and payouts can be provided (1) through the definition of the metric, or (2) through the definition of adjustments. For example, consider a globally dependent business with a significant amount of operations in developing nations. In reviewing its past three years of performance, the company noted that fluctuations in exchange rates have had a material impact on measured profitability. The compensation committee may choose not to hold executives accountable for managing currency risk by defining and measuring performance on a "constant currency" basis, using exchange rates for translation in effect for the same prior-year period (effectively eliminating the impact of currency fluctuations during the current year). Alternatively, the committee may choose to hold executives partially accountable by adjusting measured results for certain one-time currency-related items, such as charges related to currency devaluation and hyperinflationary accounting.

Compensation committees can consider the following actions:

■ Review the historic impact of "one-time" gains and losses or extraordinary items on measured performance and associated payouts. It is important that companies understand where their plans may be vulnerable to external pressure, the frequency with which such factors present themselves, and the sensitivity of the plan's payouts.

■ Consider the definition of each metric used in the incentive plan. A metric itself may explicitly define what an executive is (and is not) accountable for doing. Consider the items included in the definition of the metric, whether and the extent to which such items are within the control of the executive, and whether such items are relevant to determining "core" company performance.

■ Consider the definition of allowable adjustments to incentive plan metrics. Most companies use an "adjusted" performance measure (e.g., adjusted EBITDA, adjusted operating income, etc.). Adjustments to such measures are often broadly defined in underlying plan documentation, allowing the compensation committee to exercise judgment in determining whether to include or exclude certain items. Common adjustments to measured performance generally exclude the impact of acquisition and integration-related costs, restructuring costs and asset impairments.

Pitfall 3: The Incentive Plan Doesn't Support Company Strategy

Incentive plans at their very best can be incredibly powerful in supporting and driving corporate strategy and results. A well-designed incentive plan makes clear what the company and its stakeholders value and for what they are willing to pay. A poorly designed incentive plan can do just the opposite, by driving the wrong behaviors or by simply focusing executives on erroneous and inconsequential outcomes.

Since the 2008-2009 recession, almost all organizations have reconsidered their strategies. While many companies have simply made adjustments to their strategy, others have worked to completely transform their business.

When an incentive plan does not evolve with the direction of the company, some common problems may include:

■ The incentive plan does not motivate executives to reach the newly established company goals; or worse, the plan motivates behaviors that work against (or are counter to) the company's strategy.

■ The incentive plan has failed to evolve and is no longer connected to a company's goals. Consider a company that has been historically focused on profitability while growth is key under its new strategy. If the incentive plan does not evolve with the new strategy, there can be an inherent misalignment between the objectives of the company and stakeholders and the way executives are incented.

- The incentive plan is leading strategy rather than supporting it. Incentive plans are best designed to support strategy and not to lead strategy. Without a clear company direction an incentive plan often becomes a "cash delivery system" and not a tool that drives performance.

Here are some ideas of what to do:

- Management and the compensation committee should review the incentive plan against company strategy on an annual basis, making sure that incentive measures and goals are still relevant. A review may range from an assessment of measures (and their associated weightings) to a wholesale examination of the entire plan.
- If a company is in the process of redefining its strategy, it is critical that the company first establish its strategy and then design its incentive plan to support the strategy. Designing an incentive plan in opposite order often leads to a disconnect between the plan and desired outcomes.

Today's organizations are more agile than ever, able to adapt their businesses to rapidly changing markets and volatile economic conditions. Combined with greater scrutiny on pay-for-performance, it is imperative that companies continually review the design of their incentive plans. Such examinations should be conducted with a focus on balancing business needs and strategy with market practices, while actively soliciting feedback from the compensation committee, the board of directors and plan participants.

Umbrella Plans: A Means to Assure Tax Deductibility Under Section 162(m)

An employer generally can deduct, for income tax purposes, reasonable compensation paid to its employees for personal services rendered. However, public companies can face the hurdle of IRC section 162(m), which bars the deduction of compensation in excess of $1 million paid to certain top executives in a tax year unless a performance-based exception is satisfied. The employees who potentially are subject to the section 162(m) limitations are known as "covered employees" and consist of the company's CEO and its other three highest paid executives (other than its CFO).

Performance-Based Exception to IRC Section 162(m)

Not all compensation is subject to the deduction limit imposed by section 162(m). Specifically, compensation that constitutes "qualified performance-based compensation" is exempt; its key requirements include:

- The compensation must be payable solely upon the achievement of pre-established performance goals.
- These goals must be objective and must preclude discretion to increase award sizes.
- The ability to attain the goal must be substantially uncertain at the time the goal is established.
- The plan and performance measures must be subject to shareholder approval.
- Performance goals must be administered by "outside directors."
- Prior to payment, the company's compensation committee must certify that the goals were attained.

In order to provide flexibility in a company's incentive plan structure while preserving section 162(m) deductibility, the concept of an "umbrella plan" (so known because there is a plan over or within a plan that protects the deduction) was developed and is now widely used.

Types of Umbrella Plans

An umbrella plan commonly falls in either of two categories:

- Shareholder-approved plan document contains a lengthy list of objective performance measures and a limit on the maximum incentive award for any participant. If these requirements are satisfied, the compensation committee selects from the metrics set out in the plan document and establishes a bonus pool formula (subject to the individual participant maximums). Negative discretion then is applied by the compensation committee to reduce the award levels produced by the bonus formula to implement the desired incentive structure (such as contained in participants' scorecards).

- Shareholder-approved plan document with a specified formula that funds a maximum bonus pool for participants. After using a section 162(m) compliant metric or metrics to establish a fixed bonus pool and the maximum percentage of the pool that can be paid to any participant, the compensation committee uses negative discretion to allocate the pool in line with performance based on employee scorecards.

Plans Using List of Performance Measures

This approach starts with obtaining shareholder approval of a plan document that includes an exhaustive list of performance measures (sometimes referred to as a laundry list) along with a maximum incentive award amount that may be paid to any individual. The individual maximum awards specified in the formal (shareholder-approved) plan should be larger (generally much larger) than the maximum amount an individual could be awarded according to underlying plan.

The compensation committee establishes through a written resolution a bonus pool formula using one or more of the shareholder-approved measures contained in the plan document within the first 90 days of the performance period. The bonus pool formula should be established at levels higher than the possible maximum bonus that would be awarded pursuant to the underlying plan. Also, as mentioned above, the amount paid to a participant pursuant to the bonus pool formula cannot exceed the individual maximum contained in the plan document. The compensation committee may use negative discretion to adjust the award downward from the earned amount, with such reduction commonly made to the amount indicated in the underlying incentive scorecard.

This list of performance measures must be reapproved by shareholders at least every five years to remain section 162(m) compliant.

Specified Formula Pool Plan

The specified formula pool uses a section 162(m)-compliant formulaic financial metric to fund a maximum bonus pool amount payable to participating individuals. The formula is used to calculate the maximum aggregate amount of the pool, and this pool amount is then considered the "outside plan." Within the amount funded, a scorecard would then be applied (the "inside plan") to allocated plan amounts and negative discretion used by the compensation committee.

Benefits and Drawbacks

In determining the approach to provide in the shareholder-approved plan document, it is important for companies and compensation committees to consider the benefits and drawbacks of both types of umbrella plans.

Plan Using List of Performance Measures

Benefits:

- "Cleanest" alternative and easier to communicate to participants and shareholders
- Well-regarded by the market and its use is prevalent among public companies

Drawbacks:

- Requires every measure to be objective and included in the shareholder-approved plan. Despite the typical lengthy lists of metrics, from time to time a company may not have considered a certain measure that it now would like to use but is unable to do so without an amendment approved by shareholders.

Specified Pool Formula Plan

Benefits:

- Provides greater flexibility in choosing performance measures while allowing for section 162(m) deductibility
- Has some market prevalence and is well-regarded as a tool to use for tax-deductibility

- Shareholder approval only required every 10 years unless change financial funding formula

Drawbacks:

- Potential for poor optics if maximum achievement is set too low and the additional performance goals are not closely related to pay-for-performance
- If the outside plan threshold is not achieved, no awards can be made under this type of plan

Other Considerations

With an umbrella plan, compensation committees are afforded the flexibility to determine appropriate annual incentive pay for top executives and still achieve corporate tax-deductibility. This can be an important consideration in light of shareholder derivative lawsuits that have claimed corporate waste and other breaches where the incentive compensation paid was not deductible due to a failure to satisfy section 162(m). (See Chapter 26.) While these cases have met with little success in the courts, the time, effort and professional fees involved in defense against such claims can be costly. Accordingly, in addition to timely action by the compensation committee, it is critical that all design requirements and shareholder approvals are met so that any umbrella plan is section 162(m) compliant.

CHAPTER 5

Public Company Long-Term Incentive Compensation: An Equity-Based Focus

By Tony Wu and Bryan Kligman

For senior executives at public companies, equity-based LTIs usually are the largest component of the pay package, often exceeding base salary and annual incentives by several multiples. Owing to the multi-year vesting periods and the potential for significant rewards, LTIs are a powerful and highly visible tool in retaining top executive talent. In addition, equity-based compensation is the principal agent in aligning company leadership with shareholders and reinforcing pay for performance.

In the 1980s through the early 2000s, stock options dominated LTI plans. More recently, changes in accounting, governance reforms, market downturns, shareholder scrutiny, and concerns about high dilution levels have combined to alter both the design and use of LTIs. More than any other factor, however, the required expensing of stock options under accounting rules adopted in 2004 prompted significant strategic changes in LTI practices.

In addition to accounting rule changes, updated proxy require-ments for compensation disclosure began drawing attention to practices and plans that previously might have been known only to a handful of company insiders and board members. Further, disclosure requirements demanded that companies explain *why* certain plan elements were used in addition to *what* existed. Thus, it became incumbent upon executives and compensation committees to rethink and re-evaluate their equity plans based on their specific business needs and strategies, all while taking into consideration how their shareholders were likely to view their plans.

Companies have broadened their approaches and applied a more strategic lens to LTIs and now often use a portfolio approach to making LTI grants by spreading more value over a combination of vehicles. The biggest gains have been seen in performance-share plans and performance-vested restricted stock plans that combine both share price increase and other key companywide performance to determine incentive value.

Many issues have to be addressed in designing LTI programs: the potential value of company shares, management's perception of share value, the optimum number of shares authorized for use, the effect of run rates, and stock overhang, to name only a few. In this environment, setting performance goals has taken on a heightened importance in LTI design. Many companies are challenged just setting annual goals, let alone having to project multiple-year targets. Determining accurate performance measures that trigger appropriate plan payouts is, of course, crucial to the success of these plans, and often the most difficult. Our objective is to provide practical insights on how companies can transition to a more balanced, strategic approach to LTIs.

This chapter:

- Examines how LTIs fit into an overall pay strategy and what compensation committees and senior management must do to address the share dilution and pay-for-performance issues relating to LTIs.

- Discusses the design flexibility available to companies seeking to include performance conditions in full-value stock awards. Considerations such as leverage, performance measures, goal setting, performance periods and eligibility for performance-vested plans also are addressed.

- Reviews the key accounting issues relating to LTIs, focusing on performance shares and performance-vested restricted stock.

- Recommends that companies examine their stock option program for efficiency and perceived value from both shareholder and executive perspectives.

Strategic Considerations for Long-Term Incentive Plans

Direct compensation in its many forms — base salary, annual bonuses and LTIs — is the single greatest expense for most companies in the United States. Accordingly, employee rewards represent a significant component of the financial strategy and decision process for any successful business.

Because the compensation system is such a large part of an organization's overall financial structure, it is strategic almost by definition. Nowhere is the strategic nature of the compensation program more evident than in the design of executive LTI programs. Specifically, an LTI program is:

- Likely the key element in a company's ability to attract and retain top executive talent — those individuals who develop and implement strategic business plans
- Costly and creates significant multi-year liabilities, creating long-term commitments for the company
- Highly visible; no board of directors or compensation committee wants to be in the position of defending compensation practices similar to excessive arrangements that have been reported at some well-known and respected organizations.

With the increases in proxy-related disclosure requirements, shareholders of public companies gained more and better information with which to evaluate a company's LTI program. As these shareholders began paying more attention to these disclosures, and as they were given more power with which to affect a company's compensation decision-making, LTI practices began changing. Gone are the days in which companies would simply disclose that their program designs were a function of market practices and competitiveness; the SEC and shareholders began demanding that companies demonstrate the link between their programs and their strategy. Proxy advisers have also played their part in shaping LTI design as winning over shareholder support continues to be important to companies in the say-on-pay era.

Understanding Constraints in Granting Long-Term Incentives

LTI issues go beyond pure compensation design. They introduce issues relating to accounting, tax and use of a company's share pool — each of which provides some constraints. LTI awards entail real expense and potential dilution of shareholder value, adding levels of complexity when compared to other elements of the executive pay package.

These constraints are critical for all companies to understand as they look to balance their HR objectives with the cold, hard facts of their LTIs' effect on financials and share availability.

Key questions in this process include:

- How many shares are available for the company to grant?
- When will the available pool of shares be depleted?
- What is the company's current stock overhang relative to peer and shareholder benchmarks?
- What will be the expense impact of each type of share granted? How well does that expense correlate to perceived value on the part of recipients?
- What are the tax implications — to the recipient as well as the company — of the different LTI vehicles being considered?

Knowing the Hot Buttons

The landscape for LTI compensation changes annually, and every company needs to know what market trends suggest and what shareholders watch. As the largest part of an executive's compensation package, LTIs tend to attract significant shareholder attention on issues that relate to dilution of their share value and the pay-for-performance orientation of the company's program.

Some of the key questions companies need to ask regularly go right to the heart of these hot buttons:

- What is the right level of shares for the company to use annually (i.e., run rate)?
- Do additional equity grants provide additional motivation or retention value to an executive who already has a significant stake in the business?

- Do executives own enough shares to demonstrate adequate alignment with shareholders? Are the company's share ownership and retention guidelines/requirements set at the right levels?
- How long is "long term"? Should changes be considered that better align the vesting of these incentives with the time horizon for the company's business challenges?
- How much (if any) of the company's LTI mix should be performance-vested vs. service-vested?
- What should happen to unvested shares upon termination? Should they vest immediately, continue to vest, or not vest at all?
- What should happen to unvested shares upon a change in control? Should they vest immediately or continue to vest?
- To what extent does the LTI design "check the box" from a proxy adviser perspective?

While none of these questions necessarily has a single right answer for every company, many shareholders will have strong opinions on them. No compensation committee should ever be surprised by shareholders' reaction to its company's LTI program, which puts pressure on the compensation team to ensure that each and every one of these issues is given adequate attention and planning.

Performance Shares and Performance-Vested Restricted Stock

Regulatory and corporate governance developments, combined with the refinement of a key design feature, have breathed new life into the use of performance shares and performance-vested restricted stock in LTI programs. Full-value stock award plans like restricted stock — long-favored by recipients but often loathed by skeptical investors — have shown an increase in use since the stock option expensing rules changes. Today, however, the inclusion of performance criteria is an essential feature in these plans to meet shareholder demands for good governance and paying for performance.

Service-Based, Full-Value Plans (Restricted Stock and Restricted Stock Units)

Executives who receive traditional service-based, full-value awards are generally granted as either restricted stock (RS) or restricted stock unit (RSU) awards.

- RS: Award of actual shares with current ownership rights and subject to vesting (based on time and/or performance). Actual shares are issued at the grant date (with a restrictive legend on any certificate) but typically held by the company or in escrow until vesting. RS cannot be transferred until vested. Recipients are generally treated similarly to actual shareholders as both dividend and voting rights typically accompany such vehicle.

- RSU: Award of units (a bookkeeping account) representing a contractual right (but no current ownership rights) to receive payment (generally in shares but may be made in cash) at some point after vesting. No shares are issued until the time of actual payout/delivery (assuming equity "settlement"). RSUs cannot be transferred until they are converted into actual shares. Since the award of an RSU is essentially a contractual promise to pay at some time in the future with no shares actually issued upon grant, they do not have dividend or voting rights, although companies may provide "dividend equivalents" to mirror the availability of dividends on RS.

These awards entitle executives to actual shares or the right to shares of company stock, usually without cost, once prescribed terms and conditions are satisfied. In conventional practice, terms and conditions were limited to time-based vesting. Stay on the job for, say, four years, and the unit or stock becomes yours, either ratably over time (graded vesting) or all at once (cliff vesting) at the end of the restriction period.

All in all, this tends to be a good deal for the executive. The downside is limited (restricted stock/units do not go underwater), and the cost cannot be beat (by contrast, an executive must pay the exercise price for a stock option). Once restrictions lapse, the executive may sell shares or use cash (often from bonuses) to pay the resulting tax (at the time of vesting in the case of RS and actual payout/delivery in the case of RSUs). However, from the viewpoint of wary investors, this often is deemed too good of a deal; they tend to want to see more executive skin in the game and performance hurdles that are more robust than merely staying employed.

In concert with the increased use of full-value awards over the last decade (starting with the adoption of accounting changes under FAS 123R, now Accounting Standards Codification (ASC) Topic 718), RSUs have replaced RS as the favored type of full-value equity award for employers. The rationale for this trend can be found in one word — flexibility. From both design and administration perspectives, RSUs offer more flexibility than RS.

Adding Performance Conditions to Full-Value Awards

Recently, the use of performance shares and performance-vested restricted stock/units has surged for a combination of reasons. First, aforementioned changes in the accounting rules eliminated a compelling advantage in favor of stock options by requiring companies to recognize a charge to earnings on fixed option grants issued at fair market value. This heavily debated action evened the playing field for other compensatory equity-based programs with stock options from an accounting perspective.

Additionally, with shareholders becoming more involved in all matters relating to executive pay, companies became more focused on the levels of dilution that resulted when the majority of LTIs were granted through stock options. Using performance shares or restricted stock helps conserve shares because companies obtain more mileage from the full value of a restricted share than from the fair value of a stock option, which always will be worth less than the underlying price of the stock.

Most notably, performance shares are designed in part to respond to the perceived lack of pay-for-performance orientation from which service-vested vehicles suffer. Performance share plans (PSPs) provide a more direct link to performance than stock options or other service-based LTI vehicles by using two different levers to align pay and performance: the accomplishment of key goals (typically financial, operational or shareholder driven) that determine how many shares are earned, combined with the value of those shares earned at the end of the cycle.

PSPs are now viewed favorably by external constituencies, particularly when used as the dominant vehicle in an LTI program. At many of the largest U.S. public companies, CEOs and other C-suite executives often receive at least 50 percent of their TDC in the form of LTIs. In this pay mix, PSPs increasingly comprise at least 50 percent of the overall LTI value.

Designing Performance Share Plans

One key benefit of a PSP is the considerable design flexibility offered. However, before a PSP can be rolled out, numerous design features have to be thought through (including details). Given the significant organizational, employee and shareholder implications associated with PSPs, companies need to get it right when designing, implementing and communicating these programs. There is no one-size-fits-all approach to PSP design; rather it should support and promote each organization's unique business strategy and compensation philosophy while aligning with the interests of key stakeholders.

Leverage

PSPs usually have a degree of leverage, which refers to the relationship between performance and payout levels. Typically, these plans operate similarly to annual incentive programs in that there are scaled payouts available for performance that is both below and above target goals.

Many PSP programs contain the following three levels of performance and corresponding common payout levels (i.e., the performance/payout calibration):

- **Threshold.** A floor that represents the minimum level of performance that must be achieved before PSPs can be earned. For an absolute financial performance measures, threshold performance is generally in the range of 80 to 90 percent of target. For a relative performance measure (e.g., relative TSR), threshold performance is generally set around the 25th-35th percentile versus the applicable comparator group. In each of these cases, the threshold payout level is generally 25 to 50 percent of target.

- **Target.** The expected or planned (budgeted) level of PSP performance achievement and payout. For an absolute financial performance measures, 100 percent of plan/budget typically equals a 100 percent payout. For a relative performance measure, target is often set at the 50th percentile (median) versus the applicable comparator group, equating to a 100 percent payout.

- **Maximum.** The total PSP opportunity that may be earned for superior performance, sometimes referred to as a cap. For an absolute financial performance measures, maximum performance is generally in the range of 110 to 120 percent of target. For a relative TSR performance measure, maximum performance is generally set around the 75th percentile versus the applicable comparator group. In each of these cases, the maximum payout level is often 150 to 200 percent of target. In an effort to provide "fairness" and better align with shareholders, PSPs using relative TSR may include a limit on payout at target levels when an organization's TSR is negative over the performance period but relative performance would have resulted in above-target/maximum payouts.

A common leverage curve provides something on the order of 50 percent of target shares for achievement of threshold performance, and 150 or 200 percent of target shares for achievement of stretch performance. (See Figure 5-1.)

In both examples, shares are earned at a faster pace for incremental performance above target levels than they are below target levels. Achieving the right leverage relationship should be a function of a company's overall pay philosophy, business strategy and performance orientation. For example, a more leveraged curve may be appropriate for entrepreneurial organizations where executives are expected to take on more risk in an effort to drive the success of the business. In these situations, executives would be more generously rewarded for outstanding performance, but held more accountable for below-target performance. A flatter leverage curve, on the other hand, might be appropriate for a company with a less leveraged business strategy.

FIGURE 5-1

Examples of Varying Performance Share Plan Leverages

Performance Measures

A primary challenge with using performance shares is the difficulty in setting reasonably difficult yet achievable goals for an extended time. To fix goals, companies often rely on the forecasting abilities of their finance and strategic planning teams to develop realistic projections. However, while many companies use objectives that are absolute in nature, goals also can be relative.

Absolute goals typically are financial in nature but, increasingly, companies are adopting more strategic measurements that capture needed longer-term business transformations (e.g., sales or market share growth in a key product category). Relative goals almost always are financial in nature and look to compare the company's performance against a peer group or broader index (e.g., the company's total shareholder return or top-line growth versus its peer group). Balancing the benefits and drawbacks of each approach, many companies may use both types of measures in their plans, allowing them to balance absolute performance with out-performance.

While there is a debate about the use of objective and subjective measures in annual incentive plans, most long-term plans make use of only objective measures that are easily measurable. There are several practical reasons for this. First and foremost, in the United States, section 162(m) of the IRC stipulates that for compensation to be considered "performance-based" and, therefore, eligible for tax deductibility (where the $1 million cap otherwise would apply), associated performance goals for a few top-paid executives (i.e., CEO and next three highest paid executives other than the CFO) must be objective so that a third party can clearly determine whether the goals have been attained. These goals cannot be subject to discretionary assessments that could increase the amounts. Second, the accounting rules penalize equity-based awards that are not based on the objective performance criteria, requiring such grants to be treated with liability accounting instead of the preferred equity accounting treatment.

Goal Setting

Many companies have difficulty determining whether the respective goal levels being proposed are reasonable — if goals aren't properly set, the degree of pay and performance alignment may be skewed too far up or down. Easy goals may result in over-payment for under-performance, while stretch goals may result in under-payment or non-payment for performance that should warrant some payout.

When setting goal levels, several key parameters that drive the process and outcomes should be considered: a company's strategic plan, external performance expectations from shareholders and the market, internal performance expectations from participants (i.e., do the goals have a reasonable likelihood of being achieved?), and the odds of attaining different outcomes (i.e., threshold performance levels should be achieved most of the time, target performance levels should be achieved some of the time, and maximum performance levels should be achieved a few times). Examining historical levels of short- and/or long-term performance achievements may help provide some insight on the degree of difficulty of past goal-setting practices. For example, if actual performance achievements are frequently skewed toward maximum or threshold performance levels over the last five performance cycles, then some recalibration may be warranted.

Common chances of attaining the key performance levels are shown in Table 4-2 of Chapter 4. If goals are too difficult, participants will have low perceived value of the plan and ignore performance. If goals are too soft, the plan will not drive the performance that shareholders are seeking.

Eligibility

Performance plans typically have been limited to senior executives as they represent the key players in driving the success of the business and may cascade one to three levels down depending upon various factors such as the company's size, structure, business/compensation strategy and compensation philosophy. For example, a company with $500 million in revenues and a flat organizational structure may limit PSA eligibility to C-suite executives only; in comparison, a company with $20 billion in revenues and a multi-layer structure may provide PSAs to all employees at the vice president level and above. Current practice limits performance shares to the executive level, as lower-level employees may not always grasp the performance share design concept as it relates to their own positions. The less a participant understands about the award and the less ability to influence the outcomes, the less value that he/she ascribes to the award.

Performance Period

Most plans tend to include a three-year performance period, which is a function of the maximum length of time in which many companies are comfortable forecasting performance, as well as what is considered to be a market-standard vesting period. However, there are plans in the marketplace that are designed from one to five years. Such plans should maintain some alignment with the time horizon of the company's strategic challenges.

Accounting Considerations

A company's financial statements often affects the types of incentive compensation provided to executives. Accordingly, key accounting considerations may influence awards of performance shares and performance-vested restricted stock.

ASC Topic 718 requires that all equity-based compensation granted to employees be accounted for at fair value, measured at grant date. Stock-based awards, including stock options and full-value share plans — whether time- or performance-vested — are classified as equity awards (as opposed to liability awards), assuming payments are settled solely in company stock. Dividends or dividend equivalents (if any) paid during the vesting or performance period are not recognized as additional compensation cost unless the underlying awards are subsequently forfeited and the dividends are not repaid. However, accounting implications vary depending on the type of measures selected.

Performance Conditions

For awards that may vary on the basis of performance conditions (as opposed to market conditions), accruals are recognized over the amortization period and are intended to reflect the probable payout outcome. At the end of each reporting period, the company has to assess the likely performance outcome. Expense recognition then tracks payout amounts based on this estimated performance outcome until the next period when this process is repeated.

If the probable performance outcome changes during the subsequent reporting period, expense accruals need to be adjusted to track new estimated corresponding payouts. Because the number of shares that can be earned likely will differ from target levels, the tracking of awards can cause volatility in compensation expense, as predictions for the likely outcome of shares earned will vary by reporting period. Expense accruals will fluctuate over the course of the performance period depending on whether probable performance outcomes go up or down. (See Figure 5-2.) One advantage of linking performance shares to a performance condition is the reversal of the expenses if the performance condition is not met. Examples of performance conditions include revenue, earnings, cash flow or return-based efficiency measures (e.g., return on equity).

Market Conditions

For performance awards that may vary on the basis of market conditions (in which the stock price is a factor in triggering the award's vesting), the grant-date fair value is determined based on a Monte Carlo valuation model, simulating all possible outcomes over the term of the award. The resulting output is a single value incorporating the economic effect of the market condition over time. Expense is fixed at grant date and amortized over the performance period. (See Figure 5-3.) The expense is irreversible if the market

FIGURE 5-2

Expense Accruals and Performance Award Outcomes

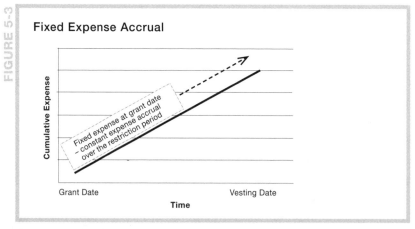

FIGURE 5-3

Fixed Expense Accrual

condition is not met. Examples of market conditions include stock price and total shareholder return.

Income Tax Deductibility

To obtain income tax deductibility under IRC section 162(m), a PSP must be approved by shareholders and contain one or more objective performance metrics, thereby qualifying as performance-based compensation. Goals must be set either prior to the beginning of the performance period or within 90 days of the beginning of the performance period with the outcome substantially uncertain and no more than 25 percent of the performance period having passed. Unearned shares typically do not carry voting rights, and participants may or may not be paid dividend equivalents throughout the performance period.

Other Considerations

Other design implications for a PSP are:

- **Share usage.** Performance shares are full-value awards and often are counted as more than one share toward the equity pool (i.e., shares available for award issuance) for the share usage and ISS' burn-rate calculations. Depending on the plan's leverage curve, companies typically reserve their shares at stretch payout levels up front to ensure that the number of shares required is available at the time of payout. If the actual number of shares paid out is less than reserved, the excess number of shares reserved is available for future grants. To avoid an "against" vote recommendation from a shareholder proxy advisory firm, burn-rate levels typically need to be kept within a range of market-standard levels.
- **Number of tranches.** The number of award tranches also has an effect on the ultimate design. Assuming a three-year performance period, a company may issue one award tranche at grant that spans over the entire performance period, or three award tranches, one tranche at the beginning of each year of the performance cycle. One award tranche simplifies the accounting requirements, as this award is considered to only have one grant-date fair value. The latter, multi-award tranche design requires the company to

determine a grant-date fair value for each award tranche. This not only adds to the accounting complexity, but the administrative complexity as well (e.g., tracking of performance for each award tranche).

■ **Grant process.** LTI awards typically are granted annually. With such an approach, multiple awards overlap, therefore creating "glue" in the position. Executives are less willing to leave three award cycles on the table if another opportunity presents itself. However, with three award cycles come three sets of overlapping performance measures; a commitment generally must be made to the nature of metrics selected, as vastly different overlapping metrics may dilute the performance message and confusion as to which goals to focus on may arise. Therefore, rather than measuring goals annually, three-year cumulative goals are measured to determine award payout.

Growing Use of Performance Shares

Performance shares are playing a more prominent role in an executive's total compensation package as pay for performance, corporate accountability and shareholder value creation have increasingly become focal points in today's executive compensation environment. Performance shares clearly have an advantage over time-vested equity vehicles. Design flexibility, a direct link to performance, favorable accounting treatment, and the perceptions of shareholders have made performance shares a favored long-term incentive compensation delivery vehicle in the boardroom. However, a properly designed plan requires careful thought, rigorous modeling and refinement, as even the slighted design decisions may have lasting program implications. While the complexities may seem overwhelming, PSPs are increasingly viewed as the best answer in balancing executive pay, shareholder interests and financial performance.

Stock Option Efficiency and Perceived Value

While the accounting changes that required the expensing of stock options spurred companies to look at different plan designs, stock option efficiency (from both a shareholder and an employee perspective) also has become an issue for consideration.

Stock options have low share-usage efficiency relative to other equity vehicles. To deliver the same expected equity value to employees, a company has to grant significantly more stock options than full-value restricted shares, which have built-in value at grant.

Since the introduction of stock option expensing, companies must consider the expense efficiency of stock options. In this process, two critical questions are being asked about their LTI plans:

- What is the stock option value actually realized by employee per dollar of expense? While stock options have the potential to deliver significant value to option holders, they may have zero realizable value unless they are in the money when exercisable. In companies where share price performance is poor, companies will incur expense for a vehicle that delivers no value to employees.
- What is the gap between the perceived value of stock options and the expense taken by the company? The binomial and Black-Scholes stock option valuation models provide an expected value of stock options. In theory, stock option recipients should value these options at the same levels produced by the valuation models. In reality, however, an employee's perception of the stock option value is typically much less than the expense value, creating a potentially significant inefficiency.

Perceived Value

For certain employees at some companies, the perceived value of stock options can be less than 50 percent of the option valuation. This means that, for every dollar of stock option value granted, the recipient credits the company with delivering less than 50 cents of value. Simply put, the employee would believe that a cash payment of 50 cents or less would be a fair exchange for a stock option grant.

The degree to which this discount exists involves a number of factors, including:

- **The company's recent share price history.** For companies with strong share price history where stock options have vested in the money, the perceived value of stock options is likely to be much higher than in companies with stagnant price history.

- **Salary level and personal wealth situation.** Higher-paid employees such as executives tend to value stock options higher than lower-paid employees. In large part, this perception may be due to the fact that lower-paid employees generally have nearer-term cash needs and are more inclined to focus on the potential that a grant may yield little or no gain.

Examples of Perceived Value

Company A: Changing the LTI Mix to Increase Perceived Value

Company A is considering a move from stock options to time-vested restricted stock and wants to increase the perceived value of the LTI grant while maintaining the same current expense. The company grants an employee $90,000 worth of LTI value through 30,000 stock options, with a $9 current share price and a $3 option valuation.

However, the company's recent share price performance has been modest. Some previous grants are currently underwater, and an internal survey finds that most employees value the stock options significantly less than the expense value

would suggest, discounting the expense value by approximately 33 percent (for a value of $2 per stock option). As a result, the employee values the $90,000 grant at approximately $60,000.

In switching to time-vested restricted stock, the expense value of each restricted share will be $9, or three times each stock option, utilizing 10,000 shares to create an LTI grant with the same $90,000 expense. A survey by the company determines that employees tend to give roughly a 12 percent "haircut" to restricted shares (or $8 per option), for a perceived value of $80,000.

Company A	Value Granted	Share Price	Expense Valuation	Perceived Value	Number of Shares Needed	Expense Taken	Perceived Value
Stock Options	$90,000	$9	$3	$2	30,000	$90,000	$60,000
Restricted Stock	$90,000	$9	$9	$8	10,000	$90,000	$80,000

For Company A, this switch from options to restricted shares results in an increase in the perceived value of the grant by $20,000, while maintaining the same expense.

■ **Personal risk profile.** Employees who are risk averse will place less value on vehicles that have the potential to finish underwater.

As companies begin looking at alternatives to stock options, it is imperative that they consider perceived value at different levels of their own organizations. Understanding how employees value these vehicles can provide significant opportunity to create LTI packages that increase perceived value, reduce share usage, limit expense and/or provide greater expense efficiency. (See "Examples of Perceived Value.")

Company B: Changing the LTI Mix to Reduce Expense

Company B is similar in all ways to Company A, but rather than looking to create the same expense, the company wants to re-create the same perceived value.

At Company A, time-vested restricted shares were substituted for stock options based on the expense relationship of $9 to $3, or a 3:1 ratio. However, when we look at the perceived value of the two vehicles — $8 for restricted shares and $2 for stock options — we see that these actually relate in a 4:1 ratio. Using the 4:1 ratio translates into a conversion of only 7,500 time-vested restricted shares, down from 10,000 at Company A.

Company B	# of Shares Granted	Share Price	Expense Valuation per Share	Perceived Value	Expense Taken	Perceived Value
Stock Options	30,000	$9	$3	$2	$90,000	$60,000
Restricted Stock	7,500	$9	$9	$8	$67,500	$60,000

Here, Company B has created the same perceived value, while reducing the expense of the LTI program by $22,500.

Share Conversion Ratios

As in Company A in "Examples of Perceived Value," many employers have long used a standard 3:1 stock option to time-vested restricted share conversion ratio based on the approximate expense relationship. For companies where the perceived value of stock options is relatively high, this ratio can re-create the perceived value.

However, in companies where the perceived value is significantly lower than the expense relationship — like Companies A and B — there is an opportunity to either increase perceived value or reduce expense. As illustrated, Company A was able to increase the perceived value of the grants with a 3:1 conversion, while Company B was able to reduce the expense of the grants with a 4:1 conversion.

Other Considerations

Clearly, the implementation of a comprehensive LTI program should not be driven by expense, perceived value and share usage concerns in isolation. In particular, maintaining adequate performance criteria in LTI packages has become more critical than ever. As mentioned, it is common for restricted share/unit plans to have performance features.

While these performance-based programs typically have a perceived value lower than that of time-vested restricted shares — as the number of shares or units to be delivered is not guaranteed — they also can be useful because fewer shares are needed and the awards may maintain a higher perceived value than stock options

Each company has different needs, business objectives, employee mixes and shareholders. Compensation committees need to look at various considerations involving expense, share usage, retention concerns, perceived value, company performance and performance leverage to determine the right course for their organization. The one-size-fits-all approach is rarely a viable one. A portfolio approach, through which multiple vehicles are used to consider these issues at different levels in the organization, is generally advisable.

As a starting point, however, companies need to understand how various vehicles support the execution of their business strategy, the extent to which employees value the different LTI vehicles being presented to them, and their alignment with shareholder value creation. By considering this information and assessing the degree of emphasis needed to be placed on each factor, companies and their boards will be best able to achieve the optimal portfolio.

CHAPTER 6

Long-Term Incentive Compensation in Private Companies and Business Units

By Daniel Moynihan and Suzanne Crafts Booher

How you compensate key employees is an important factor in successfully attracting, retaining and motivating them for the long term. As such, LTI pay is a critical component of most executive compensation packages. LTIs can help recruit and retain high-performing executives, encourage specific executive behaviors and align executive financial interests with those of shareholders. In addition, LTIs can focus executives on what is best for the organization well into the future and, if well-designed, promote superior corporate performance that directly benefits shareholders. Employers are seeking methods of compensating executives that are based on sustained, long-term performance.

While there are some differences, the basic objectives for LTI programs hold true for both public and private companies. Public companies have considerable flexibility in designing LTI programs through stock options, restricted stock, performance shares, phantom plans and other forms of equity compensation, as well as cash programs. Private companies often have to compete with public companies for talent and want executives to make decisions as if they have the same economic interests as the owners. Ongoing equity grants, however, are not usually effective in private companies. In these businesses, equity generally is illiquid and subject to numerous restrictions that cause executives to substantially discount the value they place on any such awards. Also, founder-owners (or their families) are seldom willing to dilute their ownership stakes.

The following pages focus on approaches to non-equity LTIs specifically designed for private companies and the business units within public companies where compensation strategy dictates that LTIs focus on business unit rather than corporate performance.

This chapter:

- Explains why a performance unit plan is a viable LTI for a private company and what financial and nonfinancial performance measures may be used in the plan design. We illustrate how performance unit plans actually work through two examples — a single performance factor example and a matrix example.
- Describes a value creation plan, an easy-to-administer and easy-to-understand LTI vehicle in which participants share in an incentive pool that varies up or down based on company or business unit "economic profit." Using an example, an explanation is provided about how a measure of profit is defined and how the incentive pool is determined and awarded.
- Provides an overview of how phantom equity is used in private companies, as well as within the business units of publicly traded businesses.

The Performance Unit Plan Alternative

Performance unit plans (PUPs) often make good sense for private companies. They are one of the available performance plans that link cash payments to the operating performance of the company during a multi-year performance period. Unlike annual bonuses, PUPs tie financial rewards to the company's long-term performance while avoiding prolonged financial obligations.

Under a typical PUP, participants receive a fixed number of performance units, each with a target value. Each grant of performance units relates to a performance period that typically stretches over a three- to five-year horizon. The final value of the units at the end of the cycle correlates with the achievement of pre-established performance objectives. Depending on the company's objectives, performance periods may run sequentially (end to end) or may overlap.

Performance Measurement

A PUP relies upon carefully selected performance measures to evaluate executives' contributions. Performance measures must be well understood and performance expectations must be well communicated if a program is to be effective. A properly designed PUP focuses executives on achieving desired results and promoting actions consistent with the business strategy.

Financial and Nonfinancial Performance Measures

Nonfinancial measures can be quantitative (e.g., market share, product mix, productivity, cost position) or qualitative (e.g., customer satisfaction, quality, service level, process excellence).

Financial measures are more traditional and typically found on company accounting statements. They typically are income-based (e.g., net income, operating income, earnings per share, revenue) or return-based (e.g., return on equity, return on assets, return on capital).

The overriding role of financial performance is to link behavior with value creation. As this link becomes more straightforward and transparent, the measures generally become more effective. The selection of financial measures often requires a balance between accuracy and complexity. The financial measures that most accurately reflect the value of the company tend to be the ones that are the most complex.

What and How to Measure

The performance measurement involves two decisions: what to measure and how to measure. Performance measures identify what to measure, and performance goals determine how to measure by establishing target levels of performance against those measures. Goals can be established using internal or external benchmarks. While internal benchmarks (or absolute goal-setting method) have been the most common approach, external standards (or relative goal-setting method) are becoming more prevalent.

At the end of the performance period, actual performance against objectives is evaluated. Based on this evaluation, the performance unit value is determined. Each unit has a target value if the plan's target performance is achieved for the period. The actual performance unit value varies depending upon the long-term performance during the period. It is common in most plans to have a threshold performance level so that the performance unit has no value if the threshold level is not achieved. A performance range is set, which determines the payout at threshold, target and maximum levels. The unit value for threshold performance typically is 50 percent of target value. Likewise, a maximum performance level is established correlating to a maximum unit value, which commonly is set at 150 percent to 200 percent of the target value.

Single Performance Factor Example

In the single performance factor approach, only one measure is used to determine the incentive payout. While perhaps the simplest structure (because it uses only one measure), it does not diversify an executive's incentive opportunity. (See Figure 6-1.)

In this example, the awards are generated in a range of zero to 150 percent times the target award based upon sales growth performance versus goal. Under other designs, multiple factors may be considered with the total payout opportunity representing the sum of performance on all measures.

Matrix Example

In a matrix approach, two measures are used to determine the incentive payout. This method is more complex than the single factor, and an advantage is that the combination of the two measures can be weighted differently at varying performance levels to reflect strategic priorities. (See Figure 6-2.)

Looking at a matrix of performance measures, if a company was below target in sales but above target in earnings before interest

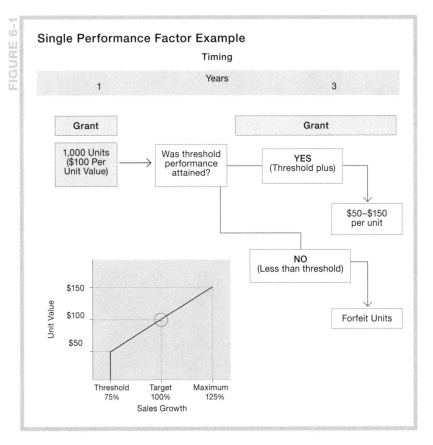

FIGURE 6-1

Single Performance Factor Example

and taxes (EBIT) margin, the plan still can pay out at 100 percent of target. (See "Advantages and Disadvantages of PUPs.")

Overall, a PUP can be easy to administer and explain, and it provides an alternative to a stock-based program in which such an equity award is not practical or desirable.

The Value Creation Plan Approach

In many cases, a viable alternative to stock-based LTI awards can be found through the use of a value creation plan (VCP) that shares a portion of earnings above a pre-established threshold with executives. A VCP can be understandable for participants and relatively simple to administer based on measurable returns at the business-unit level or consolidated level (for private companies).

FIGURE 6-2

Matrix Using Sales and EBIT Margin

EBIT Margin Performance	% Payout (0% Payout)	95% / $0.950 billion	97.5% / $0.975 billion	100% / $1 billion
110% / 11%		$104.5 MM / 100%	$107.25 MM / 125%	$110 MM / 150%
105% / 10.5%		$99.75 MM / 75%	102.38 MM / 100%	$105 MM / 125%
100% / 10%		$95 MM / 50%	$97.5 MM / 75%	$100 MM / 100%
95% / 9.5%		$90.25 MM / 37.5%	$92.63 MM / 50%	$95 MM / 75%
90% / 9%		$85.5 MM / 25%	$87.75 MM / 37.5%	$90 MM / 50%

0% Payout ⟵

Sales Performance

In essence, each VCP participant has an ownership interest in an LTI pool that grows or shrinks based upon the private company or business unit's performance relative to the annual expected return on investment in the entity. A VCP eliminates the need to settle upon a method to value company stock (for private companies), set multi-year performance goals or establish peer group or index benchmarks.

Designing the Program

To establish a VCP, both a measure of profit and return must be defined and understood by all participants. Examples of profit measures include EBIT, net operating profit after taxes (NOPAT) and bottom-line net income. Examples of return measures include return on equity and return on invested capital (debt and equity). The threshold return must be periodically adjusted as the cost of investment funds and/or debt-to-equity ratio change. Further, as the private company's or business unit's capital base grows, so too would the required profit to meet the expected threshold return to investors.

$112.75 MM	$115.5 MM	EBIT $
175%	200%	Payout as a percent of target
$107.63 MM	$110.25 MM	EBIT $
150%	175%	Payout as a percent of target
$102.5 MM	$105 MM	EBIT $
125%	150%	Payout as a percent of target
$97.38 MM	$99.75 MM	EBIT $
100%	125%	Payout as a percent of target
$92.25 MM	$94.5 MM	EBIT $
75%	100%	Payout as a percent of target

102.5%	105%
$1.025 billion	$1.050 billion

Sharing Ratio

When a VCP is created, a sharing ratio needs to be established whereby a portion of the private company or business unit's annual economic profit is contributed to an LTI pool. The sharing ratio is based upon market target awards and determined at the start of the plan and held constant for a defined period. If an economic loss occurs (i.e., earnings below the expected threshold return), then the sharing ratio's proportion is deducted from the incentive pool. The annual contribution (or deduction) is then allocated among the plan participants' account balances using a predetermined formula.

This two-step exercise occurs annually over the life of the plan. To mitigate risk for the participants, a floor could be placed upon deductions from the incentive pool; a corresponding limit could be placed on annual contributions to the pool to limit the company's liability. Special provisions would be crafted regarding a potential sale of the company/business unit or if the private company completes an initial public offering.

Example

For an example of how a VCP could work, consider the co-founders of a debt-free private company who want to establish an LTI plan for their senior executive team but are unwilling to dilute their ownership in the company. The co-founders decide to set up a VCP

Advantages and Disadvantages of PUPs

Advantages:

- Risk/reward balance can be precisely engineered.
- No shares are required.
- Design can result in low or zero payments during sub-par performance cycles.

- Charge to earnings is capped because there is a maximum payout.
- Can be used to reinforce mid-term performance objectives.
- Relatively easy to communicate.

Disadvantages:

- Difficult to set long-term performance goals.

- Subject to liability accounting treatment.

that rewards executives for NOPAT above a threshold return on the co-founders' equity in the company.

In this example, the sharing percentage of NOPAT that exceeds the company's cost of capital would be added to the incentive plan pool annually and allocated to the individual participants' accounts according to formula. To the extent that NOPAT is lower than the cost of capital, the incentive pool would be reduced using the sharing percentage. (See Figure 6-3.)

Vesting for each year's contribution to the LTI pool typically would be over three to five years, and distribution of a portion (e.g., one half) of the vested amount could be provided for at that time. The remaining portion of the vested balance could be required to remain in the pool until a fixed date in the event of a below-threshold performance year (which would cause the pool to shrink). Distribution could even be in the form of parent-company stock for participants who are employees of a business unit of a publicly traded company.

The design would need to take into account the potential application of the tax rules governing nonqualified deferred compensation plans under IRC section 409A. If section 409A applies to the specific design, its deferral requirements would need to be satisfied to avoid taxation and penalties when there is no longer a substantial risk of forfeiture (e.g., on vesting).

A VCP rewards investors before rewarding executives by motivating the executive team to focus on attaining an earnings level above

FIGURE 6-3

Illustration of a Value Creation Plan

A	Calculate NOPAT at end of year	$5,000,000
B	Calculate owners' equity	$40,000,000
C	Factor in cost of capital ...	X 10%
D	... to get to threshold return	$4,000,000
E	Subtract threshold return from NOPAT to get economic value creation	$1,000,000
F	Apply the sharing ratio ...	X 15%
G	... to get contribution to incentive pool	$150,000
H	Allocate contribution among plan participants (as shown below)	

$$\frac{\text{Individual's target}}{\text{Sum of participants' target}} \quad X \quad \text{Contribution to pool}$$

the cost of the investors' capital. For executives in business units, a VCP provides a performance metric directly connected to their business unit's financial performance, which they can influence more directly than the parent company's overall stock price. A VCP can be easy to administer and explain, and it provides executives an alternative to company stock where such an award is not always practical or desirable.

Phantom Stock

A tool that has languished in obscurity at public companies, phantom stock recently has shown signs of emerging there while continuing its more common usage at privately held firms. In the appropriate situation, phantom stock can provide valuable attributes of equity and help with motivation, focus and retention.

The basic concept of a phantom stock program involves a company's agreement or promise to pay the recipient of an award an amount equal to the value of a certain number (or percentage) of shares of the company's stock. Commonly structured through the award of units, a phantom stock program enables a company to make an award that tracks the economic benefits of stock ownership without using actual shares. Because phantom stock is a contractual right and not an interest in property, the tax event for the executive and the employer occurs at the payment in settlement of a properly designed phantom stock arrangement.

Phantom stock plans are shadows that mimic their real equity counterparts; phantom stock and shadow stock are terms that often are used interchangeably. Although shares of real stock can be traded at will, phantom shares or units take on value only when key contingencies or vesting conditions are met. A phantom stock plan typically does not require investment or confer ownership, so its recipient does not have voting rights. It is essentially an upside opportunity, as participants' investments typically are limited to their services; they stand to gain from any upside growth of the company.

Valuation

In making awards under a phantom stock plan, there is a determination of the value of a phantom share or unit in connection with awards to one or more participants. Valuations also will be needed for periodic reporting to participants (and to actual shareholders and the SEC if used by a public company) as well as for determinations of amounts payable at the time of settlement.

Phantom stock programs can be simply designed. However, they should be created to meet the company's specific needs and objectives in protecting the unique knowledge and skill base that is represented by those key employees selected for awards. The two types that are most prevalent are:

- The appreciation-only plan (much like a stock appreciation right)
- The full-value plan, where the award includes the underlying value of the unit (like a restricted stock unit).

Generally, a phantom stock plan or agreement spells out how the program operates and how payments are determined, along with other various details, often including:

- Eligibility criteria
- Vesting schedule
- Valuation method or formula

- Performance measurement
- Settlement and payout events
- Handling of various termination events, including:
  - Retirement
  - Death
  - Disability
  - Dismissal (involuntary)
  - Resignation (voluntary)
- Restrictive covenants
- Form of payment
- Provisions for the sales of the company
- Any funding vehicle

Design and Accounting

Accounting is a key challenge of phantom stock. Historically, phantom plans have been viewed as undesirable from an accounting perspective because of the resulting liability accounting treatment. This creates volatility on the company's income statement, which is something that concerns most financial officers. Generally, for accounting purposes, phantom shares must be treated as an expense over the required service period, and the company does not receive its income tax deduction until the benefits are paid out. This timing is similar to other equity awards, but can prove to be not as advantageous in periods when the value of the award increases. With liability accounting, the accounting expense and corresponding tax deduction are the same. When real equity is used, the company may get a tax advantage, as the expense can be locked in at grant while the tax deduction can grow as the value of the equity grows.

In addition, coming up with cash to cover phantom payouts can be tricky. Phantom stock plan gains (in appreciation-only programs) or current fair value (in full-value programs) must be paid by the company versus the public markets which is the case when using publicly traded equity. Finally, phantom stock programs typically are subject to the complex rules applicable to nonqualified deferred compensation under IRC section 409A, so care must be taken in their design.

Why Use Phantom Stock for LTI Awards?

Phantom stock can help in getting an executive team to think and act like equity partners. It creates a sense of ownership in the success of the business because having phantom stock means the participants have "skin in the game." The concept of being an equity partner by having phantom stock can create the same feeling of connection as the more traditional equity tools (e.g., stock options, restricted stock).

In addition to its incentive components, a phantom stock program involves deferred compensation and can act like golden handcuffs in retaining key executives. Phantom stock most often is used by privately held companies, but (as previously noted) some publicly traded organizations are using phantom stock or similar cash-based LTIs as well.

Phantom stock plans can be especially useful in providing the economic benefits of equity without diluting shareholders. Because recipients of phantom units lack voting rights, a company can issue these units without altering the governance of the company or worrying about dilution issues. Phantom stock does not directly dilute the value of real outstanding shares. Phantom stock awards do, however, have a significant effect on cash flow at payout. This is why some plans have a conversion feature and may pay out in actual stock.

Another advantage to a company is the ability to design an award so that an executive receives no benefit unless vesting conditions are met and, under the appreciation-only model, the company's value has increased. The fair market value of the stock is commonly used by public companies, while private companies have various approaches. For example, a professional valuation may be preferred but viewed as too costly; many companies then turn to book value. Other approaches include a formula using revenue, EBITDA, net income, or a combination of relevant measures; a formula also can help with consistency of the valuation over time.

There are many reasons a company would consider a phantom stock arrangement:

- A public company may find that it has insufficient authorized shares to award the desired amount of awards that require actual stock.

- A company's leadership may have considered other plans but found their rules too restrictive or implementation costs too high.
- The owner(s) may desire to maintain actual and effectual control, while still sharing the economic value of the company.
- There may be ownership restrictions for certain types of entities (i.e., sole proprietorship, partnership, limited liability company), such as the S-corporation 100-shareholder rule.
- The objective is to provide equity-type incentives to a restricted group of individuals.
- A corporate division that can measure its enterprise value and wants its employees to have a share in that value even though there is no real stock available.
- A desire to focus on an event or contingency (e.g., sale, merger, IPO).

Typically, a phantom plan can provide a more flexible alternative that is not subject to the same restrictions as most equity ownership plans. For many, the simple desire to use an equity-like vehicle without giving up true ownership may be reason enough to implement. In considering a phantom stock program, the advantages and disadvantages in Table 6-1 should be evaluated.

Who Is Using Phantom Stock?

Phantom stock is not only a private-company phenomenon. Our research of proxy filings found some well-known, publicly traded companies that are using this tool to attract, retain and motivate select groups of employees.

Phantom stock is a traditional LTI vehicle rather than a fad. While trends come and go, cash-based LTI plans do have a place in the executive compensation portfolio. While these plans generally are simple and provide flexibility to the company, they also can raise various issues that must be considered carefully. In the appropriate situation, a phantom stock plan can keep the company spirit alive in the executive suite.

TABLE 6-1

Pros and Cons of Phantom Stock

Advantages:

- Allows employees to share in the growth of the company's value without being shareholders
- No equity dilution, as no actual shares are awarded
- Powerful retention tool when combined with vesting
- Board/compensation committee has flexibility to design plans based on their own discretion
- Can be tied to overall company or business unit results
- No employee investment required
- Can provide for dividend equivalents
- Design can permit phantom stock to be converted into actual equity
- No income tax until proceeds are converted to cash or real stock
- Potential tax deferral of employee compensation
- Retirement benefit opportunity.

Disadvantages:

- If paid in cash, can be a financial drain on the company's cash flow
- At a private company, may require outside valuation on an annual basis
- Company needs to communicate financial results to participants
- Payments to employee are taxed as ordinary income
- May affect the overall value of the business in a transaction
- IRC section 409A rules add complexity and difficulty in achieving objectives.

CHAPTER 7

Performance Measurement for Incentive Pay Plans

By Matthew Kleger and Adam Kahle

The importance of pay for performance as a principle of executive compensation philosophy can hardly be understated. Entire books and hundreds of articles and conference presentations have been devoted to showing the techniques and strategies needed to align executive pay with company performance. As has been the case over the past several years, the focus on executive pay — especially the dollar amounts reported in the news — has distracted attention from performance, which should be the focal point of any pay-for-performance discussion.

There is no unified, standard way to address the performance side of the equation, and various metrics are in use. The use of multiple performance measures — financial, strategic, operational and individual — is appropriate when performance is measured on a holistic basis and viewed through multiple lenses. That said, total shareholder return (TSR) is increasingly becoming the focus of performance from a number of different perspectives. While TSR is seldom used as a performance measure within short-term incentive programs, it can be very helpful in measuring senior management performance within LTI plans when balanced with other performance measures that more accurately reflect the current status and expectations of long-term growth.

One of the biggest challenges within both short- and long-term incentive design is determining the most effective performance measures and measurement approach given each company's unique set of facts and circumstances. Once a metrically sound framework is in place, the goal-setting process can be a relatively unambiguous process for some companies, while others may struggle to set "meaningful" goals in context of the current state of the business, competitive landscape, performance measure(s) being utilized, and shareholder and senior management expectations.

This chapter:

- Discusses performance measurement approaches and considerations for incentive plans.
- Addresses the conditions under which an effective performance/ payout calibration takes place and the threshold, target and maximum performance levels used for goal-setting purposes.
- Discusses how performance should be defined and measured and introduces a "cash value added" approach that connects corporate performance metrics with shareholder return.
- Explains in more detail the techniques used in incorporating TSR in LTI plan design. Taking a "high-definition" approach in choosing and implementing a TSR comparator group is recommended — one that entails testing, weighting and ranking the comparator group companies. Examples of when not to use TSR also are reviewed.

Performance Measurement Approaches and Considerations for Incentive Plans

From a performance measurement perspective, companies measure goals on an either absolute or relative basis:

- **Absolute (internal approach).** Performance goals are measured vs. internal plan (budget/target). An internal approach requires a strong planning process and is difficult in industries in which external events can have a dramatic effect on results. Performance goals usually are effective when there is rigor around the goal-setting process and goals are based on the company's strategic, financial and operating objectives. This technique can be enhanced if shareholder expectations are incorporated in the process.

- **Relative (external approach).** Performance goals are measured vs. an external comparator group. A relative or external approach measures the company against a comparator group of companies that are affected by similar macroeconomic factors, compete in the same market and/or have similar products. This method eliminates the need to set internal company performance goals because it focuses on how the company performs against its comparator group. It also mitigates the risk of setting the goals too high or too low. Depending upon the company and performance goals being utilized, a comparator group may consist of a compensation peer group, custom peer group or broad market index.

Relative performance measurement is seldom used within STI plans and typically reserved for performance-based LTI programs. The choice of performance measures is also a key consideration in establishing absolute vs. relative performance measurement. Absolute performance measurement is typically utilized when long-term performance measures are based on profitability (EPS, EBITDA, etc.), revenue/sales, cash flow (free, modified, etc.) and/or capital-efficiency (ROE, ROIC, etc.). Relative performance measurement is typically employed when long-term performance measures are based on TSR or stock price (relative TSR is discussed in additional detail below). A potential drawback to a relative approach is that selecting a comparator group may be difficult for some companies. It may be particularly challenging for firms with a unique business model or in a consolidating industry. Also, the relative approach sometimes can result in unintended payouts. Even if a company out-performed the majority of its comparator group companies, it is possible that its absolute performance was poor and created "negative value" for shareholders. This situation can be addressed in the following ways:

- The compensation committee may apply negative discretion in determining the incentive payouts. Therefore, the compensation committee would have the ability to pay reduced or no incentives if the company did not create any shareholder value.
- In addition to the relative performance measurement versus the comparator group, an absolute threshold (or "circuit breaker") can

be established under which reduced or no incentives are paid if the threshold performance level is not achieved (i.e., if the company does not reach an $X level of EBITDA, reduced or no incentives are paid, depending on the terms). In cases in which the circuit breaker is tripped, all incentive payments become discretionary.

- In the case of relative TSR, a cap on the payout regardless of relative performance versus the comparator group in the event that the company's absolute TSR is negative over the performance period (current trend is to set the cap at target).

In selecting a performance measurement approach, companies should consider several factors:

- **Management process.** How much rigor and structure is in the process? How much information is available to management regarding shareholder and analyst expectations and peer company metrics?
- **Strategic priorities.** What are the company's business objectives and ability to forecast performance based on the company's life cycle and maturity?
- **Company performance.** How volatile is the company's performance on an absolute basis and relative to peers historically?

Setting goals for incentive plans is a subjective process that requires much discussion and consideration. The board of directors and management should be able to provide sound rationale for the goals and approach selected.

Performance and Payout Calibration for Incentive Plans

With the increased scrutiny on executive compensation and greater transparency due to enhanced disclosure requirements, having a pay-for-performance compensation philosophy is practically a must. Companies not only need to show a relationship between executive pay and business performance, but also must demonstrate that they pay the appropriate level for commensurate performance. The pay-for-performance calibration/relationship should create and reinforce shareholder alignment.

A main challenge in designing an incentive plan (when based on absolute performance) is being able to forecast company performance and set goals at the right level, especially for periods longer than one year. Executives are motivated, and the likelihood of desired performance increases under incentive plans when the following conditions are met:

- Executives have a line of sight in which they understand the performance goals and view them as realistic and achievable.
- There is a clear link between performance and pay.
- Executives view the pay associated with the incentive plan as meaningful (i.e., large enough to justify the effort required to achieve the performance goals).

If performance goals are not appropriately set, there can be negative consequences. If performance objectives are set too high, executives will not be motivated, knowing there is little likelihood of achieving the targets. At the other extreme, if executives consistently and easily achieve performance targets, they are being sent the wrong message that superior performance is not required to receive a meaningful incentive payout.

As noted in discussions of incentive programs in preceding chapters, STI plans and performance-based LTI programs typically have pre-established performance levels:

- **Threshold.** A floor that represents the minimum level of performance that must be achieved before an incentive can be earned.
- **Target.** The expected and/or planned (budgeted) level of achievement or a realistic goal that is achievable and meaningful.
- **Maximum.** The total incentive opportunity that may be earned for superior performance, sometimes referred to as a cap.

The level of performance relative to target that should correlate with threshold and maximum payout levels can be difficult to calibrate. A simplified approach would be to set the threshold performance level at 80 or 90 percent of target performance and set the maximum performance level at 110 or 120 percent of target performance. For example, if revenue is the performance metric and the target is $1 billion in revenue, a maximum performance level based on

120 percent of target, or $1.2 billion, may be reasonable. However, if TSR is the metric and 10 percent TSR is the target, 120 percent of target (or 12 percent TSR) likely would set the maximum goal too low.

Calibrating threshold and maximum goals appropriately can depend greatly on the performance measure. One way to test the reasonableness of the goal-setting process is to estimate the probabilities of achieving the performance levels and compare them to standard achievement frequencies (as illustrated in Table 4-2 in Chapter 4 and also discussed in Chapter 5 in the section titled "Performance Shares and Performance-Vested Restricted Stock").

Say on Pay? What About Performance?

A pay-for-performance debate has long dominated the corporate governance agenda. While great progress has been made in enhancing transparency and aligning the interests of management and shareholders, there has been surprisingly little consensus on what constitutes best practices in performance management. Boards and investors must hold management accountable for achieving performance objectives that are comprehensive, actionable and value creating.

For compensation professionals, aligning executive pay with performance is the great work in progress of our time. The plot is well understood — align management with investor objectives by rewarding executives for their enterprise's performance and voilà ... all stakeholders are satisfied.

So why does the drama continue to escalate? Because the mainstream focus to date has been on the pay side of the equation.

While significant and important progress has been achieved, the critical problem of effectively assessing performance remains largely unaddressed. Unless and until this changes, the plot will continue, intensifying during worsening economic times.

Defining Performance

Pay-for-performance depends entirely on the definition of performance. While executive pay is an easy target, it is a distracting sideshow to the management imperative of assessing and improving corporate performance. So why has progress been so elusive? The two primary reasons — comparability and complexity — are well-known:

- First, establishing standards for industries or enterprises that have different economic dynamics can be contentious at best. The question "Who had a better year, the World Series champion or the Super Bowl winner?" illustrates the point.

- Second, "corporate performance" math is difficult to measure and not necessarily supported by historical accounting measures. Much like a horse race, corporate performance is best thought of as a firm's position at any given point in time relative to its long-term objectives. While the past is certainly prologue, current expectations define performance, not vice versa. It is a world in which "What have you done for me lately?" is trumped by "What can I expect from you tomorrow?"

Measuring Performance

As noted earlier, relative TSR is increasingly becoming the focus of performance for a variety of reasons, including:

- Preference by large, influential institutional shareholders and other key stakeholders;

- Prevalence as a performance measure within large public company long-term incentive plans;

- De facto definition of performance per pay-versus-performance disclosure requirements established under the Dodd-Frank Wall Street Reform and Consumer Protection Act of 2010; and

- Usage as the singular definition of performance for Institutional Shareholders Services' quantitative CEO pay-for-performance assessment.

For some companies, there are very good reasons to use relative TSR as a performance measure for LTI plans. For example, in mature businesses that are cyclical and/or significantly affected by external factors, relative TSR can be an excellent way to assess the achievements of management in the prevailing market, economic and regulatory context. Conversely, relative TSR is of limited validity and application for the following types of organizations:

- Companies targeting substantial growth;
- Firms in a turnaround situation;
- Companies that are not competing with others for customers or investors to any meaningful extent; and
- "Grow or die" companies.

For these types of organizations, absolute performance is what matters most. If relative performance is to be used at all, it might be used as a multiplier or modifier to the short- or long-term incentive award rather than as a primary measure.

While TSR can be an appropriate measure, it is imperfect and there are some concerns with using this singular metric as the standard bearer for measuring performance:

- **TSR depends on two random, arbitrary points in time.** The same company can simultaneously be the best among its peers for one timeframe and the worst for another.
- **TSR is not actionable.** Theoretically speaking, expectations on earnings and future performance, coupled with supply and demand, should be the primary considerations affecting share price. Instead, share prices are influenced by many factors outside the control of executive decision makers. External perceptions, interest rates and geopolitical activity are some of the many factors that contribute to positive and negative share price growth. The case of Enron demonstrated the ill and unintended effects of CEOs who attempt to make TSR actionable.
- **TSR is a short-term performance measure.** Irrespective of the timeframe selected, TSR fluctuates with the daily vagaries of the capital markets. It is possible, for example, for an enterprise to have achieved a five-year TSR of 20 percent one day and 0 percent the next. Can CEO performance actually go from top quartile to bottom quartile in a single day?

Ultimately, corporate performance must be assessed based on a broad framework of interrelated metrics that influence current expectations. To succeed, the framework must, first and foremost, be economically sound. The "performance mathematics" must ensure that as levers are pressed, expected values are achieved and perceptions are influenced accordingly. Performance measurement also must be comprehensive and balanced. History is replete with pay-for-performance issues stemming from improvement in measured revenue growth offset by non-measured asset expansion. Finally, the assessment approach must be easy to implement. If it cannot be readily understood and tracked by all stakeholders, it will not work.

Figure 7-1 is an example of a performance management framework that connects capital market expectations with actionable enterprise operating metrics. The framework begins with establishing a corporate performance measure that is highly correlated to TSR. Measures like cash-value added (CVA), summarized in Table 7-2 (using the "residual value" definition), have become attractive choices in recent years because of their efficacy and simplicity. Forecasted CVA has a strong correlation to TSR because it is tied directly to the discounted cash-flow valuation of the enterprise.

While CVA is important because it is the sum of the moving parts of performance, the actionable levers of growth, profitability

FIGURE 7-1

Performance Management Framework

Shareholder Value
(i.e., TSR)

Corporate Performance
(i.e., cash value added)

Growth
(i.e., revenue)

Profitability
(i.e., ROS)

Asset Management
(i.e., ROIC)

Sales Metrics
(i.e., price, volume, market share)

Operations Metrics
(i.e., direct costs, SG&A, TCO/ TCL, CAOEX)

FIGURE 7-2

Cash-Value Added (CVA) Defined

Cash-Value Added:	Operating cash flow – capital charge
Operating Cash Flow:	Net income + depreciation +/- changes in net working capital
Capital Charge:	Total invested capital x weighted average cost of capital

and asset management are the important focal points. By establishing plans and targets in each of these areas in accordance with forecasted CVA, performance improvement can be measured and effectively managed for the long-term. From a board and investor point of view, the framework provides the rest of the story to the TSR metric and enables effective assessment of performance in the context of executive pay.

Although this approach is not immune to the aforementioned issues of comparability and complexity, it is a useful paradigm for establishing a standardized methodology regarding corporate performance management. As investors become increasingly frustrated by subpar returns, they will shift their attention from pay to performance. Boards and management that take action now will be well-served by staying ahead of this inevitable plot twist.

Incorporating Relative TSR in Performance-Based LTI Plan Design: A High-Definition Approach

When incorporating a relative TSR measure into a performance-based LTI plan, not all companies take a high-definition view in selecting and implementing a TSR comparator group, despite the fact that the choice of comparator group can have a big effect on both performance and payout outcomes. Similarly, high-definition thinking may allow an organization to reduce the level of random "noise" in the comparator group, which may in turn make the use of relative TSR more appealing to executives who often are suspicious of its use as a performance measure.

Historically, the common approach with relative TSR plans was to base the comparator group on the most obvious alternative investments for a shareholder. This reflected the origins of relative TSR in the relative performance-driven bonus plans operated for mutual fund managers themselves. In the early days, this often meant simply using the S&P 500 or some other very broad comparator group. However, hindsight and experience have exposed this as low-definition thinking. Such broad comparator groups include a high degree of randomness due to the very different degrees of volatility and cyclical exposure faced by different sectors and businesses. In addition, when looking at the stock market in high definition, we see that the U.S. shareholder base has become more diverse in the past 10 to 15 years and the alternative investments are not always obvious.

With this richness and diversity in both the shareholder base and the nature of potential alternative investments, it becomes necessary to think about relative TSR in a different way. In essence, this means considering which businesses face broadly similar economic, market, regulatory and operational challenges. This generally includes direct business competitors and/or businesses with a similar profile in terms of complexity, structure, products, sectors and locations. Size also can be a factor, but wider size variations can be accepted for TSR than would be appropriate when selecting a peer group for compensation benchmarking purposes.

Of course not all businesses have competitors that look like them or face the same challenges. For example, in some highly consolidated sectors there may only be a handful of competing firms, and some of these may not be listed on a stock market. In these circumstances, assuming that TSR remains a valid metric, it becomes necessary to choose on the basis of factors such as:

- **Correlation:** How well does the historical TSR of different sectors correlate to our company/sector?
- **Volatility (beta):** How does the historical share price volatility for different sectors compare to our company/sector?

Having developed a potential comparator group, it is important to model and test this group. This means tracking TSR for the potential comparators over several overlapping historical performance periods and computing what the plan would have paid in these scenarios. This modeling allows the following key questions to be addressed:

- Do the performance outcomes fit with what we believe about the historical performance of our business?
- In a small group, are any comparators miscorrelated? Why? Does the miscorrelation invalidate the outcomes? Is this likely to recur?
- In a larger group, are many sectors miscorrelated to us and our main competitors?
- In a global group, are any countries miscorrelated?

Ideally, this exercise answers whether the proposed comparator group is suitable and/or highlights any necessary modifications. It is possible that the modeling will produce a set of notional historical payments that seem to be driven by random factors rather than the performance of the business. In this event, either the proposed comparator group needs to be significantly revised or the use of relative TSR as a measure needs to be re-thought.

Some companies may have a small number of highly relevant comparators and a larger number of companies with whom they have some similarity. In this case, the aim is to make sure the comparator group is large enough to be robust without it being dominated by the less relevant comparators. The answer here could be to weight the companies in the comparator group such that the most relevant companies have a larger effect on the result.

When assessing performance against a comparator group, there typically are three approaches:

- **Sample percentile ranking.** This is the simplest and most common approach, and would be the low-definition default choice. However, under this approach incentive payments are sensitive to the level of clustering of comparator companies. Therefore, incremental improvements to TSR may have a very large or very small effect on plan vesting/payouts.
- **Percentage outperformance.** An example of this approach provides for full vesting/payout where TSR is at median plus 10 percent per annum, with linear interpolation used between median and this level. This approach avoids material differences in incentive awards arising from small differences in performance. However,

this approach does require a percentage outperformance target to be set for full vesting/payout.

■ **Smoothed ranking.** This is a compromise option between the two approaches described above. For example, TSR at median- and upper-quartile companies is calculated with vesting/payout between these points calculated by linear interpolation. Again, this avoids material differences for incentive awards arising from small differences in performance.

Simple percentile ranking works best for very large comparator groups. Otherwise, the other methods are preferable. If the comparator group is very small, the percentage outperformance approach generally works best.

Any high-definition approach requires active consideration of the following issues:

■ **Start and end dates within the performance period.** Depending upon a company's objectives and intent, TSR is generally measured over one of the following periods — calendar year, fiscal year or grant date to vesting date.

■ **Share price averaging period.** Generally, the authors recommend an averaging period of at least one month (typically 30 to 90 days) at both the beginning and end of the performance period as a "spot price" approach is not aligned with the desired intent of the program.

■ **Treatment of companies leaving the comparator group.** This typically depends upon the comparator group being used to measure relative performance and reason for exit (acquired, taken private, bankruptcy, etc.).

■ **Termination provisions.** It is important to define the provisions around relative TSR performance, vesting and payout in the event of various termination scenarios (CIC, by the company "without cause," by the executive for "good reason," etc.). These provisions should be addressed up front and are generally memorialized in the individual LTI award agreement, LTI plan document or employment agreement.

CHAPTER 8

Executive Retirement Benefits and Deferred Compensation

By Melissa Rasman and Ron Seifert

Deferred compensation arrangements can help employers attract and retain key executives by furnishing benefits beyond the basic executive compensation package. These executive retirement programs have become increasingly prevalent in recent years. They are found in various forms in two-thirds of all organizations, and in an even higher percentage of larger publicly traded companies.

Broadly defined, a deferred compensation arrangement consists of an individual agreement or a plan whereby an organization pays compensation to one or more of its employees at a future date for services rendered in a prior year. The term "deferred compensation" encompasses both tax-qualified and nonqualified arrangements. Due to the limits on contributions and benefits under qualified plans, nonqualified programs generally are used for executive deferred compensation arrangements.

Employers typically use two basic categories of nonqualified deferred compensation plans: non-elective plans (commonly referred to as supplemental executive retirement plans [SERPs]) and elective deferral plans. The key difference is that employers fund non-elective plans, whereas employees contribute their own earnings to elective plans. Some employers offer plans that provide both non-elective and elective deferred compensation.

This chapter:

- Discusses the strategic objectives of a SERP program and the technical considerations that affect SERP design. Examples are furnished of three customized design alternatives depending on the status of the SERP participant.

- Explains why the costs of a SERP are a crucial consideration and the five basic principles that underlie executive pensions. There also is a discussion of the rationale behind SERPs, including the role that executives themselves play in a SERP design.

- Reviews the purpose and objectives of an elective deferred compensation program and the applicable tax and accounting rules that govern these plans. Key features and disadvantages of these plans also are discussed.

- Addresses the use of performance-based SERPs that reward criteria other than, or in addition to, the passage of time to motivate and reward executive performance. Plan features that an employer may wish to consider are described.

SERP Design and Organization Strategy

Supplemental executive retirement plans, as the name suggests, are designed to supplement a company's existing qualified retirement plans. Although executives generally are covered by the same qualified retirement plans as the rest of the employee population, tax-qualified retirement benefits are subject to limits on:

- Salary taken into account for plan purposes
- Benefit levels that can be provided (in the case of defined benefit plans)
- The amounts that can be contributed to a participant's account for a given year (in the case of defined contribution plans).

Due to these restrictions, the overall benefit levels provided under qualified plans are lower for the executive population relative to their compensation level than for the general employee population. To make executives whole for the effects of these limits, employers commonly establish SERPs. Further, organizations often design a SERP to provide a higher level of retirement income (relative to an executive's compensation) than is provided under their tax-qualified plans. These richer SERPs usually are designed to attract and retain executives. A Hay Group survey of executive benefits found that the most popular income replacement ratio is 60 percent, which for many highly paid employees would be impossible to achieve through tax-qualified retirement plans.

A SERP must be unfunded, and coverage must be limited to a select group of management and other highly compensated employees; otherwise, legal mandates under the Employee Retirement Income Security Act of 1974 (ERISA) would make a SERP unworkable in most cases. Generally, SERP benefits are taxable to the executive (and deductible by the employer) when paid, subject to two key exceptions:

- Employees of tax-exempt employers subject to IRC section 457(f) are taxed when their benefits are no longer subject to a substantial forfeiture risk (i.e., are vested).

- Executives of any type of employer may be taxed as vested benefits accrue if provided under a plan or arrangement that fails to meet the legal constraints on timing of benefits elections, distributions and funding under IRC section 409A (which are discussed in the third section of this chapter).

Design flexibility has been critical to the popularity of SERPs. A SERP can be used to:

- **Attract mid-career hires.** Help supplement benefits to executives who are hired later in their careers; this can be an important recruitment tool for high-performing executives.

- **Assist in succession planning.** Offer an executive early retirement to allow for necessary succession planning.

- **Attach golden handcuffs.** Retain an executive who may consider leaving for either retirement or a competitor.

- **Provide competitive benefits.** Close the gap between the existing qualified plans and what the market offers.

- **Reward executive performance.** Better align the interests of executives and shareholders.

A SERP's value to an executive and its strategic impact can be affected by certain critical factors, as discussed in "Key Value Parameters."

Key Value Parameters

Replacement Ratio

The target percentage of an executive's pay that the SERP is designed to pay annually during retirement. It is designed to help an executive maintain his/her accustomed standard of living in retirement. As previously noted, the most popular replacement ratio is 60 percent of an executive's total cash, with nearly 80 percent of organizations with SERPs providing ratios in the 50 to 70 percent range.

Definition of Pay

The pay definition is critical to understanding SERP value. A 60 percent replacement ratio can look very different depending on whether it is pegged to salary versus total cash (salary plus annual incentive) or total direct compensation (total cash plus LTI).

Most organizations use total cash in their definition of compensation for SERP purposes. About one-quarter of organizations define compensation as base salary only, while a small (and declining) number include long-term incentives. Arguably, using LTIs in defining pay is inappropriate. An LTI is intended as capital accumulation for the long-term, and it should not be replaced in a program that is designed to re-create a comparable post-retirement standard of living.

Average Pay Period

SERP values can be substantially affected by the final-pay averaging period. In companies where pay leverage and the resulting year-to-year differences are low, choosing a highest period will have little effect. But in companies with highly leveraged pay packages, such a plan could result in a significant windfall for executives. The most common choices are the highest consecutive three- and five-year periods.

Definition of Service

In this context, service refers to the minimum amount of time an executive must work with the company to earn a full retirement benefit. Retiring with less than the plan's service minimum usually requires pro-rating the targeted replacement ratio.

For companies that have a tradition of long-tenured executives, the service period may make little difference to executives. But for the increasing number of companies that recruit top executives from competitors later in their careers, the service period may be a critical determinant in the recruiting package. The typical minimum service period is 15 or 20 years. However, special provisions are sometimes crafted to recruit key executives closer to retirement.

Vesting

The vesting schedule also can have a significant effect on a SERP's value. The most prevalent practices are based on an executive's tenure with the company, with roughly

Examples of Customized Design Alternatives

Different situations may call for different designs. In examining three familiar scenarios, common design considerations are noted.

First, consider the mid-career hire. Assume that a struggling company is dramatically changing its market strategy and the current executive team has little such experience. The company hopes one-half of the SERPs using a cliff-vesting schedule that provides 100 percent vesting after a specified period of years of service (e.g., three, five, ten years), and the remaining organizations using either graded vesting, 100 percent immediate vesting or vesting at a particular age.

Retirement Age

Allowing executives to receive full benefits at an earlier age is becoming more popular. Consistently, the prevalent retirement age has been 65, but there continues to be notable prevalence for unreduced early retirement at ages 60 or 62.

Careful consideration should be given to any lowering of an unreduced retirement age. While there may be strategic reasons to facilitate an executive's early retirement, such changes can substantially increase the SERP's cost. In addition, company stakeholders may not benefit if the early retirees are vital to the company and no adequate succession plan is in place.

Actuarial Assumptions

The actuarial assumptions used to convert an annual target benefit to a lump sum can be significant. In practice, the selection of these assumptions — which include the assumed interest and mortality rates — can be both subjective and negotiable.

Balancing Design Considerations

Each component of a SERP can be used more effectively to achieve desired results when companies do a better job of ensuring that their SERP design is driven by organizational strategy.

Organizations must ask critical questions regarding both strategy and the current makeup of the executive team. For example:

> How important is retention of the current executives in helping the organization meet its strategic objectives?

> Has the succession plan provided a strong enough executive pool with the right skills and competencies to lead the company where it needs to go?

> Does the organization need to recruit a new executive from a competitor to better enable that strategy?

> Is the current retirement package competitive enough to prevent executives from being poached by a competitor?

Generally, it is beneficial to have one program design that can serve most of the executive population. However, in many cases, the need to retain or attract particular top executives may necessitate a customized plan design.

to attract an executive from a competitor that has had success with a similar strategy. The design considerations here will be around making the SERP's upside attractive while also building in performance leverage.

Second, consider the golden handcuffs situation in which a company wants to retain its successful CEO by motivating the executive to retire later rather than earlier. Here, design considerations are around giving the executive more opportunity to obtain a larger SERP payout by staying past age 65.

Then there is the typical rising executive who is being promoted from a senior manager to a top executive. While the company's strong preference would be not to lose such an executive's talents, the board may believe that, given the company's strong succession plan, a replacement can be found if needed. Design considerations focus on increasing leverage to influence performance, with the understanding that consistently poorer performance could result in low payouts.

Each of these situations may call for a different approach to SERP design. (See Table 8-1.) In each case, the mix should be tailored to the organization's particular needs and objectives.

Executive Pensions/SERPs: An Approach Based on Core Principles

With enhanced disclosure of executive pensions, especially large (and arguably abusive) arrangements for top executives have attracted the attention of shareholders, proxy advisers and the press. Relevant questions to consider are:

■ Are the programs reasonable and appropriate?
■ Is the true potential cost reasonably determinable?
■ How were they designed and approved in the first place?

TABLE 8-1

Alternative Approaches to SERP Design

	Replacement Ratio	Pay Definition	Pay Period
Mid-Career Hire	40%	**Total direct** (total cash + LTI)	3-year period average
Golden Handcuffs	60%	**Total cash** (base + bonus)	Highest 3-year period average
Rising Executive	50%	**Total cash** (base + bonus)	3-year period average
Typical Case	60%	**Total cash** (base + bonus)	3-year period average

Why the Cost of Executive Pensions Is Important

Executive pensions can be quite expensive, often constituting a significant portion of the value of an executive's total compensation. Historically, many executive pension arrangements were not fully and clearly disclosed to shareholders, although this was significantly improved by the enhanced disclosure rules issued by the SEC starting in 2006. However, even now the costs may not be well understood.

The most highly leveraged executive pension is the defined benefit SERP. Defined benefits (DB) plans are back-loaded, with the funding cost increasing substantially as pay increases, particularly as the executive gets closer to retirement age.

For example, assume a long-serving executive covered by a 60-percent-of-final-salary defined benefit SERP is appointed CEO two years before retirement. Further assume that this resulted in his base salary increasing from $1 million to $1.5 million. While his projected annual pension benefit increased from $600,000 to $900,000, the single lump-sum cost increased approximately $3 million. Even spread over his two remaining years, this would cost roughly $1.5 million per year, or 100 percent of his annual salary per year. This is before any bonus is even included in the pension formula. It would not be surprising to find that no board or compensation committee member was aware of this leverage and that the salary decision was made without even considering the consequential pension cost.

Although a fairly extreme example (but based on a real case), this situation illustrates just how important pension issues can be. One-year value transfers of 50 percent to 150 percent of base salary to executives

Minimum Service	Vesting Requirements	Retirement Age
10 years	5-year graded	60
15 years	10-year cliff	70
20 years	15-year graded	65
15 – 20 years	15-year graded	65

through final pay executive pensions are common. The closer to retirement age this occurs, the more this hidden cost is leveraged. If incentive plans appear unlikely to pay out, final salary pension plans can provide a strong motivation for an executive to negotiate a salary increase.

Core Principles

Employers should reflect on certain core principles as guidelines for appropriate practice in developing executive pension programs:

- **Core Principle 1:** The provision for an executive pension is part of the rewards package the executive receives for work carried out for the organization and, as such, should be treated as part of the total compensation package, not as a separate entitlement.

- **Core Principle 2:** Realistic cost estimates of any pension proposals should be disclosed to compensation committees or other decision makers. In the case of DB plans, the cost estimates should reflect the value being transferred to the executive as well as the leveraging and phasing of that transfer — not simply the current cost charge or contribution. Salary comparisons — internal or external — and salary adjustments should consider the added effect due to significant differences in pension costs.

- **Core Principle 3:** Aside from any pension provision required by law or under a tax-qualified retirement plan available to all employees, the executive should determine the extent, if any, of the total compensation package that is apportioned to a pension.

- **Core Principle 4:** The provision of executive pensions generally should be made on a defined contribution (DC) basis (rather than on a DB basis). This DC pension (e.g., a percentage of base salary) then should be a component of the total compensation package each year. The particular amount of that component each year can be actuarially determined to produce target benefits each year of retirement, just like a DB SERP. Under a DC approach, deferred compensation is shown as an account balance that recognized the cost attributable to each year of employment.

- **Core Principle 5:** In accordance with enhanced executive compensation disclosure rules, the cost of executive pensions must be more fully described. In particular, DB plans often contain potentially costly ancillary benefits and special features in addition to the basic target replacement ratio. Examples are subsidized (unreduced) early retirement provisions, the inclusion of LTI awards in the definition of compensation, granting additional years of service for short-term executives, providing unrestricted joint and survivor benefits, and numerous other features.

Rationale

Providing a sound overall compensation package for a top executive was the focus in developing these core principles.

- Senior executives are, relative to most employees, highly paid. They have more opportunity during their working lifetimes to acquire significant assets or wealth to support that lifestyle in retirement.

- In addition, senior executives have more flexibility to determine and apportion the income level to spend currently versus save for retirement. Because this apportionment can vary substantially from person to person, it is more appropriate to allow the executive to make this decision than the employer. It is less appropriate for the employer to take on the financial risks associated with providing a high level of guaranteed benefits or to determine the extent to which executives should defer consumption.

- Executives should have the opportunity (and responsibility) for choosing the level of retirement income or target replacement ratio that they need and re-apportioning their total pay accordingly. In this process, executives can use an equivalent DC schedule that will produce this target. In other words, executive pensions should be considered more of an elective deferred compensation plan, although structured as employer-funded SERPs.

- Most executives are intelligent, responsible individuals who are relied upon by their employers to make sound decisions on complex issues in their work. They often have responsibilities regarding asset values far in excess of their own pension assets. It is therefore appropriate that they take responsibility for determining the portion of their compensation packages allocated to retirement benefits.

Which Pay Components Should Be Used in Determining Pensions?

Variable pay has become a standard portion of executive compensation packages, and the level of retirement income generally is considered relative to pay. However, retirement income is not expected to be as volatile as pay can be from year to year. Accordingly, some judgment should be applied in targeting an executive's fixed retirement income to a variable rate of compensation while in active employment.

It can be appropriate to include annual bonuses in the definition of pay for purposes of determining pension contributions or benefits. Annual bonuses can be considered as part of the standard of living developed for an executive over the years. However, LTIs represent special awards that are intended to be capital accumulation devices in and of themselves (as is a SERP). Therefore, the inclusion of LTI in the definition of annual pay for pension purposes is redundant and inappropriate.

In some circumstances, the inclusion of annual bonuses in the pension formula is purely cosmetic. For example, an annual pension of 60 percent of base salary at retirement is the same as a pension of 50 percent of total cash compensation for an employee with a 20 percent bonus. A company may believe that one approach appears less controversial than the other even though they both produce the same benefit.

Removing Executive Distractions

A common argument is that DB plans enable an executive to ignore his/her personal financial security concerns and focus on the company's business, as opposed to the distractions attendant with the variations in a DC structure.

If the employer wants to take such a paternalistic approach, this can be addressed by providing a basic level of DB protection. Beyond such a minimum, the second core principle would be applied.

Elective Deferred Compensation Arrangements

Nonqualified deferred compensation (NQDC) plans that are funded by executives through elective deferral arrangements also can help employers attract and retain key executives by furnishing benefits beyond the basic executive compensation package.

A nonqualified plan is not required to meet the coverage, vesting, funding or fiduciary responsibility rules of ERISA. Most of ERISA's reporting and disclosure requirements and the tax-qualification requirements under the IRC also are inapplicable. However, a nonqualified arrangement does not receive the favorable tax treatment accorded a qualified retirement plan.

Because nonqualified plans are exempt from the most restrictive provisions of ERISA and the IRC, they can be designed to cover selected executives. In fact, these plans generally cannot be made available to rank-and-file employees.

Elective deferred compensation plans enable an executive to defer payment of a portion of his/her compensation to a future date. Under a properly designed plan, executives of for-profit businesses can defer tax on compensation until they receive it without risking forfeiture if they voluntarily terminate employment; executives of tax-exempt organizations do not have this option due to special tax rules applicable to tax-exempt employers. Therefore, elective plans are a more valuable benefit in the for-profit sector.

Purpose

Elective NQDC plans are similar to section 401(k) plans in that a covered employee may elect to set aside a portion of his/her compensation for payment in the future. Such plans have several advantages:

- **Deferrals of compensation in excess of the statutory limitations on qualified plans.** Nonqualified plans can make up for regulatory limits on pre-tax contributions to tax-qualified plans, such as section 401(k) plans, and can recognize pay that may not be taken into account under a qualified plan. Because nonqualified plans allow executives to defer compensation above the statutory limitations, they can be used to supplement retirement benefits under a company's qualified retirement plans and provide for other future financial commitments.

- **Reduction of executive's current income taxes.** Current taxable income is reduced by the amount of compensation that is deferred.

However, compensation will be taxed at ordinary income tax rates that are in effect when distributions are received. If the executive is in a lower income tax bracket when distributions are made (compared to the applicable rate when compensation is deferred), there may be additional income tax savings. On the other hand, if the applicable tax rate is higher, the executive could pay more in taxes than if the compensation had not been deferred.

- **Tax-deferred accumulation.** Income tax is not paid on earnings credited to a deferred compensation account until distributions are received, allowing the deferrals and earnings to compound on a pre-tax basis.
- **Recruitment and retention of key employees.** An employer can use these plans as a recruitment incentive and retention tool. Many executives seek arrangements to supplement the company's retirement plans. In addition, these executives may be more likely to continue employment to avoid triggering a taxable distribution upon termination or, if vesting is deferred, forfeiting all or a portion of the benefit accrued.
- **Coverage and design flexibility.** Because there are no coverage, eligibility or nondiscrimination requirements applicable to nonquali-fied plans, an employer can provide these benefits to a select group of executives or highly compensated employees; coverage of other employees could subject the plan to the reach of ERISA. Because there are fewer formal requirements applicable to NQDC plans than to qualified plans, nonqualified programs are simpler to establish and maintain. In particular, nonqualified plans have no funding requirements.

Taxation and Accounting

General rules on how NQDC is taxed and how it is treated under the accounting rules are summarized in Table 8-2.

Under a taxable employer's deferred compensation arrangement that satisfies applicable tax law standards, neither the compensation nor the earnings on the deferrals is taxable to the individual until received. When the employee recognizes taxable income and incurs tax liability, the company receives a tax deduction in the same amount. In most cases,

TABLE 8-2

How NQDC Is Taxed and Treated Under Accounting Rules

	Company Accounting	Company Taxation	Individual Taxation
Compensation Earned	Charge to earnings	No tax deduction	FICA tax
Compensation Received	No charge to earnings	Tax deduction	Ordinary income tax

the company will have recorded an expense on its books at the time the compensation was earned, even though the tax deduction might not apply for many years.

Applicable Tax Laws

Although NQDC plans have fewer restrictions than qualified plans, specific rules must be followed to accomplish the deferral of an employee's taxable compensation.

- **Constructive receipt.** If an executive can obtain funds at any time upon request or has control over them, the amounts are currently taxable under the long-standing doctrine of constructive receipt, regardless of whether the executive actually obtains the money. To avoid constructive receipt, a deferred compensation agreement must be entered into before the deferred income is earned or available; the arrangement also must substantially restrict the executive's ability to access the funds until a predetermined time or event (at which time it will become taxable). These requirements were formalized as part of IRC section 409A.

- **Section 409A.** IRC section 409A imposes a series of requirements on NQDC arrangements; its rules govern when deferral elections may be made and when they may be modified, when deferred amounts may be distributed, and how they may be funded. Unless an exception applies, a nonqualified arrangement must meet these requirements in form and in operation. Section 409A accelerates income taxation and imposes a 20 percent tax penalty, as well as interest payments, on a covered executive if a plan is noncompliant. See "Section 409A and Elective Deferred Compensation Plans" for more information about specific rules that can apply.

To avoid current taxation of deferred amounts under the economic benefit and constructive receipt doctrines, nonqualified plan benefits must be unfunded and subject to the claims of general creditors. In the case of the company's insolvency or bankruptcy, the executive's right to receive payments may be no greater than that of any other general unsecured creditor. Although nonqualified plan benefits must be unfunded, they typically are informally funded, with funds set aside in trust accounts to cover the plans' liabilities while maintaining exemption from most ERISA requirements. These funds remain assets of the company and are within the reach of creditors in the event of insolvency or bankruptcy.

Informal funding can increase participant security but falls short of true funding. Two common informal funding devices are:

■ **Rabbi trust.** An employer-established grantor trust into which the employer determines how much money or other assets are placed

Section 409A and Elective Deferred Compensation Plans

Initial Deferral Elections

In general, elective participant deferrals are irrevocable and must be made before the start of the calendar year in which the related services commence. The election must identify the amount to be deferred, the length of period of deferral and the form of payment. For performance-based compensation relating to services performed during a period of at least 12 months, a participant's initial deferral election may be made at any time before the six-month period prior to the end of the performance period — if it meets certain criteria. For example, participants in a bonus plan that has a calendar-year performance period could make deferral elections regarding such bonuses anytime on or before June 30 of the calendar year in which the amounts are earned.

Changes to Deferral Elections

A subsequent participant election to delay a payment or change the form of payment must not take effect for at least 12 months and must further defer the payments for at least five years. If the payment is scheduled to be made on a fixed date, the subsequent deferral election may not be made sooner than 12 months prior to the date the amount is scheduled to be paid. In general, these restrictions also apply to changes to distribution provisions initiated by the employer.

Distributions

Payments of deferred compensation may only be made at a specified time or under a fixed schedule that is objectively determinable, or upon certain specified events — separation from service, death, disability, change in the ownership or effective control of the company or unforeseeable emergency, in each case as defined by the IRC and tax regulations.

for the provision of benefits. These assets must remain subject to the company's creditors.

- **Corporate-owned life insurance (COLI).** Death proceeds or loans are used to recover benefit payments provided by the plan. COLI involves an employer's investment in cash-value life insurance policies that insure the lives of selected executives. The company pays the premiums, retains ownership and receives tax-free proceeds when the participant dies.

If assets are transferred outside of the United States or restrictions are triggered by an employer's poor financial health, section 409A accelerates income taxation and imposes penalties on executives covered by informal DC funding arrangements.

Section 409A also penalizes certain officers and top-paid employees of any public company that maintains a tax-qualified DB plan if the employer sets aside assets to pay deferred compensation in specific

---

Acceleration of Payments

Deferred compensation payments generally may not be made before the permissible payment date or event specified in the plan. This anti-acceleration rule effectively bars distribution of benefits upon plan termination, except under very limited circumstances.

Six-Month Delay to Specified Employees

Payments to a specified employee of a public company triggered by a separation from service must be delayed at least six months following the separation, except in the event of disability or death of the specified employee. For purposes of this provision, "specified employee" generally includes "key employees" of public companies as defined in the "top-heavy" rules governing benefits provided under tax-qualified retirement plans.

Restrictions on Setting Aside Funds

Section 409A limits the ability of an employer to informally set aside assets to pay deferred compensation benefits.

Economic Benefit

Under the economic benefit doctrine, income realized in any form by an executive is taxable upon grant if:

> It has tangible, quantifiable value that the executive has in effect received, and

> There is no substantial risk of forfeiture.

> The economic benefit doctrine was formalized in IRC section 83, governing when transfers of "property" are taxed.

circumstances: while in bankruptcy, within six months of terminating an underfunded plan or while the plan is less than 80 percent funded under "at risk" funding rules.

Plan Design

In designing an elective deferred compensation plan, decisions on certain key features are needed:

- **Eligible deferral sources.** Which elements of compensation are allowed to be deferred? Base salary, annual incentive, cash-based LTI and/or RSU?
- **Deferral period.** What is the period for deferring compensation? Will payments be triggered at termination, retirement, death, disability, change in control or on a specified date? When will payment be made after the relevant trigger?
- **Form of payout.** What are the permissible forms of payment? Lump sum or installments? If the trigger is an employee's termination, the form of payment must be the same for each year's deferral.
- **Investment options.** Deferral accounts are usually credited with a return that can be fixed, based on a variable rate or floating rate (e.g., prime rate, U.S. Treasury bill rate), or tied to a hypothetical investment alternative (e.g., mutual fund).

These design decisions are also important for nonelective deferred compensation plans (e.g., SERPs).

Potential Disadvantages

Despite their many advantages, NQDC plans also have drawbacks. Disadvantages to consider when evaluating such plans include:

- **Current tax deduction unavailable to employer.** An employer cannot claim a current deduction for any NQDC amounts until the employee receives the amount as income.
- **Unfunded plan.** Deferred amounts under an NQDC plan are merely an employer's promise to pay the employee in the future. Because these amounts must remain subject to the claims of the employer's creditors in the event of insolvency, a company's obligation to pay may become an empty promise if it becomes insolvent.

- **Restricted access to money.** In general, participants do not have access to deferrals until the selected payment date or event.
- **Possible higher tax rate.** The applicable tax rate when payments are received may be greater than when funds are deferred, reducing the overall return on the deferrals.
- **Risk of tax penalty for section 409A violation.** If the employer fails to comply with the operational and written documentation requirements of section 409A, the executive will owe ordinary income tax earlier than expected, plus a substantial tax penalty.
- **Securities law registration.** An employee's interest in an elective deferred compensation arrangement is considered a security, subject to registration under federal securities and state blue-sky laws, unless an applicable exemption applies. Most deferred compensation plans are exempt from federal securities registration, but may need to be registered in certain states where employees reside.

An executive's opportunity to defer compensation can be an effective recruitment and retention tool, so employers should consider making available nonqualified plans that are tailored to their particular circumstances. Executives usually appreciate being able to defer compensation in excess of the statutory limits. Before proceeding, an employer should understand the financial implications of the postponed tax deduction for the deferred compensation. An employer also must ensure that its nonqualified arrangements comply with the requirements of IRC section 409A and are designed to be tax effective for eligible executives.

Performance-Based SERPs: An Alternative Approach to Executive Benefits

In designing executive compensation programs, a key objective is to align the interests of executives and shareholders. Efforts have centered mainly on current compensation and wealth-building opportunities, such as stock compensation and other LTIs. Retirement benefits, on the other hand, typically have been viewed as a reward for long service rather than as a motivator of executive behaviors. In the current era of increased scrutiny of executives' total pay packages and greater shareholder activism, employers may want to include executives' retirement benefits in the mix of performance-based rewards.

Simply stated, a performance-based SERP places one or more performance conditions on an executive's accrual of benefits. SERPs are extremely flexible; there are many ways to design such a plan and various performance conditions that can be appropriate.

Performance Conditions

A fundamental principle of a performance-based SERP is that some criteria other than the passage of time (e.g., achievement of a measure of performance) must occur for a retirement benefit to be accrued. One approach is for the employer to establish the same performance measures as used for the executives' incentives, such as revenue, profitability or cash flow targets. Alternatively, an organization may choose to personalize the performance measures, such as achievement of individual sales targets, improvement in a business unit's profitability, or other personal goals. The performance measure can even be an event, such as a predetermined milestone in product development, emergence from bankruptcy, or completion of a transaction (e.g., initial public offering). In determining which performance measure(s) to establish, an issue is assessing and setting the degree of difficulty for attainment. How high should the bar be set? The decision is based entirely on the employer's goals for the SERP regarding the executives' behaviors that the employer wishes to motivate.

As executives achieve the performance measures determined under the SERP, objectively judged positive results should occur. Shareholders and other stakeholders presumably would be pleased that the executive group as a whole is accomplishing its goals or, in the case of personalized performance measures, that the executive is generating positive results for the organization. Such favorable occurrences can create an environment in which stakeholders are better able and more willing to accept the executives' rewards as reasonable.

Applying the Performance Conditions

In a performance-based SERP, application of the performance conditions falls into two categories: benefits accruals and vesting.

Benefit Accruals

If performance dictates whether a benefit is accrued in a given year, the SERP would operate in exactly the same way as a traditional SERP, except that at the end of the performance period an objective measure of performance determines whether that year's benefit accrual is added to the total accrual.

For example, if the DB SERP pension amount is calculated as 2 percent multiplied by final salary multiplied by years of service, then whether the performance goal is achieved could determine whether that year of service would be added to total years of service in the participant's benefit formula. If a DB SERP pension is calculated as 60 percent of final pay, prorated by years of service divided by 15 (not greater than one), then the achievement of the performance goal could determine whether that year of service would be added to years of service in the formula.

A DC SERP operates even more simply if performance measures are applied to benefit accruals — simply add the annual account allocation, or not, based on whether the performance goals are achieved.

Of course, rather than an all-or-nothing accrual entitlement, a proration of the accrual can be applied in either a DB or DC design.

Vesting

Achievement of performance targets also can dictate whether an executive attains a vested (non-forfeitable) right to collect the benefits that have accrued under the SERP. Essentially, vesting is a design overlay on top of the pattern of benefit accruals under the SERP. In designing a SERP, vesting can be done according to a schedule, phasing in over some number of years, and/or can begin at some age. Alternatively, vesting can occur 100 percent (so-called "cliff" vesting) at some defined age or service point in time. Depending on the employer's goals for the SERP (i.e., in terms of retaining executives), the vesting schedule can be structured for earlier or later vesting in an executive's career.

For example, a phased-in vesting schedule might be 20 percent vesting per year beginning at age 55, subject to the achievement of personal performance goals. If the employer is a tax-exempt employer, it is important to consider, when establishing the vesting criteria, that vesting of nonqualified benefits generally triggers taxation to the executive of the value of the vested benefit.

Financial Considerations

The economic value of a pension benefit is based on the ultimate value of the benefits to be paid. Therefore, depending on the nature of the performance measures applied to the accrual or vesting of the SERP benefits, the economic value of the plan may or may not change. If, however, the performance measures instituted under the SERP truly provide for an uncertainty regarding whether some (or all) of the pension will be received by the executive, then the economic value of the pension will decrease, manifesting itself in one of the following ways:

- To the executive, it may mean that the perceived benefits provided by the SERP may decrease or the actual benefits payable under the SERP will decrease, each in comparison to a SERP without performance measures.
- To the employer, cash required to fund the SERP benefits may decrease, and accounting expense also may decrease.

Employers designing a performance-based SERP should consult their actuaries on quantifying these financial impacts.

Use of Performance-Based SERPs

Employers may want to add performance measures to the design of their SERPs to motivate certain behaviors among their executive team.

With proper design, the approach can be very effective. As is the case with most nonqualified arrangements, there can be a great deal of flexibility in developing a performance-based SERP. The various design features should be considered in conjunction with the other incentive-based pay and benefits plans sponsored by the organization to ensure that the performance-based SERP complements, rather than duplicates or conflicts with, other programs.

CHAPTER 9

Executive Nonretirement Benefits and Perquisites

By John Putnam and Andrew Shapiro

Though not as prevalent as in the past, special executive health and welfare benefits and perquisites can be important adjuncts to executive pay packages. Perquisites of various kinds are found in most U.S. companies and are very prevalent outside of the United States. Whether offered in cash or in kind, perquisites cover a broad range of services and benefits — personal use of corporate aircraft, financial planning, company cars, home security and physical exams being among the most common. Typically offered to a select group of employees, executive health and welfare programs (e.g., death, disability, injury, paid time off) usually are add-ons or extensions to existing plans available to all employees.

Most perquisites have been in decline for many years. Shareholders and institutional investors continue questioning the reasonableness and costs of perquisites because there is no obvious link with performance. Tax law requirements can result in some or all of the perks' value being taxed as income to the executive. More significantly, in its major overhaul of the executive compensation disclosure rules in 2006, the SEC lowered the financial threshold for aggregate perquisite disclosure for named executives and directors, thus giving a much clearer picture of the extent of perquisite use in publicly held companies.

Health and welfare plans also may trigger additional taxes to executives. Nonetheless, they represent value to executives and, like perquisites, should be reviewed to ensure that they use company funds efficiently and align with executive compensation and corporate strategies. Health and welfare benefits and perquisites that clearly benefit both the company and the executive without engendering unacceptable criticism, such as those affecting the health and safety of the employee, likely will continue to be offered, while others will be reduced or eliminated.

This chapter:

- Analyzes perquisites in large U.S. companies, with a discussion of which perquisites are the most costly to the company, which are likely to be discontinued and which may survive.
- Discusses the trends in executive health and welfare benefits, including the various kinds of executive life insurance, short- and long-term disability benefits, health-care benefits, and vacations.

Executive Perquisites

Executive perquisites (perks) have been under fire for many years, so it was no surprise that the SEC targeted them in its 2006 reworking of the executive pay disclosure rules.

Companies now must break out perks that have an aggregate value in excess of $10,000, while the prior rules only required disclosure of perks that were worth more than $50,000 or 10 percent of cash compensation. Because most companies limited their perquisite disclosures to what was required, pre-2007 proxy statements did not furnish a true indication of the prevalence of various perks.

Most research found that most companies now are disclosing all perks, even if they total less than $10,000 in value. Of course, some organizations follow the reporting requirements precisely and do not disclose the smaller perks.

Prevalence of Perks

Looking for developing trends related to executive perks, Hay Group examined the proxy disclosures of large public companies regarding CEO perks furnished in recent years. Looking at large public companies, almost all provided at least one perk to their executives. The most common perk was personal use of the corporate aircraft, followed closely by financial planning and company cars. Other notable perks were home security, physical examinations, supplemental life insurance, spousal travel and club memberships.

Why Focus on Perks?

In dollar terms, perks are a very small slice of the pay pie. Then why have perks drawn such criticism from investors and corporate watchdogs? The media need to grab public attention and often focuses on outliers — examples from corporate America that are at an extreme (i.e., the largest or smallest amounts). While these examples typically are not representative of the entire sample, they can make interesting news and great headlines. (See "The Outliers.")

Companies Discontinuing or Eliminating Perks

With investors gaining a better look at executive perquisites in post-2006 disclosures, many corporate boards re-examined the perks furnished to the company's executives. As part of the process, some employers discontinued selected (or even all) perks. In fact, since 2006 most companies have reported the discontinuance of at least one perk. The perks most frequently eliminated have been income tax gross-ups, country club membership dues, spousal travel, company cars and financial planning. Companies in recent years have reported perks that, for the most part, related to the overall health and well-being of the recipient executives. Typically, companies have not cut back on most security-related perks for the CEO, such as personal use of the corporate aircraft or home security or a security driver. These security-related perks became very common after the terrorist acts of Sept. 11, 2001. Many companies specifically disclose that these perks are primarily for security purposes.

Will Perks Continue Declining?

Because the safety of senior executives is critical for U.S. companies, companies appear likely to retain perquisites that enhance executives' safety. Similarly, because it is in the interests of both companies

The Outliers

Where companies reported a substantial amount of CEO perk value, we reviewed the text to look for outliers. Aside from the use of corporate aircraft, the largest perk values were for the cost of home security, tax gross-ups, supplemental life insurance, a company car and driver, personal and spouse travel, and financial counseling. The smallest perk values, all under $1,000, were for the cost of physical examination, health club membership, personal entertainment, airline club membership and gifts.

Personal Aircraft Usage

Personal use of the corporate aircraft, when provided to senior executives, typically is the most costly executive perk. The value of executive perks appears in the "All Other Compensation" (AOC) column in the proxy's Summary Compensation Table, along with the value of discount stock purchases, company contributions to defined contribution plans and company payment of insurance premiums. The median value of a CEO's personal use of the corporate aircraft recently has exceeded 50 percent of the AOC total value.

Companies also are continuing to put limits on how much plane usage the CEO and sometimes the other executives can use per year or by month. The limits are typically stated as a defined dollar amount or as a specific number of hours per year. We have also seen the limits stated as a number of trips per year.

Unusual Perks

We also examined proxy statements for descriptions of unusual perks, but it appears that larger companies have deliberately discontinued using perks that tend to stand out. There are still perks that involve the use of corporate facilities (e.g., company barbershop, boats, hunting and fishing clubs, company helicopter) and those that involve organizations providing company products or product discounts (e.g., tire program, theme park use, merchandise discount program).

and their senior executives to manage the health of such executives, physical exams are likely to survive.

On the other hand, companies probably will continue curbing various club memberships (e.g., country clubs, health clubs, airplane clubs), free sporting and entertainment event tickets, and tax gross-ups, as they are finding insufficient benefit to justify the criticism received from groups such as proxy advisers and the media.

From time to time during the past two decades, cafeteria perks or perks allowances appeared on the verge of becoming popular. The approach involves granting an executive an annual dollar amount that the executive then allocates among a select group or menu of executive perks. While few companies report perks allowances, recently several have decreased or eliminated allowances and replaced them with a one-time salary increase. Of course, critics are quick to point out that this approach may have an adverse cost effect for the company as base pay increases also raise the costs of items based on salary, such as annual bonuses, target LTI amounts, life insurance and retirement benefits.

Executive Health and Welfare Benefits

Executive benefits and perk programs are designed to attract and retain key employees and frequently are designed specifically for certain executives. While retirement benefits have received much attention, the focus here is on the nonretirement benefits components, often referred to as health and welfare programs. This terminology groups together the benefits received for certain specific life events: death, disability, illness, injury and paid time off, each addressing common health and welfare needs.

Executive health and welfare benefits are not particularly scrutinized because they usually follow the "same for all employees" approach that is found at a majority of organizations today. "Top up" benefits are found in less than one-half of U.S. employers, with the prevalence rising as the size of the organization increases. Clearly, cost is an issue, as most of these benefits are provided at little or no cost to the executive. But the real value of any extra benefits may not be appreciated because the covered executives, like most employees, only focus on these benefits when they actually are needed.

From an examination of health and welfare benefits, some insight was gained into the trends observed regarding these benefits. Because executives should consider their health and welfare needs as carefully as their retirement and post-employment requirements, this section concentrates on the "why" as much as the "what" for each key coverage area.

Death Benefits

Executive term-life insurance comes in many forms and designs, with each serving a variety of purposes. The typical life benefit provides coverage often based on a percentage of salary above that provided to all other employees. This benefit may be implemented because the basic coverage levels have caps or upper limits that preclude the executive from coverage of a full multiple of salary. For example, a two times salary basic plan with a maximum of $400,000 would clearly create a shortfall in intended benefits for anyone making more than $200,000 a year in salary. Thus organizations may create a separate insurance class for the executives with higher limits or purchase individual coverage for the additional amounts. In either case, because it only is intended to make up for lost benefits, the full cost usually is paid by the firm.

While many other forms of life insurance are available to executives, all involve more permanent coverage instead of the typical term insurance.

Key-person life is an individual policy owned totally by the employer and is provided by only a very small percentage of employers. The most common reason for the coverage is to protect the employer against the sudden loss of a key executive. Other purposes include funding for retirement income and increasing the individual's estate. The organization pays the full cost of the policy and receives the full proceeds.

Disability Benefits

Short-term salary continuance and/or accumulation-of-days programs like PTO provide further coverage for executives. In salary continuation programs, this often takes the form of a 100-percent-of-pay benefit for the entire short-term disability period or an additional number of days (generally about a week) in a PTO bank.

Special long-term programs are provided by about one-third of organizations, with the majority of the cost covered by the employer. Where employers provide these extra benefits, the larger organizations lead the way. In addition, more than two-thirds of the health-care industry provides these additional disability benefits, perhaps because of their health mission.

The design of these plans is intended to increase the level of coverage through various approaches, including:

- Shorter waiting periods for commencement of benefits
- Higher monthly maximum benefits

- Higher percentage of salary benefits (typically up to 70 percent of base pay)
- The definition of disability based on only the executive's current occupation
- Easing the maximums or expanding definitions all increase the value of this benefit if and when an executive incurs a disability.

One key item executives need to remember is that whatever portion of the premiums are paid by the employer, that same portion of the benefit, if received, also is taxable income.

Health-Care Benefits

Due to the scope of health-care coverage commonly provided by U.S. employers for all employees and the tax-free nature of these benefits, few special executive health-care benefits are offered. Those furnished to executives usually focus on simple additions that have no tax impact because the taxes would be assessed on the full actual medical costs, not just the premiums.

In about half of companies, executives have initial waiting periods for eligibility waived so their coverage begins with the start of employment. An annual physical examination previously was another key executive benefit, as companies and executives each understood the importance of maintaining a healthy executive team. However, as health-care reform has taken effect, all employees have annual physicals covered at 100 percent under preventive-care mandates. Thus, except for a few situations in which the executive can obtain these physicals at high-end clinics, this no longer is seen as an executive perquisite.

Finally, very few organizations offer a formal medical expense reimbursement plan; their scarcity likely reflects the high cost of the premiums. To avoid tax implications, these plans must be fully insured and provide for reimbursement of medical expenses incurred by the executives and their dependents in excess of the amounts covered by the underlying basic plans. Most core plans are designed to cover catastrophic costs, so these reimbursement plans really provide coverage for the first-dollar type co-payments and deductibles in the base plans up to the annual out-of-pocket maximums.

Executive Vacations

"Executive vacations" do not mean luxury suites or fabulous resorts — rather they refer to having more time away from the job. This is a much more critical benefit outside of the United States; our European colleagues really do take significant time off each year. However, in the United States, only about one-third of organizations provide additional vacation days to executives.

For those that do, it typically takes the form of an additional five vacation days and/or waiving the service schedule so the executive receives the full number of vacation days regardless of tenure with the organization.

Usually, U.S. executive compensation and benefits focus on retirement and LTIs. However, all executives need to understand their full suite of health and welfare programs and make sure their individual and family needs are met, just as they are expected to achieve the goals of their organizations.

CHAPTER 10

Stock Ownership Guidelines and Share Holding Requirements

By Cory Morrow and Kevin McLaren

Shareholders, the business media and institutional investors all favor the notion that executives and outside directors should own a significant number of shares in the companies they manage or oversee. Share ownership guidelines have been around for many years and now are found in most large, public companies in the United States. Less prevalent, but noteworthy, are holding requirements.

For executives and outside directors, share acquisition through stock option awards has no financial downside. If the options are underwater, they are not exercised and the recipient loses nothing; when they are in the money, the recipient may exercise and sell the shares immediately, thus capturing an already known financial gain while relinquishing share ownership. Shareholders, on the other hand, must wait — sometimes for years — before they realize a similar gain and run the risk of seeing their investment shrink. Hence the question: Do stock options (as well as other equity-based incentive vehicles) truly align executive, outside director and shareholder interests?

Ownership guidelines attempt to reverse this deficiency by requiring recipients to achieve and maintain a certain level of share ownership — usually a multiple of salary or the board retainer — for a designated time period. The level of required ownership increases with rank in the organization. Despite the favorable optics of mandated executive and director share ownership, some question whether it truly is needed. In up-market times, guidelines usually are easy to achieve and can seem superfluous when senior executives already own shares far in excess of what typical guidelines require. On the other hand, in a market downturn, guidelines can be difficult to achieve, especially for recent hires.

This chapter:

- Discusses the pros and cons of stock ownership guidelines and describes an approach for establishing an ownership guideline program. In addition, it describes typical aspects of using such guidelines (including which shares qualify, shareholding periods and time frames for fulfilling guidelines).

- Outlines alternative approaches currently gaining attention under which executives and outside directors are required to hold shares for a specified period or until (or even beyond) retirement.

Use of Share Ownership Guidelines

The majority of U.S. public companies use some form of share ownership guidelines for executives and outside directors. Implementing these guidelines publicly demonstrates a board's desire for executives to share in the same rewards and risks as shareholders.

For executives, ownership guidelines typically only apply to the CEO, direct reports and in some case second-level reports. Most commonly, share ownership guidelines are expressed as a multiple of base salary, with greater requirements for higher-level jobs within an organization. Table 10-1 illustrates typical share ownership guidelines as a multiple of base salary; however, there is a wide variance in the level of ownership requirements.

TABLE 10-1

Typical Share Ownership Guidelines

CEO	5x
Direct reports	3x to 4x
Key executives	2x to 3x
Senior managers	1x to 2x

Usually, participants are given a reasonable time period — typically five years — to obtain company shares and meet the set ownership levels. Once the required level is reached, participants are expected to maintain those levels throughout their employment with the company. For purposes of determining compliance with the guideline, company stock that the participant owns outright, vested shares in employee benefits plans, and unvested restricted shares (which vest solely on the passage of time) commonly are typically included. However, unexercised stock options usually are not counted.

Guidelines are similar for outside directors. Most commonly, share ownership guidelines are expressed as a multiple of a director's annual board cash retainer. Unlike executives where the multiple corresponds to the executive's position, all outside directors are subject to the same multiple. Similarly, directors are provided with an "accumulation period" — typically five years — to obtain company shares and meet the set ownership levels. Given the typical practice of providing the majority of a director's compensation in stock, directors are often able to achieve the ownership guidelines by holding the shares delivered to them through these grants.

Potential Concerns With Share Ownership Guidelines

Although share ownership guidelines are viewed positively by the investment community and encouraged by corporate boards, they are not without issue:

- In a rising stock market, the required ownership level can be trivial in comparison to the amounts earned from company equity programs, allowing recipients to sell substantial amounts of equity while still satisfying the established ownership guidelines.
- Conversely, if the share price does not appreciate, employees are faced with purchasing shares using their personal resources or relying on the company to ease its enforcement of the guidelines; neither alternative provides a positive result.
- Timing also can cause problems. Depending on the time of hire, share ownership guidelines may not be equally difficult for all

participants to achieve (i.e., newer hires could have difficulty complying due to higher exercise prices than tenured employees).

Some company executives and outside directors believe that providing consistent equity award grants and encouraging responsible behavior around equity disposition (e.g., limited sales) are sufficient safeguards, making share ownership guidelines unnecessary.

Net Shares Retention Alternative to Ownership Guidelines

In view of some of the potential concerns with share owner-ship guidelines, companies have explored other approaches to consider in lieu of, or in tandem with, share ownership guidelines. A net shares retention plan is an alternative that can increase share ownership levels, create a retention tool and strengthen the alignment of interests between executives, outside directors and shareholders.

The key feature of a net shares retention program allows a partici-pant to build share ownership while permitting diversification. This approach has been gaining popularity, including its use in combina-tion with share ownership guidelines.

When a participant exercises his/her stock options, has the vesting restrictions lapse on a time-vested restricted stock award, or receives an earn-out of performance shares, the individual may sell enough shares to cover payment of the exercise price and resulting taxes. The participant then is required to hold a specified percentage of the net shares for a designated period of time. The participant may sell the remaining net shares and the funds to diversify his/her personal portfolio. (See Figure 10-1.)

The holding requirements typically range from 25 to 75 percent of the net shares. A typical holding period is three to five years, although some companies may require executives and directors to hold the specified net shares until termination of employment or termination from the board.

With each exercise, lapse of vesting restrictions or earn-out, the participant builds his/her share ownership position while having the opportunity to diversify personal assets. Shareholders are protected

FIGURE 10-1

Net-Shares Retention Plan Approach

The employee exercises 1,000 options with an exercise price of $10 and a fair market value of $20.

The employee sells 700 shares to cover the exercise price ($10,000) and taxes ($4,000).

The employee is required to hold 50 percent of the net shares (150 shares).

The employee may sell the remaining 150 shares.

from executives cashing out completely after short-term run-ups in the stock price.

Paying for Long-Term Performance

Some organizations have adopted hold policies requiring executives and outside directors to keep a significant portion of their stock awards until retirement and, in some instances, into retirement. The focus of hold policies is to more strongly link executive equity-based compensation — the primary component of their pay packages — to long-term performance. There are several forms of hold policies, including:

- Retention ratios
- Long-term vesting
- Temporary holding requirements used in conjunction with traditional stock ownership guidelines.

Retention Ratios

The retention ratio is the most common hold design, requiring that an individual retain a fixed percentage (typically 50 to 75 percent) of the after-tax portion of earned equity awards until he/she leaves the company. Although less common, the holding period also can be extended for a period of time into retirement (i.e., hold through retirement).

The key is that the retention ratio applies to earned equity awards. When an executive or outside director receives shares of company stock (e.g., a stock option is exercised, restricted stock vests), a portion of the net shares must be retained for the duration of the executive's career or director's tenure. The net shares apply to the profit or gain shares that remain after the payment of taxes and, in the case of stock options, the exercise price. Because the equity awards already are earned, the executive or director is not in danger of losing the awards if he/she leaves the company.

For example, a company may require executive officers or directors to retain at least 75 percent of common stock and equity awards (less allowances for the payment of any option exercise price and taxes) made to them while they are employed by the organization or serving on its board. Under this approach, a portion of an individual's net worth is tied to the company's share price. Proponents argue that the approach motivates executives to strive for superior performance of the share price on a long-term basis.

Some companies not only require executives to hold a portion of their equity until they leave the company, but also to hold a portion of their equity into retirement. This approach, while worth noting, is not as common as "hold until retirement" policies.

Long-Term Vesting

Under the long-term vesting approach, a portion of an executive's equity grant does not vest until retirement. One consequence is that an executive cannot sell a portion of the equity grant until retirement, even if the executive is permitted to exercise unvested stock options. This is a notable difference between the retention ratio and long-term vesting approach. Under the retention ratio design, the ratio only applies to earned equity awards and, if an executive leaves before retirement, he/she is not in danger of losing the awards. Under the long-term vesting approach, the awards are forfeited if the executive leaves before retirement age. This feature likely explains why the long-term vesting approach is far less prevalent than the retention ratio design.

Temporary Holding

A temporary design, as the name implies, requires an executive or outside director to hold his/her equity awards only until the traditional ownership guidelines have been met. For example, a company may require its executive officers and directors to hold 100 percent of their equity awards (net of taxes and exercise price) until stock ownership guidelines are satisfied. After achieving the guidelines, recipients would be required to hold 75 percent of equity awards for one year. The temporary design is intended to provide a "stop-gap" until traditional ownership guidelines are met.

Benefits of Hold Policies

Hold policies take share ownership guidelines to another level by tying equity grants to the duration of an executive's career (or director's tenure) with the company. A company and shareholders may obtain significant benefits from such policies, including aligning executives' long-term net worth to superior and sustained stock price performance. Hold policies also reinforce stock ownership guidelines and support the notion that executives and directors should have a long-term equity stake in the companies they manage or oversee. Additional benefits of adopting hold policies include:

- **Focus on long-term performance.** Hold policies encourage executives and directors to take a long-term approach to stock ownership, which arguably aligns their interests with those of shareholders. In addition, hold policies force participants to analyze the effect of their short-term decisions on the long-term company results. If an individual is required to hold a significant amount of his/ her wealth until retirement, he/she likely is more likely to focus on long-term, rather than short-term, value creation and/or excessive risk-taking actions and decisions.

- **Size of equity awards.** There has been some investor concern that executive stock ownership guidelines have not kept pace with the size of executives' equity awards. Investors may argue that that equity pay packages have increased and there has not been a corresponding increase or adjustment to an organization's stock ownership guidelines. Hold policies help support the alignment between the size of equity awards and increase in executive ownership.

- **More effective than traditional stock ownership guidelines.** As mentioned, criticism of traditional stock ownership guidelines is that in periods of rising stock prices, the number of shares a recipient is required to retain decreases. Hold policies add another layer to traditional stock ownership guidelines, not allowing an executive or director to decrease his/her stock ownership level based on rising stock prices. Conversely, hold policies also help alleviate unequal burden between long-tenured and new executives and directors in periods of declining stock prices. New executives and directors will not need to allocate a large portion of their compensation to satisfy guidelines.

- **Investors' pay scrutiny.** With the spotlight on executive compensation and particular scrutiny of C-suite compensation, hold policies can send a strong message to investors. Equity awards that are subject to hold policies help enforce the desired long-term behavior and performance.

These policies also aid in counteracting the notion that executives can time a market sale (e.g., an ability to sell equity shortly after vesting could lead executives to focus on short-term prices). Hold policies may mitigate potential short-term swings and/or gains.

Potential Pitfalls

The appeal of retirement-based policies is understandable. Hold polices may lead executives to focus more on the long-term results while addressing investor concerns that executive stock ownership levels have not kept pace with the increasing equity awards. However, hold policies, like many executive compensation provisions, also may create contrary incentives. Potential pitfalls and negative consequences of hold policies can be far-reaching:

- **Encourage early retirement.** Hold policies could potentially encourage executives to retire prematurely. For example, if an executive believes that the company's shares are overvalued and will likely fall in the near future, a hold-until-retirement policy could encourage the executive to retire early and cash out at a higher stock price (subject to any blackout periods and insider trading restrictions). This can be a significant issue, particularly for organizations with high-value executives who may be difficult to replace. In addition, the executives with the largest equity stakes, and potentially the executives who generated the biggest returns for the company, would have the greatest incentive to retire early.

■ **Focus on short-term results near retirement.** Executives who have a significant portion of their wealth tied up in equity compensation likely will be very focused on the company's performance one to two years prior to their retirement. That is, a hold policy may create an incentive for executives to focus on short-term company results prior to retirement to ensure that they can cash out at an optimal stock price.

■ **Weighing of hold-beyond-retirement policies.** One way for companies to help avoid this issue is to require executives to continue to hold their equity after they leave the company — namely hold-beyond-retirement policies. This should cause executives to be less focused on the stock price at the time of their retirement. However, the approach could be perceived as unfair to executives whose long-term wealth now would be in the hands of their successors. The hold-beyond-retirement provision could be tempered by requiring the executive to hold the equity only for a relatively short-period (e.g., six months) after retirement, minimizing the potential effects of decisions outside of their control.

■ **Impact on younger executives.** Some executives may view hold policies as excessive, particularly younger executives who are not planning to retire for many years. Hold policies may create recruitment and retention issues for executives who are in demand in the market and have the option to move to another company with a comparable total rewards package without the restriction of hold policies.

Shareholder Review

Share ownership guidelines, net share retention plans and hold-until-retirement policies have been positively received by shareholders, boards of directors and industry watchdog groups. Hold policies are still a minority practice in the United States, but increased corporate governance and disclosure of executive pay may encourage a wider adoption of ownership policies that include hold-until-retirement and post-termination holding periods. As compensation committees review their share ownership guidelines and assess whether hold policies are appropriate for their executive officers and outside directors, they should at the same time review the totality of their companies' compensation programs to ensure that all policies and practices encourage and engage executives and directors to achieve common strategic goals.

CHAPTER 11

Executive Employment Contracts and Post-Employment Arrangements

By Bill Gerek

Whether through individual agreements or programs covering a group of select executives, top management at U.S. companies typically have one or more financial protections should certain events occur affecting the status of their employment. Most common are employment contracts, severance programs, change-in-control (CIC) arrangements and post-employment consulting agreements.

While these arrangements share a long history, particularly in publicly held companies, there recently has been much discussion on whether they are needed or desired. For example, employment contracts often simply state the obvious regarding salary, bonus and other elements of pay. Because post-termination restrictions (often the key contractual benefits obtained by companies) can be difficult to enforce, agreements may unduly favor executives. Further, CIC arrangements, whether in an employment contract or in a separate plan or agreement, may go beyond the key objective of encouraging executives to stay until a transaction has been completed.

Nonetheless, these arrangements have numerous supporters. Companies are justifiably concerned about losing key employees in a restructuring, and employees want financial protection if they are made redundant in a transaction over which they have no control. And, in special circumstances, companies may continue to need the services of key employees once they have retired.

Like all other aspects of executive pay, employment contracts and post-retirement arrangements have garnered considerable attention from shareholders, proxy advisory groups and the press. They are concerned about policies that potentially result in windfalls to executives and excessive accounting and tax charges to the company. Moreover, through say-on-pay voting, shareholders can now voice their opinions on executive pay at public companies and can use this forum to press companies to revisit their policies and justify their actions.

The ultimate question for a company is what makes sense given its particular corporate culture, business objectives and likelihood of a restructuring or a key executive retiring in the near future. Eligibility, costs and the specific purposes of any compensation arrangements need to be carefully weighed; what other companies do should not be the primary consideration.

This chapter:

- Outlines the reasons for having employment contracts, describes their pros and cons, and discusses the key provisions and issues companies should address in designing and refining their use of executive agreements.
- Discusses CIC design features such as eligibility, definition of change in control, single- and double-payout triggers, benefits continuation, equity acceleration, and structuring cash payments.
- Describes how to handle unvested equity under various kinds of termination events and the accounting and tax issues that must be addressed. The chapter also analyzes the criticism and widespread abandonment of excise tax gross-ups, and compensation committee considerations in complying with the proxy vote on golden parachutes under say on pay.
- Suggests possible rationales for post-retirement consulting arrangements, including how payments might be structured and the abuses that often are found in such agreements.

Executive Employment Agreements: Why, When and What

Questions around whether an employer should have an employment agreement with one or more of its top executives, along with the associated practices, often are prompted by negotiations with a potential top executive hire or a reconsideration of existing arrangements with the current executives. The heightened focus on good corporate governance in recent years has caused many companies and compensation committees to re-examine the rationale for, and terms and conditions of, executive contracts.

In determining whether and when to use contracts for executives, it is critical to examine an organization's specific facts and circumstances and to understand why employment agreements have been used or are under consideration. It generally is helpful to review the basic approaches for executive contracts and then consider the pros and cons of these agreements.

Approaches

The use of employment agreements for executives can vary considerably among companies, often depending on the organization's culture and the views and philosophy of the board of directors, the compensation committee and the CEO. We see four basic approaches:

- **Contracts not used.** Some employers do not use contracts at all, instead relying on general policies or more limited agreements to address specific issues such as severance, change in control, confidentiality and noncompetition.
- **Only for top-team "new hires."** Other companies limit employment agreements to new-hire situations, especially those in which a sought-after executive is reluctant to join a new and largely unfamiliar organization without the protections of a contract. A related question is if and when either the entire contract or certain executive protections should "sunset."
- **Use for top executive team.** Many organizations extend employment agreements to some or all of the top executive team. Certain organizations may have a contract with only their CEOs, while others may enter into written agreements with a dozen or so executives.

- **Broad use among executives.** A few companies use employment agreements to document their employment relationships with all executives above a certain level (e.g., vice president).

Rationale for Contracts

An executive contract sets out the key terms and conditions of the employment relationship. While contracts typically address salary, annual incentives, LTIs (often equity-based), benefits and perquisites, there is little need for a formal contract if the objective simply is to memorialize these items.

Generally, the most important reasons for an employment agreement are to:

- Specify and make clear what an executive will receive upon various events resulting in a termination of employment (e.g., death, disability, retirement, resignation, resignation for good reason, dismissal and dismissal for cause).
- Address the impact of a change in control of the employer.
- Impose reasonable post-employment restrictions upon an executive (e.g., restrictive covenants addressing matters such as confidentiality and nondisclosure, non-competition, non-solicitation of employees and/or customers, and non-disparagement).
- Specify how and where disputes are to be resolved (e.g., through arbitration in a stated locale under identified rules versus through court litigation in a stated locale applying the law of an identified state).

If properly drafted, employment contracts can help secure the future services of key employees critical to the organization's success. These agreements establish the respective rights, duties, obligations and responsibilities of the parties at a harmonious time; from this perspective they can be likened to premarital agreements.

Arguments Against Employment Agreements

While both the employer and the executive can be well-served by documenting the employment relationship through a contract, another view is that such agreements are either unnecessary or unduly favor executives. Arguments sometimes advanced against executive employment agreements include:

- **Pay for failure.** The heightened focus on executive compensation has highlighted instances in which an executive dismissed for poor performance was entitled to large severance pay based on the terms of an employment agreement. This view maintains that any payments would have been more reasonable if no contract had been in place and the executive had to negotiate a severance package in connection with his/her termination.

- **Performance equals security.** Some maintain that the protection provided by an employment contract is unnecessary for a top executive who is doing a good job and that an executive should not have this protection if he/she is not performing well. However, turnover levels among CEOs and other senior executives (a shorter job "life expectancy") have caused many executives to believe contractual protection is necessary for at least a limited term — especially for new outside hires.

Key Provisions and Usage

Severance and CIC protections usually are the most critical provisions for executives, while employers seek the benefits of restrictive covenants and clawback provisions.

Both parties receive certainty (assuming the agreement is well-drafted) of the terms that will apply in identified circumstances (especially various termination events). From an employer's perspective, a contract may discourage a competitor from recruiting an executive in jurisdictions that provide for tort damages for interference with the relationship of an executive under contract. An agreement may enable an employer to determine which state law will apply where there are contacts in multiple jurisdictions and, if desired, mandate arbitration of disputes regarding employment matters.

Rather than simply limit the use of executive contracts, an objective should be to improve the contents of executive agreements. A consensus is developing regarding best practices that should be considered for employment agreements. (See "Checklist for Considering a New Contract or Evaluating an Existing Contract.")

Checklist for Considering a New Contract or Evaluating an Existing Contract

- ❏ **"Evergreen" renewal.** Evergreen provisions typically call for automatic extension of renewal unless a specified advance notice is given. Procedures should be implemented to review agreements before any such extension becomes effective. In any case, an employer's advance notice not to extend the contract term or renew the agreement should not trigger severance pay.

- ❏ **Critical definitions.** The definitions of "change in control," "cause," and "good reason" should be particularly scrutinized. In reaction to some widely publicized severance payments to executives who were dismissed or resigned after poor corporate performance, companies may seek to expand cause definitions and constrict good reason events.

- ❏ **Calculating pay.** Where any payments are based on pay, a determination is needed on what amounts should be included. Some companies consider only base salary, while many others use salary plus annual incentive; very few include LTIs, especially because that is viewed as a poor pay practice that can produce excessive payouts. Also, the term "annual incentive" can be variously defined, so the method of its calculation should be specified.

- ❏ **Potential cost of retirement benefits or enhancements.** Shareholder groups may object to provisions that provide "deemed service credit" to increase an executive's retirement package (often coordinated with SERP benefits). Where that approach may be needed to recruit a mid-career executive to make up for benefits foregone at a former employer, the cost should be calculated and understood, with the rationale clearly documented and discussed in an effort to counter potential opposition, especially by proxy advisory firms.

- ❏ **Severance pay.** Any severance payments should be conditioned on the executive's agreement to reasonable restrictive covenants. Depending on what is permitted (and enforceable) under the laws of the relevant jurisdiction(s), covenants relating to non-competition, non-solicitation (of customers/clients and employees), nondisclosure of confidential information, and non-disparagement of the employer should be considered.

Considerations in Change-in-Control Design

In view of corporate governance considerations, special rules affecting nonqualified deferred compensation and broad executive pay disclosure requirements, it has become critical for companies to examine their CIC programs. As part of their compensation disclosures, companies are required to identify and quantify all potential compensation payments for named executive officers (NEOs) in connection with any termination of employment, including a change in control.

One result has been increased attention to and scrutiny of CIC provisions. Compensation committees must understand the rationale around CIC plans to be able to defend and justify the plans to shareholder activists as well as for strategic business reasons.

Purpose

Before evaluating CIC provisions, it is necessary to understand their objectives. The main premise behind such arrangements is

❏ **Overall cost analysis.** The potential costs for all payments directly or indirectly affected by an executive's contract should be determined on a worst-case (most costly) basis. These costs should be reviewed periodically to make sure the compensation committee understands how changes in base salary, for instance, may affect these payments (e.g., where a target bonus is a multiple of base salary).

❏ **Vesting on a change in control.** Accelerated vesting may be appropriate when there is a non-cause dismissal of the executive following a change in control or the executive would have no continuing equity interest in a merged entity. In other cases, it may be appropriate to continue the vesting or provide for discretion in the board to accelerate vesting as appropriate under the circumstances, although there is mounting criticism of the latter approach.

❏ **Trigger event.** Any CIC severance benefits should require a "double trigger" for payment rather than simply the CIC event ("single trigger"). Thus, there would need to be a change in control and an involuntary termination of the executive within the change period (commonly one to two years after the change).

❏ **Section 409A.** The potential application of IRC section 409A (regarding nonqualified deferred compensation arrangements) should be considered when determining payment provisions. Because there are various exceptions and alternative approaches for compliance, section 409A can affect design and not merely legal language.

❏ **Responsibility for drafting.** The employer should have the contract drafted by its advisers, not by someone representing the executive's interests. The drafting process should be within control of the board. Also, a general counsel should not be put in the position of negotiating contract terms with an executive to whom he/she may report.

to protect shareholder interests by mitigating potential distractions to key executives regarding their future employment with the company in the event of a change in control.

However, critics of CIC arrangements question whether such payments are necessary because many executives already have accumulated significant wealth from the company, especially individuals with long tenure. The counter-argument is that severance is needed to protect the executive from losing his/her job due to an event that is outside the executive's influence. A severance program would be designed to bridge the executive financially for a reasonable period while he/she seeks another job. At times when the market for talent is particularly competitive, companies also use CIC arrangements to recruit executive candidates. A candidate who is considering multiple job offers will consider the potential payments in evaluating and comparing the total packages.

Design

In reviewing a company's CIC plans, there are several design features to consider:

- **Eligibility.** While often available to a broader group than are employment contracts, most companies limit CIC programs or policies to the upper tiers of executive ranks (particularly focusing on the CEO and his/her direct reports). Some companies include another level of senior management or even a third tier.

- **Definition of change in control.** The following are the most common triggers used for defining a change in control:
  - Acquisition of voting stock (generally ranging from 20 to 50 percent)
  - Merger, consolidation or reorganization
  - Change of board composition
  - Sale of substantially all of the company's assets
  - Liquidation or dissolution of the company.

Most companies use some or all of these triggers in their definitions of change in control, the terms of which may appear in agreements, policies and plans. The tax regulations under IRC section 409A also contain guidance on the thresholds for certain events that may need to be considered.

- **Triggers.** Payouts upon a change in control generally are triggered under three basic scenarios:
  - **Single Trigger.** Only a change in control need occur.
  - **Double Trigger.** Both a change in control and an involuntary termination (other than for cause) or a constructive termination (i.e., a resignation for good reason) must occur within a certain period (generally one to two years after the change in control). Some programs also are triggered when a change in control is after a dismissal if the event was the result of negotiations underway during a stated period (e.g., six months) prior to the executive's termination.
  - **Modified Single Trigger.** A double trigger is in effect, except for a short (generally one month immediately after the first anniversary of the date of the change in control) period during which a voluntary termination results in a payout.

Until recently there often was a distinction between the trigger for cash severance under CIC arrangements and the trigger for acceleration of vesting under equity plans. While the long-time majority practice has been a double-trigger approach for cash severance, single triggers prevailed for equity incentives to provide accelerated vesting. However, expanded disclosure rules and criticism from proxy advisers (among others) caused companies to reconsider such equity single triggers. In just a few years we witnessed a rapid decline in single triggers for new equity awards as compensation committees acted to limit practices that could not be easily justified (after all, critics claimed that an executive should not need accelerated vesting and payout if he/she is still employed). (For more on accelerated vesting of equity, see "Equity Vesting Acceleration upon a Change in Control" later in this chapter.) Modified single triggers have come under attack because they permit executives to resign after a certain period following a CIC event and receive payment even if he/she had not been actually or constructively terminated. Best practices and good governance now call for double triggers for new equity awards as well as for cash severance payouts.

- **Cash severance.** Most arrangements provide for cash severance expressed as a multiple of pay that is paid in a lump sum. Now that separation amounts payable in installments are potentially subject to the deferred compensation rules of IRC section 409A, installment payments have become much less common. There may be two or three tiers of multiples that correspond to levels within the organization. Among larger companies, three times pay has been the prevalent multiple for the CEO, while smaller companies usually provide two to three times pay. Organizations commonly provide one full multiple less in cash severance to the next level or tier below the CEO.

Cash severance usually is determined as the relevant multiple of either base salary or base salary plus annual incentive. There are also variations on how annual bonus is defined, including:

- **Target.** Target incentive for the year of change in control.
- **Average.** Average incentive paid during a prior number of years.

- **Highest.** Highest incentive paid during a prior number of years.

Target is the most frequently used annual bonus definition, followed by some form of average incentive.

- **Benefits continuation.** Most companies also provide continuation of health and welfare benefits upon termination in the event of a change in control. The period of continuation usually is coordinated with the period represented by the cash severance multiple. In designing these arrangements, care must be taken to avoid unanticipated income tax consequences to the executive, including consideration of IRC section 409A.

- **Equity acceleration.** For equity plans, companies typically provide CIC protection in the form of accelerated vesting of equity awards. As previously noted, the once-typical approach of a single trigger for equity acceleration has been questioned, and a double trigger has surpassed it for new awards and agreements. A double trigger prevents an executive from cashing out his/her equity before normal vesting if the individual remains employed.

- **Excise tax treatment.** IRC section 4999 imposes an excise tax on a "disqualified individual" if parachute payments made in connection with a CIC exceed the safe-harbor limit, which is three times the individual's "base amount" (the average of the individual's total taxable compensation paid by the corporation for the five years preceding the year of the change in control). However, the excise tax amount is equal to 20 percent of all parachute payments in excess of one times the base amount. IRC section 280G provides that such "excess parachute payments" are nondeductible to the employer. Companies address this excise-tax issue in various ways:

  - **Gross-up.** The company pays the executive's excise and related income taxes to keep the executive "whole" so that the individual receives the same after-tax amount as he/she would without the imposition of the excise tax.

  - **Modified gross-up.** The company provides a gross-up only if the payments exceed the safe harbor by a certain percentage or amount (e.g., 10 percent or $100,000). If not, payments are cut back to the safe-harbor limit to avoid any excise tax.

- **Cut-back.** The company cuts back all payments to the safe-harbor limit to avoid the excise tax.
- **Valley provision.** The company cuts back parachute payments to the safe-harbor limit only if doing so would result in a higher after-tax amount for the executive.
- **Do nothing.** The company requires executives to pay any excise tax.

While the provision of a gross-up previously was the most common practice, its use has fallen sharply due to harsh criticism by shareholder groups, proxy advisory firms and the media. Once potential gross-up payments were included in disclosures under SEC proxy rules, compensation committees focused on the magnitude of the total potential cost of gross-ups. As a result, cutback and valley provisions have increased in use as most public companies have eliminated parachute tax gross-ups for new awards or agreements.

Compensation committees should regularly review CIC programs and confirm the plan design is serving its intended purpose(s). They also need to understand the potential payments and costs that could be triggered in the event of a change in control. A sharp increase in the company's stock price or a large equity grant can result in millions of dollars in payments.

Handling Unvested Equity Awards at Termination

An executive's employment termination raises the issue of whether unvested equity awards should be forfeited or their vesting should be accelerated or continued. While too often an afterthought in designing equity programs and related agreements, the approach taken can greatly affect the amounts ultimately received by a terminating executive.

When negotiating employment agreements and drafting equity plan documents and individual award agreements, companies should consider how they wish to address various possible termination events. With heightened governance scrutiny by advisory firms and public outrage over perceived excesses in executive compensation, a company's treatment of unvested equity is especially important.

Background and Relevant Termination Events

Like most compensation decisions, the particular facts and circumstances are paramount in the treatment of unvested equity. Where an employment agreement is involved, the executive's input may be part of the negotiation process; in recent years the views of shareholders and their advisers have played an increased role. The treatment of unvested equity generally is addressed in a company's equity plan document and/or individual award agreements. In some cases a company may include language that gives authority to the board of directors or compensation committee to apply discretion to accelerate vesting.

Potential accounting and tax considerations also need to be examined so that the company can structure the arrangements in a favorable manner and avoid inadvertently triggering adverse accounting or tax consequences.

The basic employment termination events are:

- Death
- Disability
- Retirement
- Termination by the company (dismissal) without cause
- Dismissal for cause
- Termination by the executive (resignation) without good cause
- Resignation for good cause
- Termination in connection with a change in control.

Other than death, each company will have its own definition for each of the termination scenarios, but most companies' definitions address common themes. In the following discussion of various termination events, those that often are treated similarly are grouped.

Death, Disability and Retirement

When an executive dies, becomes disabled or retires during the course of employment, the relevant award agreements and equity plans need to be examined to see if there is a provision that allows for either the continued or immediate vesting of all or a portion of unvested awards. Some companies take an executive- or beneficiary-friendly approach on the view that none of these events reflects any wrong-doing, poor performance or disloyalty on the part of the executive. In designing equity incentive plans and award agreements, companies should review the potential tax and accounting consequences of acceleration of vesting on death or retirement.

When unvested stock options are accelerated in any of these scenarios, there typically is a reduction in the exercise period; the new period commonly is the shorter of the remaining option term or one or more years from the date of acceleration; on occasion companies allow option exercises for up to three years after the termination event.

Other companies and their advisers take the position that no such acceleration of vesting is warranted in these circumstances. The view is basically that, in an atmosphere increasingly focused on performance, these awards have not been earned at the time of death, disability or retirement and that any payment would be a windfall. Also, the existence of life or disability insurance may be viewed as a replacement for any awards that may be forfeited upon these employment terminations. In particular, with respect to accelerated vesting on a defined "normal retirement date," companies need to understand the accounting and income tax consequences of the plan or award design so as not to be surprised by any truncated financial expense for the company or earlier (pre-separation from service) income tax obligations for the executive.

Termination by the Company for Cause or by the Executive Without Good Reason

When an executive is dismissed for cause (generally including fraud and gross negligence in the definition) or resigns without good reason (typically including a material reduction in duties), it is rare for a company to allow continued or accelerated vesting on any portion of unvested equity awards. In these circumstances there would be no reason to allow executives to receive compensation other than what was legally required (generally what was accrued up until the date of termination). The definitions of "cause" and "good reason" need to be carefully crafted to the company's particular situation and often are highly negotiated in employment contracts.

Termination by the Company Without Cause or by the Executive for Good Reason

Considerable debate can be had on the appropriate handling of unvested equity awards when an executive is dismissed without cause or he/she resigns for good reason. An analysis of data indicates that unvested equity awards most commonly are forfeited when an executive is terminated without cause or resigns for good reason. While a dismissal (or good-reason resignation) may not be due to any fault of the executive (especially if during an economic downturn), most employers do not view this as sufficient reason for accelerating vesting (at least absent a change in control) and prefer to focus on rewarding and retaining current employees. Some companies, however, focus on perceived fairness concerns and see value in recruitment and retention efforts by providing vesting protection to actually or constructively dismissed employees.

Termination in Connection With a Change in Control

Vesting acceleration considerations can be especially important in connection with a change in control. As previously mentioned under "Considerations in Change-in-Control Design," single-trigger acceleration is now disfavored. Where CIC protection is determined to be useful, proxy advisory firms and shareholder groups now favor double triggers so that executives who simply quit after a CIC event are not benefited.

Accounting Considerations

All share-based compensation is accounted for under Accounting Standards Codification (ASC) Topic 718. ASC 718 requires that all share-based awards granted to employees be accounted for at "fair value." Basically, when an unvested equity award accelerates upon a termination event, the service condition of the original award is not expected to be satisfied because the employee is not expected to render the requisite service. Thus, the compensation cost for the original, unvested award should be zero at the date of the modification as none of the awards are expected to vest. The incremental fair value is equal to the full fair value of the modified award, which represents the total cumulative compensation cost that the company should recognize for the award. On the modification date, the company would reverse the compensation cost previously recognized for the unvested award, if any, and recognize compensation cost equal to the full fair value of the modified award, which is fully vested.

Income Tax Considerations

Three (extremely simplified here) income tax provisions are of particular importance regarding unvested equity upon termination:

- First, unless certain exceptions apply, under IRC section 409A, a publicly held company may not make any payments of deferred compensation to certain key employees within a six-month period after a separation from service. Both the relevant plan documents and actual administration of the program need to satisfy section 409A to avoid harsh tax consequences for the recipient of any such accelerated awards that are determined to constitute deferred compensation.

- Second, companies need to consider IRC section 280G, as the acceleration of unvested equity on a change in control is valued in determining whether any of certain officers and other "disqualified individuals" has received an "excess parachute payment" that is subject to excise tax (under IRC section 4999) payable by the individual as well as the loss of the corporation's income tax deduction for such payment. If section 280G is not considered until after a change in control, it may be difficult to avoid parachute tax consequences. (The potential application and impact of sections 280G and 4999 are explained in more detail later in this chapter.)

- Third, IRC section 162(m), currently applicable only to the CEO and the next three highest paid executives (other than the CFO), contains requirements for a public company to obtain an income tax deduction for performance-based compensation in excess of $1 million for the year. Compensation will not qualify as tax-deductible performance-based compensation if payment may be made on an involuntary termination of employment or retirement without regard to whether the applicable performance goals are satisfied.

Looking at the Relevant Facts and Circumstances

While it can be helpful to see how other companies handle unvested equity upon various employee termination events, a company's focus should be on what approach best advances its particular objectives. Various factors — including accounting and income tax considerations and views of proxy advisory firms — need to be weighed. Recruitment, motivation, retention and cost may be evaluated differently at each organization; with an understanding of the key issues and approaches, an informed decision can be made.

Equity Vesting Acceleration Upon a Change in Control

Equity-based compensation — whether in the form of stock options/ stock appreciation rights (SARs), RS/RSUs or performance shares/ performance units — is an integral part of executive LTI programs. A common provision in the governing documents addresses how an executive's unvested interests are treated if there is a change in control of the company. Because a significant portion of an executive's wealth often is tied to the value of equity-based compensation, the conditions for accelerated vesting are particularly important.

As discussed in the section of this chapter titled "Considerations in Change-in-Control Design," most equity plans include either a single or double trigger for acceleration of vesting upon a change in control, with a modified single trigger used at some companies. Thus, upon the relevant trigger, all unvested stock options become immediately exercisable, all outstanding RS or RSUs are immediately vested and are no longer subject to forfeiture, and all performance-based shares would be vested and paid in accordance with the governing document.

A Trend Toward Double Triggers

As previously discussed in this chapter, single triggers for equity acceleration on a change in control now are viewed quite negatively by shareholders, investors and proxy advisers, leading to the rise in double triggers. While certainly not exhaustive, Table 11-1

TABLE 11-1

Single and Double Triggers: Pros and Cons

Single-Trigger Approach	
Advantages	**Disadvantages**
■ Allows certain executives to share in the value they have created for shareholders. ■ Provides for a built-in "retention award" that can eliminate the need for a cash retention arrangement through the date of closing. ■ Does not affect the current stock prices, as outstanding equity awards are treated as a sunk cost by the buyer. ■ Beneficial when acquiring company is going to terminate the existing equity plan or does not convert the unvested equity of the acquired company into its own stock.	■ Can be viewed as a windfall for executives who would not be terminated by buyer. ■ No retention value after the closing of the transaction. ■ Incentive for executives to only focus on near-term stock price of the company. ■ Acceleration generally constitutes a parachute payment under IRC section 280G.

Double-Trigger Approach	
Advantages	**Disadvantages**
■ Viewed by corporate governance and shareholder advisory groups as the preferred approach — a best practice. ■ Acts as a key retention tool for senior executives who are instrumental to the integration process. ■ Alleviates the need for additional retention incentives in the form of cash or additional equity. ■ Aligns executive and shareholder interests due to the long-term value of the acquiring company. ■ Protection for the executive in the event of termination of employment due to a change in control. ■ Not necessarily considered a parachute payment under IRC section 280G.	■ Executives, unlike shareholders, may not immediately share in any increase in value of company stock (or acquirer's stock). ■ Potential loss of income to the executive if unvested awards are not converted into the acquirer's stock.

highlights some notable advantages and disadvantages of single- and double-trigger acceleration.

Implementing the Elimination of a Single Trigger for Equity Acceleration

If a company decides to eliminate existing single triggers for the acceleration of vesting on equity-based compensation, it must address the practicalities of how best to implement the change, taking into account anticipated employee reaction, expectations for some quid pro quo, and any contractual rights under current awards and agreements. Some companies may determine to make only prospective changes — whereby any future programs and agreements will have double triggers — but leave existing arrangements unchanged until they expire. Others may choose to negotiate with executives to give up the single triggers, perhaps in exchange for some other benefit.

Impact of IRC Section 280G

An important factor to consider in the treatment of equity in CIC scenarios is the potential exposure to the golden parachute ramifications of IRC section 280G. Section 280G denies an income tax deduction to a corporation for "excess parachute payments" made in connection with a change in control. A related provision, IRC section 4999, imposes a 20 percent excise tax on any person who receives compensation that, under section 280G, is deemed to constitute an excess parachute payment.

As part of the complex calculation to determine if any person has received excess parachute payments, the accelerated value of unvested equity awards is taken into account. This accelerated value is determined under different methodologies depending on the type of equity vehicle but, in many cases, represents a significant portion of the total value an executive is deemed to receive upon a change in control. When a single-trigger acceleration approach is used, all unvested awards are immediately vested and must be taken into account for purposes of the section 280G calculation.

If the value of equity acceleration (when taken into account with all other payments contingent upon a change in control) triggers an excess parachute payment, then the company will lose valuable income tax deductions. To compound matters, if an executive is grossed up for any excise tax that may be imposed, this gross-up protection could potentially cost the company almost three times the initial excise tax, as these gross-up payments are considered additional excess parachute payments that become subject to the excise tax as well. These excise tax gross-up provisions are extremely costly to shareholders when taking into account the amount of cash that is required to cover the gross-up payment and the additional income taxes on compensation deemed to be nondeductible.

When the double-trigger acceleration approach is used, there is no immediate value under section 280G because unvested awards are not necessarily accelerated upon a change in control. However, if in connection with a change in control an executive is terminated by the acquiring company without cause or the executive resigns for good reason, then all unvested equity is immediately vested and such acceleration generally is calculated in the same manner as the single trigger. Thus, a double-trigger approach may result in a parachute payment while the single-trigger approach clearly will constitute a parachute payment.

While the discussion around the merits of the single- versus double-trigger approach continues, one thing is certain: double-trigger acceleration provisions are being considered and implemented by more companies than ever before.

Parachute Excise Tax Gross-Up Considerations

As mentioned, excessive amounts payable on a change in control may be subject to a loss of tax deduction to the company and an excise tax on the employee under the golden parachute provisions of IRC sections 280G and 4999, respectively. Over the years many corporations determined that a gross-up for the effect of the parachute excise tax was the preferred approach for working around the excise tax.

Excise tax gross-ups have attracted significant negative attention and been criticized as poor or problematic pay practices. With the advent of say on pay and say on parachutes, combined with the increased influence of shareholder advisory groups, excise tax gross-ups have become uncommon for new awards and agreements. Nevertheless, it can be helpful to examine why many companies used gross-ups (as some still do) for senior executives.

Inequity of Parachute Excise Tax and Argument for Tax Gross-Ups

In determining the amount (if any) of parachute payments subject to the 20 percent excise tax on excess parachute payments, the relevant income tax regulations start with a disqualified individual's base amount. The base amount is the average — for the five years immediately before the year of the change in control — of an employee's box 1 income from Form W-2. If the aggregate present value of all payments made to an executive that were contingent upon the change in control at least equals three times the base amount, then all payments made in excess of one times the base amount are subject to the 20 percent excise tax.

The particular facts regarding any employee can produce quite different income and parachute tax consequences. Thus Table 11-2, captioned "Example: Parachute Excise Tax Calculations and Comparison," illustrates how the excise tax can be unfair. While this example may be extreme, it highlights the potential inequity of the excise tax:

- Executive A took all of the cash he could from the company and did not align his interests with those of shareholders. As a reward for cashing out every year, A pays $0 in excise tax.

- On the other hand, Executive B did everything that the company and shareholders would prefer — she deferred cash and did not exercise stock options, thereby cementing her long-term interests with those of the company. By doing the right thing from a corporate governance perspective, as well as taking less cash annually, B gets hit with an excise tax bill of $1,555,000. (Of course, many executives postpone exercising stock options simply in hopes of maximizing their ultimate returns.)

This example illustrates why excise tax gross-ups originally became prevalent in senior executive employment agreements. The gross-ups leveled the playing field for similarly situated executives who

TABLE 11-2

Example: Parachute Excise Tax Calculations and Comparison

Executives A and B each earn $1 million in base salary and receive a $2 million bonus for each of the five preceding years. In addition, both A and B could exercise stock options worth $500,000 per year.

Executive A exercises all of his stock options every year during the five-year period, while Executive B does not exercise any of her stock option awards. Also, A does not defer any of his base salary or bonus while B defers 25 percent of both base salary and bonus on an annual basis.

In the year of a change in control, both A and B receive a $10 million golden parachute package. The table below illustrates the components of the parachute excise tax calculation for each executive and compares the tax due for each executive.

	Box 1 W-2 average	2.99* x base amount	Parachute payments ($10 million) greater than 2.99* x base amount?	Subject to 20% excise tax	Amount subject to 20% excise tax	20% excise tax
A	$3,500,000	$10,465,000	No	No	$0	$0
B	$2,250,000	$6,727,500	Yes	Yes	$7,775,000	$1,555,000

*2.99 used as short-hand approximation of calculating just below three times the base amount.

may have acted differently with respect to stock option exercises and deferrals of compensation.

Mounting Criticism and Pushback Against Excise Tax Gross-Ups

With the advent of expanded disclosures (see Chapter 14), shareholders, their advisers and various business media became increasingly critical of excise tax gross-ups. Gross-ups have been targeted as a poor or problematic pay practice in say-on-pay voting. Where a say-on-pay vote is unavailable (e.g., at publicly traded companies with biennial or triennial say-on-pay votes), shareholders still may express their displeasure by casting "withhold" or "against" votes regarding compensation committee members who approve arrangements with these gross-ups. In addition, the presence of this type of perquisite will negatively influence a company's scoring on various governance ratings.

In their annual proxy statements, companies are required to estimate and disclose termination payments under different scenarios as of the last day of the reporting year. While the average investor may not understand how the calculations are derived, he/she does know that these payments and related gross-ups are very expensive. This negative attention — and particularly the threat of a negative say-on-pay vote and/or withhold or against vote recommendations on compensation committee members — caused companies to review their attitudes toward golden parachute payments and any associated excise tax gross-ups. Boards generally have eliminated excise tax gross-ups in any new awards or arrangements, often by restricting golden parachute payments so that they are cut back to ensure the IRC section 4999 excise tax is not triggered.

Compensation Committee Considerations

Say on pay raised the stakes for compensation committees regarding the use of excise tax gross-ups. Compensation committees no longer deal only with the public scrutiny and proxy adviser oversight. As previously noted, publicly held companies generally now are required (under the Dodd-Frank legistlation) to provide shareholders with an advisory, nonbinding vote on the pay (as described in its annual proxy statement) of its NEOs. In addition, a separate advisory, nonbinding vote of shareholders is required on golden parachute compensation for a company's NEOs in connection with an acquisition, merger, consolidation or certain other business transactions.

Compensation committee members need to understand that if any new or materially amended executive agreement or award contains a parachute excise tax gross-up, they should expect to have to defend their position to shareholders to rebut a negative say-on-pay recommendation from proxy advisory firms.

Without excise tax gross-ups, some executives have turned to other approaches to avoid or limit the potential application of any parachute excise tax. Some alternatives may not align with shareholder interests, such as a reduction of compensation defer-rals, earlier stock option exercises (followed immediately by sales of shares so acquired), and holding only the minimum amount of company stock to satisfy any stock ownership guidelines. In addition, compensation committees will continue to explore with their advisers various ways of mitigating any potential excise tax through compensation design practices, including consulting and non-compete agreements that can shift compensation from contingent upon a change in control to reasonable compensation for future services.

Post-Employment Consulting Arrangements: Are They Appropriate?

Companies often enter into post-employment consulting agreements with outgoing or retiring executives. However, as executive pay is subjected to ever-increasing scrutiny, questions arise: Are these arrangements justifiable? If so, what terms are appropriate?

Sometimes there is a plausible rationale for these arrangements, such as transition to a new management team or passing knowledge on from an outgoing executive. All too often, however, these consultancies simply are a going-away present provided gratuitously by the board without the expectation of any meaningful services from the executive. In the extreme, they can be clearly inappropriate and represent excessive compensation with no pretense of a justifiable rationale. Yet they persist, even appearing in employment agreements negotiated well in advance of actual termination.

In the nonprofit world, particularly in academia, there have been cases involving an emeritus designation of retired executives and professors. These arrangements may include the equivalent full-time salary with far less than full-time responsibilities. Questions can arise regarding whether meaningful services are being provided to the employer. (See "Common Abuses and Issues in Post-Employment Consulting Arrangements.")

Design of Consulting Arrangements

Because a consulting arrangement should be limited to those circumstances in which there is a particular need to retain the executive's services, the design and terms of any such agreement should be customized to the particular situation. (See "Justifications for Consulting Arrangements.") Following is a discussion of key design considerations.

Common Abuses and Issues

Among the more frequent abuses:

> Compensation rates that are too high (as a percentage of full-time pay)
> Consultancy periods that are too long
> Coverage of spouses under the agreement
> Inclusion of executive benefits and perquisites that would not otherwise be paid to outside consultants
> Arrangements negotiated too far in advance of the consulting period (thereby presuming the need for the executive's services)
> Promises made as an entitlement regardless of the executive's success while active.

These lead to a series of questions:

> Does the payment really represent additional severance?
> Is the arrangement a retirement benefit in disguise?
> Should the amounts be viewed as deferred compensation?
> Whatever the characterization, is it acceptable as such?
> Why doesn't the employer just call it a retirement plan?
> Who actually cares? The board or the compensation committee? Shareholders? The public? The tax authorities?
> Who has the responsibility for determining reasonableness?

Retainer

A retainer to be available for special projects can be sufficient, but the facts and circumstances should be carefully considered. Even if the executive is expected to be called upon for less than the prescribed time, this does not necessarily affect the appropriateness of the arrangement, but rather is part of the overall situation to be evaluated. In fact, this approach has significant prevalence in post-retirement contracts.

Determination of Value

The value of any post-retirement consulting arrangement to the employer reasonably could be based on a number of alternative theories, including:

- A direct assessment of the value to the employer of assigned consulting projects, regardless of time spent and regardless of results.

> ### Justifications for Consulting Arrangements
>
> Clearly there are situations in which a post-employment consultancy is supportable, including:
>
> > Transitions in which knowledge needs to be passed to the new management team
>
> > Proprietary knowledge that must be protected from leakage to competitors
>
> > Special projects that otherwise would require an outside consultant
>
> > Experienced executive is needed to represent the company in relationships with customers, investors, regulators or other special groups
>
> > Outgoing executive might be key to maintaining or further developing business through long-standing relationships
>
> > Changes in control, especially in which the executive's expertise is required on a temporary basis during the post-merger period.

- Project results, rather than hours spent (i.e., the "finder's fee" theory). If the value to the employer is sales, this can be a function of relationships and results, not necessarily time. For example, if there was a significant sale negotiated during an afternoon of golf, it was not likely a direct function of time.

- The value of the executive's availability in potential situations.

Structuring Payments

The structure of the consulting payments could be built around:

- A proration of pre-retirement salary.

- A dollar retainer amount per year during which the individual's services are available (e.g., a "bench player" that can be called into play if and when needed, but who is barred from "playing" for anyone else during the prescribed time period).

- A consulting arrangement based on an agreed-upon hourly rate, against which the former executive bills time on assigned projects.

Total Compensation Package Approach

What appears to be most important to the IRS — especially for tax-exempt organizations — is the aggregate of the compensation package for post-employment services. Basically, the absence of certain payments (or the provision of lower amounts) can offset "excesses" in other components. To the extent that one or more components of the total package may be less than amounts that otherwise would be acceptable, there may be "credits" available to balance any otherwise excessive portions.

In this process, consideration might be given to pay components such as retirement benefits, post-retirement medical benefits and severance benefits. In terms of what an employer receives, there may be a need to value a covenant not to compete when that covenant has significant value to the employer. This approach can be especially helpful in developing the reasonableness of an executive's compensation under the intermediate-sanctions provisions of the Taxpayer Bill of Rights II (the legislation that restricts executive pay to reasonable levels at tax-exempt organizations).

Retirement Benefit

One common approach is for the employer to provide the CEO with a target retirement benefit of an annual life annuity equal to 60 percent of final average pay (base plus bonus). This formula assumes a reasonable length of service with the employer and inclusion of benefits under the company's qualified retirement plan. If an executive's base plus bonus averaged $1 million for the final three years, such a formula could have a lump-sum present value at age 65 of approximately $3 million. The absence of this type of program can help justify additional benefits on the basis that a major portion of a "normal" executive compensation program was lacking. Under the total package approach described above, the value of a consultancy agreement might constitute a substitute for the value of a typical retirement program for similar executives.

The Pseudo-Retirement Plan

While in some cases an employer may install a SERP arrangement retroactively just before retirement, care is needed to assure that there is sufficient rationale for this retroactivity. Because this approach involves crediting service in excess of actual work for the employer, a public company would need to consider the likely opposition of proxy advisory groups to that aspect of the program. Another caution exists when the outgoing executive already has a sufficient retirement program in place; a consulting agreement could be redundant.

The Retainer Approach

In another example, a compensation committee and an executive enter into a post-employment consulting agreement on a retainer basis, with the purpose of reserving 25 percent of the executive's time during a five-year period. The compensation committee concludes that there is sufficient value to the organization to have that resource contracted under the terms of the agreement and available to provide a range of duties as needed.

As a general rule, it should not be unreasonable for the executive and the compensation committee to enter into such an agreement and for the executive to be paid reasonable amounts, assuming that the executive does in fact reserve or otherwise make available 25 percent of his/her time. However, in this case, the five-year duration of the payments generally would be excessive for a management transition or for a non-competition restriction.

Should We Plan Ahead for Executive Consulting?

One especially problematic use of post-retirement consulting arrangements is when they are agreed to far in advance of any separation discussions. Too often such use is really just additional post-employment pay for the executive. A compensation committee would have a better reason to consider such a post-employment consulting arrangement (assuming it otherwise makes sense) at the time the executive transition is being negotiated. At least then there would be a relationship to performance rather than making commitments without a determination of the need for such services.

PART II

Governance, Disclosure and Compensation Committee Initiatives

CHAPTER 12

Compensation Committee Governance

By Brian Tobin and Sonja Mertens

Sound governance practices are critical for compensation committees as they work to make well-grounded and defensible executive pay decisions. These practices provide a framework within which appropriate pay programs can be designed and tailored to the needs of the company. The nuances of these programs, as well as the rationale behind potentially contentious elements, then can be communicated to shareholders and other stakeholders through required disclosure as well as voluntary outreach.

However, having governance practices in place does not always mean they are followed in practice. As such, the assessment of compliance with policies is another crucial component of the compensation governance equation that should be regularly evaluated.

A responsible and diligent compensation committee works to ensure strong governance is present in its decision-making processes, both in policy and practice. As executive pay decisions are ultimately the responsibility of the compensation committee, these controls are of vital importance in protecting the company as well as individual committee members from legal and/or reputational risk related to executive pay programs.

This chapter:

- Reviews the role and responsibilities of the compensation committee, including establishing a compensation committee charter and an annual calendar of quarterly meetings.

- Offers practical advice on conducting board and committee self-assessments.
- Outlines the roles of key players in compensation governance.
- Summarizes required factors for assessing the independence of compensation advisers and provides guidance on the evaluation of their performance.
- Presents a "governance scorecard" to aid compensation committees in understanding their responsibilities as well as the details of the plans and payouts they approve and monitor.
- Suggests actions for consideration by compensation committees seeking to maintain or improve voting results related to the say-on-pay provisions of the Dodd-Frank Act.

Responsibilities of the Compensation Committee

The compensation committee generally has responsibility for:

- **Compensation philosophy.** Establishing and periodically reviewing a compensation philosophy that is aligned with the company's strategic objectives.
- **Executive compensation and benefits programs.** Establishing and providing oversight of base salary structures, all incentive plans, retirement plans, employment agreements, severance arrangements and other pay programs and policies (e.g., clawbacks, share ownership requirements, etc.).
- **Performance assessment.** Assessing the CEO's performance; monitoring and reviewing performance targets and results for top executives.
- **Oversight of executive compensation administration.** Approving compensation adjustments, incentive payouts and equity grants for the CEO and other top executives.
- **Risk assessment.** Reviewing potential risks associated with compensation programs and policies as well as internal controls for their mitigation.
- **Compensation-related disclosure.** Reviewing and recommending the CD&A for inclusion in annual proxy statements.
- **Succession planning.** Managing the succession planning process and regularly evaluating succession plans for the CEO and his/her direct reports.

- **Compensation for board of directors.** Recommending compensation for the board of directors.
- **Board communications.** Maintaining regular communication with the entire board on its activities and recommendations.
- **Committee charter and calendar.** Maintaining and regularly reviewing a committee charter and annual calendar of activities.*
- **Self-assessment.** Assessment of committee performance.*

* Responsibilities are described in greater detail later in this chapter.

Generally, the compensation committee should be composed of three to five directors. Given the ever-increasing complexity of the executive compensation environment, all members of the committee should have significant HR or compensation experience.

To comply with New York Stock Exchange (NYSE) and NASDAQ standards, each committee member must be considered independent under enhanced requirements. Notably, the board of directors must consider all factors relevant in determining whether members have any relationship to the company that would preclude independence from management, including the source of compensation and the existence of any affiliate relationships.

Compensation Committee Charter

A clear, succinct compensation committee charter is vital for establishing a mutual understanding of the purpose, governing principles and responsibilities of the compensation committee among the board, the committee and the CEO.

The compensation committee generally is responsible for developing the charter and submitting it to the board for approval. The charter should be a living document and reviewed annually to assess its continued relevance and compliance with relevant statutory and regulatory requirements.

Topics typically addressed include:

- **Purpose.** Why the compensation committee exists and what its ultimate objectives are.
- **Membership, composition and procedures.** Number of members, selection and removal process for members and the chair,

independence standards, frequency of meetings, quorum, and other governance procedures established by the board.

- **Duties and responsibilities.** The committee's specific accountabilities regarding executive compensation programs, potential material risks associated with compensation programs, disclosure, succession planning, etc.
- **Executive session.** Ability to convene without management present.
- **Advisers to the compensation committee.** Authority to select and retain external advisers including consultants and legal counsel and requirement to assess adviser independence.
- **Reports/communication to the board.** Frequency and content of communications with the board.

Care should be taken to ensure that the charter does not require the committee to take any action unless it is prepared to carry out such duty, as failure to do so may expose the organization or individual committee members to the risk of litigation. For this reason, some advocate that the duties and responsibilities laid out in a charter be written largely in general terms to mitigate the risk that a breach can be definitively proven.

Public companies must disclose whether a charter has been adopted by the compensation committee. Both the NYSE and NASDAQ require the adoption of a charter addressing certain items, as summarized in Table 12-1.

Annual Compensation Committee Calendar

As part of its annual planning process, the compensation committee should establish a calendar of activities to guide it in fulfilling its duties through the year. Most compensation committees should plan to meet at least four times per year, with the possibility of additional meetings where circumstances warrant. Typical items included in the planning process are included in the sample compensation committee calendar in Table 12-2.

Board and Committee Self-Assessments

Board assessments are mandatory at all companies listed on the NYSE. While there is no similar requirement for NASDAQ-listed companies,

TABLE 12-1

Compensation Committee Charter Requirements

NYSE Requirements	NASDAQ Requirements
Compensation committees must have a written charter that addresses:	Compensation committees must have a written charter and must review and reassess the adequacy of this charter on an annual basis.

■ The purpose and responsibilities of the committee, including:
  – Reviewing and approving corporate goals and objectives relevant to CEO compensation, evaluating the CEO's performance in light of goals and objectives, and determining and approving the CEO's compensation level based on this evaluation
  – Making recommendations to the board with respect to non-CEO executive officer compensation as well as incentive compensation and equity-based plans that are subject to board approval
  – Preparing the disclosure required by Item 407(e)(5) of Regulation S-K, specifically the compensation committee report related to the review and recommendation of the CD&A to the board for inclusion in relevant disclosures
■ An annual performance evaluation of the compensation committee
■ The rights and responsibilities of the committee related to retaining and evaluating the independence of compensation consultants, legal counsel or other advisers
	The charter must address:
	■ The scope of committee responsibilities and how those responsibilities are carried out, including:
	  – Structure
	  – Processes
	  – Membership requirements
	■ The committee's responsibility for determining, or recommending to the board for determination, the compensation of the CEO and all other executive officers
	■ That the CEO may not be present during voting or deliberations on his/her compensation
	■ Specific responsibilities and authorities related to retaining and evaluating the independence of compensation consultants, legal counsel or other advisers

The charter should also address:

■ Committee member qualifications, appointment and removal
■ Committee structure and operations, including authority to delegate to subcommittees
■ Committee reporting to the board

many NASDAQ companies have adopted a process for board evaluation. As a component of good governance, many other organizations, even private companies and nonprofit organizations, have adopted the practice of conducting an annual review of the performance

TABLE 12-2

Sample Compensation Committee Calendar

First Quarter Meeting	Second Quarter Meeting	Third Quarter Meeting	Fourth Quarter Meeting
Review (and approve) incentive payments for the fiscal year just ended	Review compensation committee charter	Review and approve board compensation for the coming year	Review competitiveness of executive compensation and alignment with compensation philosophy
Finalize input on CD&A and proxy statements	Perform committee self-assessment	Review results of shareholder votes from annual general meeting	Review (and approve) base pay changes (if any)
Develop the compensation committee calendar for the year	Assess performance of adviser(s)	Review total executive compensation	Review (and approve) incentive plan performance goals for the coming year
	Review executive succession plans	Structure for the coming year, including base salary ranges and incentive targets	

Ongoing / as warranted

Receive periodic updates on company performance related to incentive compensation

Evaluate CEO performance relative to established goals

Board communication

Review executive employment contracts / severance payments in the event of executive turnover

Consider regulatory changes and market trends in compensation and governance

of the board and its committees. Board assessments are examined in depth in Chapter 20 where the four main methodologies for evaluating the board are discussed — namely surveys, interviews, research and observation.

The value in these assessments can be maximized if companies move toward a method of self-assessment that fosters dialogue and discovery, including a combination of methods such as coupling interviews and surveys. Many boards and committees are now adding another component to the assessments — individual director performance. While various methodologies may be adopted for such assessments, often the most informative is a director peer review, in which directors provide feedback on the performance of others and receive feedback from their peers. As noted in Chapter 20, legal counsel should advise the committee on how it might safeguard the director peer review process to avoid the risk of potential litigation based on negative feedback.

To build a more robust view of board and committee performance, management's perspective can also be incorporated into the review process. While not all boards welcome management feedback on their performance, those that do have found it often yields especially useful guidance. Not only can this exercise prevent the board and its committees from becoming insular, but it can also surface important issues and enhance the working relationship between the board and management.

In practice, not all of these feedback methods need to be implemented at once or even conducted every year. However, finding ways of evaluating performance that bring multiple perspectives together is key to maximizing the effectiveness of assessment.

Key Players in Compensation Governance

The compensation committee has additional resources to assist it in discharging its accountabilities, including senior leadership, internal HR staff, and external, independent advisers. (See Figure 12-1.) Each has a critical role to play in ensuring strong corporate governance principles are developed and approved at the board level then cascaded down through the organization and ingrained in compensation-related decision-making at all levels.

Independence of Advisers

The compensation committees of public companies must have the authority to retain compensation consultants, legal counsel or other advisers (collectively referred to as compensation advisers), and they are directly responsible for the oversight of their work. However, before selecting any such adviser the committee must take into consideration at least six identified factors regarding their independence, including:

- The provision of other services to the issuer by the person who employs the adviser

FIGURE 12-1

Key Players in Compensation Governance

Compensation Committee

Senior Leadership	Internal HR Staff	Consultant
Accountabilities	**Accountabilities**	**Accountabilities**
› Implement the compensation philosophy for executives	› Coordinate compensation committee activities	› Understand the business
Provide direction for plan administration	› Monitor and assess performance for all employees	› Share best practices and market trends
› Establish individual performance and development plans for executives other than the CEO	› Take responsibility for executive communication, plan documentation and legal review, data/survey collection	› Counsel on the appropriateness of the compensation philosophy
› Provide executives' annual salary plan to compensation committee	› Act as critical link to strategic planning process (metric management, succession planning, etc.)	› Counsel on the relationship between the compensation philosophy and program design
› Recommend incentive targets and goals	› Understand regulatory environment	› Counsel on the detailed design and implementation of compensation programs — understanding and communicating the implications of various designs on the business
› Measure performance of executive group	› Provide feedback on compensation program effectiveness	
› Communicate results on incentive performance		› Provide current market data
› Understand regulatory environment		› Attend key meetings
› Provide feedback on compensation program effectiveness		

- The amount of fees received from the issuer by the person who employs the adviser as a percentage of the total revenue of the person who employs the adviser
- The policies and procedures of the person who employs the adviser that are designed to prevent conflicts of interest

- Any business or personal relationships of the adviser with a member of the compensation committee
- Any stock of the issuer owned by the adviser
- Any business or personal relationships between the executive officers of the issuer and the adviser or the person employing the adviser.

These six factors represent the minimum required for consideration under SEC rules, though additional factors may be adopted by individual exchanges. Neither the NYSE nor NASDAQ have adopted specific additional factors, though NYSE standards call for compensation committees to consider all factors relevant to the independence of a compensation adviser. Accordingly, compensation committees at NYSE-listed companies may need to assess independence through a broader lens.

While compensation committees are required to assess the independence of advisers, they are not prohibited from selecting and retaining compensation advisers that are not independent. A committee would need to consider if it would be willing to disclose and explain the retention of a non-independent compensation adviser.

In assessing the independence of compensation advisers, a variety of approaches may be used to obtain information. While some compensation committees use questionnaires only requesting specific information related to the six identified factors, others expand their areas of inquiry to include additional questions designed to fully explore any perceived independence issues.

Assessment of Advisers

While not required, a recommended best practice is an annual assessment by the compensation committee of any adviser(s) it has retained to assist in navigating the various issues involved in executive pay decisions and board governance.

The compensation committee should:

- Determine how well its advisers understood the company, its particular circumstances, and the role of various compensation elements in achieving the organization's goals and objectives.

- Assess the advisers' effectiveness in applying this understanding to support the committee in fulfilling its annual responsibilities.
- Evaluate the usefulness and timeliness of work completed by the adviser at the request of the committee.
- Consider any other services the adviser may have provided the company and whether they were approved by the committee.

After considering these elements, constructive feedback should be provided to the adviser(s) where warranted, including both areas of strength and opportunities for improvement.

The Governance Scorecard

Good governance calls for a compensation committee to take a regular, comprehensive look at the practices and programs that make up the organization's executive compensation system. While the explanation and rationale required as part of the CD&A have encouraged compensation committees to be more aware of pay programs, a full review may still be very enlightening for committee members.

One approach to such a review process is the "governance score-card" — a series of rated elements that focus on key issues in compensation committee governance and executive compensation. Although the specific rating criteria should differ between companies based on the particular circumstances, the main elements of a scorecard address fundamental questions that are generally relevant to all companies. (See Table 12-3.)

Objectives of Governance Scorecard Criteria

Under the SEC's proxy disclosure rules, CD&A disclosure of executive compensation programs should address the "how" and "why" as well as the "what." The governance scorecard approach helps committee members think through the context required for this disclosure, going beyond current plan design to also include the process and rationale for decisions.

Accordingly, the governance scorecard should be designed to provide the compensation committee with a structured view of key compensation plan governance and design elements from the

TABLE 12-3

TABLE 12-3: Sample Governance Scorecard

Category	Sample Criteria
Governance	■ Is the compensation committee well-structured and following practices that would be considered appropriate? ■ Does the committee operate effectively and independent of excessive management influence? ■ Are committee members sufficiently knowledgeable in HR/compensation matters? ■ Does the compensation committee have appropriate access to independent advice? ■ Is the compensation committee's charter appropriate and regularly reviewed? ■ Are the duties and requirements found in the charter actually followed in practice?
Compensation risk	■ Is a thorough analysis of the risk profile of compensation programs conducted regularly? ■ Are all relevant risk areas considered (e.g., financial risk, reputational risk, operational risk, etc.)? ■ What measures are in place to mitigate risks that have been identified? ■ Is there an appropriate balance between short- and long-term incentives? ■ Are there appropriate controls on the use of discretion and judgment in compensation awards?
Competitiveness	■ Are the compensation plans not only competitive with the external market, but also appropriate for the internal needs of the business? ■ Is the peer group representative of the company's competitive market for talent? ■ Is actual compensation provided to executives consistent with the compensation philosophy?
Plan design	■ Are compensation plans adequately thought through and appropriately focused on performance? ■ For a public company, are necessary compensation plans approved by shareholders? ■ Are there issues of dilution? Overhang? ■ Have the potential effects of relevant income tax regulations (e.g., IRC sections 162(m), 280G, 409A) been considered during the design process? ■ Are benefits and perquisites consistent with good practice and adequate for the needs of the business? Have they been re-evaluated recently?
Alignment	■ Are plan design and pay mix aligned with organizational culture and the financial and operational goals of the company? ■ Are compensation awards appropriate to support business strategy and for both expected and realized results? ■ What is the degree of anticipated difficulty in achieving goals? Are the targets sufficiently challenging? ■ Is truly exceptional performance rewarded properly?
Executive agreements	■ Do severance, change in control and any other terms of executive contracts and agreements satisfy a legitimate business need? ■ Do they provide adequate protection for executives while aligning with shareholder interests?

perspective of an external, independent observer (e.g., shareholder, proxy adviser, analyst, regulator, etc.).

Using the scorecard to identify areas of concern provides a guide for where time and energy should be focused. This then helps to ensure the right questions are being asked and appropriate changes are being made in light of the regulatory, business and economic environments.

Approach to Scorecard Use

The intent of a governance scorecard is not to judge compensation program elements as "right" or "wrong," but to provide an assessment of:

- Its fit with the business needs of the company
- Alignment with good business practices
- Appropriate degree of concern for shareholder interests.

The classic stoplight approach, or simple rating of A, B or C, with rationale as appropriate, provides a good starting point for discussion.

- Green light/A, signaling alignment: The company has elements that clearly support and emulate best practice and good governance principles.
- Yellow light/B, signaling caution: There are some potential gaps between best practice and the company's approach. However, the gaps are sufficiently limited in scope, severity or potential material risk that they need to be addressed only if there is a perceived need.
- Red light/C, signaling misalignment: There is a clear gap between good governance and company policies and practices. When contemplating changes in executive compensation, these issues take priority.

Say on Pay

Say on pay, a non-binding advisory vote of shareholders to approve the compensation of a company's NEOs (as such compensation is disclosed in its annual proxy statement, including the CD&A, compensation tables and narrative disclosures), is mandatory for U.S. public companies.

- Under Dodd-Frank, a say-on-pay vote must be held at least once every three years.
- A separate vote of shareholders on whether the mandated say-on-pay vote subsequently will be held annually, every two years or

every three years — a "say on frequency" — is required at least once every six years.

The say-on-pay and say-on-frequency votes are advisory only and may be disregarded by the compensation committee and the board. However, voting results reflect shareholders' views on the appropriateness of the executive compensation program. As such, committees choosing to ignore this feedback from shareholders risk facing negative implications for future say-on-pay votes and the re-election of compensation committee members to the board. (The disclosure and certain other aspects of say on pay are discussed in Chapter 14.)

Negative Say-on-Pay Votes

Negative say-on-pay votes typically signal shareholder dissatisfaction related to executive compensation programs, individual terms for NEOs or the company's response to past voting results. While negative votes are not the norm, shareholders who vote down management's say-on-pay proposal most commonly do so due to concerns related to:

- Pay for performance
- Excessive executive pay (e.g., well above peer median values)
- Generous severance packages
- Outsized sign-on bonuses
- Failure on the part of the company to address low voting support for specific compensation committee members.

A negative or relatively low say-on-pay vote puts pressure on compensation committees to review, justify and in some cases adjust programs and policies that affect the compensation of NEOs. In the event of such a voting result, compensation committee members may feel compelled to conform to a standard advocated by proxy advisers, institutional advisers or activist groups.

Rather than solely focusing on standards and common market practices, however, compensation committees seeking to maintain or improve their say-on-pay results should consider engaging in one or more of the following actions:

- Reviewing compensation plans
- Monitoring the pay-for-performance relationship

- Improving disclosure
- Increasing shareholder outreach.

Findings from reviewing compensation plans and the pay-for-performance relationship can provide an indication of whether adjustments to compensation programs are warranted and, if so, what specific concerns may need to be addressed. Whether or not adjustments to compensation plans are deemed necessary, additional clarity and effort in explaining the rationale behind certain potentially contentious practices may still be advisable.

Reviewing Compensation Plans

Say on pay amplifies the attention devoted to any problematic component of executive pay. As such, a compensation committee and its advisers should evaluate each element of the company's pay program (including its rationale) and compare it against a "hot button" checklist. The following is a sample of areas to examine:

- Compensation philosophy. Peer group, target pay positioning, objectives
- Compensation program design. Base salary, pay mix, incentive structure
- Annual incentives. Targets (e.g., percent of salary), metrics, number of metrics, leverage curve, clawbacks
- Long-term incentives. Types of programs, vesting type (time, performance), metrics, number of metrics, leverage curve, deferrals, clawbacks for all programs
- Equity use. Share allocation, burn rate
- Risk assessment. Processes for the identification of potentially material compensation risks and internal controls in place
- Contractual elements. Existence and terms of employment contracts, severance, CIC benefits.

Such a checklist, tailored for a company's particular situation, can be used to evaluate specific pay practices and assess the overall executive compensation program. In determining which areas should be included on the checklist, the compensation committee must understand which practices may be especially sensitive in their next say-on-pay vote.

Monitoring the Pay-for-Performance Relationship

The primary purpose of evaluating pay-for-performance is to validate compensation levels within the context of company performance, both against internal business plans and relative to external peer organizations.

The pay-for-performance relationship is often assessed via analysis of realizable or realized pay in addition to the Summary Compensation Table disclosure of targeted pay opportunity. Realized pay represents actual take-home pay for an executive during a specific time period, and realizable pay represents the total amount of vested and unvested potential earnings. Such analyses incorporate multiple definitions of pay, enabling committee members to review compensation outcomes from more than one perspective.

Findings from analysis can then be included in disclosure to shareholders as a component of annual communications.

Increasing Shareholder Outreach

Increasing consideration during the decision-making process is also being made to shareholder and other stakeholder reactions, with outreach to investors and proxy advisers becoming more common.

A company should maintain regular communications with its major shareholders to gain their insights on perceived strengths and weaknesses of the executive pay program. Interaction with shareholders can facilitate understanding of concerns and provide an opportunity for a company to discuss the rationale behind the compensation program throughout the year, not just at the time of proxy filing (when investors and advisers may be unavailable or have little time to engage). Critical issues can be discussed and, where elicited, suggested modifications can be considered.

Before launching a communication or outreach program, it generally is helpful to develop a formal strategy with investor relations and in consultation with compensation advisers. This strategy may involve the formation of a working team that includes representatives who are knowledgeable about the company's executive compensation programs and may interact with shareholders and proxy advisers.

In developing this team, a company generally starts with the members of the compensation committee and then considers including:

- A member of the governance committee (depending on the individual's role in board-shareholder communications)
- The chair of the board
- The CFO
- General counsel
- The head of HR
- A senior executive in investor relations.

Company representatives should be informed on what types of information and disclosure can be provided. During the process of obtaining input from various shareholders on matters such as proposed equity compensation plans, companies must take care not to run afoul of SEC Regulation FD (Fair Disclosure) by sharing material, non-public information.

Going Forward

At the core, management and compensation committees want to develop and maintain pay programs that:

- Provide a competitive advantage in attracting and retaining talented executives.
- Align compensation programs with business strategy.

As such, companies will continue to strive for appropriate — and often unique — pay programs that reflect the needs of their businesses and motivate executives to perform.

However, as compensation committees "color outside of the lines" with executive compensation design, they need to ensure they retain a focus on clearly communicating the intricacies of compensation programs and the rationale behind decisions to stakeholders. By engaging in outreach and increasing the level of attention paid to their proxy statements, compensation committees can work to obtain high positive levels of say-on-pay votes while ensuring compensation programs meet the needs of the company.

CHAPTER 13

Compensation Committee Tools

By Brian Tobin and Tim Bartlett

One of the most important duties of the compensation committee is to make compensation decisions that align executive and shareholder interests while supporting the strategic direction of the company. Ideally, the compensation committee should consider a number of different perspectives and sources of information to fulfill these duties.

The reality, however, is the compensation committees often organize meeting agendas in response to specific issues. At one meeting, the committee may decide on salary increases; at another, it may determine annual incentive awards; at a third meeting, the committee may discuss severance agreements. The result is a piecemeal approach that often fails to assemble the parts into a cohesive whole.

This chapter focuses on the tools that boards and compensation committees can use to help them make more informed decisions regarding executive pay.

This chapter:

- Identifies five critical issues that compensation committees should consider in the meeting planning process.
- Explains how tally sheets can bring to light the true costs of the executive pay program and offers guidelines for customizing a tally sheet to a company's particular executive pay program.
- Discusses four fundamental questions that should be applied in a fitness review to the key aspects of executive compensation (base salary, annual incentives, LTIs, benefits, employment contracts,

and severance and change-in-control arrangements) to ensure that they can withstand external scrutiny.

- Provides an approach that enables companies to calculate executives' current and future wealth; with accumulated wealth analysis, companies can better align company and executive needs.
- Examines issues involved in the clawback of compensation paid when a financial restatement, fraud or other identified event leads to a finding of unearned or inappropriate payment.

Maximizing the Compensation Committee Calendar

Many compensation committees recognize the need to take a big picture approach to executive compensation decision-making. A critical element in this process is meeting-planning. This means thinking more holistically about the relationship between pay and performance and how compensation issues align with core business issues at the company.

In making decisions regarding meeting-planning, we see the following critical areas that committees should consider:

- Linking business strategy to human capital strategy through an evaluation of how the company makes money, and consideration of whether the executive compensation plans align with the business cycle. Plans meant to drive performance and business in a previous business cycle may not be relevant today. Similarly, committees should consider whether compensation programs are fully aligned with the company's business and talent strategies now and in the foreseeable future. A significant item to review is the extent to which a company's incentive plans are focused on value creation and financial performance, and whether, in totality, the programs actually reinforce the business model, strategy and vision. The end result is that each meeting should include a conversation on the state of the business, market dynamics, future goals and how well the current philosophy is working, followed by a consideration of whether any changes are appropriate.
- Governance and risk management oversight to ensure that a company's practices, policies and procedures fit the business, its

philosophy, business stage and life cycle. Part of this oversight involves taking a hard look at the short- and long-term incentive plans. A process of regular evaluation can help ensure that these programs are working as planned, and that the metrics in each plan are achieving the desired business results without causing excessive risk. In this sense, risk oversight and risk management serve to protect a company's assets while also creating long-term value.

- Considering the manner in which the executive compensation programs support executive team succession planning and the development of top talent. Committees should inquire at each meeting regarding any difficulties in recruiting or retaining top talent, and ask HR leadership about the development of talent throughout the business.

- Assessing the committee's level of compensation knowledge and if further education or training are needed. A key element in the committee's oversight of executive compensation programs is to ensure that its members have a regular source of updated information on compensation developments. Continuous learning at the committee level will only foster better discussions and serve to mitigate risk around compensation planning.

- Assessing the extent to which executives understand the rationale and design of the pay programs. Two key elements in this are determining (1) whether executives can identify the link between business goals and driving results for the organization, and (2) whether executives can see how their actions can affect compensation. The committee should clearly document the roles and responsibilities for developing executive pay, communication strategies and content, and the respective roles of the committee, management and advisers. The committee should also ensure and understand the processes in place to allow investors to share their input with the board, the committee and management.

In addition to maximizing the committee calendar to provide perspective on executive compensation issues, the following sections provide an overview of several tools available to the committee to aid in its assessment of executive pay.

Starting Points for a Discussion on Executive Pay

Much of the committee's work cannot be completed without establishing an overall perspective on executive compensation in the then current business and regulatory environment. Some critical areas for consideration and action by the entire board of directors to guide actions by the compensation committee include:

- Agree upon what success would look like for the company considering current and short-term business conditions.
- Identify the key executives in this context.
- Agree upon the critical actions and behaviors required from these executives.
- Determine the key areas of business risk and the timeframes over which these may be resolved.
- Identify any new constraints on the company's freedom to act arising from known shareholders' views, regulatory considerations, tax impacts and other legal concerns.

Executive Compensation Fitness Check

Executive compensation is a focal point of potential vulnerability for companies. The media, shareholder groups, proxy advisers, various prominent boards and commissions, and Congress all have described executive compensation as a motivating force behind a purported decline in corporate responsibility.

Compensation committees should periodically conduct a "fitness check" to ascertain whether the company's executive compensation programs can effectively withstand external scrutiny.

Fundamental Questions

Four fundamental questions typically are addressed when conducting a fitness check:

- Are the compensation programs and policies consistent with shareholders' expectations?
  - Do executives' share ownership standards, share retention requirements and stock sale/option exercise procedures align their interests with those of shareholders?

- Do cash and equity programs encourage no more than the level (and nature) of business and investment risk expected by shareholders?
- Are plan designs and approval processes sufficiently transparent?
- Is the board governance process adequate with respect to compensation?
- Are executive incentive (both cash- and equity-based) programs, retirement vehicles and deferred compensation opportunities fair to both the shareholders and executives? Are they tax-effective?
- Is the amount of shareholders' equity dilution appropriate?
- Are the payments, terms and conditions of severance and change-in-control policies reasonable in both favorable and adverse scenarios?
- How has the business and share price performed in the past several months?
- What is the status of executive share ownership requirements?

■ Are the programs appropriately competitive and defensible? Are all elements of the rewards and benefits structure:
- Appropriately positioned?
- Internally equitable?
- Externally competitive?
- Consistent with good pay practices?
- Consistent with an appropriate peer group?
- Reflective of scope of business and role/accountability?
- Appropriately balanced for both short- and long-term rewards and motivation?
- Consistent with an articulated and supportable rewards strategy?

■ Are the programs and payments linked to corporate strategy and business performance?
- Does the design drive actions and strategies that enhance value while also promoting ethical behaviors?
- Are the goals and rewards tied to significant improvements in business operations or company finances?
- Do the rewards encourage no more than the desired level of business risk?
- Are the arrangements comprehensive and comprehensible?

- Are the programs consistent with best practices?
- Is the annual incentive plan rewarding the right outcomes and encouraging the right behaviors?

■ Are relative executive rewards levels and relative performance aligned appropriately?
- Do the history of payouts under incentive programs and the levels of compensation increases correlate to recent business performance and drivers of shareholder value?
- Are the rewards levels based on proper broad-based and industry-specific peer groups?
- Does relative TDC correlate to TSR?
- Does actual pay delivered correlate to a corresponding degree of performance against relevant value drivers (e.g., cash flow, earnings-per-share growth, return on invested capital, market share, new-product sales, customer satisfaction)?
- Are the number, weighting and reinforcement of rewards measures appropriate?
- What is the status of LTI grants and potential impact to attraction, retention and motivation issues?

In addressing these questions, consideration must be given, at a minimum, to five key aspects of executive compensation:
■ Base salary
■ Short- and long-term incentives
■ Executive benefits (including retirement and insurance arrangements)
■ Employment contracts
■ Severance and change-in-control arrangements.

In addition, a separate review should be conducted of the board's own compensation programs and its governance processes related to executive compensation.

To reinforce an independent perspective, an independent outside adviser should be retained who should report directly to the chair of the board's compensation committee for the fitness check. Because the specific components of any fitness check must be customized to an organization's circumstances and objectives, the scope of any review varies from company to company.

Tally Sheets: Adding Up the Cost of Executive Compensation

Due to an increased scrutiny of executive compensation, corporate boards have turned to "tally sheets" to obtain a comprehensive view of the true size of executive pay packages. A tally sheet is a detailed compilation of all major components of executive compensation, including base salary, annual incentives, LTIs, retirement programs, and various benefits and perquisites.

While the particulars vary from company to company, the essence of a tally sheet is a summary of an executive's total pay package. To present a true picture, a tally sheet should consider not only what an executive receives during employment, but also what he/she may receive upon the various events that may result in a termination of employment. The value of tally sheets has been recognized as an important tool for compensation committees, and their use has become a common (and best) practice. A substantial majority of public companies already are using some form of tally sheet.

Board members at some companies may not have a big picture perspective on all elements of compensation, particularly the benefits, perquisites and termination pay that an executive may receive. For example, this can occur where different elements of compensation and benefits packages are addressed at different times, perhaps without considering how a change in one piece may affect another. Tally sheets can provide boards with a holistic and long-term look at each pay component, the relationships among these elements, and the potential future value of each element under different scenarios — particularly those causing a termination of employment.

As previously noted, decisions on executive pay often are made on a piecemeal basis. Compounded by the fact that many compensation committee members serve on a rotational basis, the committee may lack the historical or other perspective to make comprehensive pay decisions. Too often tally sheets have revealed unexpectedly high (even shocking) aggregate pay packages, causing directors to experience "holy cow!" moments. (See "Benefits of Tally Sheets.")

Benefits of Tally Sheets

Understanding the Costs of Executive Terminations

A compensation committee should be aware of the aggregate value of amounts payable to the CEO and other top executives upon termination of employment. These scenarios should include retirement, death, disability, dismissal, dismissal for cause, voluntary resignation, resignation for good reason and termination in connection with a change in control. To simplify the presentation, those termination events that call for the same payouts can, in many cases, be grouped. By understanding what has been promised under executive contracts and various programs, directors can avoid surprise or embarrassment. Tally sheets help ensure that compensation committee members are aware of the cost and timing of potential payouts, as well as the terms and conditions that trigger payment.

Revealing the True Value of Executive Benefits and Perquisites

Although compensation committees have been accustomed to tallying top executives' base salaries, annual incentive pay and LTIs, they sometimes may overlook benefits and perquisites. Compensation committees need to know more than the types of benefits provided; they must understand the value of the benefits and perquisites. Before approving executive pay changes, compensation committees should understand the costs, tax treatment and financial accounting consequences of these modifications to their benefits and perquisites program.

Creating Greater Alignment With the Company's Compensation Philosophy

When decisions on various components of an executive's total pay are made at different times throughout the year, the compensation committee needs to consider how each program fits in the company's overall compensation philosophy. Tally sheets look at the compensation and benefits in totality, allowing the compensation committee to determine the appropriate mix by considering relationships among pay components. A compensation committee should test its tally sheets annually against its compensation philosophy and determine whether the pay philosophy is delivering the appropriate value over time.

Tally Sheet Guidelines

While any tally sheet has to be tailored to a company's specific programs, following are some suggested basic guidelines on the level and scope of data that should be included:

- A recent history (e.g., three to five years) of base salary, target annual incentives, actual annual incentives, LTIs, benefits and perquisites
- All vested and unvested equity awards

- The current spread values of all outstanding vested and unvested stock options and stock appreciation rights (SARs) and the current value of all other LTI awards
- The estimated size of the next LTI plan payout and any other LTI plan cycles in progress
- The current value of an executive's interest (both vested and unvested) under all tax-qualified retirement plans and under all nonqualified SERPs, as well as a projection of future payouts.
- The amounts payable on various termination events (as identified).

Tally sheets can be valuable tools for boards in making the most appropriate executive pay decisions. Because compensation committees are responsible for executive pay, it is essential that members are fully aware of all elements of compensation. No compensation committee should feel comfortable in approving an executive pay program without understanding its potential costs, especially payments due after employment terminates.

Use of Realizable Pay: Measuring Pay for Purposes of Pay-for-Performance Alignment

Another tool that has been used by compensation committees in recent years is the concept of realizable pay. In the evaluation by companies, shareholders and proxy advisers on how to measure pay for testing pay-for-performance alignment, realizable pay has become the term used to describe the total compensation value that an executive may realize given actual stock and company performance as of a specified date. It is with long-term equity awards where the distinction between TDC value as reported in the summary compensation table of the annual proxy statement and the calculation of realizable pay exists.

The basic concern with using grant values is they are essentially reasoned guesses of the expected value of the equity award at the time of grant. Over time, such values may not correlate to actual amounts being realized by executives from the grants (which values ultimately could be significantly more or less). This method also looks at pay prospectively, extending beyond the period for which performance is measured. For example, a CEO's performance shares can appear as $5 million in grant value; however, if threshold performance is not achieved and the shares do not vest, the awards do not produce anything realizable. Accordingly, the concept of realizable pay was developed to address this issue. In general terms, realizable pay figures would substitute the grant date value of equity used in the summary compensation table with the value of the equity awards that executives may receive based on actual stock price performance as of a specified date.

Accumulated Wealth Management: Is It Worth Examining?

Compensation committees are continuing to gain a better understanding of the total wealth potential of an executive's past, current and projected future compensation and benefits. In the same manner, an increasing number of companies are taking accumulated wealth into account when making pay decisions. Given the expanded disclosure of executive pay, this trend likely will continue.

Why is accumulated wealth analysis important? From an executive's perspective, accumulated wealth provides security, independence and the funding of retirement objectives. To the extent that accumulated wealth enables an executive to retire, it can open opportunities for identified candidates to develop and move up in the organization. From a company's perspective, the say-on-pay process has heightened the emphasis on making sure that pay appropriately reflects performance, causing companies to question what pay for what period is compared with performance.

Overview of Accumulated Wealth Analysis

An accumulated wealth analysis starts with an examination of awards and accruals under all company-sponsored wealth-accumulation vehicles, particularly an executive's equity interests and retirement benefits (including deferred compensation). While companies may develop and conduct the analysis in various ways, the clear goal is to understand the total wealth position/potential of the executive. A key objective of executive compensation is the creation of wealth for those who enhance shareholder value through successful management of entrusted resources. Accumulated wealth can be especially large where total shareholder returns are strong.

Examining Equity

Because the vast majority of public companies deliver a sizeable portion of compensation in the form of equity-based vehicles (e.g., stock options, restricted stock, performance shares), the process includes the consideration of these grants.

- **Gains from past grants:** The analysis begins with ascertaining the compensation an executive has realized from past grants. While vested grants have lower retention value, retained equity has wealth accumulation value that becomes increasingly important as the executive contemplates retirement.

- **Outstanding equity:** Outstanding equity, whether vested or unvested, should be included in the accumulated wealth analysis because such grants have true economic value. One complication to including outstanding equity is projecting the future gains/losses in stock price for the model. This can have a dramatic effect on the value of stock options (i.e., stock options only have value at prices above the exercise price, while time-vested restricted stock retains some value at all stock prices short of implosion of the company). Additionally, compensation committees should consider the mix of vested and unvested awards when making future pay decisions.

- **Future grants:** A consideration of projected future grants provides information regarding the future value of all equity vehicles at retirement. Again, this type of analysis requires modeling of future stock price, but will often yield that "ah-ha" moment when the compensation committee realizes the potential wealth accumulation assuming continued grants at the current level.

How Much Is Enough?

The obvious use of the wealth-accumulation analysis is to determine how much wealth has been and will be created. It certainly can be argued that an executive with 100 to 200 times salary in accumulated wealth through his/her stock-based compensation does not need further motivation/alignment via company stock performance. On the other hand, one to four times salary is not enough to provide an executive with financial security, nor the ability to retire or change his/her venue in retirement. Also, current compensation and the opportunity for more wealth operate to motivate and retain the executive.

It is in the middle, and not at the extremes, where compensation committees must discuss and develop a strategy around how much is enough. The objective is not to reduce compensation as much as to understand at what point additional wealth is offset by an executive's desire to enjoy the fruits of his/her labor. Simply turning off the spigot is not a viable alternative because the executive could choose to work for a competitor that is more than willing to pay going market rates with the full complement of incentive plan awards. Rather, it is important to align rewards with shareholder value as well as executive needs and desires.

Alignment With Shareholders?

Suggestions have been made that the true use of an accumulated wealth analysis should be to ensure alignment in wealth creation of the executive and the shareholders. While shareholders contribute capital, executives contribute sweat equity in earning their wealth. Therefore, converting income to wealth should be an objective. In its simplest form, one would compare the value that could be realized based on accumulated grants and cash to actual company performance.

For example, CEO-realized compensation may be examined during a five-year period and compared to a peer group of companies. A comparison of total shareholder return would be included in the analysis. Ideally, realized pay positioning would align with performance (e.g., pay at the 75th percentile would align with the 75th percentile of total shareholder return).

Revisit Severance Agreements

Severance agreements and contracts often are structured to provide an executive with what might be viewed as a form of insurance policy to cover the loss of income stemming from the loss of a job.

Using the accumulated wealth analysis can help directors determine if there is a need for such term insurance going forward. Is there a level of accumulated wealth that makes the term insurance provided by a severance agreement unnecessary?

Succession Planning Tool

The use of the accumulated wealth analysis as a tool in succession planning is an often overlooked application. As companies lean more toward developing executive talent in-house, they need to understand and strategically manage the amount of wealth each future leader has accumulated to date and his/her future earning potential.

In the case of succession planning, the board and the executive team ideally would build up enough ownership over time to align the wealth creation of the executive with shareholder value creation, as well as ensure the incumbent stays and performs until a viable successor can be established.

An accumulated wealth analysis is another valuable input for compensation committees when managing an executive's total rewards. As boards are pressed to consider past compensation decisions when reviewing current compensation, it is expected that the adoption of this practice will increase among boards and the application will evolve. Because the accumulated wealth analysis is fairly new to most compensation committees, they need to be wary of setting arbitrary caps on compensation and avoid trying to immediately align with industry norms; rather, a more productive approach would involve engaging in a dialogue based on the company's and executive's particular circumstances.

Recouping Executive Pay: Clawbacks

Clawbacks have emerged as the primary means to recover "erroneously awarded" incentive-based compensation from current and former executives. In this context, "erroneously awarded compensation" refers to incentive compensation that would not have been received in light of an accounting restatement by the company. As corporate governance groups and shareholders advocated for the adoption of general policies or terms in executive agreements and incentive plans to enable a company to recapture bonuses and other incentive-based rewards in appropriate circumstances, companies increasingly developed clawback provisions suited to their own particular circumstances.

Initially spurred on by fairly narrow recovery provisions in the Sarbanes-Oxley Act of 2002, Congress included clawbacks in the terms for troubled institutions that received U.S. Department of Treasury investments under 2009 bailout legislation. Congress then moved to center stage with the inclusion of mandatory, fairly rigid clawback requirements (subject to relevant SEC rulemaking and the implementation of stock exchange listing standards) in the 2010 Dodd-Frank legislation applicable to public companies. It took the SEC until August 2015 to issue proposed rules on clawbacks requiered under Dodd-Frank.

In general, Dodd-Frank contains considerably broader recapture rules than the clawback provisions under Sarbanes-Oxley. For example, Dodd-Frank's clawbacks apply to any executive officer (not just the CEO and CFO), do not require any misconduct (just simply the requisite restatement described in the next section on "Putting Clawbacks in Context"), and cover a three-year (rather than 12-month) period. Public companies subject to Dodd-Frank's mandates also should consider including any additional features or processes that address the organization's particular circumstances or facilitate administration.

Putting Clawbacks in Context

Traditionally, a clawback was a formal policy or a provision in an employment agreement or in a compensation plan that permitted a company, often in its discretion (typically exercised by the board or compensation committee), to recapture cash and/or equity incentive payments from certain employees — generally senior executives — for one or more reasons (set out in the particular program or agreement). Putting aside the statutory and regulatory mandates noted above, a policy or provision might provide for a clawback if:

- An executive has been deemed responsible for fraudulent actions.
- Incentive payments were based on misstated financials, especially if the result of fraud or negligence.

- An executive has violated enforceable noncompetition provisions or other restrictive covenants.
- An executive has been responsible for defined actions detrimental to the company.

Clawbacks can be designed to be triggered by any one of the events identified in the policy or provision; definitions of covered events and the consequences have varied considerably across companies. The most common triggers among the largest U.S. public companies are a financial restatement by the company (e.g., Dodd-Frank's "required ... accounting restatement due to the material noncompliance ... with any financial reporting requirement under the securities laws ...") or an executive's ethical misconduct. The next most prevalent event is a violation of a noncompetition agreement.

Covered Compensation

As clawbacks grew in prevalence (and became the subject of legal mandates), the definition of "covered compensation" became more expansive. Initial provisions focused on cash-based bonuses; recently, clawbacks have broadened to include equity compensation — both vested and unvested stock awards. Research indicates that the vast majority of policies included both cash and equity incentive compensation (e.g., "incentive-based compensation [including stock options awarded as compensation]" under Dodd-Frank) in their definition of compensation subject to clawback.

Board Considerations in Developing a Clawback Policy

Before adopting clawback provisions, boards and compensation committees need to think through both the legal requirements and the possible application of the clawback provisions. The implementation of a clawback policy surfaces administrative and compliance issues that need to be reviewed and thoroughly discussed.

Which Employees Need to Be Covered Under the Policy?

Recoveries under Dodd-Frank extend to "any current and former executive officer," which of course bring to mind some practical difficulties inherent in recouping pay from a former officer. Beyond the required group that a clawback policy must cover, we find that the further down in the organization that the recovery provision extends, the more likely the provision will be viewed favorably by corporate governance groups.

Which Compensation Elements Should Be Covered?

As previously noted, Dodd-Frank requires the recovery of any incentive-based compensation if the other conditions for a clawback are met; companies may decide to extend compensation recoupments even further. Base salary typically is not covered in clawback arrangements because base compensation is not usually linked to specific performance objectives. While awaiting rulemaking on clawbacks under Dodd-Frank, some companies adopted provisions that directly link their clawback provisions to all performance-based pay (including both cash and equity compensation). A clawback policy required by Dodd-Frank should, for example, address how to implement the repayment of gains generated by stock sales if the stock price was affected by misstated financial information.

Where Should Clawback Provisions Be Included?

Some companies adopt clawback policies that then are incorporated by reference into the relevant plans and agreements; this approach works well for compying with the Dodd-Frank mandates as it is relatively simple to implement. Other companies include clawback language in all employment agreements and incentive plan documents.

Looking Ahead

While clawbacks are often viewed as a common sense solution to "undeserved" executive compensation, various facts and issues specific to a company's circumstances should be considered in designing any clawback policy that extends beyond the Dodd-Frank mandates. Because U.S. public companies are compelled by Dodd-Frank to adopt claw-back provisions, companies need to understand which components of their executive pay programs may be subject to clawback. From a design perspective, whether an award is covered by the clawback rules may affect its attractiveness, as executives generally prefer to receive awards that are not subject to clawback.

CHAPTER 14

Disclosure of Executive Pay

By Bill Gerek

Executive pay disclosure goes hand in hand with other legislative and regulatory attempts to achieve accountability and transparency in all matters relating to corporate governance. The SEC's expanded disclosure rules adopted in 2006 and 2009 and the 2010 Dodd-Frank legislation (including SEC rules adopted thereunder) have considerably altered the disclosure landscape. Companies must now provide more detailed tabular information, additional narrative in the CD&A, information on the qualifications of directors and their fees, the degree of risk-taking inherent in pay programs, and the rationale behind the company's leadership structure.

The disclosure of so much information in numerous public documents, each with a distinct reporting schedule and format, makes the work of the compensation committee increasingly more difficult and time-consuming. This is especially true when it comes to disclosing equity compensation, comprised as it often is of several different vehicles and overlapping grants over multi-year periods. The actual total value of equity pay granted and realized over time may be quite different from the snapshot that appears each year in the proxy.

In addition, the need to communicate with shareholders effectively regarding say on pay, coupled with expanded SEC and stock exchange disclosure requirements, has undoubtedly resulted in longer proxy statements. This trend will likely continue, as the remaining disclosure rules required by Dodd-Frank ultimately are implemented (as of this printing). Consequently, compensation committees need to collect and analyze data in a way that allows for a more complete understanding and communication of reported values.

This chapter:

- Reviews the purpose of the CD&A, its connection with the new compensation committee report, and issues and actions to make the CD&A a more meaningful document.
- Discusses the key issues of the SEC's 2009 final rules expanding proxy disclosure in public companies, including the requirement to discuss the extent that pay programs might encourage harmful risk-taking, equity awards to directors, and the company's leadership structure.
- Provides a three-part mechanism for measuring executive pay to better understand how pay programs interact over time and facilitate the communication of executive pay programs to shareholders.
- Reviews say on pay, say on parachutes, clawback policies and other provisions of Dodd-Frank related to executive compensation.
- Discusses the reasons that companies should plan for continued scrutiny by major stakeholders, their advisers and regulators, and ways in which companies and their compensation committees may better prepare for each proxy season.

Challenges of the Compensation Discussion and Analysis

In 2006, the SEC adopted substantially expanded executive compensation disclosure rules that were described as a wake-up call by the director of the SEC's Division of Corporation Finance. Of particular importance is the CD&A section that was added as a required component of annual proxy statements. Companies have been forced to focus not just on the "what" but also the "why" in executive pay disclosure.

Objectives of the CD&A

In its commentary on the CD&A, the SEC envisioned the section as an "overview providing narrative disclosure that puts into context the compensation disclosure provided elsewhere" for a company's NEOs. The expressed objective was to explain material elements of these executives' compensation. Critical to this process are seven questions that should be addressed:

- What are the objectives of the company's compensation programs?
- What is the compensation program designed to reward?
- What is each element of compensation?
- Why does the company choose to pay each element?
- How does the company determine the amount (and, where applicable, the formula) for each element?
- How does each element and the company's decisions regarding that element fit into the company's overall compensation objectives and affect decisions regarding other elements?

At the time of the 2006 rulemaking, executive pay disclosure at many companies had become standardized — even largely boilerplate — and often furnished little meaningful guidance on how executive pay actually is determined. In requiring a CD&A, key SEC goals were to encourage much more thoughtful analysis by compensation committees in determining executive pay and to have these pay considerations thoroughly disclosed. Many statements in the CD&A require significant elaboration; it is not sufficient to state that "pay is based on performance" or that "compensation is targeted at the median of comparable (or peer) organizations." Rather, how these standards are applied needs to be described, along with relevant policies, factors and regulatory impact.

In addition, the latest trends in shareholder engagement call for companies to begin preparing for the proxy season sooner and with greater deliberation regarding their compensation plans and programs. The proxy should tell a company's compensation story, but the decisions behind the story need to balance any shareholder concerns about its compensation programs with how these arrangements support the company's business strategy and objectives. We believe that the best way to demonstrate this balance is to show due consideration of shareholder issues coupled with effective shareholder engagement; the CD&A section of the proxy should clearly explain the compensation committee's final decisions and why they were made.

Relation of CD&A to the Compensation Committee Report

Although the CD&A discusses compensation policies and decisions, it does not address the compensation committee's deliberations because it is not a report of the compensation committee; rather the CD&A is the company's responsibility. However, the 2006 SEC rules also mandated a new form of compensation committee report that requires the committee to state whether:

- It has reviewed and discussed the CD&A with management, and
- The committee recommended to the board of directors that the CD&A be included in the company's annual report and proxy (based on the aforementioned review and discussions).

Potential Liability Under the CD&A

While the compensation committee report is considered "furnished" to the SEC, the CD&A is a filed document. This technical distinction means that the CD&A is considered to be part of the proxy statement and the disclosures are covered by the Sarbanes-Oxley Act of 2002 certifications required of principal executive officers and principal financial officers. The potential liability was designed to increase attention to the statements made.

Issues to Address in the CD&A

The CD&A is principles-based (rather than rules-based), and the SEC intends that it furnish perspective on the numbers and other executive pay information contained in required tables and elsewhere. A significant challenge presented by the CD&A has been articulating the rationale underlying the components of the executive compensation package for each NEO. The SEC's rulemaking provided nonexclusive examples of potentially appropriate issues that might reasonably be addressed in the CD&A; each should be considered in light of the organization's particular facts and circumstances. The CD&A must be comprehensive in scope; a company should describe any compensation policies it applies, even if not covered in the SEC's examples. The discussion also should address post-employment arrangements relating to compensation.

Besides the breadth of its requirements, the CD&A calls for greater depth than had been customary in compensation committee reports. While a CD&A generally should avoid repetition of the exhaustive information presented in tables and other portions of the proxy, it should identify material differences in compensation policies and decisions applicable to individual NEOs. Considerable thought and effort can be required to determine what should be discussed and then to prepare the appropriate explanation —which is supposed to be written in plain English (a standard not often met).

Areas That May Require Particular Attention

The examples provided by the SEC include some items that previously received scant attention in most proxy statements. In expanding the scope of executive pay disclosure, the SEC implicitly furnished its views on items that should be considered in executive compensation design.

- The SEC identified the familiar concept of benchmarking as a particular subject for disclosure. Information is needed on the benchmark for any material element of an executive's compensation, including the component companies (peer group) used for the benchmark. This requirement has increased the focus on having an appropriate peer group and choosing reasonable benchmarks. In comment letters from the SEC during the first few years of proxy filings under these rules, benchmarking was one of the main sources of SEC inquiries.

- One example from the SEC suggested discussing how gains from prior option awards are considered in setting other elements of compensation. By identifying the topic, the SEC implied that compensation committees should look at this issue.

- The well-publicized concerns some years ago at dozens of companies regarding the timing (a concept broader than backdating) and pricing of stock options caused the SEC to specifically provide for extensive disclosure regarding the timing and pricing of option grants. Various elements and questions were identified by the

SEC for disclosure; these should be considered in determining the appropriate use and design of stock options in a company's executive pay program.

- Another example refers to a company's equity ownership guidelines and mentions any policies regarding hedging an executive's economic risk of such ownership. Many organizations have since developed hedging policies rather than state that they do not have any such policy. As mentioned later in this chapter, hedging policies were addressed in Dodd-Frank and extended to all employees and directors.

- Because the impact of the accounting and tax treatment of a particular form of compensation is one issue that the SEC views as potentially appropriate for discussion, an organization might consider the role played by various regulatory provisions (e.g., the $1 million deduction cap and the detailed regulation of nonqualified deferred compensation under IRC sections 162(m) and 409A, respectively, and the accounting impact under ASC Topic 718) in selecting the form and design of awards.

Recommended Actions

The following actions should be useful for most companies:

- Start the process early each year. Based on anticipated changes, future proxy seasons likely will involve more input from a wider group of stakeholders than ever before (e.g., legal/corporate secretaries, HR/compensation professionals, communication, marketing, investor relations, shareholder advisory firms and board members). Every party with responsibility regarding a CD&A needs to appreciate the significant effort that can be required to satisfy the disclosure standards — a narrative approach that considers a lengthy list of issues. A critical factor in managing this compliance process involves having sufficient time to fully vet all compensation issues that might need to be discussed.

- Develop an overall understanding of the objectives and requirements for the CD&A, working with advisers as needed.

- Internal personnel and external advisers (ideally including attorneys, accountants and compensation consultants) should work together and undertake the preparation of a "mock" CD&A. Generally it is helpful to take the company's most recent CD&A as a starting point, but then view everything with fresh eyes to assess its applicability for the relevant year. New information is added, irrelevant material is deleted, and the whole reconsidered in light of the particulars of the company and its industry as well as relevant legislation and rules, economic considerations and a host of other factors. A key focus is on clarity, organization and presentation. When the parties actually commence this process, they realize how much is involved in crafting a focused discussion of the appropriate issues for the CD&A.

- Many companies now dedicate a section of their annual proxy statements to addressing expressed and potential concerns of shareholders. Consequently, more companies include discussions of how a compensation committee or board responded to such issues, as well as whether (and, if so, how) compensation programs were modified.

- Inevitable scrutiny follows certain policies (e.g., parachute tax gross-ups). A company needs to provide a strong rationale for any important programs or provisions that are likely to be controversial.

- The compensation committee should be involved. While a company has responsibility for the preparation and filing of a proxy statement and the CD&A, it is the handiwork of the compensation committee that is being explained in the CD&A. The SEC clearly expects that compensation committee decisions will be affected by the knowledge that they will be subject to disclosure.

- Once an organization understands the scope of the tasks involved in crafting the CD&A, it should identify any issues that need to be addressed and information to be included. As instructed by the SEC, each company needs to focus on its particular facts and circumstances. Minutes of compensation committee meetings, reports of internal staff and consultants, and various plan documents and summaries may be helpful to examine as part of this process.

- A draft CD&A should be circulated among the working group for comment. During an iterative review process, all parties should keep in mind the ultimate goals of a clear yet comprehensive overview of the company's executive pay determinations.

Enhanced Disclosure of Executive Pay

The regulation of executive compensation accelerated in 2009 as Congress, the Obama Administration and various regulatory agencies all added their voices to the debate surrounding sound executive pay practices. Near the close of 2009, the SEC adopted final rules further expanding proxy disclosure of executive compensation for public companies. Following is an overview of these SEC rules and some of the key compliance issues.

Relationship of the Company's Compensation Policies and Practices to Risk

Under the 2009 rules, public companies must discuss compensation policies and practices for all employees — not just NEOs — to the extent that risks arising from them are "reasonably likely to have a material adverse effect" on the company. Companies need to identify and then review all compensation arrangements to determine whether there are potential risks that might trigger disclosure. Any problems discovered in the review process then can be fixed or appropriately mitigated.

The SEC furnished examples of situations that could potentially trigger discussion and analysis:

- A business unit of the company carries a significant portion of the company's risk profile.
- A business unit has a significantly different compensation structure than other units.
- A business unit is significantly more profitable than others within the company.
- Compensation expense at a business unit represents a significant percentage of the unit's revenues.
- Compensation policies and practices vary significantly from the overall risk and reward structure of the company.

In assessing the degree of risk, companies can consider any compensation policies and practices designed to alleviate risk or balance incentives (e.g., clawbacks and recoupment policies, bonus banking, stock ownership requirements). The type of disclosure is determined on a case-by-case basis, but may include:

- The general design philosophy of compensation policies for employees whose behavior would be most influenced by the incentive programs.
- The company's risk assessment or considerations in structuring its incentive compensation policies.
- The ways in which the company's compensation policies relate to the realization of risks resulting from the actions of employees (e.g., through the use of clawbacks, holding periods).
- The company's policies regarding adjustments to its compensation practices to address changes in its risk profile.
- Material adjustments the registrant has made to its compensation policies or practices as a result of changes in its risk profile.
- The extent to which the registrant monitors its compensation policies to determine whether risk management objectives are being met.

As a topic that relates to all employees and not just NEOs, risk-related disclosure should have its own section in the proxy statement and generally not be included in the CD&A. Importantly, the SEC does "not require a company to make an affirmative statement that it has determined that the risks arising from its compensation policies and practices are not likely to have a material adverse effect on the company." In view of this limitation on the disclosure that is required, companies have been split on whether they should take the next step to voluntarily make such an affirmative statement that they maintain no such unreasonably risky compensation programs.

Disclosure Regarding Fees Affecting Independence of Compensation Consultants

The disclosure rules require a company to disclose the fees paid to a compensation consultant if the consultant furnished consulting services related to executive or director compensation as well as other services to the company. However, fee disclosure is not required if the fees paid to the consultant for additional services did not exceed $120,000 during the company's fiscal year. When disclosure is required, it must include:

- Aggregate fees paid for executive and director compensation consulting services
- Aggregate fees paid for other services
- Whether the decision to engage the consultant for other services was made or recommended by management and whether the committee or board approved the other services, if the consultant was engaged by the compensation committee.

Disclosure on the Qualifications of Directors and Nominees

Under the disclosure requirements, a company must discuss the particular experience, qualifications, attributes or skills that qualify an individual to serve as a director for the company, based on the company's business and structure at the time the disclosure is being made. However, the rules do not require disclosure regarding the specifics that qualify the individual to serve as a committee member. Disclosure is required for all directors, even if they are not standing for re-election in the applicable year, and should include:

- Any directorships at public companies held by each director at any time during the past five years (instead of only disclosing currently held directorships)
- Certain legal proceedings involving any director or executive officer during the past 10 years (instead of five years)
- Whether and how diversity is considered when identifying director candidates.

The SEC has not defined diversity; rather, each company is allowed to define it as it determines to be appropriate for its particular circumstances (e.g., experience, skills, education, race, gender). If a policy on diversity exists, the company must disclose how the policy is implemented and how its effectiveness is assessed.

Discussion of Company Leadership Structure

A company is required to disclose whether and why it has chosen to combine or separate the CEO and board chair positions, along with the reasons why the company believes that this board leadership structure is the most appropriate for it at the time of the filing. If the same person serves as CEO and chair, the company needs to disclose whether and why the company has a lead independent director and the role of the lead independent director in the leadership of the board. As discussed later in this chapter, Dodd-Frank confirmed this requirement through a statutory mandate.

In addition, the rules require companies to describe the board's role in the oversight of risk (which may include credit risk, liquidity risk and operational risk). For example, a company may describe whether the entire board reviews risk or if there is a separate committee. Further, a company may find it helpful to discuss how risk information is communicated to the board or relevant committee members.

The Continuing Challenge of Appropriate Disclosure

The 2009 rules:

- Responded to some criticisms of the 2006 overhaul of the SEC disclosure rules relating to executive compensation;
- Addressed various executive compensation issues that became important after experience with companies' disclosures; and
- Generally expanded the scope of required disclosures.

Companies are faced with the challenge of accurately explaining their programs and policies in a way that is sufficiently detailed yet understandable and meaningful to investors and other interested parties.

Measuring Executive Pay: The Equity Compensation Challenge

The 2009 changes in proxy disclosure rules caused a shift in the method and outcome of future years' executive compensation reporting. The reported numbers that tend to be the focus of media, pay critics and analysts do not always capture the true story of executive pay.

Understanding Reported Values of Executive Pay

The complex structure of executive compensation, dominated by various forms of equity and cash-based LTIs, can lead to significantly different interpretations of pay. These differences result from the interaction of varying approaches to data collection, analysis and reporting. Ensuring that all relevant data are collected for incorporation in the analysis, applying meaningful analytical tools to construct pay models, and reporting the information in a way that recognizes the complexity of pay practices all are essential for board-level decision support. Increased disclosure requirements, governance pressures and continued media attention make it imperative that pay values are understood and clearly communicated — internally and externally.

Effect of Prior Year's Compensation Actions

Special circumstances underlying a previous year's equity awards can be misinterpreted the next year. As an illustration, in 2009 many companies acted to address the results of a depressed stock market, increased market volatility, poor business results and the effects of those conditions on executive pay. These special, often one-time actions held potential for misinterpretation — either because they might be deemed part of annual pay or, conversely, because they might be excluded from pay calculations altogether. Such decisions made during the data-collection process can lead to a flawed analysis as true pay levels resulting from these items are not represented properly. A particular executive's compensation often can only be interpreted properly by understanding pay actions on a before-and-after basis.

In the 2009 example, companies that implemented stock option exchange programs canceled many years of stock options and re-granted some or all of those at a more favorable price. Merely reporting the Black-Scholes value of the re-grant as an element of 2009 pay oversimplified the total compensation implications.

Some of those companies excluded officers from their programs yet took other action — such as skipping or deferring the normal annual grant — that also needed to be considered. A company whose compensation peer group consists of several companies that made these types of pay decisions may have raised its executives' pay levels without recognizing these dynamics.

These complexities highlight the need for heightened attention to a three-faceted approach to executive equity compensation interpretation — collection, analysis and reporting.

Data Collection

Discussions of executive compensation focus primarily on single-year values, forming the root of many misunderstandings. But executive equity awards often are developed as part of a multi-year plan. SEC proxy disclosure rules recognize this through the required three-year reporting format for the Summary Compensation Table and the multi-year aggregations in other tables. A common example is when an executive receives a large new-hire equity grant, often two to four times the size of a typical annual grant, and then receives no equity award the following year(s). The single-year approach often leads to the conclusion that there has been a pay cut or an elimination of LTI awards when pay in year two is compared to that of year one.

Much of the important detail is contained in footnotes and narrative in the proxy statement, without which the tabular figures may be misinterpreted. In addition, many pay actions not captured in the tables are nevertheless disclosed in the CD&A section or appear in Form 8-K filings subsequent to the issuance of the proxy statement. Given the dated (look-back) nature of tabular information, these additional sources are critical to understanding the true current market for executive pay. The complexities of executive equity compensation have long required a multi-year, multi-source perspective and any economic turmoil can increase the importance of this approach.

Data Analysis

While the valuation of equity instruments receives much attention, the variations in fair value that may result from volatility or expected life assumptions are less significant than the effects on deemed value from a series of decisions that guide the equity compensation calculation. Such analysis often is bypassed and the fair value resulting from the reporting process — typically what appears in SEC filings — is accepted as the pay value without any further consideration. Compensation committees and executives need to understand these dynamics to ensure effective pay decisions.

Volatile equity markets can result in equity grants with an unprecedented variation of values relative to business fundamentals and significant intra-year variations in relative grant values. For example, looking back to 2009, assume two companies whose share prices directly track the NASDAQ index both granted stock options in 2009, the first in early March and the other in early September. The first company reported grant-date fair values approximately 50 percent lower than the second company, but by the end of 2009 provided intrinsic value that was 260 percent greater. Variations of this magnitude were unprecedented in the history of executive pay and teach important lessons. An unusually large number of companies awarded stock options in February through April 2009 near the market low, and in many cases those grants quickly accumulated value far greater than the artificially low Black-Scholes value that was reported in SEC filings. Ironically, many of those companies granted a larger number of shares to offset the lower fair value at the time, exacerbating this effect.

These dynamics require that companies understand not only what was granted (i.e., stock options, time-vested shares, performance-based shares, cash LTI) and how much was granted, but when it was granted. In addition to understanding award type and timing, the emergence of performance features requires attention to the effect of performance contingencies or accelerators, thresholds and targets, absolute versus relative performance measures, and the interaction of time-based and performance-based conditions. Also, as publicly-traded companies now typically have stock ownership guidelines and share retention requirements (see Chapter 10), the risk-reward balance has changed. Thoughtful analysis is required to understand the real effect on executive pay value resulting from the interaction of these features.

Data Reporting

With proper data collection and analysis, pay can be reported in ways that provide a meaningful picture of executive pay practices over the past years. A single snapshot of pay is not adequate for telling the story in this complex environment. Merely viewing pay as a single number may lead a compensation committee to reach flawed conclusions about the company's competitive position in the market. Scenario-based pay projections — incorporated into tally sheet and wealth accumulation analyses — will provide the compensation committee and the executive team with a point of view consistent with other business decision processes.

Pay Granted, Earned and Realized

A greater scrutiny of pay values introduces a need for the multi-dimensional view of pay, with at least three possible pay views to be considered. This approach requires taking pay analysis beyond a grant-based focus to a dynamic view of the life cycle of executive pay — when granted, earned and realized.

Under current SEC rules, equity incentive figures in the Summary Compensation Table are reported on an "earned"' rather than a "granted" basis. The fair value of all equity awards made during the reporting year are deemed to have been what was "paid" to the executive for that year rather than what was accrued for accounting purposes. There are lengthy and complex arguments around which of these two methods is preferable, and why, but sound pay analysis does not force an either/or decision. It is important to understand what was granted, the incremental amount earned, and — as media organizations often do — the pay realized over a period of time to obtain a true picture of executive pay. Thus, we have seen the development of supplemental disclosures to show "realized pay" or "realizable pay" (with still some notable variance among users in the meaning of these terms), depending on the organization and what it believes most helpful in understanding the compensation of its executives.

While no single analytical structure will make sense for all companies, compensation committees and executive teams should:

- Think through the three data processes (collection, analysis and reporting) in the context of three alternative views of pay (granted, earned and realized), and
- Ask a series of questions to ensure a comprehensive approach. Table 14-1 illustrates the types of questions that may help guide a year's analyses and decisions.

Various tools — tally sheets, wealth accumulation models, "walk away" value calculations and scenario-based analysis — address some of these issues. A methodical approach can help a company understand the tools being used and the rationale for using a tool to the exclusion of others. It can be helpful to view these alternatives in this three-by-three analytical framework to capture the issues surrounding the collection, analysis and reporting of equity compensation data and recognize alternative measurement points of grant, earning and realization to ensure a clear understanding of market pay levels and practices.

Further Executive Pay Disclosure Under Dodd-Frank

While broadly targeting the financial services industry, including provisions that address consumer and investor protection, the Dodd-Frank legislation contains important executive compensation and corporate governance provisions that apply to most public companies regardless of industry. To a considerable extent, Dodd-Frank left the specifics of the new requirements to rule-making by the SEC and then inclusion in listing standards by the securities exchanges.

Most of the executive compensation provisions of the Dodd-Frank legislation added new disclosure requirements for public companies. Following are the basic terms of key executive compensation and corporate governance disclosure provisions enacted

TABLE 14-1

Data Processes of Collection, Analysis and Reporting

	Granted	Earned	Realized
Collection	Did we capture all of the grants and actions taken last year? Have we properly categorized "annual" pay actions	Did many of our peers grant during the market lows? How is that affecting reported grant value and fair value?	Were there significant realization events that created compensation not captured in the typical proxy and survey formats? Have we compared vested but unexercised in-the-money option gains?
Analysis	Have we explored the stock price patterns of our peers and reviewed scenario-based pay values?	Have we analyzed competitors' changes in vesting schedules, acceleration provisions, and holding requirements to understand changes in earnings opportunities?	Have we conducted an historical analysis of realized pay to understand how this may be affecting current grant patterns?
Reporting	Have we accounted for new hires, promotions, terminations, founders and special qualifications of incumbents?	Are we considering risk-adjusted differences in pay values: options vs. time-vested full-value awards vs. thresholds and targets on performance awards?	Do our tally sheet and wealth accumulation tools capture realized value including post-vesting accumulation?

in Dodd-Frank. The effective dates of the various parts of the act varied; certain changes were effective on enactment (July 21, 2010), while other provisions only were designed to take effect either after a transition period or after the regulatory authorities promulgated rules fleshing out the statutory mandates. The SEC devoted its initial focus to the Dodd-Frank provisions with specified effective dates and only began to address the last group of statutory provisions affecting executive pay disclosures in 2015. Dodd-Frank undoubtedly is having a substantial effect on executive pay processes at most public companies.

Understand Investor and Proxy Advisory Policies

Companies should understand the key policies of various parties that now weigh in on executive compensation, especially those that may affect the acceptance of their compensation programs. Accordingly, the regular review of the current policies and past recommendations of proxy advisory firms and major investors should identify programs that risk adverse reaction from these groups, allowing companies to reconsider their programs or explain their effectiveness from the company's viewpoint. Modification or engagement (or a combination of the two) may help avoid the negative consequences that could follow a violation of such policies.

FIGURE 14-1

Review of Investor and Proxy Advisory Firm Policies

- Review proxy advisory firm policies
- Review major investor policies
- Are any of your programs at risk of a "no" vote?
- Explain effectiveness of programs
- Engagement

Say on Pay

Resolving a long-running debate on whether and how to obtain the views of shareholders on executive pay, Dodd-Frank requires a public company to provide shareholders with a nonbinding vote to approve the compensation of its NEOs. A say-on-pay vote must be held at least once every three years, which started with the first annual shareholders' meeting occurring after Jan. 21, 2011 (six months after the date of enactment). As of the same effective date, and at least once every six years thereafter, shareholders must be afforded the right to vote on whether a say-on-pay vote occurs once every one, two or three years.

A company's say-on-pay vote covers the compensation shown in its CD&A and Compensation Tables (including narrative disclosures). Effective communications with shareholders is especially important in connection with a say-on-pay vote. Before a vote a company should make an effort to address potential shareholder concerns with the goal of obtaining strong majority approval. After either a negative vote or one with a narrow approval margin, outreach to large shareholders to obtain their feedback can help the company understand shareholders' concerns so that they can be addressed.

Advisory or not, a failure to respond effectively to a high level of dissatisfaction may result in "withhold" or "against" votes regarding the re-election of compensation committee members.

Say on Parachutes

Executive compensation payments and other benefits triggered by a change in control of the organization (golden parachutes) are common at U.S. companies. However, well-publicized examples of particularly large payments to executives sparked controversy over the authorization of what some perceived to be overly executive-friendly arrangements. The initiatives regarding say on pay ultimately led to the related requirement of disclosure and a nonbinding shareholder vote regarding executive compensation arrangements related to proposed change-in-control transactions — coined "say-on-parachute" votes. The disclosure for a say-on-parachute vote is required in any proxy for a shareholders meeting at which shareholders are asked to approve an acquisition, merger, consolidation or proposed sale of all (or substantially all) of the company's assets. A say-on-parachute vote is not required if the parachute arrangements already have been subject to such a vote, although the conditions imposed by the regulations regarding this provision limit its utility.

Compensation Committee Consultants and Other Advisers

Two critical and related issues involve the ability of a compensation committee to engage compensation consultants, legal counsel and other advisers, and the independence of any advisers so retained. Dodd-Frank contains separate provisions that authorize a compensation committee to retain a compensation consultant, independent legal counsel and other advisers, with the committee to "be directly responsible for the appointment, compensation and oversight." A company is required to provide appropriate funding, as determined by the compensation committee, for any advisers so retained. With respect to compensation consultants (but not the other advisers), proxy disclosure is required regarding whether the compensation committee has retained a compensation consultant, whether that consultant's work led to any conflict of interest, the nature of any conflicts and how those conflicts are being addressed.

With respect to independence, a compensation committee "may only select a compensation consultant, legal counsel or other adviser ... after taking account the factors identified by the [SEC]...." The SEC's rulemaking identified factors that may affect independence, and the securities exchanges subsequently adopted listing standards within the bounds of the SEC rules, including six general factors contained in the SEC's rules. After considering these factors and other considerations that it deems relevant, the compensation committee then is free to select a compensation adviser but must disclose how it has resolved any potential conflicts.

Pay-for-Performance Disclosure

Dodd-Frank mandated that the SEC craft rules that require a public company to disclose in the proxy statement for its annual share-holder meeting a "clear description" that "shows the relationship between executive compensation actually paid and the financial performance" of the company, taking into account any changes in the value of the company's stock and any dividends and distributions. The disclosure may include a graphic representation of the required information. As expected by most experts, the SEC's rulemaking read the last portion of this statutory language as a requirement to discuss performance in terms of TSR.

Some companies have developed their own analyses of the relationship between executive pay and performance to enhance their proxy disclosures; Figure 14-2 is one such approach. With the SEC's rulemaking efforts in mind, publicly traded companies ultimately will need to address pay-versus-performance disclosures. In addition to discussions of performance related to TSR, companies may find it useful to present and explain performance using other metrics. These comparisons often involve trends in either reported or realized/realizable compensation versus company performance on an absolute basis (e.g., year-over-year growth) or relative (performance versus peers). In any case, since the relationship of executive pay and

FIGURE 14-2

Approach for Additional Pay-Versus-Performance Disclosures

Is plan aligned with company financial performance

If not, explain why and what adjustments will be made

If so, explain the evidence to show alignment

What financial measures determine success and why do they work?

Carefully consider how to accurately and persuasively present pay-for-performance programs in the proxy performance is of particular interest to investors, a company generally should address the issue in an executive summary of the CD&A.

CEO Pay Ratio Disclosure

In an effort to address the debate about internal pay equity, Dodd-Frank imposed an especially burdensome provision requiring the SEC to mandate a new compensation ratio pay disclosure. The required disclosure (applicable for various SEC filings, not simply a company's annual proxy statement) consists of three items:

- The median of the "annual total compensation" of all of the company's employees except its CEO
- The CEO's total annual compensation
- The ratio of the two numbers.

A company with many employees in low-wage countries likely will find that its pay ratio is significantly higher than at an otherwise comparable company whose employees are concentrated in high-wage countries. In its final rules adopted in August 2015, the SEC provided that the comparison of CEO pay was to be made to that of the company's median employee. Much of the SEC's rulemaking was devoted to how a company may determine such median employee and then that individual's compensation. Other than some limited exceptions, all employees (including non-U.S. and part-time employees) need to be considered in determining the median employee. In addition to the required disclosures, companies can include additional information that may provide context regarding the company's pay practices and the reported pay ratio.

Clawback Policy

Dodd-Frank requires public companies to develop, implement and disclose what is commonly called a "clawback policy" for the recovery (from current and former executive officers) of incentive compensation based on certain financial information where there has been a required accounting restatement due to material noncompliance with a financial reporting requirement. At a minimum, in the event of a restatement, a company needs to recoup any excess incentive-based payments made based on inaccurate information in the previous three years. The required timing of a company's compliance with these standards is tied to the effective date of final SEC rules on such recoveries and the company's fiscal year.

In general, the clawback rules under Dodd-Frank are considerably broader than the clawback provisions of Sarbanes-Oxley. For example, Dodd-Frank's clawback provisions apply to any executive officer (not just the CEO and CFO), do not require any misconduct (just simply the requisite restatement), and cover a three-year (rather than 12-month) period. Key features of a clawback policy under Dodd-Frank include who is subject to the policy, the triggers for a recovery, and what elements of compensation are subject to the policy. While clawback policies have become a widespread and best practice, every existing policy will need to be reviewed and updated for compliance with final SEC rulemaking.

Consideration should be given not only to the Dodd-Frank requirements, but also to any additional features or processes that address the organization's particular circumstances or facilitate administration. A company complying with best practices might extend its clawback policy to recoup excess compensation paid as a result of (a) ethical misconduct, or (b) a restatement of financial statements unrelated to changes in accounting rules or interpretations.

Employee and Director Hedging

Under Dodd-Frank, the SEC must require each public company to disclose in its annual proxy statement whether any employee (not just an executive officer) or board member is permitted to purchase financial instruments "designed to hedge or offset any decrease in the market value of equity securities" granted as compensation or otherwise owned by such employee or director. Because equity hedging strategies can enable an employee or director to limit the effect of holding requirements commonly imposed on top executives and directors, the provision aims to shed light on any such actions and indirectly encourages companies to bar or limit such hedging. Even before Dodd-Frank, SEC rules already called for the disclosure of policies regarding hedging; one notable effect of the legislative provision is the extension of such disclosure to all employees as well as directors.

Investors increasingly expect companies to implement and enforce anti-hedging and anti-pledging policies. While prior transactions may be difficult to unwind, companies should adopt prospective policies against hedging and generally pledging. If no policy exists, companies should explain how they mitigate risk associated with these practices.

Perquisites

Perquisites continue to be scrutinized by shareholders (as discussed in Chapter 9). In light of years of reduction or elimination of various perks, the trend is toward limiting perquisites to those that directly relate to legitimate corporate purposes. Companies should be prepared to explain how perks are justifiable; examples have been ones that directly assist the executive in focusing on his/her company responsibilities, or enhance the security and health of the executive and his/her family.

Double-Trigger Equity Vesting

As discussed in Chapter 11, double-triggers have become the favored approach regarding both cash payments and equity vesting in connection with a change in control. Such policies generally prevent payments of cash severance and accelerated vesting of equity (time and performance-based) upon a change in control unless the executive is terminated without cause or terminates employment for good reason within a specified time following a change in control. The market increasingly views double-trigger vesting as a "best practice" in compensation. Any company with a single-trigger change-in-control provision should explain in its proxy the rationale for the provision and why it is in the company's interests to maintain such a provision.

Disclosures Regarding Board Chair and CEO Structures

The SEC was directed by Dodd-Frank to issue rules requiring a public company to disclose in its annual proxy the reasons why the company has chosen either the same person to serve both as board chair and CEO or two different people to serve in those positions. Basically, Dodd-Frank provides a legislative mandate for what companies already were required to do under the SEC's proxy disclosure rules.

How to Approach Disclosures

In drafting proxy disclosures, companies should be careful to avoid embellishments that can prompt litigation. Disclose what is material, address what may be unfavorable, and explain why a program, award or provision works for your company, but be careful of "overselling." Tell your story the right way and don't forget to engage shareholders.

CHAPTER 15

Risk in Executive Compensation

By Dana Martin

Risk management in public companies continues to evolve following financial services crises and an ongoing public focus on executive compensation. The SEC took steps to inhibit executives from profiting through excessive risk-taking by requiring public companies to consider whether any of their compensation plans create risk-taking incentives and, if so, to disclose in their annual proxy whether a materially adverse effect on the company is reasonably likely. Risk management, not traditionally within the purview of the compensation committee, is now an important item on the committee's agenda.

Incentive plans encourage executives to aim for the maximum rewards permitted under the plan. While these plans seldom resemble the bonus arrangements that figured so prominently in the financial crisis, risk is, nonetheless, a necessary element in executive pay. How should companies and their compensation committees go about taking on the burden of risk-reward analysis and ongoing monitoring? What are the red flags that alert boards to a high-risk situation?

The best way to do this is through a balanced, fact-based approach that allows for a prudent exposure to risk without compromising sustainable long-term growth. The results, however, should not be so balanced that the creative spirit is curbed. Companies will not benefit from a watered-down incentive program in which the business needs and priorities unique to the company are not underlying factors. While risk-adapted incentive plans require a thorough and complex decision-making process, boards and management gain from internal effectiveness and enhanced external defensibility.

This chapter:

- Addresses the key questions compensation committees need to ask in determining if compensation programs potentially pose a business risk. There also is a checklist for risk assessment and a discussion of the role compensation systems played in the financial industry downturn.
- Discusses how a balanced approach to risk addresses pay elements and mix, LTIs, performance measures, goal setting and payout structures.
- Examines how the prevalence of performance awards in LTI plans may encourage risk-taking by executives.
- Offers an approach to benchmarking executive pay that supplements the usual two-dimensional snapshot approach with a third dimension that provides an in-depth analysis of executive pay under various scenarios over time.

Background to Risk in Executive Compensation

Public and regulatory attention remains on the design of certain executive pay incentives; the concern is that the structuring of the incentives may promote overly risky behavior in attempts to earn especially large payouts. As a result, the assessment and management of risk in executive compensation has been the subject of various legislative, regulatory and corporate governance initiatives intended to limit excessive risk. In designing and evaluating executive pay programs, risk now is a critical factor.

According to a common definition, "risk" involves the possibility of suffering harm or loss in the pursuit of an objective. The issue of risk in compensation programs typically has centered on the downside of the equation — the probability and consequences of failure. However, executive compensation programs historically focused on the positive side with little regard for the potential negative outcomes. Business decisions should be made to create an appropriate balance between risk and return — not to maximize both. During difficult times, shareholders look to the board of directors for guidance on these difficult issues.

Following the debacles at Enron and WorldCom at the start of this century, there were concerns that the boards of these companies (and no doubt at many others as well) did not fully understand the complexity of the company's financial structure. As a result, Sarbanes-Oxley was enacted to force corporate boards to address weaknesses in financial controls. In fact, one of the most significant effects of the statute was to require that a qualified financial expert be included as head of the audit committee at a public company. This, in turn, drove significant changes in board composition, qualifications and compensation.

Financial difficulties later in that decade directed blame in a different direction — failed risk oversight by the board. Risk management failures have been viewed as a leading cause of economic problems. A consensus developed that one of the drivers of overly risky business decisions was the highly leveraged design of pay programs in the banking and financial services sector.

In the past, the management of risk generally was lodged in the audit committee or the full board. As a result of the focus on the effect of incentives on behavior, compensation committees have had to evaluate executive compensation in a new light and address the age-old link between risk and reward.

Going Forward

The issue of determining performance risk and factoring in time horizons adds complexity to the design of executive compensation programs. Some suggest the use of long holding periods for equity awards to focus on the creation of long-term value. Other techniques may involve fail-safes such as bonus banks or clawbacks so that organizations can recoup some of the incentive pay they have disbursed if a longer time horizon shows performance results actually were poor.

In aligning pay incentives with risk management, compensation committees need to monitor compensation programs and any potential link to risky behavior. To properly manage risk, companies also must provide greater authority to risk managers.

Programs that have features similar to the following can be considered high-risk and suspect in the current compensation environment:

- Low salary relative to incentive (e.g., 10 percent salary/90 percent incentive mix)
- Focus on annual performance rather than long-term sustained results ("swing for the fences" behavior)
- Uncapped upside
- Excessive use of stock options
- Use of multi-year recruiting guarantees.

Other quasi-regulatory bodies also have become involved. As part of its evaluation of business strength and financial condition, Standard & Poor's added an enterprise risk management assessment. Certainly there is a need to be more aware of the potential risks in designing compensation programs. Compensation committees should undertake a formal evaluation of compensation policies and practices to determine their potential effect on enterprise risk.

While few compensation plans promote the level of risk that was historically built into Wall Street's incentive structure, there are other elements of risk that can harm the company short of bankruptcy, a forced sale or a total collapse. To name a few:

- Exposure to criticism/public image with shareholders and customers
- Difficulty with proxy voting on proposals regarding executive compensation and/or share availability
- Board embarrassment, particularly regarding severance arrangements
- Having to make payments for chance occurrences or were wildly disproportionate to the value created.

Key questions for a compensation committee involve both philosophy and design.

Do Plans Reflect Strategy?

Are the metrics aligned to promote balance between short- and long-term objectives? Many banking practices were entirely focused on short-term behavior and results. Going forward, this is viewed as inappropriate in most cases.

Does the Compensation Committee Understand All Potential Scenarios?

For example, has there been a conscious and detailed analysis of all executive compensation plans (severance and CIC payments as well as incentives) to understand the complexities and potential consequences of certain events and decisions? The use of tally sheets enables compensation committees to approach executive compensation decisions by evaluating the overall combined exposure to the company from all sources.

Further, the compensation committee should take a careful look at the possible behaviors and business decisions that would trigger large payouts. A common example might be plans that could encourage executives to look for risky acquisitions to promote top-line growth at the expense of returns. Similarly, CIC payments may be so rich as to drive strategy, regardless of whether they are in the best interests of the shareholders.

Is There Too Much Weight on One Metric?

Good plan design suggests that there be balance in the metrics selected (e.g., a combination of growth, profitability and sustainable returns). The risk here is that too much emphasis on one issue can significantly detract from, or even impede progress on, other important performance metrics.

Are the Plans Diluted With Too Many Metrics?

Is there a risk that the plans are so balanced that they fail to provide direction or proper weighting to strategic objectives?

Is the Leverage in Executive Compensation Reasonable?

In at least the financial services sector, the traditional view of executive compensation was that "high risk, high reward" was a good thing. Plans in many cases were designed with significantly escalating rewards for performance. While there may be sound reasons for high levels of award opportunity in some cases, events have demonstrated the need for compensation committees to evaluate the risk of promoting excessive and risky business activities in search of the "big score."

Are Controls in Place to Mitigate Risk in Executive Compensation?

Checks and balances to consider include:

- Clawbacks for payment in prior years that ultimately were shown to have been unearned or based on financials that had to be restated (perhaps including events that extend beyond the parameters set in Dodd-Frank).
- Consideration of "bonus banks" to smooth out the variability in annual payouts and provide the company with a vehicle for reversing previously "earned" bonuses.
- Multi-year performance periods (three years or more) rather than excessive focus on short-term gains.
- Holding requirements on shares/meaningful ownership guidelines (even up to and after retirement).
- Caps on plan upside to limit the potential for unexpected or windfall payouts.

Once a thorough assessment of compensation is completed, the compensation committee can evaluate the effect of plan features relative to the risk factors involved. In speaking about risk in October 2008, John White, at that time the head of the SEC Corporation Finance Division (but expressing his own views), phrased the risk disclosure issue in words that still ring true:

"Ask yourself this question: Would it be prudent for compensation committees, when establishing targets and creating incentives, not only to discuss how hard or how easy it is to meet the incentives, but also to consider the particular risks an executive might be incentivtized to take to meet the target — with risk, in this case, being viewed in the context of the enterprise as a whole?"

What Changes in Executive Pay Arrangements Are Occurring (or Are Likely to Occur) as a Result of the Focus on Risk?

While most executive compensation plans are not a threat to the business, there have been some changes in the overall framework of best practices in executive pay design.

- Shift to a longer-term focus in plan design and a more rigorous alignment of payment to the timing of the result. In reference to the risky acquisition strategy noted earlier, rewards may be matched to the timing of expected corporate benefits, not at the close of the deal.

- Changes in plan design that reduce the impact of single metrics. It is not uncommon to find similar measures used in both short- and long-term incentives. Although neither plan may be excessive in itself, the double usage may concentrate risk and create problems.

- Greater consideration of both absolute and relative performance measures. Over-reliance on one or the other can result in unintended payout results.

- Increased use of modeling tools so that compensation committees can better understand the potential effect of compensation decisions. Had the directors at financial companies better understood the disastrous effects of a down economy combined with high leverage, the painful consequences at many companies might have been limited or even avoided.

- Greater attention to plan caps and more modest leverage in plan design. Companies have recognized the usefulness of compensation committee discretion — especially negative discretion — in plan awards to address not only what was achieved, but also how it was attained.

- A continuing re-evaluation regarding the use of stock options. Stock options are a form of compensation with high potential returns, but with no real downside prior to exercise.

- More consideration of compensation risk as part of the overall board risk-assessment process. This has been the central theme in the current focus on risk in the compensation process.

A concern in the current focus on risk is that it may have a negative effect (hopefully temporary) on the creativity and entrepreneurial spirit that has propelled U.S. business success. There needs to be a continued emphasis on taking reasonable risks and aligning the rewards with the gains produced.

Risk Assessment: Initial Process and Checklist

Risk and reward are the two ends of the compensation spectrum. Compensation committees have continuously tried to balance these components — risk (in the form of stretch goals) and reward (enough to make the risk worthwhile). But how much is too much? The SEC requires all public companies to evaluate their risks from compensation arrangements.

The SEC's rules require that every publicly held company discuss in its annual proxy statement whether any of its compensation plans or practices (for executives and nonexecutives) create risk-taking incentives that are reasonably likely to have a material adverse effect on the organization. From a practical viewpoint, the result is that every public company needs to examine each of its compensation programs to:

- Be assured that no such potential risks exist, and
- Fix or otherwise mitigate any potential risks that may be uncovered.

Organizations and compensation committees must develop a process to assess and then manage the possible risks posed by the compensation programs they maintain or oversee. As part of the initial process, it is useful to develop a checklist to guide the analysis. However, any process and checklist needs to be tailored to a company's specific circumstances — real thought and analysis are needed, not simply a "check-the-box" compliance mentality. The initial process for assessing risk involves:

- Creating a project team (which might well include a senior risk officer, inside and outside legal counsel, a senior HR or compensation officer, and a compensation consultant) to assess the level of risk for each of the distinct compensation programs to be reviewed against a key set of criteria.

- Collecting and reviewing the organization's existing written and unwritten pay policies, practices and plan documents as well as similar items pertaining to the company's enterprise risk management.

- Conducting the compensation risk assessment and identifying for the compensation committee the risks that the organization faces that could threaten its value or have a material financial, operational or reputation effect on the company. Identify the features of the organization's executive and nonexecutive compensation policies, practices and supporting management processes that could induce executives and employees to take those risks.

- Analyzing the results of the risk assessment and discussing how to mitigate and manage any such excessive risks, and/or establishing a process and timetable for revising those compensation and incentive programs that contain excessive risks.

Checklist for Risk Assessment

Table 15-1 is a sample checklist containing generally relevant criteria for use in assessing the risk profile of compensation programs. To determine the risk exposure of each program, consider determining the potential probability and cost of a worst-case scenario. It is helpful to characterize (or rank) potential cost and risk on a grid as high, moderate and low, at times using a red, yellow and green "stoplight gap analysis" as a visual means for characterizing and addressing levels of risk.

Review

The financial industry crisis spawned an increased focus on potential risk in compensation programs. Companies, regulators and advisers all attempted to address the various factors that contribute to risk in compensation programs, but many important issues still remain. For instance (and most basically), there is no universal definition of what is meant by "risk." While the SEC has eased the reporting burden for public companies by limiting required disclosure to risks that are "reasonably likely to have a material adverse effect on the company," the core issue remains.

TABLE 15-1

Risk Assessment Checklist	Risk managed effectively	Caution	Risk not managed effectively
		(Check one)	
Alignment and balance in performance metrics			
Is there risk in division or subsidiary reward performance metrics not aligning with corporate reward metrics?			
Is there a risk in one financial measure dominating employee focus at the expense of other key performance measures?			
Is there a risk in short-term measures dominating employee focus at the expense of long-term performance measures?			
Overall:			
Corporate financial protection and use of hurdles			
What is the degree of risk in team and individual goals requiring incentive payouts in a year when the corporate entity did not meet baseline financial or profit-ability goals?			
Are hurdles appropriately set that balance corporate protection and reasonable prob-ability of an incentive payout?			
Overall:			
Alignment of pay with market competitiveness			
What is the degree of risk in organization pay levels and target earning opportunities not aligning with marketplace practices?			
Is there risk in eligibility criteria not being consistent internally?			
Overall:			
Impact on motivation and engagement			
What is the degree of risk in current incen-tive plans not providing optimal motivation and results?			
Are employees aware of and committed to the principles behind the intent of the incentive plan?			
Overall:			

Risk Assessment Checklist	Risk managed effectively	Caution	Risk not managed effectively
		(Check one)	
Appropriate use of management discretion			
What is the degree of risk in the usage of management discretion in incentive plan payouts where the criteria may or may not directly align with corporate performance?			
Are the principles and rules of discretion consistently known and applied?			
Overall:			
Plan effectiveness			
What is the degree of risk in incentive plans not being perceived as effective and motivational by managers and employees?			
Overall:			

Upon review of a company's proxy statement by the SEC (perhaps as part of the SEC's triennial reviews), a failure to show the company conducted a risk assessment in compliance with these rules could prompt queries on specific programs. Aside from any input or feedback from the SEC, ideas are exchanged among companies and their advisers. Reasonable approaches also are developed after considering information disclosed in filings during the most recent proxy season. In any case, the initial process and checklist provide a solid starting framework for a company's compensation plan risk assessment.

Executive Pay for Sustainable Performance: Restoring Investor Trust

Investors increasingly require that executive pay be tied to sustainable performance measured by economic profit to take account of both total capital deployed and risk. Companies must develop effective risk management practices and review employee rewards to ensure sustainable performance.

Despite unprecedented fiscal and monetary interventions by governments and central banks, the global economy remains highly volatile. Uncertainty in markets persists because investor and creditor trust remains significantly impaired. Investors now are demanding from management greater transparency, accountability and long-term performance sustainability than ever before. But transparency in financial services is a difficult goal to attain. Financial instruments are pioneered daily, and it is difficult to adequately describe the complexities of a single transaction, let alone a diverse global portfolio. The continuing debate on marking-to-market focuses on this issue and is further complicated by the significant claims attached to any one asset at any point in time.

Keeping Rewards in Context

Rewards systems have certainly contributed to the problem and need to be radically overhauled. However, changing rewards so that executives suffer if there is a financial crisis is not the whole solution. Financial crises are infrequent, so they only affect the executives in place at the time; they are also generally (almost by definition) not anticipated, so the possibility of a collapse tends not to affect executive behavior. Therefore, in addition to changing rewards:

- Financial services companies must continue to improve their risk assessment and ensure that they are not betting the company on a single investment or on investments that are likely to be correlated in an economic or financial crisis. Given the long timescales, this has to be a governance and regulatory responsibility, not driven by rewards — although part of top executive rewards should be for doing this well.

- Companies also need to build up reserves against the inevitable losses from time to time, as insurance companies do. Arguably the excess of the risk-adjusted required return over the risk-free rate is an "insurance premium" that should be reserved against future losses, not paid out in bonuses (or dividends).

Achieving Risk-Adjusted Rewards

Executive rewards must be based on measures of corporate performance that take account of the risks to shareholders' capital inherent in the business strategy. Notwithstanding complexity, investors will no longer be satisfied with the "too complicated" excuse on risk-adjusted performance management.

Corporate performance must be assessed based on a broad framework of interrelated metrics that influence current expectations. To succeed, the framework must first and foremost be economically sound. The "performance mathematics" must ensure that as levers are pressed, expected values are achieved and perceptions influenced accordingly. Second, it must be comprehensive and balanced. As Peter Drucker reminded us, "we manage what we measure." History is replete with pay-for-performance issues stemming from improvement in "measured" revenue growth offset by "non-measured" expansion in assets or risk. And finally, it must be easy to implement. If it cannot be readily understood and tracked by all stakeholders, it will not work.

Two measures that should be considered to tie executive pay to performance are TSR and economic profit (EP). TSR is a strong de facto measure of long-term corporate performance, despite the difficulties of defining a peer group to measure relative performance and the potential effect of short-term price fluctuations. EP is fundamentally the return on capital deployed net of its risk-adjusted cost. It is an essential measure because it ensures that return is calculated in the context of both the scale of capital deployed and its inherent riskiness. While this is a more complicated calculation for financial services companies because these companies are essentially "spread" businesses, EP can be superior to other metrics like earnings per share and EBITDA because these do not consider risk and capital deployed.

However, TSR and EP must be managed through a performance framework. Figure 15-1 is an example of a performance management framework that connects TSR and EP with actionable enterprise operating metrics. From a board and investor point of view, the

FIGURE 15-1

Performance Management Framework

framework provides a holistic approach that enables effective assessment of performance in the context of executive pay.

While this approach is not immune from the aforementioned issues of comparability and complexity, it is a useful paradigm for establishing a standardized approach to performance management. Investors have made clear that a failure to tackle the problem will no longer be tolerated. The restoration of trust begins with executive pay for sustainable risk-adjusted performance.

Designing Incentive Plans in Today's Risk Environment

Incentive plans continue to receive increased scrutiny, sometimes even cast as the villain in organizations' rewards programs. In particular, incentive programs have been cited as a cause of excessive risk-taking for short-term gains at the expense of long-term sustainable performance, which can ultimately contribute to business failures. However, incentive plans are essential for linking pay with performance, placing needed emphasis on critical near-term and long-term business priorities and motivating employees to achieve challenging goals. Based on studies and work with clients, balance seems to be a key to designing incentive plans that accomplish these objectives, but also mitigate unhealthy risk.

The primary objective of a balanced program is to ensure that no single compensation element is driving a specific outcome at the expense of other key outcomes. Where do we look for balance? Some answers can include:

- Pay elements and mix
- LTI elements
- Performance measures
- Goal-setting
- Incentive payout design.

Pay Elements and Mix

We begin by looking for balance in the overall mix of compensation elements. Not only do we assess the competitiveness of each element of pay, but attention also is focused on the mix of pay.

- How much is being delivered in fixed versus variable pay?
- What is the ratio of short-term compensation versus long-term compensation?
- How much is delivered in cash versus equity?

Many of the answers depend upon the roles and levels within the organization. For executives, a large percentage of the total pay mix is typically delivered in long-term, variable pay. Because many positions below the executive level do not have the same line of sight to long-term results, fixed base pay typically becomes a larger portion of the mix as one travels down in the organization. Similarly, the focus generally is more on variable annual incentives rather than on long-term programs in moving down from the senior-executive level.

A growing number of companies are delivering a portion of annual incentive earnings in the form of deferred stock or "banking" the bonuses for payout at some point in the future based on future performance. These features further reduce the incentive for risky behavior to achieve unsustainable short-term gains.

LTI Elements

There are several choices regarding LTIs, each serving a unique purpose with its own set of advantages and disadvantages. Stock options and stock appreciation rights link directly to shareholder interests and are of value only when the share price increases; however, these can be a temptation for inappropriate risk-taking to achieve the increases. Time-based restricted stock provides opportunities for ownership and serves as a retention device, but it can be viewed as a giveaway. Performance-based share and cash plans align with critical strategic performance, but it can be difficult to set challenging yet realistic long-term goals in light of market uncertainties.

When it comes to managing risk, once again balance generally is the best approach. Our research has found that most large public companies are taking a portfolio approach to LTIs, making grants in two or even three vehicles.

Performance Measures

Performance measures are arguably one of the most difficult aspects of incentive plan design. Choosing the right metrics in the right combination can stymie even the best of experts. There are some general rules, however, when it comes to managing for risk and, not surprisingly, a critical one is about balance.

Incentive plans, whether short- or long-term, that use multiple metrics (particularly more than one financial/operating metric) reduce the risk of driving performance of one metric to the detriment of other measures that are important to the long-term success and viability of the company. Metrics that present a balanced view of how the organization is performing are favored, particularly combinations of profitability, growth and sustained return measures, and reduced reliance on top-line growth measures. Additionally, it is important to consider qualitative measures that emphasize strategic priorities.

Goal-Setting

Another challenge in the design of an incentive program is being able to forecast company performance (especially for periods longer than a year) and setting goals at the right level. If performance goals are not set appropriately, there can be negative consequences.

Generally speaking, goals should be challenging, but attainable. If goals are set too high, we see two alternative unsatisfactory outcomes:

- Executives may not be motivated if they perceive there is little likelihood of achieving the targets.
- Executives may take excessive risks to try to reach very difficult goals.

Conversely, if goals are set too low and the incentive plan is paying out more frequently and at higher levels than is intended, the company is at risk of paying incentives for mediocre (or even poor) performance and not achieving an appropriate return on its investment.

There are two basic approaches companies can use in setting standards:

- **Absolute.** Goals are set based on the company's year-over-year performance and/or budgets. An internal approach requires a strong planning process and is difficult in industries in which external events can have a dramatic effect on results. Performance goals are usually effective when there is rigor around the goal-setting process and the goals are based on the company's strategic and operating objectives.
- **Relative.** Goals are focused on how a company performs relative to its competitors or peers. A relative or external approach measures the company against direct competitors that are affected by similar macro-economic factors and compete in the same market or with the same products. This approach mitigates the risk of setting the goals too high or too low. However, the approach can sometimes result in unintended payouts: If a company outperforms the majority of its peers, it is nevertheless possible that it produced negative value for shareholders, including negative profitability or negative total shareholder return.

Plans that allow management and the compensation committee to use discretion in determining achievement of results, and ultimately the corresponding payouts, further mitigate risk. Plans that are entirely formulaic are viewed as contributing to the potential for risk and unintended, negative consequences for the company. More and more, companies are also including clawback features (even beyond the strictures of the Dodd-Frank Act) to recoup incentive awards that may be deemed in the future to be based on unearned performance results or financials that later were restated.

Incentive Payout Design

In designing incentive arrangements, one critical item is the structure of the relationship between performance and payouts. Typically this is a range, from threshold to maximum, with incremental pay for incremental performance. To mitigate risk, the program should have upside and downside potential. All-or-nothing plans, whereby a participant receives a fixed award for achieving a target level of performance, but nothing for just missing the target, are viewed as contributing to potentially risky behavior. Additionally, the slope of the line (i.e., the relationship between performance levels and the associated payouts) can vary. Flatter slopes that require greater performance for incremental payouts are generally more appropriate in today's risk environment, but must be balanced so that stretches in performance are not unrealistic.

One of the most important features in the payout design, when it comes to risk, is limiting the upside potential with a predetermined maximum level of performance and payout (capping the plan). Caps prevent windfall earnings that may not represent achievements attributable to management or may be from unsustainable levels of performance. Another important feature that mitigates the risk of a company making payouts when it cannot afford to do so is a financial trigger. The trigger typically is established as a minimum level of corporate-wide profitability (or similar measure) that must be achieved before any incentive payouts can be made. The cap and trigger can work in tandem to provide balance in the overall payout structure and mitigate potentially risky scenarios.

Be Careful Balancing

So, balance is good. But can there be too much balance? The key is to achieve balance in the areas where the risk outweighs the benefits.

Beware of watering down your overall program and losing focus. Achieving balance at the expense of putting in the right program that will motivate and retain your people could reduce the return on your investment.

There is no one right way to design an incentive plan. There are a variety of plan designs that work well in different companies for different reasons. The organization's rewards strategy, and the purpose and intent of the incentive programs, should guide the design of the plans to ultimately drive performance.

Benchmarking Executive Pay: The Third Dimension

It can be reasonably argued that making decisions on executive pay is one of the most important responsibilities of the board, and in particular is the most important responsibility of the compensation committee. If nothing else, decisions on executive pay are certainly one of the most visible, and can be one of the most controversial, decisions made at the board level. Each year the annual proxy of a public company must disclose how much each of the top five executives is paid, how the incentive compensation plans work, and why each element of pay was included. Further, the proxy must include an assessment of the risk level built into the incentive plans in order to disclose, as previously noted in this chapter, whether any incentive plans that "are reasonably likely to have a material adverse effect on the company." "High risk, high reward" is no longer considered a reasonable compensation strategy (if it ever was).

Executive pay has always been a subject of interest in the popular press. Following each proxy season the leading newspaper in nearly every major U.S. city publishes a story on the most highly paid CEOs in the area. The data may not always be accurate, but is almost always the source of serious discussion and shareholder activism.

Since 2011 public companies are required to provide shareholders with an opportunity to vote on the overall executive pay package via say on pay. The vote is advisory and nonbinding and, in theory, could be ignored by the board. But what responsible board could ignore the will of the shareholders? And if it did, how long would the shareholders continue to elect them to the board? Shareholder activist groups are already taking an active role in shaping the votes, and in some cases shareholders have filed suit against the company and against individual members of the board as a result of failed say-on-pay results. Nonbinding indeed!

The Problem

Given this environment, boards — particularly compensation committees — must be certain that they are following a rigorous, fact-based approach to decisions on pay. As part of this process, most committees engage an independent third party to provide data on market pay levels, short- and long-term incentive plan design and provide advice on what may be appropriate for their company. The core of this information typically is a detailed proxy study that compares the value of the package offered to company executives relative to the value provided to executives at a select group of peer companies.

The common analysis of executive pay follows a two-dimensional approach.

- The first dimension is simply the value offered to peer group executives — base salary, annual and long-term cash incentives and the grant-date fair value of equity grants. This dimension provides a snapshot of what was paid.

- The second dimension provides the committee with the mix of pay elements — how much of the value was provided by cash, stock options, restricted shares, performance shares, restricted stock units and other incentive vehicles. This dimension can be illustrated by a pie-chart that can illustrate how much of the executive pay is fixed (base salary, restricted shares) and how much is performance-based, at-risk.

But in looking at this market snapshot, are committees getting a full and true picture of the competitive landscape and the potential risks inherent in any compensation plan? We think not.

As a simple example, assume two executive pay packages as set out in Table 15-2. In looking at this data, the casual observer may conclude that these executives are paid the same, when clearly

TABLE 15-2

Comparison of Composition of Pay Packages

	Executive 1	Executive 2
Base	$1,000,000	$1,000,000
Target annual incentive	$500,000	$500,000
Option grant	0	$1,000,000
Restricted share grant	$1,000,000	0
Grant date price	$10	$10
Total value	$2,500,000	$2,500,000

the realized value of what they will earn as their equity grants mature may be very different based on factors such as market change and performance.

Although the grant value of equity is the same (in dollars) based on the concept of fair value, the number of shares used for an option grant will typically be greater than that of a restricted share grant. For this example, assume an option on three shares deliver the same fair value as one restricted share, which means:

- Executive 1 would receive 100,000 restricted shares
- Executive 2 would receive 300,000 stock options.

As the share price changes over the term of the award, the value to the executive differs substantially. Thus, assuming both grants will be fully vested after three years, Table 15-3 illustrates the different outcomes of two executive compensation packages depending on the level of the change in the price of the company's shares.

Clearly, these alternative grant strategies do not produce the same effect, and as an issue of good corporate governance, compensation committees need to be aware of the effect that plan design can have on value. Specifically, as an enhancement to the traditional proxy analysis, good corporate governance might suggest that these committees also look at the volatility of potential outcomes — the third dimension.

TABLE 15-3

Comparison of Outcomes of Pay Packages

	Executive 1	Executive 2
	100,000	300,000
Potential price change	Shares' value	Options' value[1]
95%	$950,000	$0
100%	$1,000,000	$0
110%	$1,100,000	$300,000
120%	$1,200,000	$600,000
150%	$1,500,000	$1,500,000
200%	$2,000,000	$3,000,000

[1] Value expressed as actual realized value, not Black-Scholes

What Is the Third Dimension?

The third dimension is a method of evaluating not just the snap-shot, but the potential outcomes of plan design given a number of different stock performance scenarios over time. Using data provided in company proxies, a careful analysis can determine the effect of plan design on each executive's total compensation (base salary, annual and LTIs and retirement benefits/deferred compensation). Data can be provided for the NEOs both in the absolute and relative to peer companies.

The Range of Outcomes

Figure 15-2 provides an array of potential outcomes expressed in dollar values highlighting the potential exposure of the company to unexpected costs, as well as the potential values of the compensation plan relative to competitors.

Why Is This Analysis Critical to the Compensation Committee?

As discussed, the simple answer is it provides the committee with an in-depth look at executive pay over time, not just a snapshot approach common to most compensation reports. In addition, having this data is consistent with the general trend in compensation disclosure requirements for more analysis and consideration of "what if"

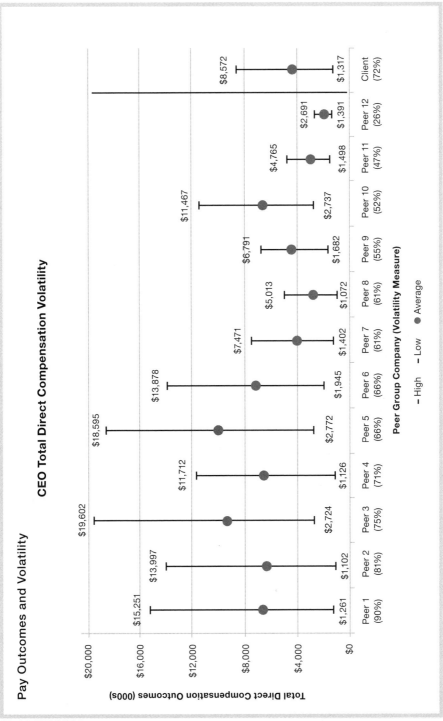

Pay Outcomes and Volatility

CEO Total Direct Compensation Volatility

FIGURE 15-2

scenarios. Best practice already expects that the committee will look at tally sheets to review executive pay in its totality. How much better to add performance scenarios and outcomes?

It also provides the committee with a more robust illustration of compensation risk for the required disclosure in the annual proxy statement. Too much risk and leverage creates an incentive for risky (and ethically challenged) behavior from executives. Too little risk and leverage may create a competitive disadvantage and/or internal dissatisfaction with the alignment of executive rewards with the results delivered to shareholders.

Following the collapse in the financial services industry in the 2008–2009 economic downturn, many compensation committee members confessed that they had not fully grasped the potential impact of outcomes in highly speculative compensation plans. The volatility analysis suggested would have gone far in providing committees with full disclosure and may have helped prevent disaster.

While a "volatility of outcomes" discussion is not (yet) required as part of the proxy disclosure rules, the trend is clearly in the direction of more disclosure regarding the relationship between pay and performance. Shareholder groups are demanding visibility and Dodd-Frank requires that companies illustrate how the company performed regarding pay versus performance. Can it be long before progressive, well-governed companies begin showing not just what happened in the prior year, but what could happen? If nothing else, it provides a proactive defense for committees against legal action by disgruntled shareholders.

PART III

The CEO Life Cycle

Introduction

By Irv Becker and Christine Rivers

What is the CEO Life Cycle?

What is the most important concern of the board? Leadership continuity — and more specifically, ensuring the right CEO is in place — is the most important concern of the board. The board's most daunting set of responsibilities are the activities involving the CEO — succession, performance evaluation and compensation. We are calling this the CEO life cycle.

If it were up to many directors, they would just as easily delegate these functions — and in many cases they do. Sadly, this delegation is often made to the CEO him/herself who, as discussed in the next three chapters, is not the person who should be doing this work.

However, progressive and well-governed boards not only face these activities head-on, but they proactively manage them. That is, boards need to build the related tasks into their calendars and develop processes around them to ensure these efforts receive the focused attention they deserve.

What Does This Look Like?

It begins when the necessary components of the CEO life cycle — succession, performance evaluation and compensation — that are part of the standing agenda of every board meeting. Not just when the issue is imminent, but ongoing. There is a process based on trust and candor that begs for real conversations. When the CEO and members of the board (usually the chair or a lead director) have ongoing performance-related discussions, matters tend to stay on track. It becomes what they do, what they talk about, what they worry about. It can be as simple as, "How are you doing? How are things going? What is getting in the way?"

Part of the process is the board doing its own intelligence-gathering. This may include visiting headquarters and other field locations, observing and interacting, so that engaging in conversations with other members of the C-suite becomes a natural component of the way the board works. It's not micro-management; rather, it's keeping the lines of communication open.

Lastly, it's rooted in the strategy. Whether it's succession planning, performance evaluation or compensation, the strategy is the foundation — otherwise it's not relevant. When the strategy is the starting point, the questions become, "Are we prioritizing the right things? Is the CEO spending his/her time on the right activities? Is the board ensuring alignment of strategy to compensation, performance evaluation and the profile of the next CEO?"

When the board ensures this laser-like focus on the three components of the life cycle, the organization's probability of success exponentially increases. It's holistic, integrated and relevant.

Optimize Organizational Effectiveness

The activities discussed above are the tangible aspects of the CEO life cycle — the work the board must do. But how should the board act? How can boards approach these pursuits in a way that enhances meaning, ensures greater purpose and optimizes organizational effectiveness?

The answer lies in the way the board and the CEO interact, the relationship they have, the relationship the board builds with the senior management team, the way the CEO brings information to the board and the intent of the CEO to engage the board in meaningful conversation. It's what occurs in-between the tangible, concrete activities that essentially make up the way they work together. The real value in aligning these activities is the ability to have one conversation, built on one foundation, that tells one story and has clear priorities, as the CEO and the board build trust and credibility together.

CHAPTER 16

CEO Evaluation

By Dave Wise and Stephanie Sloan

A key, but often overlooked, responsibility of the board of directors is to assess the performance of the CEO, which includes providing feedback and supporting continued growth and leadership development. When measuring CEO performance, boards and compensation committees ideally should have information that looks at CEO performance from several relevant perspectives, including both the "what" has been achieved and "how" the CEO has achieved it. Furthermore, boards should provide ongoing, regular feedback throughout the year to keep the CEO informed of how his/her performance is viewed by others and whether he/she is on track with expectations. All too often, boards fail to provide input on a regular basis and evaluate performance by primarily relying upon financial performance, neglecting just as relevant nonfinancial considerations. This chapter focuses on how boards can more effectively assess the CEO and provide relevant feedback to guide and improve performance.

This chapter:

- Explains how a formal performance management process, which includes regular check-ins and ongoing performance dialogue, leads to improved performance and a more collaborative CEO-board relationship.
- Maintains that nonfinancial assessment measures in combination with financial metrics can give a more complete picture of CEO performance.

■ Discusses how nonfinancial performance criteria can be gathered and measured to effectively approach CEO assessment.

Performance Evaluation Process

Effective evaluation of a CEO is a process, not an annual event. Establishing a clear performance appraisal and feedback process in the beginning, particularly with a new CEO, creates a clear standard of how the CEO and board will work together on an ongoing basis to share information and feedback. It also establishes the role that the board plays in governing how well the CEO is leading the business. If approached in a collaborative, supportive fashion, the performance appraisal process should lead to a strong relationship between the board and CEO. In that way, directors can effectively provide the guidance and wisdom necessary to steer the CEO through rocky times and build the trust needed to improve CEO performance. This reduces surprises and allows the CEO and board to establish comfort in a regular dialogue of how the organization is doing and particularly how the CEO is performing relevant to board expectations. We have seen too many times the situation when a CEO hears for the first time there are concerns with performance as he/she is "asked" to leave the company.

News stories describe far too many situations where the board, although concerned with the CEO's performance, made only half-hearted efforts at providing feedback. Then sometime later the company has a crisis, resulting in the CEO's dismissal and creating major trauma for the company and its people. In many cases this scenario is preventable through an appropriate CEO performance evaluation process and regular performance dialogue.

The process starts with being clear and aligned on the strategic intentions and objectives of the business. This clarity enables the board and CEO to establish a clearly articulated set of performance metrics that go beyond financial metrics. Once the metrics are identified, the process continues with:

■ Examining these metrics on a regular basis to discern how the company and the CEO are performing;

- Providing performance feedback throughout the year, so the CEO is well aware of how he/she is performing;
- Rewarding and incentivizing the successful accomplishment of these key indicators; and
- Considering other leaders who can carry out the business plan should the CEO exit the company for a foreseen or unforeseen reason (succession planning).

These efforts to establish a clear performance evaluation process, can pay huge dividends. An effective and well-managed CEO performance evaluation process:

- Creates a shared understanding of CEO performance expectations between the board and the CEO and sends a clear message regarding what the board considers important;
- Provides the platform for monitoring progress and providing ongoing discussions regarding performance throughout the year; and
- Enables the board and the CEO to communicate effectively on performance-related issues.

This approach also minimizes the angst and emotion around having an annual milestone performance event. As the board becomes more accustomed to this integrated and established approach, the evaluation of the CEO naturally becomes a continual endeavor and a central focus of board activity on a year-round basis. By doing so, performance discussions can happen regularly and involve an ongoing dialogue, ideally scheduled on a quarterly basis and built into the board calendar.

Performance Objectives Tied to Longer-Term Business Strategy

We believe boards should address the CEO's performance by anchoring the evaluation process squarely in the company's forward-looking strategic business and organizational priorities. By doing so, directors then become better able to manage the CEO Life Cycle — consisting of performance evaluation and the alignment of the CEO's compensation to short- and long-term performance objectives, as well as CEO succession.

In an ideal situation, the performance evaluation process is integrated into a successful onboarding process with a new CEO. This establishes clear roles and responsibilities at the outset and sets the stage for a stronger, more collaborative CEO-board relationship.

Regardless of when the evaluation process is created and implemented, boards must determine what they are trying to accomplish. What are the expectations for the CEO? What needs to be achieved this year that aligns with the longer-term strategy? What battles will the CEO be accountable for winning? How will those challenges and opportunities be quantified so that they can be measured?

These answers are found through the creation of a CEO role profile that is built upon the company's strategy. The CEO role profile is foundational to performance evaluation, as this strategic blueprint guides the evaluation and related incentives. The role profile articulates the strategic objectives that the CEO is expected to achieve both in the long- and short-term as well as the related CEO accountabilities. It defines what successful strategy execution actually looks like. Based on these clearly outlined strategic goals, performance metrics can be established that enable regular CEO evaluation and feedback.

These efforts articulate and drive priorities and enable the board and the CEO to gauge progress throughout the year. Boards can then evaluate the CEO against criteria that matter. And through regular reviews of the CEO's progress, directors will encourage evaluations that achieve clarity, consistency and the right outcomes.

Performance Measures

Today, when establishing objectives and measuring CEO performance, boards tend to over-rely on financial metrics to evaluate the CEO. Perhaps this is to be expected; financials are the most obvious way to assess how the organization, and by association the CEO, is performing. Financials are preferred as they typically are easy to quantify and less prone to generating debate about accuracy. However, in the current environment of heightened scrutiny and accountability, boards are increasingly concerned with both what was achieved and how it was accomplished.

Although a board must always hold CEOs accountable to the financial outcomes, we know that not everything a CEO does well will show up in annual financial results. For this reason, today's CEO metrics should include elements of strategy execution and organizational capability development. Board discussions about CEO performance evaluation should include financial metrics, but also talk about progress against key strategic milestones, like targeting a new market or changing the customer profile or even building talent capabilities to meet future changes in the business. These are the initiatives, whether they're in the incentive plan or not, that boards must review and provide regular feedback upon.

Financial Versus Nonfinancial Metrics

The CEO is responsible for the entire enterprise, so quantitative metrics like earnings per share or return on invested capital are good measures of his/her accomplishments. These financial measures, of course, are very important. They reflect the growth and profitability of the company and determine the amount of dividends that can be distributed to shareholders. Furthermore, these measures are numerical and objective, not easily open to manipulation and have a major effect on shareholder value.

However, financials are limited in gauging the extent of the organization's value creation process. By their nature, financials are lagging indicators and only tell part of the story. In case after case of corporate malfeasance, a CEO's need to drive financial metrics caused some individuals to cut corners.

A CEO can decide to sub-optimize one area to "make the numbers;" however, such a short-term fix is not a sustainable strategy. Further, a CEO can underspend on research and development, reduce capital expenditures or even "sell market share" through profit-boosting higher prices. Other short-term solutions include underpaying key resources or not providing them with the right career opportunities. Eventually these individuals will quit, undermining the organization's progress.

All of these actions potentially can destroy future value. It is typically only after these mistakes have snowballed that they come to light, all too often destroying shareholder equity and ruining careers in the process. Board members need to track a variety of performance measures in the CEO's scorecard, such as shaping the culture, developing leadership capabilities, and collaborating with the board and other constituencies. This can help ensure that short-term financial gains are not incentivized over long-term performance and sustainability metrics.

Today, more experienced boards are demanding increased accountability from CEOs for setting corporate culture, demonstrating organizational leadership, building organizational capability and sustainability, and demanding ethical behavior. While publicly traded companies also need to consider the objective, performance-based compensation requirements of IRC section 162(m), a board can help meet its oversight mandate by incorporating nonfinancial metrics into its evaluation of CEO performance.

Nonfinancial Metrics

Nonfinancial metrics are different from non-quantitative measures. Even if a measure is not financially driven, it can still be quantified and assessed. There still must be tangible, measurable targets set for goal achievement, in order for the process to work. For example, fuzzy objectives like "improved executive team morale" are difficult to measure and quantify. Specific goals such as "scores at or above the 75th percentile on the employee engagement survey compared to Fortune 500 norms" provide clearer targets for the CEO.

These nonfinancial metrics can be established at the beginning of the appraisal process through discussion between the board and the CEO about the business strategy and the implications for CEO evaluation. There should be concrete goals for CEOs who go beyond financial results and address core issues like those described below. By establishing these benchmarks, boards can clarify what they expect from the CEO to drive financial performance in both the short- and long-term. Through regular and accurate feedback against established benchmarks, boards can support CEOs in improving their performance on how objectives are achieved.

Nonfinancial measures could include:

- **Succession:** Has the CEO hired and developed a sufficient pipeline of talent to ensure orderly succession should key executives leave?
- **Values:** Has the CEO articulated and embodied a strong set of values that serves as the bedrock for organizational performance?
- **Diversity:** What steps has the CEO taken to ensure a diverse, inclusive and fair workplace?
- **Employee engagement:** How connected are the employees to the organization? What do turnover statistics and employee climate surveys reveal?
- **Strategy:** Has the CEO been able to create and align others with a compelling business strategy to take the organization forward in a competitive external business environment?
- **Structure:** What steps has the CEO taken to create the right structure to enable the company to execute the strategy?
- **Culture:** What cultural attributes are evident within the company? Is it the right culture to help execute the business strategy?
- **Customer satisfaction:** Are the company's customers satisfied with the company's products and services? Are key customers being retained?
- **Organizational capability:** Is the human capital of the organization being effectively developed for future success?
- **Core organization processes:** Are key operational processes being improved?

One example of a nonfinancial metric that can be used for CEO evaluation is the climate that the CEO creates for his/her top team and whether the CEO is maximizing the team's effectiveness and their talent potential. Research finds a strong relationship between leaders creating positive work climates and organizational performance. Through anonymous feedback collected from direct reports, the CEO can gain a better understanding of how the work atmosphere is enabling or undermining organizational performance.

Another option is to obtain feedback from a variety of key stakeholders. When using a 360-degree evaluation, the process should be inclusive in gathering data from a wide range of sources and protecting the anonymity of the respondents. Data should be gathered from multiple sources in evaluating the performance of a sitting CEO. The CEO has many constituencies, and it is important to be inclusive when evaluating his/her performance. Look to gather a variety of inputs in providing the most relevant data to help guide performance improvement. The board itself is one of the most important bases of performance improvement feedback.

Because the feedback from constituents is highly sensitive, the utmost care needs to be established in data collection and storage and deciding who is privy to the results. Data can be obtained using online collection tools or through the use of external consultants who can conduct confidential interviews, providing aggregate feedback to the CEO. At the beginning of the evaluation, it is critical to establish who will have access to the data and how it will be used.

In summary, CEOs are being evaluated continually on their business results by stakeholders and employees. The use of several types of measures is advisable in CEO evaluations. A confluence of data points increases the CEO's confidence in the accuracy of measurement. By employing multiple ways of measuring performance, the credibility of the conclusions is enhanced. By also adding nonfinancial metrics to the mix, CEOs can gain a more holistic view of their leadership and tease out the critical factors that contribute to their long-term leadership effectiveness.

Feedback

Performance evaluations and performance feedback are familiar to virtually all executives, including CEOs, in their rise to the top. Throughout their careers, CEOs have been rigorously evaluated and provided feedback on areas and opportunities for improvement. Somewhat surprisingly, however, once an individual becomes a CEO, the quantity and quality of such input often diminishes. In our experience, the performance evaluation process commonly becomes less thorough and less meaningful the more senior the executive.

Providing this input to anyone is never easy, and giving feedback to a CEO can be especially daunting. However, most modern CEOs developed in environments where performance feedback was provided, and that process should continue once an individual becomes a CEO. In fact, the quality of the performance feedback itself can directly affect the strength of the board-CEO relationship — as well as the success of the company.

Good executives are sensitive to the truism that "the higher you go, the less feedback you receive," and the best CEOs seek input from others to accurately gauge their performance. Unfortunately, direct reports can easily be intimidated by those senior to them and may not provide honest evaluations of the CEO even when invited, generally due to perceived career risk. An organization's board is in a unique position to provide evaluations and feedback regarding CEO performance, but frequently relies upon compensation itself to send that message. We would argue that compensation and related incentives can be used to support the desired messages, but shouldn't be used as the only medium to send the message: it cannot replace the dialogue needed to provide real feedback.

Furthermore, providing effective feedback should be a continual process, not a one-time annual event. If feedback is held back until a year-end evaluation, there could be unwelcome surprises that derail the positive spirit that should underlie the entire undertaking. However, if board members are able to provide input to the CEO on an ongoing basis, the likelihood of mid-course corrections increases.

The use of an objective third party may be helpful to provide the feedback and/or coaching necessary to assist the CEO in getting the most out of the evaluation data. While a board member who has the ear of the CEO may be effective in providing performance feedback, a professional experienced in executive assessment and coaching can facilitate the process in an objective way, with less apprehension.

Summary

Successful boards take an integrated view toward performance evaluation, in context of pay and succession, but also on the foundation of strategy. What's more, integrating these themes improves the quality of the CEO-board relationship and heightens the CEO's opportunity for success, as it opens ongoing dialogue and transparency. By taking time to create the CEO role profile, then relentlessly selecting, evaluating and rewarding against it, boards can deliver long-term benefits. With so much on the line, directors shouldn't leave this to chance.

We believe that improving CEO performance evaluation provides a significant opportunity for boards. The development of a stronger process for evaluating and communicating CEO performance should yield greater clarity on roles and expectations, which ultimately should produce improved, sustainable organization performance.

By devoting more attention to developing a strong CEO performance evaluation process, an organization should see the following benefits:

- Improved and more constructive relationship between the board and CEO
- Clearer alignment of organization strategy with CEO capability
- A shared understanding of expectations
- A way to link compensation and succession planning
- The ability to correct the course before it's too late (i.e., spot and address potential problem areas and CEO blind spots)
- Greater organizational stability and sustainability as well as performance.

CHAPTER 17

CEO Succession Management

By Ron Garonzik, Katie Lemaire and Jane Stevenson

Companies and boards have recognized the critical nature of chief executive officer (CEO) succession for the current and future performance of the organization. Without the requisite attention to a rigorous process for managing CEO succession, a company may flounder, miss opportunities and lose ground to competitors. An understanding of the core elements and issues in a well-developed process for CEO succession planning is necessary to provide a solid foundation for an organization.

This chapter:

- Discusses the risks in managing CEO succession.
- Identifies common pitfalls in CEO succession planning.
- Sets out key steps in developing a succession planning process focused on the organization's particular facts, circumstances and business strategy.
- Considers how to manage the transition in CEO succession.

The Risks of CEO Succession

Managing CEO succession is one of the most important and riskiest challenges that boards of directors face. Whether it is for emergency succession or as a result of a planned transition, these public decisions have a significant impact inside companies as well as externally.

Few decisions can be more devastating to a company than picking the wrong CEO, whether internal or external. Negative outcomes can include backlash in the financial markets, internal disruption, loss of key talent, misguided strategic direction, an inability to meet performance objectives and bleak results for shareholders. The CEO may simply be ill-suited to the corporate culture, providing leadership that fails to foster team effectiveness among senior executives and engage the broader organization.

And while most CEO hires are internal, hiring externally is not always a better solution. Our research demonstrates that CEO turnover in the United States costs a minimum of 2.5 times direct compensation in immediate severance and replacement costs, including the costs associated with buying out forfeited equity-based awards and compensation for the risk of moving to another company.

Inconsistency in the way CEO succession is managed can lead to suboptimal outcomes. The Conference Board's 2015 CEO Succession Practices study points to considerable variation in assigning accountability for succession — from standing committees to the full board. This can result in working processes that reflect different planning and decision making biases and risks treating CEO succession as a separate, discrete activity. In our work with boards, we observed the inherent value in treating CEO succession as part of a continuous cyle across CEO performance evaluation and compensation and anchored to strategy — what we term the CEO Life Cycle. The result should be one interconnected set of conversations, grounded in the organization's business and organizational imperatives.

The Securities and Exchange Commission (SEC) has also recognized the significance of CEO succession planning. Prior to 2009, CEO succession was deemed to relate to a company's routine, "day-to-day" business matters. The SEC had taken the position that proposals regarding the adoption and disclosure of written and detailed CEO succession planning features were excludable from proxy statements, as such information "related to the termination, hiring or promotion of employees." The SEC eventually changed course, thereby recognizing the fundamental importance of the disclosure of CEO succession plans (Staff Legal Bulletin No. 14E; October 27, 2009), in accepting that "CEO succession planning raises a significant policy issue regarding the governance of the corporation that transcends the day-to-day business matter of managing the workforce". With this change, CEO succession was open to the scrutiny of shareholders and became a more obvious priority for boards.

CEO Succession: One Size Doesn't Fit All

Boards often need to plan for two types of CEO succession. In nearly 40% of cases that the Hay Group has studied, CEO transition is triggered by the removal, the unexpected resignation or the death or disability of the current CEO. The Conference Board CEO Succession Study reminds us that while 2014 saw the lowest level of Fortune 500 CEO dismissals since 2005 (16% in 2014 vs. 24% in 2013, and 29% in 2012) due to a recovering economy and improved corporate performance, boards should remain prepared for an immediate CEO replacement at any time. In many of these cases, the replacement is an interim CEO who can hopefully inspire confidence in the company and in the markets and steady the ship until a more permanent replacement is readied. In these cases, the CEO is nearly always an "insider" who is either a current executive or an independent board member.

But the more challenging situations are the approximately 60% of transitions that should be planned. While there always will be outliers, there should be sufficient time in most organizations for an internal successor to be developed. But for a variety of reasons, many companies still find themselves unprepared for or not aligned on this important decision.

The steps outlined here can furnish directors with the comfort of better information and a process that provides the level of due diligence shareholders deserve in this all-important decision.

Step 1: Identify the Future CEO Role Requirements
When should planned succession management begin?

CEO succession should always be on the agenda of the board, even when a new CEO has been appointed. In the latter case, while the focus of the board in this period is oriented toward successful onboarding of the new CEO, the board should nonetheless arrange

FIGURE 17-1

CEO Succession Cycle

to have a written document of the requirements for the next CEO. This is particularly important for interim or turnaround CEOs.

Development of future-oriented CEO role requirements is the anchor of CEO succession planning. The steps involved in creating this profile include working with the full board to achieve alignment and agreement on the following types of questions:

- To what extent will the next CEO need to envision the strategy for the company, or will it likely be a continuation of the current strategy?
- To what extent will the company's business model need to change (e.g., global expansion, business-to-consumer versus business-to-business, etc.)?
- To what extent will the core accountabilities of the CEO need to change, for example going from a focus on external stakeholders versus internal management or leading a public versus private company?

Common Pitfalls for Boards in CEO Succession Management

Lack of board priority

CEO succession should be a continuous conversation by the board, although this is not always the case. Lack of time and prioritization, along with a worry that it may send a negative message to the sitting CEO, are concerns some boards have allowed to get in the way. However, the absence of a robust CEO succession plan can have devastating consequences on an organization. There are numerous examples of unplanned, CEO departures that could have been headed-off or at least been less disruptive with at some basic planning; there should always be a plan for emergency succession situations. Throughout a CEO's tenure the board should maintain a continuous process of building future CEOs with the development of internal candidates. Boards need to have in place a clearly defined and ongoing process of CEO succession well in advance of any transition, one that is not based on the timeline of the current CEO. Developing future CEOs begins on a CEO's first day in office and is a full-time job for the board as it works to make sure that the right people have the right experiences.

Letting the CEO Drive the Agenda

CEOs and chief human resource officers (CHROs) are typically well intended when they develop programs to build a strong pipeline of leaders capable of filling future executive roles, including the CEO position. Though a key activity worthy of board support, CEOs are often prone to developing candidates "in their own likeness" or according to their views of fit to current strategy. CHROs, in estimating fit, can provide critical input, but may not be aware of the full range of external demands of the CEO role. While the input of the CEO and CHRO is critical, it is the board's clear accountability for selecting the future CEO and ensuring that the CEO and (in many cases) CHRO actively participate in, but do not drive this agenda.

Lack of Clarity on Board Roles of Incoming and Outgoing CEOs

With evolving changes in corporate governance practices, boards must be clear on their corporate governance as they consider CEO succession. Historically, as CEOs retired, they assumed the chair of the board role. The 2015 Conference Board report on CEO succession noted that policies routinely allowing CEOs to stay on the board are waning and the number of CEOs who are jointly appointed CEO and chair are shrinking, given the growing propensity to separate chair and CEO accountabilities. Therefore, clarity on the board role for both outgoing and incoming CEOs is a key consideration of CEO succession. Boards can avoid false impressions and potential conflict by being precise on their corporate governance intentions as they consider how best to set and manage realistic expectations tied to succession.

- To what extent will the capabilities of the new CEO need to be different from those of the exiting leader? For example, the new CEO may be required to lead in a highly matrixed organization or may be relying on an empowered, interdependent executive team rather than a COO for operational decisions.

When a company has a highly effective CEO in place, there can be a temptation to use an assessment of what accounts for this this leader's success in a development of the future CEO profile. While this process can surface critical attributes and capabilities that may explain the outgoing CEO's success, what really is critical is understanding what the business needs to accomplish for the board to view it as successful. Thus, a comprehensive study should be undertaken with a fresh perspective to develop a CEO success profile based on the intended strategy for the long-term success of the business..

By proactively identifying how anticipated changes in the organization's business strategy and organizational structure will affect the requirements of the CEO role, boards can anticipate the essential priorities for the next CEO position. The resulting discussion can also help to clarify role and competency requirements for the future CEO and align the board in a common direction. The output of this effort should be a robust CEO success profile that prioritizes the key strategic challenges, accountabilities and associated behaviors that will help to assure future success. As there is always the risk of the board developing a CEO profile that is unrealistic for any one person to fill, it is important for the board to also agree on its absolute requirements versus those characteristics that are able to be developed in the role.

Step 2: Identify and Assess Potential CEO Candidates
Who should be considered a potential CEO candidate?
Once the board agrees on the future-oriented CEO profile, one of the key accountabilities of the CEO, and one that should be made explicit in his/her performance criteria, is to develop a robust pipeline of talent to support business continuity and future succession needs. When done early enough, this work is best positioned as part of broader leadership development efforts, and should include a range of senior leaders, as their levels of potential will change over time

in relation to how they respond to the development challenges that they are given. The reasons for assessing a broader pool of CEOs are threefold. First, the organization and the leaders will benefit from the insights from these assessments and the development that follows it, strengthening the overall executive talent pool. Second, there are often "dark horse" candidates who may not look as strong, but who develop to become highly qualified as time for the transition draws nearer. And lastly, once the final internal candidates are made known, there can be unwanted competition and in some cases departures.

How should current and future potential be assessed?

To ensure that this initial assessment is objective and focused on CEO potential, rather than past performance, which may not be fully representative of a leader's growth potential, multiple perspectives should be considered:

- The CEO's perspective;
- Board members' perspectives; and
- Formal, robust executive assessments by a professional third party against the future CEO requirements.

At the conclusion of the executive assessment, reports should be generated about individual capability and potential relative to the CEO profile. Feedback is typically best provided in one-one-one development planning sessions that target the highest priority risk areas to enhance the leader's candidacy. By gathering multiple perspectives, the board and the CEO will have a more complete picture of candidates' suitability and, therefore, better information to guide development efforts.

Step 3: Develop Potential CEO Candidates
How can the likelihood of a qualified CEO candidate be increased?

Simply identifying high potentials and giving them increased board exposure and general development is not enough. CEO potential candidates should have targeted development plans in place and they should be continuously evaluated against the future CEO profile. Gaps in critical knowledge and skill areas often can be addressed through gaining exposure to other parts of the organization, supplemented with formal education (e.g., on risk management or compliance), as necessary. For such stretch assignments to work, the CEO should be held responsible for ensuring the accountability of candidate progress against the plan and should furnish regular updates to the board.

But gaps in required leadership often become more difficult to address the later that they are identified and the higher the candidate is in the organizational hierarchy. For instance, a leader in a staff role with no history of leading a business will often lack fundamental leadership experiences and related competencies that are core to line management roles — the ability to translate strategic objectives into clear implementation goals, to lead large organizations and to provide direct feedback in a manner that enables team members to enhance their performance, etc. Business leaders often fine-tune these leadership capabilities over years through trial and error as they are coming up the ranks. The absence of such capability can pose serious risk unless there are focused efforts to provide leaders with the opportunity to develop these skills.

Step 4: Select the CEO and Manage the Risks

Should the board consider external or only internal candidates?
While research indicates that internal candidates are less costly and often more successful, this decision depends on multiple factors, including the quality of available internal talent, the complexity of future business challenges, the availability of qualified external talent and the desire to retain current senior executives. After the board acquires a clear picture of the internal potential successors, informed decisions can be made about whether it is necessary to consider external candidates.

A critical success factor in selecting internal candidates is to understand the discontinuous shift in accountability in moving from senior executive positions to the CEO role. Public company CEOs, in particular, have a significant focus on external interactions for which most executives (except for the CFO) are unprepared and often have other accountability areas that cannot easily be delegated to others. In this context, CEO candidates should be assessed based on their ability to manage competing internal and external priorities.

Boards often conduct external benchmarking to provide an additional point of reference on the strength of the internal candidates without the disruption of messaging, internally and externally, that an organization may go outside for a CEO. When boards do decide to conduct and outside search, it is critical to use the same platform to compare inside and outside candidates, starting with the common CEO success profile. Moreover, outside searches need not all go to a formal assessment process if internal candidates appear to be making good progress; a silent search or benchmarking study of the availability and quality of external talent may give the board the comfort it needs. Objective assessments against the CEO success profile allow the board to measure all candidates against common criteria, diminishing the influence of familiarity in final decision making. Moreover, tools such as behavioral ("critical incident") interviewing can provide a more level playing field in making comparisons between the capabilities of external candidates and the capabilities of candidates from inside the organization. While such assessments should never substitute for the board's own judgment in CEO selection, they invariably provide useful insights that boards can incorporate into a more robust view of the candidate pool.

Step 5: Manage the Transition

Once the board has agreed on the best candidate and addressed the risks that he/she and the organization face, a comprehensive on-boarding and communication plan should be developed. This plan should be tailored to the specific situation. For example, if this a planned succession, is the prospective CEO a logical successor or is he/she a "dark horse" candidate who may not be well known to investors and key customers? This plan should include not only those on-boarding activities that the CEO must undertake, but also the specific actions required of the board such as explaining the board/ management philosophy as well as how feedback from executive sessions is provided. The plan should also specify the on-boarding actions required from the outgoing CEO (e.g., introductions to key clients, regulators, investors, etc.). Because each CEO succession often creates changes in senior leadership positions, whether the CEO is an internal or external candidate, these changes need to be carefully managed and communicated.

How boards manage succession planning is often typical of how they manage their business. Some are forward-thinking, well-planned efforts that start shortly after the appointment of a new CEO, while in other cases there is a thin slate of internal candidates or an urgent need to hire externally, creating unnecessary risks for the board and the organization. By taking a longer term perspective, boards can reduce risk and more reliably fulfill their fiduciary responsibility to shareholders. And, by considering all aspects of the CEO Life Cycle collectively (CEO succession planning, compensation and performance evaluation), boards have a greater likelihood of optimizing organizational success.

CHAPTER 18

Special Compensation Issues in the CEO Life Cycle

By Irv Becker and Sydney Hilzenrath

Taking a broader view of how boards and CEOs work together is the cornerstone of the CEO Life Cycle. The three elements of the life cycle — succession, performance management and compensation — are all linked together. A holistic view of CEO compensation, from original design of the compensation program and its underlying philosophy to benchmarking and retention, is critical to aligning the goals of the board and the CEO.

There are significant transitions for a CEO, from recruitment to retirement, and each transition has different compensation issues that need to be considered by the board. Creating the right compensation program for each stage is critical to the board successfully attracting, retaining and motivating the right CEO for the company.

While compensation elements, design and strategy have been addressed throughout the book, there are special situations that should be considered through the lens of the CEO Life Cycle. The board of directors of a newly public company has a lot to think about — SEC requirements, a different governance framework, new relationships with external stakeholders and stockholders, and formalizing themselves as a board. While all of these undertakings are important and required of a public company's board, the most important responsibilities of any board are the selection, evaluation and compensation of the CEO.

This chapter:

- Examines how compensation may impact each aspect of a CEO's life cycle, from recruitment to retirement.
- Considers the different compensation arrangements often needed for outside hires compared with internal CEO promotions, including the use of employment contracts.
- Addresses compensation issues involved with an emergency CEO replacement, including an Office of the CEO.
- Provides a brief overview of the importance of CEO performance evaluation in the context of an IPO.
- Discusses the pay considerations in a newly public company and how they differ from those of a private organization, the board's primary areas of focus, any employee issues that need to be addressed, and the general concerns now faced by the board and the CEO.

Compensation Strategies for CEO Transitions

From the time of recruitment to the moment of retirement (and sometimes beyond), the life of a CEO is filled with transitions. For a board of directors, all of these transitions involve compensation decisions. The board needs to think ahead so that it can make these decisions with proper planning in ways that match the company's strategy, culture and circumstances.

Addressed below are some of the most significant compensation issues that boards should consider in these transition periods:

Recruitment

When recruiting an external CEO and negotiating that CEO's pay package, boards often find themselves at the whim of the markets. The laws of supply and demand mean that boards generally have less control over the situation when recruiting an external CEO than they do with internal succession.

Rather than pinning all of its hopes on a single candidate, we recommend that a board keep a few candidates under consideration in case it is unable to reach agreement with its first choice on a compensation package that would fit the company's existing compensation program, pay culture and internal equity structure.

With external CEO recruitment, we see considerable stress around unvested equity, unvested deferred compensation or lost pension benefits from the previous employer that the candidate would need to leave on the table. Executives often expect to be bought out or made whole of these amounts, but companies don't want to build these additional payments into the ongoing compensation structure. Typically, they would rather agree on a one-off, up-front payment that gets included in the first year's compensation numbers.

These types of deals can lead to significant up-front equity awards or sign-on bonuses that can shine a spotlight on boards from a disclosure perspective. Keep in mind that disclosures of compensation packages are available not just to investors, but to anyone, including other members of the management team. That can create conflict if those executives become upset about how the new CEO's compensation relates to their own compensation packages.

Severance Protection

CEOs recruited from outside a company typically want some sort of down-side protection. They will usually ask for severance benefits — just in case things don't work out. (In the past, CEO candidates also might have sought a parachute tax gross-up, but institutional investors objected strongly to those types of arrangements, and we don't see them much in new arrangements.)

Recruiting an external CEO can lead to other culture-related clashes around compensation. For instance, while some companies have moved away from using employment contracts, a candidate coming from outside the organization might insist on such an agreement for his/her protection (at least for an initial term of up to three years). That could create discrepancies and inconsistencies within the management team, since other executives would lack such contracts. If a board determines that it really needs a particular CEO candidate, it might be willing to make an exception and negotiate an employment agreement, but it should be aware that doing so could lead to internal conflicts down the line.

Similarly, a CEO coming from outside the organization may want his/her incentives determined and/or paid in ways that conflict with the incentive arrangements of other executives. Some CEOs may want their equity to vest based on share price appreciation. If other executives are incentivized based on profitability or some other metric that could lead to misalignment and interpersonal conflicts among the executive team.

Promotion

When a CEO is promoted from within the organization, the board doesn't have to worry as much about the negotiations around severance, employment contracts and incentives that it might with an external candidate. The biggest issue with internal promotion usually involves finding the right speed at which to raise the new CEO's compensation.

The market rate for CEO compensation could be twice as much as the executive's former total compensation. To move someone from a $5 million to a $10 million compensation package takes careful and thoughtful planning. We often work with clients on multi-year plans to bring an internally promoted CEO up to market level compensation.

Finding just the right pace to increase compensation is critically important. If an organization does not bring compensation up fast enough, it leaves the company exposed to the risk that the new CEO could be recruited away by a competitor offering a larger compensation package.

Leaving the new CEO's compensation below market rate can also project the wrong image to investors and other stakeholders. The market could interpret low compensation as a signal that the new CEO is not quite ready or that the board has low confidence in its choice.

On the other hand, bumping up compensation too dramatically also can cause problems. A new CEO's compensation package should be at the lower end of the market range. Employers should leave some "dry powder" so that they can raise compensation later to reward for maturity in the position and high performance.

As with all issues around CEO compensation, the board should make its decisions while considering the whole. In most circumstances, we recommend bringing in a new internally promoted CEO around the 25th percentile of market compensation. The board should have a plan to get the new CEO to the market median level in three to four years by pulling different levers — salary, bonuses, short-term incentives and long-term incentives.

Keep in mind that market medians will shift over time. Best practice is to anticipate market movements and monitor the performance of both the company and the CEO to fine-tune the compensation model each year in an iterative process. As the length of tenure increases, so too does the likelihood that a CEO's compensation should be at the higher end of the market-based compensation range.

Retirement

As CEOs approach the twilight of their tenure with a company, a new set of compensation questions comes into play. Boards need to consider whether they should change the mix of their CEO's compensation structure.

For instance, do stock options still make sense for a CEO nearing retirement? While options typically have a 10-year lifespan, the company's equity compensation plan may only allow the CEO a much shorter period (e.g., one to three years) to exercise options post-retirement. Since these shorter-term stock options have less value than the 10-year options, perhaps restricted stock would make more sense for a CEO near retirement?

In the best case scenarios, a CEO should be involved in succession planning and preparing his/her successor to take over leadership. If a CEO has helped pick the successor, perhaps the board does want the CEO to hold equity for at least a certain period after retirement. The equity would provide the former CEO with a vested interest in the success of the new CEO. With advance planning, the board can start making the move away from stock options and toward restricted stock or performance shares with the aim of making sure that the retiring CEO still has enough value left in his/her equity awards to feel invested in the new CEO flourishing in the role.

To ensure this smooth and unbroken chain of succession, some companies have developed a process by which an internal candidate is promoted to president, then president-CEO, then CEO-chairman. As the next CEO rises through the succession pipeline, the CEO-chairman steps down from the CEO role but retains the position as chairman of the board. As chairman, the former CEO can guide and advise the president-CEO. Then, after a year or two, the chairman (and former CEO) can step aside and the CEO can take on the dual leadership mantle of chairman-CEO until the next turn of the wheel in the leadership cycle.

Not every company follows this model. Even companies that would like to use this model may need to abandon it if a CEO leaves due to health issues or poor performance. While the joint CEO-chairman role is still common in the U.S., many governance and shareholder advisers recommend splitting the two roles to create a non-executive chairman position. Division of the chairman and CEO roles occurs frequently in European countries. If a board has given any consideration to moving away from the unified CEO-chairman structure toward a non-executive chairman, the retirement of a current CEO can be a good opportunity to make such a split.

Emergency CEO Replacement

In addition to its regular CEO succession plans and processes, a board needs to be prepared for the possibility of replacing its CEO due to a sudden emergency. Well-known public companies have faced situations where they had to replace their CEOs without delay due to illness, sudden death, internal investigations, personal scandals and other unexpected events. The board should have an established emergency plan that it can quickly launch and implement in these types of scenarios.

The ideal scenario is having an emergency successor already identified who can assume the mantle, but many organizations find themselves in situations where there is no clear emergency plan, and no logical person who can fill the role in what can turn into a multi-month commitment. This is where the "Office of the CEO" can fill a gap. The concept is to take the CEO's accountabilities and to divide them among a number of executives/board members who can cover the role together until a permanent successor is in place.

There is no one standard approach to compensation in this Office of the CEO scenario. If executives are asked to carry an additional burden during the transition, it is appropriate to compensate them accordingly. The easiest approach is to provide a temporary percentage increase (reflective of the CEO's salary) to their base pay as long as the Office of the CEO is in place. Additional pay should be linked to performance (i.e., meeting certain targets set for the Office of the CEO). Additional bonuses could be offered to executives for maintaining or increasing the share price. Typically, these bonuses would occur during the regular compensation cycle and would reflect the length of tenure for executives serving in the Office of the CEO.

Any board member who participates in the Office of the CEO should also be compensated as it is likely to be a full time commitment for an extended period of time. The cleanest and simplest approach is to pay a monthly salary that takes into consideration his/her board compensation (the director should only be paid the difference). There are two basic approaches:

- The director is paid by the board for taking on a special project (equivalent to a percentage of the CEO's salary)
- The director is paid a management fee (an enhanced annual retainer) by the organization (equivalent to a percentage of the CEO's salary)

Summing Up

From recruitment to retirement and all the stages in between, the CEO role is filled with important compensation decisions. For board members, finding the right compensation mix often is critical in attracting, retaining and motivating the right CEO who can lead the organization to success. Yet directors should keep in mind that some of the decisions they make around CEO compensation (particularly vis-à-vis severance protection) can have repercussions around harmony within the executive ranks. Even at the end of the CEO's career, compensation decisions can help ensure a smooth transition from one CEO to the next or — in the event of a sudden and unplanned CEO transition — make sure that executives and/or board members who step into the breach are rewarded fairly for their service and performance.

The CEO Life Cycle and Preparing for an IPO

During the phases leading up to the company's IPO — from initial formation around a product or service (with perhaps an advisory board having a key role) to a public company with more formal board responsibilities — much must be done to prepare for this momentous event. While the board transition is significant and must be deliberately managed and planned, CEO succession, performance and compensation are of equal importance, requiring a similar level of focus and attention.

CEO Succession

Very early on in the new company's tenure it is important to profile the skills and competency requirements of the "CEO of the future" — a CEO role profile. The CEO role profile is developed within the context of the strategy and addresses critical questions, including:

- Given our strategy, what does the next CEO need to do?
- How will such a CEO accomplish these objectives?
- What are the "must-win battles" necessary to get there?
- What leadership characteristics are critical in this journey?
- What is the needed board/CEO relationship for the company to thrive?
- What culture does the new CEO need to create and promulgate throughout the organization?
- How will the CEO work with his/her management team and hold them accountable for execution and, in turn, how will the management team create the conditions for those in the organization also to be successful?

A board is only able to truly understand what it needs in a CEO by going through this exercise. The findings can be quite illuminating; many times the assessment of the CEO against the profile reveals a sub-optimal "fit" between the current CEO and future role requirements. This should not come as a surprise, as the skills and competencies needed to build an organization at an early stage are quite different than what it takes to run a public company, where the focus is on building organizational infrastructure, capability and overall positioning the company for growth. So while the current CEO may be the right person for now, he/she may not be (nor want to be) the best choice to take the company forward. That said, many CEOs successfully transition into the public company role; however, for boards that don't proactively assess the role, it's often not without growing pains and potential mishaps along the way.

Other Board Priorities

Similar to the considerations around CEO selection and succession, CEO compensation and performance evaluation are areas that the board of a newly public company needs to take up formally without delay. Different from a private firm's board, the board of a public company may be under a regulatory mandate to evaluate the CEO and must disclose the CEO's pay. Given these new strictures, boards need to be deliberate and sophisticated in how compensation matters are handled, if for no other reason than the optics of doing this poorly now can affect the investment (i.e., the stock price).

The CEO Dashboard

Establishing high clarity is the most important component in establishing the criteria for CEO performance. A CEO dashboard is intended to highlight company priorities and becomes the agreed-upon criteria between the CEO and the board. While the CEO dashboard is important in any organization regardless of its current phase, it is of primary importance when moving onto a public stage, where the optics of CEO performance are heightened and new stockholders are eager to grow their investment. Although the financials have traditionally dominated the dashboard, it is increasingly a trend, and a healthy one at that, to include other categories that receive some weighting toward the incentive of the CEO. For example, issues related to company sustainability, leadership continuity, governance and crisis management all impact an organization and therefore are important for the CEO to manage.

CEO Performance Evaluation

Taking this to the next level is the performance evaluation process. While the "what" is important, the "how" is equally so. At this stage the CEO and the board must jointly determine how success will be defined in each area. For example, if ensuring leadership continuity is a key dashboard metric, what does success look like? How will it be measured? What weighting does it have toward the incentive? And, just as importantly, how will the board deliver feedback?

Why wait until the annual review when a robust discussion of how the CEO is doing against the backdrop of a newly public company can take place at regular intervals throughout the year? In fact, here is a place where the board can have a significant impact — guiding and advising the CEO of the newly public company on the factors that have been determined to be critical to the company. What better way to get this new relationship on solid footing than to open the door to these important and game-changing conversations?

CEO Compensation

Lastly, we consider the link to pay:

- The pay considerations in a newly public company and how are they different from those of a private organization
- How to address any issues that may arise with employees since the pay of the CEO now must be disclosed
- General compensation concerns faced by the board.

The CEO pay process and the board's role also may undergo a significant transformation when a company transitions from private to public. The board governance process changes, with more significant and formal decision-making responsibilities and public disclosure of the board's process. The disclosure of that information can create an enormous amount of angst for the board and the CEO as the level of pay becomes subject to third-party scrutiny for the first time. Shareholders, their representatives, media, and friends and family all become aware of how, and how much, the CEO has been paid and the wealth that has been accumulated in the company, with shareholders allowed to opine through the company's say-on-pay vote.

Although the new governance and disclosure processes are daunting, a real advantage of this progression is that the board's compensation tools are enhanced; the addition of public-company equity creates a new lever for the board to press to motivate and reward CEO activities. While a potentially unsettling process, a thoughtful approach to developing the CEO's pay program should relieve some of the board's concerns in this new environment and instead become an opportunity to reflect on its principles for developing an effective CEO pay program.

Successfully Transitioning from a Privately Held to a Publicly Traded Company

Retaining and motivating the CEO and other key members of the management team through and following the IPO is important to shareholders, and therefore the success of the offering. A meaningful amount of unvested equity is what shareholders want to see. The opportunity for equity ownership is a powerful motivator that supports executive retention and aligns the interests of executives and the investors; we call this CEO "holding power."

CEO Holding Power and IPO Grants

Pre-IPO equity plans come in all shapes and sizes with unique provisions. Evaluating the amount of equity and the potential value over a three- to five-year period following the IPO under different performance assumptions helps the board evaluate the retentive value of the existing unvested equity grants. It also informs the decision-making process regarding the need and magnitude of a grant to be awarded concurrent with the IPO. This process is as much art as science, with benchmarking providing the framework of what others have done, but with board, executive, and adviser experience, and perhaps potential investor input, providing the qualitative insights.

When IPO grants are made, they are often larger than annual grants and, given the magnitude of the awards, often have a longer vesting period to support CEO retention and to provide balance for the shareholders. This extended vesting cycle creates a staggered value and vesting benefit by allowing post-IPO grants to build value over shorter time frames, creating an equity model that avoids a "cliff vesting" retention drop-off effect and instead results in a steady pattern of outstanding unvested equity to support retention and performance achievement.

The IPO equity grants can be stock options, restricted share/units or performance-based awards. The vehicle depends on various factors, including share price appreciation, dividends, dilution and the number of participants in the plan. But it is important to reinforce that retention is a primary motivator of these grants and therefore the IPO grant, or at least a significant portion, should be in the form of time-vested stock options, restricted shares/units, or a combination of the two.

Creating the Go-Forward CEO Pay Program

The post-IPO program also needs to be considered during the IPO planning period. The board should review each element of the CEO's pay to be confident that the program is aligned with the business, fair to the new shareholders and compelling to the CEO. The standard elements — base salary, annual and long-term incentives (opportunity and metrics), as well as share ownership guidelines, CIC protection, and other benefit programs — should be evaluated to create an aligned CEO pay program.

Focusing on the traditional elements of pay, base salaries may be adjusted slightly to reflect the increased demands as a public company CEO. It may take some time to get the annual incentive metrics and targets right and to consider the non-financial dashboard metrics described earlier. In any case, LTIs are the most significant element of CEO pay (60 to 70 percent in large mature companies) and, typically, developing the future approach to equity incentives is the most challenging aspect. The use of equity is markedly different in a post-IPO period. While many privately held companies have LTI programs, they look different from public company models — whether in the type and number of vehicles, frequency of the grants, value of the grants or levels of eligibility.

Equity Awards

While the IPO grants are primarily intended to drive CEO retention, the post-IPO awards will include more performance orientation to align with shareholders. This could include a performance shares concept — essentially restricted stock with performance-based vesting that is also leveraged and adjusts the shares received based on performance. We have learned from the market volatility that diversification is important and market practice has evolved so that public companies often use a portfolio concept or a combination of LTI vehicles to balance performance, retention and shareholder alignment. Accordingly, a combination of performance shares and time-vested restricted stock or stock options can be an effective model to align the interests of shareholders and the CEO in the post-IPO pay environment.

Many privately held companies issue one-time equity grants (or make awards more frequently but at irregular intervals); public firms typically grant LTI as an annual element of executive pay. The use of annual LTI grants continually reinforces long-term decision-making and supports executive retention. It may take a new public company a year or two to fully adopt this approach, but it has become the norm in CEO and broader executive pay structuring programs.

Determining the targeted value of these awards is often a new exercise for a public company board. The value is a function of marketplace norms and the board's internally driven desired mix of pay that reinforces the behaviors that the board wants to stimulate. The mix of pay (the percentage of total pay that LTIs represent) is directly aligned with the company's strategy and growth prospects. For example, there are growth-oriented companies where an entrepreneurial and visionary CEO leading the organization is motivated by the benefits of equity ownership — the ability to create and share in the value. Accordingly, in such circumstances, equity-based compensation takes a more significant role in the overall pay program. Contrast that with a non-IPO client, which emphasizes fixed compensation (implying a business in decline) — a pay program that would not be well received by shareholders in an IPO setting.

Equity Dilution

Equity incentive plan dilution informs the decision-making process around the types of awards and the levels of plan participation. The amount of equity to be shared with executives, and the resulting dilutive impact of the equity incentive plan, has become a key discussion point with shareholders in the run-up to the IPO as well as when the post-IPO company makes new requests of shareholders post-IPO. It affects the vehicles (stock options require more shares to deliver competitive value than restricted shares), participation (greater employee participation requires more shares relative to fewer participants) and the values that can be shared (and over what time frame). Market norms and investor returns matter — a recent commercial banking IPO developed its plans within a dilution norm in the 8 to 10 percent range versus a recent technology IPO in which dilution in the upper teens can be the norm.

Overall Compensation Structure

In planning for an IPO, the board's goal is to develop a compensation structure that supports the business and shareholder interests and is compelling in order to retain, motivate, drive behaviors and reward the CEO if the business is successful and provides appropriate returns to shareholders. A continuous reflection of those objectives should create the context and rationale to develop a strategically sound and defensible post-IPO CEO pay program.

Positioning for Growth

Post-IPO is the time for the organization to thrive and flourish. As with anything else, up-front planning and execution of the right levers at the right time make all the difference. Considering CEO succession, CEO performance evaluation and CEO compensation in an integrated way will increase the likelihook of success for the newly public company's strategy. Despite the best intent, organizations that take up these components separately risk loss of focus due to conflicting priorities. The CEO and the board cannot be in sync on what's important if they have not taken the time to clarify, with laser-like precision, what success looks like and how the organization will achieve it. And, lastly, since it's the entire top executive team and not just the CEO that creates enterprise value, this level of clarity and alignment becomes critical for the executive team to in turn create the conditions for enterprise success.

PART IV

The Board Life Cycle

INTRODUCTION

By Christine Rivers

The board life cycle refers to the board's journey: the continuous cycle of development, evaluation and refreshment. It's a journey that begins with selection and succession of directors to their compensation and performance evaluation, overall as a board and individually as directors. These components must be attended to continuously and in an integrated fashion for the board to satisfy its duties. And, when these components are grounded in the organization's strategy, they are not only continuous and related, they have relevance.

This is not easy territory for boards, and there's good reason why it's not. A board is a group of peers, albeit with the nuance of the chair in an oversight role, but, nevertheless, peers who come together and form a bond to execute a role with a high level of public scrutiny. And, it's quite difficult for a group of peers in this situation to be in any sort of evaluative position with each other. Even when it's clear they have a fiduciary responsibility to do so, it is a difficult activity to both initiate and undertake. They would just as easily avoid these activities — and in many cases they do.

However, progressive and well-governed boards not only initiate these activities regularly, they proactively manage them. That is, they build these activities into their calendar and build processes around them to ensure they receive the focused attention they deserve.

What Does This Look Like?

The process begins with a realization that strategy is at the foundation. "What are the skills and competencies we will need on the board to effectively oversee this organization given its strategy? How are our board members faring against that today? Do we have the right people on the board who can take us into the future?"

Next is the consideration about compensation. "Is our director compensation commensurate with what we are asking them to do? Are we able to attract the right talent to the board given the level of compensation? Or, is it too robust given our needs? Does it send the wrong message to management, our shareholders and other constituencies?"

What about director development? Peer feedback on competencies and behavior can be a powerful tool to help directors understand how their contributions are received. In the absence of assessment and feedback, directors do not have a way of knowing where they stand, which can lead to frustration (especially by those who believe some directors are not doing their job) and missed opportunities. It's surprising to hear that so many board members who have been on their boards for years have never received feedback on how they are doing; in fact it's irresponsible. However, while critically important, these activities are many times overlooked because the board chair or the appropriate committee chair (for example, governance) may not want to initiate them.

The simple solution is to accept that this cycle of activity is part of what the board must do, and make it part of the ongoing board process and board calendar. Board selection and succession, performance evaluation and compensation all should be part of an ongoing dialogue with a process; one that is based on trust, candor and real conversations. Initiated by the chair or lead director (in cases where the CEO is the chair), these activities must be continuous and integrated to be fresh and relevant. This all should be a natural part of the board's life cycle — what directors do, what they talk about, what they worry about. As tough as it is to initiate it, once it becomes part of the way of working, the value of these conversations becomes invaluable.

While a formal process is needed to generate data, there is an informal component that is quite important as well. For example, conducting "debriefs" after every meeting or at key inflection points of an event to ask, "How did we do? Could this have been better? What got in the way?" can be quite powerful and helpful as the board continually strives to improve.

As mentioned, this all is irrelevant unless it's built on company strategy. Whether it's succession planning, performance evaluation or compensation, the strategy must be the foundation as it provides the blueprint for all board requirements. Questions may arise:

- Where is the CEO taking the company?
- As a board, what do we need to possess and do to guide and oversee the CEO and management toward that outcome?
- Are we prioritizing the right things? Are we spending our time on the right activities?
- Do we have people on the board with the experiences we need to guide us in the right direction?

These are issues that the board must wrestle with as part of the ongoing process: to stay relevant and aligned. It's the board life cycle, and any board that ignores all or part of these activities or accommodates "the way we always do things" risks missteps that can have significant negative outcomes.

Optimize Organizational Effectiveness

The activities above are the tangible aspects of the board life cycle — the work the board must do. But how should the board act? How can boards approach these activities in a way that enhances meaning, ensures greater purpose and optimizes organizational effectiveness?

The answer is found in what happens in between the activities of the board life cycle: the way directors interact, the relationships they have, the relationship the board builds with the CEO and the senior management team, the way the board and the CEO share information, and the intention of the board to engage in meaningful conversations with each other and with management. It's what happens in-between the tangible, concrete activities that essentially speaks to the relationship directors have with each other and with the CEO. That is, it's the tangible components (the activities) supported by the intangible components (the relationships) that make this powerful. Of course, the critical factor here is trust; for if the relationship is not based on trust, it will fall apart quickly, and the effects of loss of trust can be disastrous.

If a board ignores any element of these activities, it is time to ask the question why, and perhaps it is time to refresh the board and its way of working. It's only when the board is operating at its peak performance can an organization be expected to do the same.

CHAPTER 19

Board Evaluation

By Andrea Plotnick and Alanna Conte

Since the early 2000s, there has been an increased focus on board evaluation. In fact, it is now a mandatory listing requirement of most stock exchanges for publicly traded organizations. The impetus for the mandatory requirements and the amplified focus is, in part, the corporate scandals which began (but did not end with) Enron, that led many observers to question whether boards were asleep at the wheel. Board evaluation has been embraced as a safety check, providing evidence that boards are armed and able to provide appropriate governance and fiduciary oversight. The practice has extended beyond publicly traded companies to include nonprofit and private organizations.

While there has been an increased reference to board evaluation as an important practice, we have three key observations:

First, listing requirements are typically not best practices — at best they are minimum requirements. Even at that, other than stipulating that an annual self-evaluation needs to take place, they are not prescriptive and do not typically spell out any further details.

Second, there is not a common definition and understanding of what board evaluation means, both in terms of scope and approach.

Third, boards may undertake an evaluation with very different objectives in mind. Some boards take a minimalist approach, amounting to a "check-the-box" exercise, while others approach evaluations as an opportunity for development and a means to maximize the effectiveness of the board and of the organization.

Board assessment with a focus on development is a win-win-win proposition — for the board itself, for the organization and for external stakeholders. Ensuring the most effective board is rewarding to board members; the right skill set among members enables effective decisions, directors are able to contribute to their full potential, conflict is handled appropriately, and processes are in place to ensure that members are truly able to exercise due diligence. The climate becomes more engaging, allowing for a more productive and strategic conversation.

A high-performing board is also of tremendous value to the organization: the board provides effective stewardship, stays away from areas it should not get involved, and reduces potential conflict between the board and CEO by bringing clarity to roles and boundaries. A board held to best practices appropriately focuses the board, and also increases the confidence of external stakeholders, that the board is doing the right things.

This chapter:

- Describes the components of a development-focused board evaluation that can be leveraged to allow the board to most effectively fulfill its roles. It addresses three levels of evaluation: the board, committees and directors.
- Discusses various methodologies for conducting the three levels of evaluation, and the advantages and disadvantages of each.
- Raises the importance of soliciting broader input than directors, to prevent an insular view. It discusses various perspectives that might be informative.
- Provides a framework that incorporates the various elements into a best practices approach.
- Flags potential pitfalls and critical considerations.

What is Board Evaluation?

Boards frequently talk about the need for evaluation, but what they specifically mean often varies, and it is not until probing questions are asked that a common understanding is reached. Part of defining board evaluation hinges on understanding the objectives of its undertaking.

Defined at its simplest and narrowest, board evaluation refers to a self-assessment — often by questionnaire completed by board members — focused on their perceptions regarding how well the board functions. While this check-the-box exercise meets regulatory requirements, it is of somewhat limited value from a development perspective.

The first issue is common to all self-assessments; it presupposes a certain amount of self-awareness and sufficient context to be able to answer questions in a helpful manner. Perceptions are not always objective and reality-based. To illustrate, asking directors to rate the effectiveness of board meetings, when they may not truly appreciate what an effective meeting looks like may not yield much useful and actionable data. Or, asking directors how well they feel that the board is meeting its roles may not be particularly instructive without the benefit of truly understanding what the various board roles are, and without input from others who interact with the board. If the goal of board evaluation is to optimize board effectiveness (to in turn, enable organization effectiveness), then a more expansive definition, and subsequently robust approach, is appropriate.

As Figure 20-1 illustrates, a full board evaluation actually occurs on three interrelated levels: the board, committees of the board and directors, including the chair of the board and committee chairs.

An Expanded Scope at the Board Level

Beginning with the board level as a unit, a robust evaluation should consider multiple facets, including:

- The composition/structure of the board;
- The roles of the board; and
- Board processes.

Board Composition

Board composition fundamentally answers the question: who is on the board? It is not about individual director assessment (although that does provide insight), but rather looking at the board as a unit

FIGURE 20-1

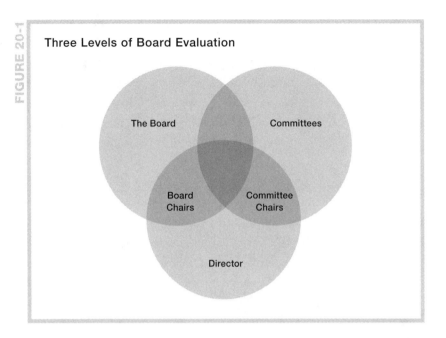

Three Levels of Board Evaluation

The Board

Committees

Board
Chairs

Committee
Chairs

Director

to ensure that, together, members have all critical areas covered, and that the composition enables the board to most effectively meet stakeholder needs.

Determining Needed Skills for the Board

An appropriate starting point is considering skills and expertise; it quickly becomes evident that one size does not fit all. Board composition (see Table 20-1) assesses the extent to which the board has the right knowledge, skill sets and mix to: provide effective oversight; deliver strategic insight; advise and mentor the CEO and management; and manage enterprise risk. Simply filling a board with "big names," which may have been fine in the past, is no longer sufficient. The combined skill sets need to adequately reflect the strategic direction, industry and stage of life of the organization, so that board members are able to make informed decisions without being completely reliant on the CEO.

Determining the right skills begins with strategy, and maintains a future focus — what is required over the next three to five years. This future lens mitigates perpetuating the status quo without due

TABLE 20-1

> **Evaluating Board Composition — Illustrative Questions**
>
> **Questions to consider regarding mix:**
> > Does the board reflect a diversity of perspectives?
> > Does the portfolio of skills and expertise reflect the full range of what is required to deliver the strategy over the foreseeable future?
>
> **Questions to consider regarding board size:**
> > Are there enough directors to effectively staff committees?
> > How does the board size compare to boards of similar "benchmark" organizations?
> > Does the board size hamper decision making?
> > Does each board member add sufficient and unique value to warrant being on the board?
>
> **Questions to consider regarding independence:**
> > Is there an appropriate ratio of external to internal directors?
> > Do directors demonstrate the confidence and experience to effectively challenge the CEO and management?

consideration for what is needed at the board level to match various organization inflection points.

The most effective means of assessing the portfolio of skills is using a skills matrix that distills the critical skills needed on a particular board, at a particular point in time, given the organization's context. As illustrated in Table 20-2, these skills form the column headings.

Covered Skills and Potential Gaps

The next step is to determine which skills are covered by which director(s), and to identify any critical holes, which could lead to blind spots. Each director is assessed against each skill area. For the purposes of looking at the portfolio of skills, the individual names are less of interest than the overall view. When current or future gaps are identified, the board has alternatives that it might pursue, ranging from board training, to specifically seeking directors with a particular skill set, to relying on external advisers who work closely with the board.

Skills matrices yield powerful insights about a board, beyond skill deficits. First, if the skills matrix focuses on the expertise

TABLE 20-2

Sample Skills Matrix

	Human Resources / Compensation	Global Operations	Finance Experience	Lean Manufacturing	General Management Experience (CEO)	Industry Expertise	Merger and Acquisition Expertise	Technology	Etc.
Director 1									
Director 2									
Etc.									

that is demonstrated at the board level, it sometimes may reveal a discrepancy with the skills a director possesses, based on his/her experience. This disconnect can often be addressed through greater role clarity for individual directors, an initial orientation discussion regarding why they, in particular, were recruited for the board, and even role descriptions that spell out specifically the skills, knowledge and expertise that the individual is expected to bring to discussions. This is often a step that is missing from the onboarding process.

Skills Portfolio and Board Diversity

Looking at the portfolio of skills provides insight into the mix of board members and overall diversity. For example, if each board member brings the same three skills to the table, and there are gaps in other areas, clearly there is an issue. While this conclusion may seem obvious, recruitment and nominating practices often indirectly lead to this being the case: relying on recommendations from current board members or recruiting all board members from the same pool can often lead to directors with similar skill sets, but also with other similar attributes — most typically: white males of a certain age, and past or current CEOs.

While board recruitment has become more sophisticated, driven in many cases by regulatory requirements, there clearly is room for many boards to develop. Attention is needed to the specific knowledge and expertise that each director has; otherwise the result can be each member adding value in similar ways, and not providing sufficient breadth. As organizations reach different inflection points, new skills may be required. A domestic company seeking to expand its global reach would benefit from a board member with global expertise who could advise, open doors, and identify and manage risks. As technology becomes more complex, new expertise may be required. The challenge for the board is to ensure adequate coverage of all key areas while limiting the board to a size that does not hamper decision making.

Further, diversity makes good business sense. The research shows that introducing diversity to the board — beginning with, but not limited to, skills — allows for problems to be considered from different perspectives and multiple angles, prevents "group think," challenges the status quo, reflects the diversity in the customer base, and can enhance the organization's reputation and brand.

The mistake many boards make is to introduce a single individual from a diversity perspective; it places undue burden on one individual, and, without a critical mass, the impact is not likely to be felt.

While diversity is clearly desirable, it is not the end goal. The goal is to have a board best structured to optimize its effectiveness. This means that diversity should always be balanced with ensuring the board is not so heterogeneous that: it cannot function as a group; it creates a situation where too many agendas are put forward; conflict management takes up disproportionate time, and it has difficulty reaching decisions.

Board Renewal and Development

Fourth, the skills matrix is invaluable in planning for board renewal. Deficiencies may be identified where education and development are required for the board as a whole. The process also can flag where an individual may no longer be adding sufficient and unique value to justify "using up" a seat, particularly in light of the need to balance skill coverage with a board size that does not impede decision making. It speaks to the point that one's relevance for a board may not be permanent — it is a state, not a trait. The issue is not about age, but about currency and relevance, so introducing director terms or retirement ages does not get at the core. Often these measures are put in place to preempt a difficult conversation.

The discussion of ongoing relevance and value-add is often the most difficult for a board chair, but with the growing complexity of risk and accelerating pace of change introduced by technology, it is a discussion that should be held with more frequency. Interestingly, sometimes just going through the skills review process can promote personal reflection and yield a more accurate self-assessment, where a director makes his/her own decision to retire from the board. At the very least, having data in hand from an evaluation can better ground a difficult conversation that is never a commentary on career or past accomplishments, but a focus on what is required by the organization to move forward and effectively provide good governance and oversight.

Independence

A fifth issue affecting board composition is independence; this is more than satisfying regulatory standards regarding independence. While many board evaluations focus on ratios of internal versus external directors, and whether directors have a material financial interest in the organization, a truer measure may be the extent to which the board is independent-minded. True independence of mind requires sufficient knowledge, skills and competencies to be able to challenge effectively, and it also requires processes to ensure that vital information is shared in a productive way, appropriate time allotted to critical issues, and opportunity to discuss issues fully using in camera sessions.

Board Roles

The next component at the board level that should be considered in a board evaluation is board roles. Board roles have become increasingly demanding, both with the complexity of risks that organizations must consider, and with the scrutiny that directors face. Boards can and should play multiple roles, and part of a board evaluation can focus on the extent to which they are fulfilling each of these roles. Four specific roles are discussed below.

Illustrative Questions for Assessing Board Roles

> Does the board set and measure annual CEO performance objectives?
> Does the board proactively plan for CEO succession, and monitor that internal candidates are actively developed?
> Does the board monitor human capital considerations, such as turnover and succession for mission critical roles, development of bench strength, and ethics?
> Does the board maintain an emergency CEO succession plan?
> Does the board effectively identify and manage risks at the enterprise level?
> Does the board advise, mentor and develop the CEO?
> Does the board proactively communicate with key stakeholders?
> Does the board approve and provide input into strategy?

Enterprise Risk Management

Enterprise risk management has become a major concern delving into areas that may not have even been on the radar 10 years ago, such as cyber-security, environmental and social impact, and reputational concerns. This is in addition to issues about corruption, supply chain and manufacturing on a global scale, as technology now allows even smaller, less sophisticated organizations to expand their global footprint. Not knowing about working conditions and safety practices in overseas plants can spell huge reputational and financial risks for an organization, as witnessed by the brand damage to certain clothing retailers from lack of sufficient international oversight. A board that is aware of risks, that can speak from experience, and that can provide counsel on navigating risks, is invaluable.

One risk area that is often overlooked relates to human capital. Boards should be requiring executives to provide a human capital dashboard report, no different than a financial report, on a regular basis. It should include measures of: overall turnover, but in particular, turnover for mission critical roles; investments in human capital; development of bench strength; and employee engagement. Relatedly, the board should be ensuring that succession plans are in place for mission critical roles.

Strategy Advice

Traditionally, the board has played a critical role in approving strategy. Of late, there has been some movement toward having boards more involved in the co-formulation of strategy to ensure complete understanding and buy-in if they are to be held accountable. Execution of strategy, however, should remain the purview of management, with appropriate controls and reporting to the board.

CEO Succession Planning and CEO Evaluation

Two board roles which often receive less attention, but are also of critical importance are CEO succession planning and CEO evaluation and development. While boards are typically on top of ensuring that strategic and financial objectives are met, CEOs are not always held accountable for making sure that the right and engaging culture is created, that they are measuring and monitoring turnover, and that they are invested in assessing and developing executives and high-potential individuals within the organization. Boards should be routinely asking questions about investment in human capital.

TABLE 20-4

Illustrative Questions to Evaluate Board Processes

> Does the board engage in effective renewal processes (succession planning, ongoing development, evaluation nomination of committee chairs)?
> Are new members effectively oriented to the board?
> Are board mandates and role descriptions in place?
> Does the board have norms of operation?
> Does the board effectively manage an annual agenda?
> Are meetings held with the appropriate frequency?
> Are meetings run effectively and do they accomplish clear goals?
> Does the board receive information critical to decision making in a timely manner?
> Does the board communicate effectively with management?

Board Processes

A board evaluation should consider all board processes associated with arming directors to best perform their jobs. The starting point is ensuring that there are clear norms in place for how the board operates, how decisions are made, and how the board engages in development. Board processes should also follow the complete life cycle of directors, from identifying, nominating and orienting new board members to establishing and managing director terms, and providing ongoing education and feedback. Processes should also be established for board succession and identification of committee chairs. A complete board evaluation should also assess communication systems within the board and with the organization, how meetings and agendas are managed, and the frequency and focus of meetings.

The Scope of a Committee Evaluation

Just as boards should be assessed to ensure optimal performance, so too should committees of the board. The starting point is to ensure that the right committees are in place, and that they are staffed with the right people. Much of the scope of committee evaluation is not dissimilar to how boards are assessed. The following questions would typically need to be addressed in a committee assessment:

- Are committees staffed with the right directors (mix, independence, skills)?
- Is the size appropriate for decision making?   .
- Are there effective processes in place for orienting and developing directors for the committee?
- Are agendas and communication packages circulated sufficiently in advance?
- Are meetings run effectively?
- Are meetings held with the appropriate frequency?
- Are directors sufficiently available?
- Is there ample and complete discussion of issues?
- Is information sufficient to make decisions, and is it provided in a timely manner?
- Are decisions reported back to the board in an effective manner?

The Scope of Director Evaluations

Assessment of directors is perhaps the most contentious of areas from an evaluation perspective. For many directors it may be the first time they have been assessed and received any kind of feedback in many years, and the process has to be handled sensitively. While some director evaluations focus on an assessment of contributions, the assessment can be strengthened by expanding the scope to focus on two additional components: (1) the skills, knowledge and expertise directors bring to the table, and (2) the behavioral competencies they display. Whereas the expectation around knowledge, skills and expertise is that each director has several critical skills needed by the board, the expectation is not that they cover the full range of skills. The expectation around behavioral competencies, however, is that each individual director should demonstrate all the competencies associated with being a high-performing director.

An assessment of the differentiating behaviors is essential to ensuring the right board dynamics, helps prevent a single-minded pursuit of results at all costs, and promotes an equal focus on how results are obtained; these are key to sustained performance. While an achievement focus is important, it needs to be displayed in combination with other behaviors; its singular pursuit can lead to short cuts, ethical lapses and short-term thinking. A director who loses control, cannot hear others' perspectives, lacks a moral compass, or cannot work with others despite exceptional knowledge and expertise, is rarely a long-term asset. Similarly, directors who are too easily swayed and lack the confidence to express their views are not as effective as they might be.

The director assessment can flag potential issues with specific directors, highlight when currency may be lacking, and raise concerns with the profile of the board as a whole.

While there is a range of important competencies, three of the most critical ones are the confidence to challenge, emotional control and listening with respect. Together they reflect an ability to be able to appropriately both weigh and challenge others' perspectives, and to be able to do so without derailing a discussion with emotional outbursts. Also important is ensuring directors understand the boundaries of their roles, and maintain the separation between oversight and management.

Director assessments should be approached with a note of caution, as they can go horribly wrong if not handled appropriately — long-standing relationships can be harmed. The assessment process should be transparent to all. Before embarking on this course, three key decisions need to be made:

- Who will provide input,
- Who will see the feedback, and
- Who will debrief each individual on his/her results and any developmental action required.

The first decision — who should provide input will be discussed more fully below. Typically it is the board chair and the individual director alone who sees his/her own feedback, although there are variations. In some cases, the governance or HR committee may also see results. In other cases, boards may decide that for the first round of assessments personal feedback is shared only with the individual director. In terms of providing input, unless the chair is highly skilled, it typically is recommended that an external, trained party provide the feedback to the directors, while the chair can be present. This is to ensure that it is delivered in the most impactful and sensitive manner, that relationships are preserved, and that the focus is on development.

Board and Committee Chairs

A special subset of directors are chairs of the board and of committees. A board evaluation should consider the extent to which they:

- Provide appropriate leadership and direction — both to the board/ committee and to management
- Promote full discussion and invite input
- Set the appropriate tone for meetings
- Manage conflict
- Allow for dissent to be expressed
- Provide needed information to make decisions

- Run effective meetings
- Provide feedback to directors, the CEO, and other key executives
- Manage board processes.

What Methodologies Can Be Used to Evaluate the Board?

Now that the scope of board evaluations has been defined, it is also important to consider the range of options for how to conduct them. There are four main methodologies, each with its own advantages and disadvantages. Some can be used as stand-alone approaches, while others are best used in combination with other approaches.

TABLE 20-5

Board Evaluation Methodologies

Surveys:
> Can be paper-based or administered electronically
> A variation is real-time polling
> Cost efficient
> Allow for a wide range of questions to be asked of a large number of people
> Unless customized, provide the least actionable insight

Interviews:
> Typically provide more candid and fuller responses than survey
> Allow for probing and discussion
> Can be time-consuming and more costly than surveys
> Limit to the number of questions that can be asked in a reasonable time frame
> Requires some expertise in design, delivery and consolidation

Research:
> Focuses on measurable and observable areas, and compares to benchmark data
> Does not provide a complete picture
> Best used in conjunction with other approaches

Observation
> Allows a third-party assessment of board dynamics, which can lead to coaching and development
> Can sometimes lead to "playing to the camera," but this dissipates over time
> Limited in application
> Best used in conjunction with other approaches

Surveys

Paper or online surveys are typically the most efficient approach. While these are inexpensive, allow a wide array of questions to be asked, and are sufficient to indicate that a board has met listing requirements, they typically do not yield the best and most actionable insight.

Adding a degree of customization to a survey, and probing issues that may be of particular importance for one's organization/board, certainly help enhance its value and the actionable insight that can be derived. Surveys can include peer assessments as a component, whereby each director is rated in terms of contributions, knowledge, skills and expertise, and competencies. Some organizations are choosing to move away from surveys to do "real time" polls, to allow for an on-the-spot discussion around results. While this type of approach can be effective, typically it is best reserved for pulse checks, to assess progress against particular areas, rather than as a baseline survey, as only a few areas can be adequately explored at a time.

Interviews

The second most prevalent approach uses interviews. While this approach often yields rich data, it is difficult to obtain the breadth of coverage that is possible through a survey approach. Typically, interviews are conducted by external parties as this tends to elicit the most candid responses. Interviews can be more costly than are surveys and require skill in designing the questions, conducting the interview and consolidating qualitative data in a useful manner. Interviews can stand alone, but they are often used in conjunction with surveys to flesh out responses and probe areas that may be more sensitive.

Research

The third approach is research-based. It is predicated on the fact that asking for perceptions should be limited to non-observable/verifiable areas. For example, asking about perceptions of ratios of independent to external directors may be less important than actually measuring the ratio, and comparing it to benchmark data from boards of similar sizes, stage of growth and industries. The research approach includes review of documentation, such as mandates and charters, board and committee minutes, communications, and strategy documents. Research is best combined with other methodologies.

Observation

The last approach is observation. It involves using an external third party to assess how the board, committee and directors interact in meetings. It allows for specific and targeted feedback around both individual and group dynamics. When observation is first introduced, it can lead to a bit of "playing to the camera," but over time, interactions become fairly normalized.

Each approach is useful and serves a purpose, but in order to gain the most from an evaluation, a multi-method approach is recommended — beginning with surveys, fleshing out further in interviews, and reviewing all objective measures. Adding on observations further amplifies the impact.

Who Should Provide Input to Board Evaluation?

One last decision needs to be made in designing an effective board evaluation: who assesses the board, committees and directors? While there is no one best answer, typically expanding input from outside the directors themselves provides more useful data. The key is to begin with the questions that are to be answered, then determining who are in the best positions to provide perspective.

Clearly board members need to provide feedback at the board level, but given the role of the board, input provided by executives who interact with the board is also critical. For example, asking directors about the extent to which they advise and mentor the CEO may yield very different responses than asking the CEO the same question. And, executives may have a different perspective of how the board functions at meetings, the quality of skills and expertise at the board table, and the degree to which directors respect boundaries of their governance role.

Two additional perspectives might also be considered at the board level: key stakeholder groups and analysts. In a world of activist shareholders, online (mis)information, and social media, boards are being increasingly called upon to transparently reach out to their stakeholders to manage risk. Sharing information and educating shareholders on vision and direction in the good times builds support and helps CEOs withstand scrutiny during bad times. By involving investors and analysts in board evaluations, boards can stay on top of how they are being perceived and build defensive strategies around the conversations shareholders are having, as well as the key points that attract activist shareholders.

At the committee level, committee members should clearly provide input, but it is also helpful to gather input from executives who support the committee.

Director assessments tend to be more contentious, in terms of who provides input. Directors are often uncomfortable providing peer assessments, but simply completing a self-assessment is of limited value. It is recommended that director assessments follow a 360-degree approach, similar to what is typically adopted for executives, whereby they complete a self-assessment, the board or committee chair provides insight, fellow directors provide input, and finally, as appropriate, executives provide input as well. More reliable and valid data come from asking for input from multiple perspectives. This approach prevents an insular view of how the board is performing.

Putting It Together — A Framework

If the objective is to create an actionable developmental plan, a more robust approach is required than simply an off-the-shelf survey. It is important to begin from an understanding of the organization's context, so as to identify appropriate comparators, and critical requirements. This step focuses the evaluation on what is important for the particular organization.

Further, using multiple methods to assess the board moves beyond self-assessments, to a more accurate read of how the board is performing. Finally, any board evaluation that does not end in an actionable plan that is monitored and reported on is of limited value. Identifying two to three high-priority areas for the board as a

FIGURE 20-2

Annual Reassessment

Determine Context	Specify Requirements	Assess against requirements	Take Action
Company strategy	Compositions, size, mix, independence	Surveys	**Composition**
Mission		Interviews	– Changes in who or size
Stage of life cycle	Compentencies: who, technical, behavioral	Competency assessments	**Compentencies**
Regulateion		Obseration	– Develop
Benchmarks/best practices	Prossesses: meetings, information, governanace	Document review	– Recruit
→		→	– Separate
	??? Mandate		**Processes**
	→		– Classify inter-accountabilities
			– Rules of engagement
			– Improve
			Roles
			– Clarify roles, expectations
			– Act on all relevant mandates

Annual Reassessment

whole, for committees, and for each director should be the outcome for the year, with a planned revisit.

Any evaluation that results in no areas for development is typically a red flag that there is something more afoot.

Critical Considerations

There are two key considerations that need to be addressed prior to launching any board evaluation. The first, largely discussed above, is around the delicacy of assessing directors. Prior to launching any director assessment, it is paramount that the process has been thought through. Beyond who provides input, who sees the data and who provides feedback, there has to be a common understanding as to what happens with the feedback and what post-assessment expectations are. Specific questions to be considered include:

- Can poor assessment results lead to asking a director to step down from the board, or are they meant to be purely developmental?
- Is development required, and how will it be monitored?
- Are documents maintained?

The last question flags a larger consideration; board evaluations are likely discoverable. A board evaluation may reveal weaknesses at the board level that could be used in claims against the organization and its directors. Before embarking on any evaluation, it is important to have a well-defined process in place regarding documentation, discarding documents and minutes with regularity, and recordkeeping, and it is appropriate to seek the advice of counsel in order to build in safeguards.

In sum, the impact and value derived from board evaluation can be tremendous, but they are also a function of the effort put in. The more robust and thoughtful the approach, the more actionable the insight that emerges.

CHAPTER 20

Board Succession Management

By Christine Rivers, Connie Schroyer and Robert Hallagan

Continuity within executive leadership, board membership, and board governance enables boards to understand and effectively oversee short- and long-term strategy. Shareholders are well served when board membership includes people with key skills, including experiences and characteristics that support strategic direction and implementation. This reduces not just the risk of poor controls, but also the related risk of not responding with focus on the current and projected environment.

Likewise, term limits for directors can provide for planned and organized refurbishment that highlight new perspectives, experiences and contributions. Governance committees do well to consider both optimal turnover and succession to the board.

This chapter:

- Describes the role of the board vis-a-vis management in creating the company's strategy.
- Addresses the skills, expertise and experiences that may be sought in board candidates.
- Examines the processes involved in the search for board members, including strategic succession management and long-term planning that approaches the search from the perspective of creating a "fit for purpose" board.
- Discusses the importance of a formal program for on-boarding directors and suggests typical components of a well-designed on-boarding process.

Formation of Strategy

Many boards today participate much more in strategy formulation with management than ever before; this is in comparison to when a board's role was more oversight and approval than real stewardship. In fact, boards may now more actively assume their oversight role while management drives the action plans and measurements.

Progressive boards aim to optimize strategy formulation by processing distinct inputs from a variety of sources and perspectives. The synthesis that emerges can be stronger than any single point of view because this type of environmental scanning avoids the pitfalls of "group think" and the challenging dialectic hones the perspectives of both board and management. Each participant in this endeavor sharpens his/her own understanding. They challenge their own thinking, while addressing the concerns and hopes of their colleagues. Together, their focused response to a plethora of opportunities transcends the older process where management developed a strategy, with or without consulting help, and a board stamped its approval.

Director Experience

To drive such a robust development and delineation of long-term strategy, boards require a diversity of skills and experience. Governance committees have the task of inventorying the areas of knowledge, skills and experiences that currently fit the chosen direction and determining which other areas should be included as the future unfolds and strategies evolve.

Also, the mix of personal characteristics that have been effective in the current culture can point to ways to add point and counterpoint to the board. For example, boards can utilize a complement of assertive versus studious types. Some directors should be well versed in finance, while others should bring an understanding of operating areas such as manufacturing, sales cultures, or lines of distribution. Consideration of these experiences in future directors brings focus to the recruitment and selection and provides a template for director evaluation and personal growth.

The question of when and where to begin is defined by whether the board considers this activity as strategic or tactical. That is, a tactical activity serves to fill a current need, as required by a director leaving or some other reason requiring the addition of a director. A strategic approach takes a long-term view, is a continuous conversation and evolves in line with the evolution of the company's strategy.

Strategic board succession has the guiding principle of "the right people at the right time." This raises important questions:

- What experiences do we need on the board next, given where our organization is going?
- What upcoming tough decisions do we expect to have to make?
- What risks will we face?
- Do we have directors on our board who have lived through these scenarios before, and were there to contribute to their organization's successful navigation through them?

Varied experiences beg for a diverse director pool, and we often discover that within such more strategic context, diversity more naturally emerges. That is, while it is important to have diversity of perspective, experience and thought on any board, leading with it as a requirement solves only part of the equation. When the primary goal is finding directors who have faced and participated in successfully steering their organizations through real challenges and opportunities, locating directors who have diversity of thought and perspective usually emerge.

From that perspective, the board can determine if it has the right mix of skills, knowledge and expertise to take the organization to the next level of its development. The results should yield a specific profile of experiences, skills, and characteristics that is diverse enough to avoid blind spots, "group think" and the dangers of stagnation. Assembling the board this way is sound practice as the board can now draw a straight line between its discernment of candidates and the requirements of the roles to be filled. Knowing what you are looking for increases the probability of finding it. Employing strategic succession management principles to board succession insures a comprehensive and on-going assessment and matching of characteristics and challenges as the future unfolds.

Starting the Board Search

With an agreed assessment of needs, the governance committee can make inquiries. There are more people seeking board membership than there are spaces to be filled. Commissioning research on available people, conducted either internally or by third parties, indicates where prospective candidates can be found. Search firms can be engaged to supply a bevy of candidates within the pools that the board suggests be investigated.

Initial contacts should be positive, representing the company well and should include a discussion of the time commitments, investment opportunities and requirements, committee work and overall expectations. Members that miss more than 75% percent of meetings are usually noted publically, so understanding the time involved and how it fits into personal circumstances should be handled upfront.

Focusing the Board Search

A company may have a governance committee that looks over the general fit of proposed candidates with the profile and whittles down to the best few who can fill the most urgent roles. Many organizations conduct some form of assessment of the best few board candidates to insure that they fit the diverse profile.

After an assessment report is considered by the governance committee, it can be shared with the full board for discussion and endorsement to move to the next stage of the process. An opportunity to meet with the full board in a formal or informal setting should allow the board to put context around the assessment report and make a final recommendation. And so, with agreement on the profile, role to be filled and assessment report, a formal background check is in order. Assuming no potential concerns are uncovered, the full board then should be in a good position to act in good faith on the next step — based on the time horizon of the need for that particular candidate's profile. Unlike more tactical board succession, strategic succession planning, by nature of its long-term time horizon, may not have a need for that particular requirement for a few years.

Often at this point, the message to those not chosen, as they may not at this time fit the requirements outlined, is to "stay tuned." In strategic board succession, needs are always evolving and the board could have a much different set of needs in the future. Having vetted candidates in the wings is helpful to ensure the desired continuity while maintaining friendly relationships with candidates who may or may not ever be selected.

On-boarding New Directors

On-boarding is a very important succession activity. New board members are not likely to be thoroughly versed on industry trends, current regulations, market dynamics, the internal financial reporting system, the history of the board and the culture of the organization. Management should participate in a formal on-boarding program so that the new member is apprised of strengths, weaknesses, challenges, quirks and the operating model of the organization. Chief financial officers (CFOs) may explain the process that leads to the pertinent financials, how these numbers are derived and why they are important for measuring performance.

Each of the lead director, the board chair, the head of investor relations and the CEO should spend time explaining the culture of the board and the organization, the usual mode of operating, the past and current interaction of the board with management, how decisions are made and what analysts' expectations might be for the company.

The general counsel should formally discuss the legal requirements of board membership, current litigation and relationships with regulators. Marketing, manufacturing, supply chain and human resources also have important stories to tell. Members should have an opportunity, first hand, to observe manufacturing, distribution and employee interaction. Ideally, tours of facilities and opportunities to speak with management and employees should be arranged. Management hosts should neither stage-manage the encounter nor sugar-coat it; these kinds of experiences can provide a primary source for developing accurate perceptions of the organization. Management also should demonstrate the appropriate relationship between it and the board.

Formal seminars are available with various board organizations where directors can learn from other directors inside and outside their own industry. Networking provides sources to address unanticipated questions. Best practices have a way of floating all boats.

Putting It All Together

In sum, a board wants to know:

- What it needs in its members,
- How to specify and describe those needs,
- Where to find appropriate candidates,
- How it should assess candidates, and
- How it will on-board new directors.

Doing so is good for shareholders, helpful for current board members and outstanding for those chosen to fill the available roles. Well-formed boards contain members who can develop a good working relationship with their CEOs for the purpose of challenging, mentoring, intelligence gathering and support for the benefit of their management team. The board needs the right set of skills and experiences to make that happen. So when board succession is well planned and executed, boards can chose the best available candidates and not hastily fill an unanticipated need. The task of overseeing strategy, offering direction, being ahead of trends and staying within regulations is enhanced by a deliberate and healthy process. Good governance supports good leadership.

CHAPTER 21

Board Compensation

By Tim Bartlett

In reaction to well-publicized corporate scandals at prominent companies, the Sarbanes-Oxley Act of 2002 ushered in the current era of governance and oversight responsibility for all directors and led to significant changes in compensation design and total compensation levels for outside directors. Subsequent legislation and rulemaking, including enhanced proxy disclosure rules, expanded governance and compensation standards under the Dodd-Frank, and new listing requirements applicable to companies traded on national securities exchanges — all have affected director pay programs.

These legislative and regulatory reforms, coupled with increased scrutiny from various stakeholders, have resulted in a steady expansion of the duties and responsibilities for outside (nonemployee) directors at publicly traded companies. Shareholders, legislators, regulators and activist watch-dog groups have increased their demands on boards. Accordingly, the roles and expectations of boards have changed substantially. Directors must provide independent oversight and informed advice. The need has grown for a more nuanced understanding of multiple areas, including strategy, finance, marketing, technology and regulations. Time commitments and involvement levels of board members have increased. To an even greater extent than before, directors are faced with the possibility of public exposure (and even litigation) for their decisions.

With the dramatic rise in the complexity, risks and challenges that boards now face, companies need to take a broader view of how they think about board service. This broader view considers the linkage that exists between three elements of the board life cycle — succession, performance evaluation and compensation. In the same manner, this new way of thinking about board service considers the relationships between boards and CEOs, the relative responsibilities of both, and how they can communicate effectively with the various constituencies they serve. Membership on a board of directors is a job that must be navigated with the utmost prudence, discretion and thoughtfulness.

This chapter:

- Addresses the overall compensation of directors and board structure.
- Considers trends and best practices in director pay programs.
- Examines the concept and role of the lead director and nonexecutive board chair.
- Notes the previous discussion of director stock ownership guidelines in Chapter 10.
- Contrasts the roles of CEO and board chairman and provides reasons why a company might want to separate the two positions.

Board Compensation Trends and Developments

Although total compensation levels and mix has varied across industries and in relation to company size, traditionally the compensation package for outside directors at publicly traded companies has included:

- Annual cash retainer
- Committee chair cash retainer
- Lead director cash retainer
- Meeting fees (board and/or committee)
- Benefits/perquisites (e.g., matching gift programs, supplemental insurance benefits)
- Equity compensation

Director pay commonly has been linked with company size, with larger companies awarding higher cash retainers and total compensation to directors.

While similarities exist when comparing current trends to historical director pay practices (i.e., level and mix of pay continue to differ across industries; total compensation levels are correlated to company size; the use of annual cash retainers and equity awards are the primary elements of director pay), several new developments regarding the structure and form of director pay are evident in the current marketplace.

Elimination of Board and Committee Meeting Fees

The elimination of fees paid to directors for board and committee meeting attendance has been a growing trend. Where the use of meeting fees has been discontinued, companies are providing increases to annual cash retainers to compensate directors for meeting preparation and attendance. Companies that use this approach commonly cite the benefits associated with the simplification of the design and administration of their director compensation programs and the removal of the need to define what constitutes a meeting for fee-payment purposes. Among companies that have retained meeting fees for directors, a minority approach is to provide for payment of meeting fees only after attendance at a pre-defined number of board or committee meetings.

Increased Focus on Work and Pay at the Committee Level

Regulatory changes continue to increase director responsibilities and oversight resulting in more work performed at the committee level. Companies traditionally have provided additional cash retainers to the chair of a standing board committee (e.g., audit, compensation, nominating, governance) in recognition of the additional duties and time involved in chairing a committee. This practice continues, with the audit committee chair typically earning a premium over the other committee chairs. While increases in compensation committee chair retainers have been common with enhanced scrutiny on executive pay practices, a gap between retainers paid to chairs of the audit and compensation committees continues to exist at many companies at many companies.

Another way that companies are recognizing the workload, including responsibilities related to risk management, for non-chair members at the committee level is to pay additional annual cash retainers to non-chair members of the committees instead of meeting fees.

Shift to Full-Value Equity Awards and Change in Determination of Size of Equity Awards

Mirroring executive pay practices, director compensation programs have increasingly moved toward full-value awards (restricted shares or common stock) to deliver equity-based pay, with stock option use becoming a less prevalent practice. For director pay programs, the decline in stock option grants may be due in part to a concern that options could encourage inappropriate risk taking, as these awards deliver value only where there is appreciation in the share price.

The most prevalent method used to determine the size of equity-based director pay continues to calculate the awards through the use of a fixed dollar value, rather than determining the equity award based on a fixed number of shares.

Vesting Periods for Equity Awards Reduced to One Year or Eliminated

The typical approach is to vest annual full-value equity awards within one year of grant. As companies move to declassify their boards in response to pressure from shareholder advisory groups, this trend likely will continue with companies using vesting schedules of one year or less to align the vesting term with the directors' annual service period. Similarly, a short vesting period for director annual equity awards can be viewed as a "best practice," as it is thought to maximize director independence because a continued service relationship is not required for a director to receive compensation.

Equity Election and Use of Deferral Programs

As director compensation levels have increased, so have the number of companies that allow directors to elect to receive additional equity awards in lieu of cash retainers or meeting fees. This practice serves to further align director interests with those of shareholders and assists directors in meeting required stock ownership levels in place companies. Similarly, a common practice at larger publicly traded companies is to require or permit directors to defer all or a portion of their cash compensation or equity awards. This practice is supported by shareholder advisory groups that encourage companies to require that directors defer equity awards through or until retirement.

Director Stock Ownership Guidelines and Holding/ Retention Requirements

Various types of stock ownership guidelines and holding period/ retention requirements for companies' senior executives and board members are discussed in Chapter 10. Although less common than for executives (especially at smaller companies), boards are increasingly determining that the use of director stock ownership guidelines and holding/retention requirements can contribute to the goal of aligning the interests of nonemployee directors at a publicly traded company with those of its long-term shareholders. Increased focus by activist shareholders and advisory groups has generated pressure to improve the alignment of director and shareholder interests, and has led to the increased use of stock ownership guidelines and holding/retention requirements.

Nonexecutive Chair Pay Practices

Organizations that transition to a nonexecutive chair structure must establish the appropriate compensation (both level and composition) for the newly defined role. To attract the right person, organizations must compensate the individual appropriately.

Reasons for a Nonexecutive Chair to Separate the Chair and CEO Roles:

- Independence. Some believe that having a nonexecutive chair provides greater independence from management in terms of board leadership. A nonexecutive chair can serve as a check and balance on a CEO. Although separation of the chair and CEO roles creates greater independence, it is not a requirement for effective board leadership. Many effective boards have an

Issues That Have Affected Board Member Selection and Pay

> The imposition or lowering of a limit on the number of boards on which a member may sit has reduced the talent pool.

> Increased obligations, time commitments and risks for directors have caused some candidates and former members to decline board seats.

> There is a shortage of top-quality candidates and a need to replace some board members with independent directors or persons with a specific expertise (e.g., accounting expert).

> A requirement under Sarbanes-Oxley stipulates that the board have a "financial expert" as a member.

> Due to concern regarding potential liability for questionable practices, many boards have been forced to examine their governance structures and independence levels.

> A call for an independent "lead director" has evolved substantially in recent years, prompted by the concern that both the chair and CEO roles often are held by a single individual. Many believe that this arrangement concentrates too much power in the hands of one person and impedes board independence.

> The board has a unique governance role, and directors should be compensated differently than executives:

  - Directors should be compensated for exercising their fiduciary oversight responsibilities, not for the company's performance.

  - Equity should be aligned to shareholders; thus, full-value shares (e.g., time-vested restricted stock) are appropriate to eliminate decisions involving undue risk.

  - Retention should not be a key strategy for board members — it can be important to avoid entrenchment of directors and to allow the board a fresh perspective.

  - Directors should not be offered benefits (e.g., retirement payments, life insurance, health insurance or perquisites).

> The scrutiny placed on financial statements since 2002 Sarbanes-Oxley legislation and concern over executive pay (the 2010 Dodd-Frank Act and more information available under expanded proxy disclosure rules) have placed extraordinary demands on committee chairs. Board members at some organizations now are being paid through new or enhanced committee chair fees for meetings with auditors, legal counsel and executive compensation consultants prior to regularly scheduled committee meetings, as well as for the additional time involved in scrutinizing and approving information being presented at their committee meetings.

> Today's investors demand high standards of corporate governance and an especially well-informed and active board.

arrangement in which the CEO and chair roles are combined and a new leadership role (lead director) is created to provide a focal point for the independent work and independent functions of the independent directors.

- **Tradition.** While uncommon in the United States, some companies have a history that dictates that the chair title be held by a separate individual.
- **Transition.** A CEO may be too inexperienced or too new to the company to be given the chair title.
- **Time considerations.** A determination may be made that the CEO should spend his/her time managing the business, and the chair should spend his/her time managing the board and its corporate oversight functions.

The decision to combine or separate the chair and CEO roles is a company-specific decision. Companies should not rely on typical market practices or governance experts in making the decision about whether the roles should be separate or combined. Governance experts typically agree, however, that all companies should appoint an independent lead director when the chair and CEO roles are combined or when the chair is affiliated (e.g., a former CEO with the company).

Essential Qualities of a Nonexecutive Chair

There are several qualifications that should be satisfied by a nonexecutive chair:

- High integrity, accomplishment and emotional maturity
- Strong leadership capabilities and the ability to lead the board's oversight and advisory roles
- Respected by all directors and senior management
- Runs meetings effectively (i.e., draws out different viewpoints and knows when to intervene to keep discussion on track)
- Good listener (i.e., keeps a finger on the pulse of the board)
- Demonstrates independence of mind
- Has the courage to step up to challenging issues, including director or CEO performance issues.

Not only should a nonexecutive chair have superb personal qualities, but knowledge of the company's industry and the company itself can be especially helpful. If company experience is lacking, upon taking the job the nonexecutive chair must strive to learn the business, the people and the company's issues from the bottom up.

Of particular importance, a nonexecutive chair should have the time available to properly discharge the duties involved. The amount of time needed varies in each situation and depends on the complexity of the organization and its issues.

Pay Practices for a Nonexecutive Chair

Recent market data have yielded observations on approaches and practices in nonexecutive chair compensation:

- The ratio of nonexecutive chair annual retainer compensation to that of other board directors commonly ranges between 2.0 and 2.5, while the ratio of nonexecutive chair total compensation to that of other board directors is approximately 1.5.
- The pay package for the nonexecutive chair position does not approach the pay levels of an employee chair.
- The compensation for a nonexecutive chair who was never the CEO is generally higher than those who are former CEOs of the company.

Setting Pay of a Nonexecutive Chair

In establishing a process for determining the compensation of a nonexecutive chair, a guiding principle should be that the pay should match the commitment and effort required by the (nonexecutive) chair role. There are several approaches and factors that should be considered in setting nonexecutive chair compensation:

- The traditional approach long had been to compensate the chair with a fee or retainer that is linked to a daily fee rate.
- A more common method for establishing nonexecutive chair compensation is using a pro-rata amount of the CEO's pay (with a decision needed on whether to include or exclude LTI values). This approach considers the perceived value and influence in the company of the individual versus that of the CEO. It also looks at the time required by the role relative to a full-time position.
- Evaluating the complexity and effect of the chair job may be a useful exercise in creating a quantitative relationship between

the CEO and the board chair. The chair's pay then can be scaled against the compensation of the CEO.

- Alternatively, discretion may be used to set compensation that the company believes is representative of market levels and equitable based on the services.
- Boards must consider that the more compensation that is given to a nonexecutive chair, the more the perception of his/her independence is diminished.

Today any pay package for a board chair is likely to be scrutinized by the public and shareholders. Regardless of the process chosen, it is important that the decisions can be explained, defended and viewed as supportable under the company's specific circumstances and the requirements of the role.

What Does a Lead Director Do?

The lead director's primary role is to manage and facilitate a board's governance process and allow the board a measure of independence from the CEO. Other duties of the lead director may include:

- Serve as an objective conduit through which directors can communicate.
- Create a process that ensures each important issue is given both analysis and consideration.
- Act as a useful director recruitment tool, allowing directors to feel more accountable to other board members and shareholders.
- Demonstrate to shareholders, regulators and the public that the board is administering governance processes that are appropriate and defensible.
- Add a visible layer of independence at a company that has a CEO who is also the board chair.
- Help develop other board members, mentor newer members, provide guidance to manage board responsibilities and advance the learning curve.
- Conduct annual outside director performance reviews.

Lead directors may not be suitable for every company. However, in today's environment, most anything a company can do to emphasize board independence and thorough governance will only help build regulator, shareholder, investor and public confidence. Given the additional obligations and duties associated with the role, lead directors commonly receive an additional cash retainer fee beyond regular board service fees.

Director Pay Practices in Private Companies

Similar to publicly traded companies, it has become a challenge for many privately held firms to recruit qualified individuals as directors. While some key differences exist in the responsibilities of board members in the public and private sectors, the basic principles and practices that apply to publicly traded companies also should be observed for private companies. According to our studies, about three-quarters of private, for-profit companies provide some sort of cash compensation, while less than one-quarter provide stock as part of such director pay.

When considering director compensation private companies, total director pay is about one-half of amounts at publicly traded companies. This can be explained by the fact that 50 percent or more of total director pay for publicly traded companies is made up of equity-based awards.

A private company may benchmark against publicly traded companies, but then apply a discount to account for the lessened responsibility for regulatory and other issues not faced in the private sector. Generally, it is better to look at the business approach of paying enough to attract quality directors and make it worth their time to serve on the board.

Director Pay Practices in Tax-Exempt Organizations

Tax-exempt organizations traditionally have not paid their directors. Today, however, with competition for director talent and increased responsibilities for board members, many tax-exempt organizations have found it necessary to pay their directors or are considering doing so. See the section titled "Considerations for Board Pay" in Chapter 25 for tax-exempt organizations.

Roles of the Nonexecutive Chair and the CEO

Role of the Nonexecutive Chair

> Plays no role in company operations
> Provides advice and counsel to the CEO
> No company officers report to him/her; CEO reports to the board
> Has authority to call meetings of the board of directors
> Chairs meetings of the board and the annual meeting of shareholders
> Chairs executive sessions and debriefs with the CEO
> Sets board agendas and oversees board information packages
> Facilitates discussion among board members on key issues and concerns outside of board meetings
> Serves as nonexclusive conduit to CEO of views, concerns and issues of other directors
> Addresses any board or director performance concerns
> May represent the company with external stakeholders at the discretion of the board and in conjunction with the CEO
> Speaks for the company in a crisis situation when CEO is unable

Role of the CEO

> Leads company operations; officers and employees report to him/her
> Attends board meetings and the annual meeting of shareholders; makes presentations on company operations
> Receives feedback from executive sessions
> Provides input into board agenda items
> Provides content for board information packages
> Communicates with the chair on various issues between board meetings
> Raises with the chair any concerns management may have about board performance, individual director performance and board composition
> Represents the company to external stakeholders

PART V

Executive Compensation in Special Settings

.

CHAPTER 22

Mergers and Acquisitions

By Brian Holmen, Jelena Jovic and Robert Hallagan

Although a business transaction undoubtedly can have significant implications for an organization, executive compensation issues are often neglected once due diligence is complete. Executive compensation is seldom a deal breaker, but it can have a substantial effect on the deal structure and future operations of the ongoing organization.

In a merger and acquisition (M&A) situation, management and HR professionals must consider whether current pay programs are properly structured to retain and motivate executives if a potential transaction looms. The companies to a transaction must also carefully consider how to address the target's outstanding equity awards as the treatment of those awards will significantly impact the deal structure and post-acquisition integration of compensation programs.

Private-equity (PE) transactions and spinoffs, like other business transactions, demand considerable preparation; compensation elements that were once a critical piece of the overall system may represent limited or even no value to executives in the new organization. Many companies also discover too late that they need to rebalance their compensation programs to reflect the new post-transaction reality.

There are numerous moving parts in an M&A transaction, many of which are focused on financing and structuring the deal. Compensation programs prior to the deal typically reflect company culture — risk-averse companies favoring fixed compensation vehicles, higher-risk profile companies preferring variable compensation. Compensation systems must be adapted to the new environment, with particular attention paid to equity awards so that the newly combined team retains high-potential performers going forward.

This chapter:

- Briefly describes common M&A transaction structures.
- Discusses retention through the M&A process, focusing on retention plan designs that incentivize employees who are critical to integration and those who are critical to post-M&A operations.
- Examines alternatives to address a target company's outstanding equity awards in an M&A transaction and common factors that impact how companies to the transaction will treat those awards.
- Describes alternatives to address a parent company's outstanding equity awards in a spinoff transaction in which a subsidiary will become a separate entity.
- Illustrates how a PE transaction is structured and outlines key issues to consider, including who typically gets equity.
- Outlines common issues that a buyer must address when integrating compensation programs following an M&A transaction.

Common M&A Structures

An M&A transaction often takes the form of:

- An acquiring entity (Buyer) merging a subsidiary corporation into a target entity (Target), a transaction commonly known as a reverse triangular merger, or
- A Buyer acquiring the stock of the Target directly or indirectly through a subsidiary. Figure 22-1 shows a common acquisition structure in which a Buyer subsidiary merges into the Target, with Target surviving as a wholly owned subsidiary. Figure 22-2 shows another common approach in which a Buyer directly (or through a subsidiary) purchases all of the outstanding equity of a Target, with Target becoming a wholly owned subsidiary following the transaction.

The form of acquisition has significant implications for the transaction (e.g., corporate and tax implications) but is generally not as

FIGURE 22-1

Acquisition: Buyer Subsidiary Merges Into Target

FIGURE 22-2

Acquisition: Buyer Purchases All of Target's Equity

important in determining how to handle the Target's compensation arrangements (absent an unusual transaction structure, such as an asset purchase in which the Buyer purchases the assets, but not the liabilities, of the Target). With the exception of a discussion of spinoff transactions, the remainder of this chapter discusses M&A transactions in which a Target will become a direct or indirect subsidiary of the Buyer.

Retention Through the M&A Process

Historically, attention in M&A transactions centered on issues related to financing and structuring the deal with lesser focus on integrating compensation arrangements. However, as companies increasingly use M&A to buy intellectual capital and critical skills, the focus has expanded to include elements such as deal synergies and successful implementation. Consequently, the ability to retain key talent has become a meaningful consideration in any M&A transaction.

M&A presents inherent retention risks resulting from uncertainties with regard to job security and future company direction, as well as perceived increases in job size and workload associated with the deal. Successfully retaining key employees, for a certain period of time or through a particular event, in the face of these negative perceptions requires a well-constructed retention strategy.

Retention Considerations

Retention strategies may contain financial and non-financial elements and should be tailored to the needs and culture of the individual organizations that are part of the deal. While a retention bonus plan is often part of the overall retention design, in deciding whether to offer such a plan companies should consider some basic questions:

- To what extent will the deal integration/implementation be negatively impacted by the departure of key employees? As M&A strategies focus on acquiring intellectual capital and skills, stakeholders are evaluating the success or failure of a transaction with regard to the effective retention of key talent.

- Can we identify key employees and job functions for successful deal integration and/or operating the new business going forward? While there is a consensus regarding the importance of recognizing and retaining key employees, the complex nature of many transactions makes this a challenging process. Absent the ability and organizational will to undertake this task, the success of any retention efforts will likely be limited.

- What is the impact of existing compensation plans and severance/change-in-control policies on employee retention? In evaluating the need for a retention bonus plan and then determining appropriate plan design, it is crucial to understand how key employees will be compensated as a result of the deal from outstanding equity awards and/or terms of employment/severance agreements. This is particularly important if the transaction constitutes a change in control (defined in equity award agreements and employment agreements). For key employees without meaningful retention "hooks" related to equity or severance, the need for a retention bonus plan is heightened.

Where the success of a deal could be negatively impacted by unwanted turnover, efforts should be made to identify critical employees who are especially at risk of leaving. If existing arrangements do not provide sufficient incentive to remain with the organization, a retention bonus plan can be a compelling element of the overall retention strategy. To be effective, the retention bonus plan should be aligned with the unique nature of the deal and account for its size and complexity. In designing these plans, companies do not have the benefit of design templates or extensive market benchmark data; rather, they must evaluate the individual characteristics of each M&A transaction and the varying retention needs for each deal.

Retention Plan Design

While the design of a retention bonus plan must fit the unique nature of the transaction, several design components are commonly considered:

- **Retention bonus plan philosophy.** Prior to designing the plan, a crucial question to address is whether the retention bonus arrangement should be a "pay-to-stay" or a "pay-for-performance" program (or some combination of the two). The answer will be driven by whether the primary purpose is to retain key employees or to drive achievement of key integration and ongoing operational objectives. If the objective is largely retention, the use of performance conditions (and resultant uncertainty regarding payouts) may undermine the value placed on the retention awards by participants. If the goal is to drive achievement of key milestones, the use of performance conditions would be appropriate in retention bonus awards to participants leading this work.

- **Program cost.** Companies generally use one of two approaches to arrive at a cost for the retention bonus plan: (1) fix a percent of the overall deal value to set the retention bonus pool to be divided among the participants, or (2) identify the participants in the retention bonus plan and set target retention bonus amounts for each, the sum of which is the total plan cost. The cost of the

TABLE 22-1

Title???

Design component	Integration-critical employees	Operations-critical employees
Retention period	Depending on the employee, companies seek to retain these individuals throughout some or all of the integration process. Generally, this period is 6–18 months post-closing.	Companies want to retain these employees long-term. Retention period typically is 1–2 years as companies use the retention bonus plan to bridge these employees to the new organization's LTI plan.
Award type	Cash is the most commonly used vehicle to deliver retention bonus payments.	Companies often use a combination of cash and equity to deliver retention bonus payments. Equity awards are favored for executives and strategically critical employees. Equity allows companies to reward the effort necessary to integrate and operate the business as well as the effectiveness of that effort (as reflected in stock price movement).
Award targets	Awards may be determined as a percent of a participant's base salary, a fixed dollar amount, or a series of amounts that grows incrementally at the achievement of critical integration or ongoing operations milestones. Awards may vary significantly based on level in the organization, the degree of criticality to integration or ongoing operations, and the perceived retention risk for an employee. While awards must be justifiable to deal stakeholders, they also need be large enough to convince participants to remain with the organization for the desired retention period. Generally, awards made to operations-critical employees are larger than those to integration-critical employees.	
Payment timing	Timing of the retention bonus payouts is an important consideration for both the company and employee. A company would prefer to delay payments until integration is complete and the new business is running smoothly; however, that time horizon may not be realistic (or retentive) from an employee's perspective.	Commonly paid in a lump sum (or two installments) at the conclusion of the post-close integration period. If paid in installments, the design is typically back-loaded so that a larger portion of the award is paid at the end of the retention period. Generally, cash and equity awards are paid out/vested if a participant remains with the organization for a fixed period of time. Vesting and payment generally occur in 2–3 installments during the retention period. Companies that want to link retention bonus payouts with performance often condition vesting on the achievement of 2–3 milestones during and/or following integration.

retention bonus plan is typically considered part of the deal and the cost is included in the M&A financial model.

- **Eligibility for participation.** A common mistake made in the design of a retention bonus plan is to apply it broadly (or evenly) across the organization. This results in retention awards being paid to individuals who did not need additional incentives to remain with the organization and the dilution of resources available to retain critical employees who are viewed as more likely to leave. Eligibility for the retention bonus plan generally should be limited to critical employees (typically executives, senior management and job/individuals critical to integration) as opposed to broad employee groups.

In determining eligibility to participate, employees are often grouped into two categories: (1) employees who are critical to integration efforts ("integration-critical employees") and (2) employees who are critical to the ongoing operations of the new business ("operations-critical employees"). Retention bonus plan designs generally differ for these groups as to the design components outlined in the following table.

Given the scrutiny applied to M&A transactions in light of their strategic importance and total cost, work to identify and retain the human capital necessary to integration and operation of the new organization is especially important and should be undertaken during the due diligence or transaction negotiation stage of the deal.

Equity Award Treatment in M&A

Of all the business strategies that companies follow in their quest to increase shareholder value, M&A transactions typically garner the most attention due to the size of the dollars involved. The same focus on increased shareholder value also has resulted in the widespread use of executive compensation packages with strong links to corporate performance. Common LTI compensation packages include some form of full value equity awards (including RSUs and PSUs). While declining in prevalence, stock options still represent a significant portion of the LTI component of executive compensation packages at many U.S. companies. One of the most critical decisions in an

M&A transaction is how the companies involved in the transaction will treat the Target's outstanding equity awards in the transaction.

Common market approaches to address a Target's outstanding equity awards in a transaction include:

- The Buyer cashing out all vested Target awards and terminating all unvested Target awards at closing of the transaction.
- The Buyer accelerating vesting for all Target awards and cashing them out at closing of the transaction.
- The Buyer cashing out all vested Target awards and assuming all in-the-money unvested awards (i.e., awards that have a purchase price that is less than the per-share consideration paid to holders of common stock in the transaction). Underwater awards (those with a purchase price that is equal to or greater than the per-share consideration paid to holders of common stock in the transaction) are cancelled. This approach may be beneficial to a Buyer when there is significant retention value represented by Target's unvested equity awards.
- The Buyer assuming or substituting for all in-the-money awards (both vested and unvested awards) at the closing of the transaction. Underwater awards are cancelled.

In most transactions the Buyer will cash out vested equity awards but a Buyer will sometimes assume or substitute for vested, in-the-money awards (typically stock options) to provide Target's executives and employees with an opportunity to benefit from any share-price increases that may occur in the Buyer's stock price following the transaction. Tax considerations (e.g., IRC section 409A) may also preclude a Buyer from cashing out Target's vested equity awards upon the closing of the transaction, in which case those awards would be assumed or substituted. In contrast, a Buyer will almost never assume underwater awards as they would provide virtually no retention value post-closing, as discussed below. In such a scenario, the Buyer can provide greater upside to Target's employees by granting new equity awards post-closing.

- When a Buyer assumes or substitutes for a Target's outstanding stock options (whether vested or unvested), tax law generally requires that the assumed or substituted stock options preserve the option "spread" of the Target option (i.e., the difference between the option exercise price and current fair market value (FMV) of the underlying stock, multiplied by the number of options). To preserve the aggregate option spread, the ratio of exercise price to FMV must be at least as high as it was under Target's stock option design. (This is why most Buyers will not assume underwater stock options in a transaction; the assumed or substituted awards would remain underwater to preserve the negative spread on the stock options.)

In Table 22-2, the ratio of exercise price to FMV for Target stock options is 60 percent ($12/$20). Therefore, the exercise price of the Buyer stock options to be issued to Target's executives must be a minimum of $30 (60 percent of $50, the FMV of Buyer's stock). The current aggregate is calculated on Target options as $20,000 (2,500 options times $8), and then the number of Buyer stock options to be granted to Target's executives is calculated as 1,000 ($20,000/$20).

Factors That Impact Equity Award Treatment in M&A

A number of factors impact how the companies to a transaction will treat a Target's outstanding equity awards, including:

- **Terms of the Target's equity plan and award agreements.** Equity plans and/or award agreements often mandate the treatment of equity awards in a transaction (typically defined as a change in control), such as requiring accelerated vesting of all or a portion

TABLE 22-2

Example: Preservation of Option Spread

	Buyer	Target
FMV	$50	$20
Exercise price	$30	$12
Spread (FMV minus exercise price)	$20	$8
Number of options	1,000	2,500
Aggregate spread (spread times number of options)	$20,000	$20,000

of unvested equity awards. In many instances, equity awards held by different individuals will have different terms (e.g., executive awards versus other employees' awards). Another factor that affects this analysis is the existence of a "double trigger" in a Target's equity awards (typically defined as a qualifying termination within a specified period, also known as protection period, following a change in control). For example, a "good reason" constructive termination trigger that is met if an employee's duties are diminished within 12 months following the transaction may be difficult for the Buyer to administer and can provide that employee with an incentive to pursue a good reason claim.

- **Cost associated with alternative approaches.** How the parties treat a Target's outstanding equity awards will have significant cost implications for the Buyer. For example, in a public company merger the Buyer will typically offer per-share consideration to Target's stockholders; each equity award that gets cashed out is therefore an incremental cost to the Buyer. In contrast, in a private company acquisition, a Buyer will typically offer a fixed price for all of Target's outstanding stock; in this form of acquisition, any Target equity awards that get cashed out will reduce the amount of the purchase price that will be paid to shareholders but will not impact the purchase price paid by the Buyer. Buyers must evaluate these considerations carefully in determining how to treat Target's outstanding equity awards.

- **Structure of the Target's equity awards.** It is difficult for a Buyer to assume or substitute for some forms of equity awards, such as certain forms of performance awards. For example, a public company performance award that includes market-based metrics (such as TSR or earnings per share) may no longer be measurable if that company becomes a wholly owned subsidiary of another entity.

- **Tax and accounting considerations.** As equity award design becomes increasingly complex, the tax rules governing those awards in the M&A context have also become more complex. Examples of tax provisions that may impact how the companies to a transaction treat the Target's equity awards include IRC sections 409A (governing deferred compensation arrangements, which include many equity award arrangements), 280G (providing for lost corporate deduction and associated excise taxes under Section 4999 regarding excess golden parachute arrangements), and 162(m) (governing corporate deductibility of performance-based compensation for certain senior executives in a public company). Discretionary accelerated vesting of unvested Target equity awards may also have accounting implications that need to be evaluated and understood before treatment of the Target's outstanding equity awards is determined.

- **Securities law considerations.** When a Buyer assumes a Target's equity awards or substitutes new awards for the outstanding awards, it has in essence granted the Target's employees the potential right to acquire the Buyer's stock. This grant may or may not be exempt from the requirement of shareholder approval by the Buyer's shareholders. The Buyer may also be subject to securities law registration requirements relating to the new awards and disclosure requirements to the Target's equity award holders in connection with these awards.

- **Target's capitalization.** In many venture-backed companies that secure several rounds of financing prior to the acquisition, common stock will sit below numerous levels of preferred stock in the capitalization waterfall. In such a scenario much or all of the transaction purchase price may be allocated to preferred stock-holders with little (or none) allocated to common stock holders and employee equity award holders. In these situations a potential Target may seek alternatives to equity to incentivize management and key employees to achieve a sale by implementing a cash carve-out plan that allocates a portion of any purchase price to be paid to plan participants before equity holders receive any transaction consideration.

- **Shareholder optics.** With the increasing scrutiny on executive compensation arrangements, including "golden parachute" arrangements, public companies involved in a transaction must also consider the optics of how they treat outstanding equity awards in a transaction. For example, a Buyer that permits full acceleration of Target's unvested performance awards at the closing of a transaction without regard to actual performance may want to consider explaining its rationale for this approach in any shareholder communications (e.g., a merger proxy) and generally should be prepared to address any shareholder and other stakeholder concerns.

Critical Steps in M&A Due Diligence

As discussed in the preceding section, numerous factors impact how the parties to an M&A transaction treat the Target's outstanding equity awards. It is critical in M&A diligence to determine early in the process:

- What Target's equity plan documents and award agreements permit and/or mandate in the transaction with respect to outstanding equity awards,
- The need to incentivize Target's key executives and employees post-closing, and
- The cost to Buyer of the alternative approaches to address Target's equity awards (for example, cashing out all Target equity awards and then granting new Buyer equity awards may be prohibitively expensive).

In our experience, these factors often influence how the M&A deal terms addressing equity awards are structured and, in the case of a public company merger, may often influence the per-share price the Buyer is willing to pay for Target's stock.

Treatment of Equity Awards in a Spinoff

Especially after a merger or acquisition, a company may decide to sell — or divest itself of — a subsidiary when it is no longer essential to its business model or long-term strategy. A spinoff is a specific type of divestiture in which, rather than being sold, a subsidiary becomes an independent company itself. In a spinoff, shareholders in the parent corporation (Parent) receive the newly issued stock of the former subsidiary (SpinCo). As a result, ownership prior to the spinoff is preserved through proportionate ownership of the Parent's stock and the stock of the SpinCo, as in Figure 22-3.

One of the critical compensation issues to address in a spinoff is the treatment of pre-spin equity awards granted by the Parent. The starting point for discussion and decisions regarding the treatment of those awards is to review the Parent's equity plan documents and individual award agreements to determine whether adjustments to equity awards are required or permitted in connection with a spinoff. Subject to any restrictions contained in the equity plan/ award documents, companies typically use one the following methodologies to handle outstanding parent company equity awards in connection with a spinoff:

■ Converting Parent equity awards held by specified employees into equity awards to acquire SpinCo's stock; this approach typically is made for employees who move to and/or stay with SpinCo. Parent equity awards held by all other employees will continue to be based on Parent's equity and will be adjusted to reflect the decrease in the value of Parent's equity as a result of the spinoff.

■ Converting all Parent equity awards (regardless of employee) into an equity award to acquire SpinCo's stock and an equity award to acquire Parent's stock (as adjusted to reflect the decrease in value of Parent's equity as a result of the spinoff).

■ Continuing to have all outstanding awards (regardless of employee) based on Parent's equity, and adjusting the outstanding awards

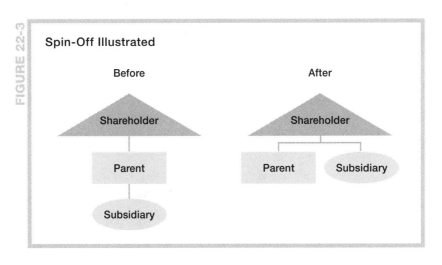

FIGURE 22-3

Spin-Off Illustrated

Before

After

Shareholder

Shareholder

Parent

Parent

Subsidiary

Subsidiary

to reflect the decrease in the value of Parent's equity as a result of the spinoff.

In our experience, the first two approaches outlined above are more common than the third. The rationale for using the first method is to ensure that employees are incentivized to maximize company value at the organization where they provide services. Also, this alternative commonly results in fewer accounting and tax complications than the other methods. The rationale for using the second approach is to incent employees to work toward the success of both companies before and following the spinoff, recognize the contributions of equity award holders to both Parent and SpinCo, and to allow employees to share in the value that they helped to create in each company.

Regardless of the method selected for treatment of outstanding equity awards, companies typically adjust outstanding Parent equity awards to preserve the aggregate intrinsic value of the outstanding awards before and after the spinoff. For stock options, these adjustments are designed to preserve the same ratio between the exercise price and the per-share value of the underlying stock as existed prior to the distribution. For time vested awards, adjustments are typically structured to maintain the award value, vesting schedule, service time and dividend rights as applied to the parent company awards immediately prior to the spinoff.

Is Private Equity in Your Company's Future?

PE firms are prominent players in M&A as these firms typically seek to acquire companies using significant leverage (debt) to finance the transaction and they seek to exit those companies through a liquidity event (typically a sale) in a relatively short timeframe, such as five years. Using leverage allows PE firms to obtain significant returns on portfolio companies that are sold at a profit.

In a typical leveraged buyout (LBO) transaction, a PE firm takes on debt in the Target's name and finances the remainder of the purchase price with cash raised from the PE firm's investors (which are limited partners in the PE fund in which the PE firm serves as the general partner). For companies targeted by PE firms, we developed the following primer on compensation and benefit considerations. In general, these deals are very complex with their own terminology. Table 22-3 provides a sampling of common terms. Following are key items to consider in preparation for an LBO transaction:

- An LBO transaction likely will trigger a change in control for the Target. As a starting point, this may trigger accelerated vesting and/or settlement of deferred compensation amounts, equity awards and/or other Target plans. Depending on a plan's payment trigger, amounts may become either payable immediately upon closing of the transaction (single trigger) or on an employee's subsequent dismissal "without cause" or resignation for "good reason" resignation during a specified window following the transaction (double trigger). Consideration must be given to the golden parachute rules of IRC sections 280G and 4999 and the conditions to avoid adverse tax consequences under IRC section 409A.

- Communicate often and early. Even if there is no actual deal, if your company is "declared" a target by the media, Wall Street or even a blogger, people will begin to develop their own theories about what is happening. Preparing employees with facts and information typically is the best approach.

- Special severance plans may be necessary. Employees may begin to receive calls from search firms. Even with a communications strategy in place, make sure that employees feel comfortable even if their jobs are eliminated.

- Inventory all current vehicles that were designed to retain employees and assess their retention ability under the current circumstances. Make sure that there are appropriate retention "hooks" that hold your most valuable employees in place before, during and after the transaction. Because many existing retention programs may have vested (e.g., equity, deferred compensation), new plans and strategies may need to be quickly designed, formalized and communicated.

- Recognize that incentive programs post-closing will likely vary greatly from the Target's plans in place prior to the PE acquisition. Many PE firms will grant a combination of performance-vested

TABLE 22-3

Common Terms in LBO Transactions

Term	Definition
Multiple of money	PE firm's estimate of the return on its initial investment (typically expressed as a 2x, 3x and so on.)
Sponsor	The private equity firm or group of firms taking part in the LBO
Portfolio company	One of the companies that is owned by a private equity sponsor
Liquidity event	An initial public offering, sale or divestiture of a portfolio company
Management promote	Equity plan in the newly private company designed to "promote" the best interests of the new private equity owners
Leveraged common stock	Preferred shares of restricted stock designed to create a tax-efficient vehicle for the management promote
Strip	Equal to option on 10 shares of stock
Buy-in	Direct investment by executives in the newly private company; can be a requirement in order to receive management-promote shares; typically capped in amount available per person and by level in the company (e.g., only available to SVP and above)

stock options (for example, performance will be tied to the PE firm's internal rate of return as of a liquidity event) and time-vested stock options to provide a combination of performance and retention incentives. Executives who are used to a broader scope of equity-award opportunities, such as RSUs and PSUs may need to be educated about the details of the post-closing equity plan (also referenced as management promote equity).

Once the deal is finalized, there still may remain a need to address various details regarding executive compensation arrangements. Considerable effort should be taken to ensure all compensation and benefit plan details are accounted for in the merger/acquisition agreement. In some cases, certain portions of the compensation packages may be subject to negotiation with the affected executives,

TABLE 22-4

Compensation and Benefits Issues Before, During and After a Transaction

Due Diligence: Pre-Transaction Planning	Deal Announced: Managing During the Transition	Going Forward: Managing the New Organization
■ Establish compensation and benefits philosophy - Market, position, mix - Different strategy (executive, salaried, hourly?) ■ Review change-in-control consequences of existing programs (e.g., acceleration of liability/payouts) ■ Measure accrued liabilities for programs with a future benefit promise (e.g., defined benefit plan, SERP) ■ Consider severance and retention plan costs - Buyer will want to know those costs on the front end	■ Create total remuneration strategy ■ Develop base pay plan - Bands/grades/other - Assess impact ■ Short-term incentives - Metrics, eligibility, etc. ■ Long-term incentives - Vehicles possible - Tax/accounting consequences ■ Audit benefit competitiveness ■ Redesign as appropriate ■ Identify appropriate vendors (e.g., TPA, outsourcers) ■ New plan documents, summary plan descriptions, etc. - New owner will want to be involved	■ Develop integrated statement of total compensation ■ Implement new compensation and benefits structure ■ Determine appropriate severance and retention policy for new organization ■ Identify administrative roles and duties (both internal/external) ■ Roll out and communicate

particularly if the PE firm has identified those executives as critical to the PE firm's strategy.

Ownership interests in the new portfolio company are often only provided to senior executives. In some circumstances, a cash-based LTI plan can be negotiated for other critical employees who do not participate in the management promote of the newly private company (e.g., corporate directors and vice presidents of a public company that is acquired by a PE firm). High-potential as well as mission-critical employees also may be included in a long-term plan with the new company.

Almost all equity interests under the management-promote plan are allocated when the deal is consummated; the remaining shares are held for new hires and targeted retention awards. Sponsors consider these awards as one-time grants that will carry management until a future liquidity event (typically a sale of the portfolio company). Sponsors often view a deal's horizon as five years or less until the liquidity event. The management promote usually will not have any feature that allows for disposition prior to this event. From the sponsor's perspective, executives need to be tied down for the deal's entire duration. This is a fairly long-term commitment for management given current rates of executive turnover and the lack of a more typical annual LTI grant program.

Table 22-4 provides some additional detail about compensation and benefit issues before, during and after a transaction. In the end, do not underestimate the compensation-related work involved and the complexity of these transactions. Changes will need to be made to many of the current compensation and benefit programs. Communications are critical during this type of transaction; keeping employees informed should help retain more of them throughout the transaction.

Integrating Compensation Programs

Integrating two sets of similar compensation programs can be challenging enough; then consider the potential difficulties when cultures, philosophies and program designs are distinctly different at the combining organizations. It can be daunting to resolve issues such as determining the appropriate compensation philosophy and reconciling compensation plan mechanics (e.g., eligibility, target award levels, award/grant processes, performance measurement, goal setting). If handled properly, these areas can be key drivers of success pre- and post-transaction.

In our experience, successful integration will typically include a review of the following factors:

- **Retention and performance incentives for the key executives and employees of the Target.** A Buyer may need to adopt a retention plan and/or provide equity award opportunities to key executives and employees to align their interests with those of the Buyer and to provide retention incentives for those executives and employees who will deliver the value to be derived from the acquisition. In transactions in which the Buyer is not assuming any of the Target's equity awards, incentives may involve Parent granting a block equity award (a larger equity grant than would typically be granted in an annual equity grant) at closing to provide holding power for Target's key executives and employees through the use of equity.

- **Integration of compensation programs.** Due diligence will inform the Buyer about the Target's incentive plans (including any short-term and long-term incentive opportunities) and successful integration will require the Buyer to harmonize Target's programs with the Buyer's business. This may result in Target participating in Buyer's plans post-closing, refinement of metrics in the Target's plans for future performance periods (or the in Buyer's plans if the acquisition is transformational for the enterprise as a whole) or a combination of these approaches. In many instances, the Target's annual incentive plan may need to be adjusted for the year in which the acquisition occurs, for example if the plan includes metrics that are difficult to measure post-closing once the Target is no longer an independent company.

- **Assessment of pay opportunities.** Executives and key employees within both the Buyer and Target may be assuming larger (or lesser) roles in the post-acquisition enterprise and adjustments to compensation opportunities may be warranted. For example, a merger of equals will result in Buyer's CEO running an organization that is twice the size of the pre-acquisition enterprise. The CEO's future pay opportunities will typically reflect this change.

- **Synergies.** Most Buyers will retain many of the Target's compensation and benefit programs for a specified period of time (e.g., through the end of the year in which the transaction occurs) to assess the programs and plan for integration. Successful integration will often include a review of the total cost of compensation and benefits of the combined enterprise and the combination/elimination of some programs to enhance cost efficiencies. Integration of benefit programs will require careful consideration of applicable plan documents and laws (e.g., tax laws, ERISA).

CHAPTER 23

Initial Public Offerings

By Brandon Cherry and Paul Hudson

In an IPO a company raises capital by offering its shares to the public via a stock exchange, such as the NYSE or NASDAQ. With a more liquid market for a company's shares and easier access to capital come numerous reporting and disclosure responsibilities and an expanded involvement of legal professionals, auditors and consultants. Upon being a public company there are also often different structures to pay programs accompanied by additional scrutiny from a larger population of stakeholders.

Companies intending to go public usually are aware that under SEC and stock exchange listing rules they will have to disclose detailed information about business operations to investors and the general public. They may not realize, however, that they can no longer rely on the compensation policies and practices in place while they were private entities. While equity compensation — typically but not exclusively in the form of stock options — garners the most attention in an IPO and generally represents the lion's share of potential financial gain for executives, other compensation elements need to be addressed before and after the company goes public.

Meaningful benefits can be achieved by realigning the executive compensation program in light of the new capital structure. Not to do so can lead to a perceived lack of alignment between executives and stakeholders.

This chapter:

- Addresses the importance of understanding the value of equity compensation in planning for and creating an IPO and discusses factors that may determine equity levels for executives hired before or after the public offering.

- Discusses the issues a company needs to address if it contemplates going public, including complying with SEC disclosure rules, likely changes to the annual incentive plan, equity compensation and dilution levels, and governance.

- Discusses the need to adopt a new compensation philosophy once the company goes public. Comparing pay levels against the competition, reviewing individual pay elements as well as target total cash and TDC, and updating employment agreements are also recommended.

Understanding Equity Compensation Prior to an IPO

Private companies often use their equity, or phantom equity designed to mirror equity, as an effective compensation vehicle to attract and motivate key employees prior to an IPO. But equity in a pre-IPO company is subject to much interpretation. Through thoughtful planning and communication, this powerful tool can have a strong perceived value to the recipient, allowing companies to potentially offer below-market base salaries, smaller annual cash bonuses or both.

However, this trade-off between cash compensation and company equity is a delicate balance and should take into consideration the potential value delivered to participants, as well as the portion of the company allotted to participants.

Understanding Value

Consider the question: "A competitor is offering me 100,000 shares; why does my current employer only offer 25,000?"

While a pre-IPO equity grant can have considerable perceived value, especially in a high-growth or momentum company, employees need to understand where their grants fit in the context of the company overall, as well as the competitive marketplace. The above question is one that compensation professionals often are asked and it can be difficult to answer. While 100,000 shares is more than 25,000, the important question is not necessarily how many shares, but how much of the company is being offered and at what price and how that fits into the overall valuation of the organization.

As companies move toward an IPO, financial analysis is used to understand potential share value. By analyzing additional rounds of financing that might occur prior to the equity event, an employee can understand how his/her individual grants will become diluted through each round of financing, as well as see the potential increase in company share price over the exercise price of his/her options. Even assuming a company proceeds all the way to an IPO, there is no way the company can definitively say what the gain at IPO will be for an individual participant; however, an estimate can be created using the overall market capitalization of the company at IPO and the estimated size of the offering. In the end, educating an equity plan participant on the value of a grant and how that grant relates to the marketplace could be necessary—sometimes 25,000 is much larger than 100,000, as shown in Table 23-1.

Determining Executive Equity

"As our company approaches an IPO, we need to hire a senior vice president; how do we determine the appropriate equity grant level?" Chances are, when a private company on the road to an IPO recruits senior managers, the shiniest carrot will be the equity award. A qualified, high-performing senior manager is not contemplating a move to a startup because the company has a generous pension

TABLE 23-1

Comparison of Potential IPO Scenarios

	Options Granted	Exercise Price	IPO Price	Option Gain at IPO
Current Offer	25,000	$2	$15	$325,000
Competing Offer	100,000	$13	$15	$200,000

plan or offers above-market base salaries. The equity grant is the lure and the question is: "How much is enough?" Unfortunately the answer is: "It depends." Important factors to consider are industry, size of the organization, additional potential dilution pre-IPO and what position the senior manager will hold.

The industry where a company operates plays a large role in the expectations and size of a pre-IPO equity grant. Generally speaking, a service-based company will offer less equity than a company operating in a high-technology market.

Companies in the technology field tend to be younger and riskier propositions given the highly competitive and fast-moving marketplace. Consequently, equity grants to technology senior managers generally are larger than those in the overall marketplace as companies attempt to mitigate the risk factor with an increase in the upside should there be an IPO.

Another key factor to consider is the importance of the company's structure in sizing executive equity grants. The size of the company, as measured in number of employees, annual revenue and/or market capitalization at IPO all correlate with the equity position at IPO — the smaller the company, the larger the equity position (share numbers, not value) awarded. A company with higher revenue, market capitalization or a larger employee base generally will have greater overall value and, consequently, the company can give away less equity to the senior managers and still deliver competitive value in its equity grants.

As mentioned, the expected dilution and the effect on individual grants is an important factor to consider when determining executive equity grants. A grant made to a senior manager hired in the period just preceding the offering will only be diluted by the IPO itself. Conversely, a grant made to a senior manager just after company formation could potentially be diluted by the IPO plus any additional rounds of financing that precede the IPO. The senior manager who comes on board just following formation is taking on a larger risk of individual dilution and the equity grant should likely reflect this inherent risk. Additionally, the earlier an executive joins an organization, the lower the probability the company will actually experience an IPO. The later a senior manager comes on board, the higher the probability the equity grant will have value in the marketplace. Consistent with equity investment, the greater the risk, the greater the potential reward.

Role and Responsibility

Finally, the company must consider the role and responsibilities of the individual senior manager being offered the equity grant. Will the senior manager have direct line of sight to the performance of the equity or does the position influence something that is measured less by company equity and more by a different company measure? An example of the position's importance in determining equity holdings can be found when looking at two senior management positions in the technology industry: chief technology officer and top sales and marketing executive.

Research suggests both positions would have similar annual total cash compensation levels but the equity held at IPO (shares owned plus shares subject to options as a percent of total shares

FIGURE 23-1

IPO Impact

outstanding) would be markedly different. In our example, a chief technology officer had median equity of more than 2.5 percent of the company at IPO while the top sales and marketing executive held less than 1 percent. Sales positions tend to have compensation geared toward annual performance while a top technology position is going to play an important role in developing company assets within the technology industry, which is critical to the creation of long-term company value.

Looking Ahead

While there is no magic bullet in determining appropriate equity grants in pre-IPO companies, there are critical questions that can be asked to narrow the focus and allow the company to make an informed decision while ensuring the executive is fairly compensated. The wild days of the late 1990s, where millionaire receptionists roamed Porsche dealerships, may be in the past, but there are still rewards for those willing to take the risk of working in a pre-IPO environment.

Preparing Compensation Programs for Public Company Life

When private companies seek to go public, they become interested in what is needed to prepare the compensation programs of a private company for the public eye. Going public through an IPO is not the end of the road; it marks the transition from operating as a private firm to doing business as a public company. Life as a publicly traded company means the company's stock is readily available for sale or purchase on a stock exchange. Public companies have easier access to capital and have liquid markets for their shares through such stock exchange listings.

The flip side is that a public company must comply with rules established by the SEC and the listing standards of the relevant stock exchange. As a consequence, a public company is required to disclose detailed information about business operations to investors and the general public. This mandated disclosure (see Chapter 14) contributes to significant differences in how privately owned companies can operate and in how publicly traded companies must function, which can materially affect compensation program design and administration. Additionally under Dodd-Frank, public companies are subject to a say-on-pay vote on executive pay by shareholders.

Required disclosure broadly falls into two categories: financial and compensation. In quarterly and annual reports, a public company must publish its income statements, balance sheets and cash flows, and management must explain these results. In the annual proxy statement (in which a company solicits the proxies, or votes, of shareholders), a company must disclose, discuss and analyze detailed information on the compensation of the CEO, the CFO and generally the other three highest paid executives (collectively, the NEOs). In addition to detailed disclosure of NEO compensation, a public company must provide information on compensation paid to all members of the board of directors. Details on the beneficial ownership of company stock of each director and NEO also must be disclosed.

Because much of a public company's compensation levels and practices are publicly disclosed, it is important that they can stand up to scrutiny and are defensible, both to shareholders and other stakeholders. Well-designed compensation plans provide competitive pay opportunities, truly link pay to individual and company performance, and communicate the behaviors and outcomes that drive shareholder returns. Before going public, a privately held company should be sure its compensation programs are consistent with public company standards; otherwise, the organization can face significant pressure from shareholders, the media and shareholder advisory firms.

Annual Incentives

Private companies sometimes have informal, discretionary bonus plans that lack clear performance criteria, funding mechanisms or targeted levels of awards. Well-designed annual incentive plans link an executive's pay to the successful achievement of goals important to company success. They also incorporate targeted incentives with base salaries so that pay mix and total cash compensation levels can be assessed.

An annual incentive plan used by a private employer (including a subsidiary of a public entity) may not necessarily be appropriate for a public company, potentially resulting in a review and modification of the plan in planning for the IPO. For example, a startup company may maintain a plan that emphasizes revenue growth as it positions for an IPO. Once public, expense control and return metrics commonly would be more appropriate than a top-line approach to incentives, although some newly public companies that seek to support aggressive growth goals may continue to focus on top-line measures like revenue. Annual incentive plans in privately held companies may also be riskier than is appropriate for a publicly traded entity given that the smaller shareholder base may have a riskier appetite than a broad-based shareholder population.

Consider an example in which a subsidiary's plan measures the unit's profit performance against a budget developed by the parent corporation. The subsidiary has no control over corporate cost allocations or the parent company's financial structuring decisions. If that subsidiary is carved out in an IPO, the new entity will have cost allocation and financial decision capability, and plan measures should be reconsidered.

Equity Compensation

Executives who join early stage startup and high-growth private companies can benefit by receiving equity compensation at then current (generally low) valuations. Companies that successfully go public can expect significant increases in their valuations, and equity compensation allows employees to share in this value creation. Of course, there are downside risks as well. Many startup companies do not succeed and even successful companies may be unable to go public when equity markets dry up or become volatile.

Private companies that plan to go public commonly use stock as an important component of their compensation programs, not just for executives but often for a broad group of (or even all) employees. This helps conserve scarce cash and links employees' interests with those of shareholders, but dilutes the stakes of current shareholders. Potential investors in IPOs typically want to see that key employees have an ownership stake in the company so that they are motivated to increase its value and minimize risk to the organization. Likewise, it is important for key employees to have some unvested equity stakes so that they must stay with the company for several years post-IPO to capture gains from post-IPO appreciation; they should not be able to just "take the money and run" as key executive departures following an IPO can cause downward pressure on an organization's share price. Further, this reinforces the idea that an IPO is not about going public, it's about being public.

Equity Compensation — Vehicles and Dilution

For many years, stock options were the currency of choice, but increasingly full-value shares (e.g., restricted stock, performance shares) are being used. (See Chapter 5 on "Public Company Long-Term Incentive Compensation: An Equity-Based Focus.") Regardless of the available award vehicles, companies need to consider several issues when evaluating equity compensation plans. A crucial question for investors, whether in private or public companies, is the dilution of their ownership stakes as a result of equity grants. The challenge is to balance shareholder concerns about dilution with the need to incentivize and retain the requisite talent.

Companies need to assess dilution from both outstanding grants and the number of shares authorized and available for future grant. Prior to going public, a company should obtain authorization for enough shares to cover projected grants for the next two or three years post-IPO (assuming dilution levels are not excessive). Acceptable dilution levels vary by industry, with high-technology and bio-technology companies generally higher than others. As a rule, potential dilution from shares granted plus those remaining for grant (also called "overhang") between 10 and 20 percent of outstanding shares is within competitive market practice with most companies coming in at the mid-point in this range.

At private companies, entity valuations and stock prices generally are low relative to similar publicly traded companies. This minimizes the charges to earnings from equity compensation, regardless of whether stock options or full-value shares are used. Once public, valuations typically are materially higher and stock prices are much more volatile. Charges to earnings will be greater, which means companies often need to be more selective regarding participation in equity compensation programs and the size and value of individual grants.

Other Issues

Prior to a public offering, a company needs to establish an independent compensation committee (e.g., no insiders such as executives on the committee). The committee should establish a charter stating its duties and responsibilities and develop a compensation philosophy that will shape its compensation decisions. Both of these will need to be publicly disclosed and should be crafted with transparency in mind. While not required, compensation committees generally directly engage an independent consulting firm for assistance with competitive market assessment and program design.

After a transition period (which needs to be carefully examined for its application to various types of awards), public companies are subject to IRC section 162(m), which limits the deductibility of non-performance-based compensation to $1 million per year for each of the CEO and the next three highest-paid executives (excluding the CFO). Non-performance-based compensation includes base salaries, discretionary bonuses and restricted stock. Formula-driven annual incentive plans and stock options normally qualify as performance-based compensation but still need shareholder approval.

Key Processes for a Newly Public Company

Compensation Philosophy

A company's compensation philosophy establishes the framework for executive compensation programs and provides a link to the underlying business strategy. A newly public company should not necessarily rely on the compensation philosophy used while it was a private entity; rather it should develop one in accordance with its new status. As part of this process, the company should define the desired role of each compensation element and its respective sensitivity to the performance of the company, business unit or individual.

Competitive Review of Compensation

Along with a change in the ownership structure (i.e., public investment), an IPO results in changes in the responsibilities of many executives and frequently the expansion of the executive team. To account for these different roles, a company may examine the competitiveness of its pay levels by identifying benchmark positions and developing competitive pay data through a mix of published and private survey sources.

When reviewing compensation levels, companies generally examine each pay element on an individual basis, as well as through a holistic, total compensation approach. While it is important that individual elements of pay be competitive and consistent with the company's compensation philosophy, a company typically would focus on target total compensation levels (total cash compensation and total direct compensation) more than on the individual pay components.

For example, a company may pay slightly below the competitive market for base salary, but provide above-market levels of target bonus opportunity and equity, thereby providing a competitive overall pay package.

Employment Agreements and Security Arrangements

The formation of a new public company may require employment or security arrangements for key personnel. Existing agreements should be examined and the need for new or updated arrangements considered. An employer is at a heightened risk of losing key employees during organizational change, especially an IPO, and the retention of key executives often is critical to the ultimate success of the IPO equity event. A company should take into account any additional risks assumed by executives during the transition and adjust compensation and severance protections accordingly.

ESPPs and Setting Policies for 10b5–1 Plans

A company preparing for an IPO might consider adoption of an employee stock purchase plan (ESPP) and setting policies related to 10b5–1 plans.

ESPP

Although more common in certain industry sectors, an ESPP is another vehicle that a board might consider before the company goes public. An ESPP allows employees to purchase company stock at a discount, and it can afford favorable tax treatment to the employee-purchaser so long as certain statutory requirements are satisfied. As broad-based plans, ESPPs can increase the interest of employees in the company's performance. When developing an ESPP, key areas for consideration are: the discount on the company's equity, the required holding period for equity, and the maximum amount an individual can purchase in a given year.

10b5–1 Trading Plan

Upon an IPO, a company and its insiders become subject to SEC Rule 10b-5 which prohibits trading by insiders on the basis of "material nonpublic information." Because trading windows vary from company to company based on dates of company report filings and certain announcements that constitute material non-public information, company insiders may have very limited time periods within which they may sell shares acquired through equity plans. However, compliance with a 10b5–1 trading plan shields the insider from SEC actions for violation of Rule 10b-5.

A "10b5–1 plan" allows an insider to trade shares at any time so long as all of the requirements of the rule are satisfied. Although a Form 4 must be filed for the transaction, the company can adequately address shareholder concerns regarding the timing of the transaction by noting in the Form 4 that it happened automatically via a trading plan rather than due to an announcement or other information.

In addition, as a company goes public, it should establish certain procedures and requirements that any person establishing a 10b5–1 plan must follow and satisfy, such as:

- Company approval — typically through its legal department — before any trading plan may become effective;
- A holding period between establishment of a trading plan and any transaction made under such plan;
- Open trading windows that would be the only times that trading plans could be established;
- Rules regarding disclosure of trading plans; and
- Limiting trades outside of a plan (if an executive has established a trading plan). Setting limitations reduces the public perception of insider trading and can stave off SEC attention on misuse of these plans.

Transaction-Specific Issues

Before developing or implementing any programs, a pre-IPO or newly public company should examine the practices of comparable organizations to establish competitive norms. When devising an appropriate comparator group, a company should consider factors such as industry, size, scope, business model, sources of recruiting top talent and strategic objectives.

The determination of competitive compensation practices for a specific transaction is more complicated than the determination for ongoing compensation elements. Developing an understanding of why a similar company implemented a compensation program is as important as discovering what it did. An employer needs to consider the nature of the transaction, the historical compensation practices at the company examined, and any information on future pay arrangements.

Points to Remember

Compensation planning during the pre-IPO stage can be difficult. However, the development of an executive compensation program that is cost-efficient, competitive, performance-based and aligned with shareholder expectations and value creation is critical to the ultimate success of an IPO.

CHAPTER 24

Bankruptcy, Retention and Other Special Situations

By Bill Gerek and Rachel Jay

In this chapter we examine compensation practices for executives at companies regarding certain special business situations or needs, including bankruptcy, executive retention, signing bonuses/awards and private-equity backed companies.

Each of the circumstances addressed involves compensation as a tool to attract, retain or motivate executive talent to support the execution of a business strategy or challenge arising from the particular facts. The covered situations involve shareholder concerns requiring special consideration in the design, implementation and communication of executive compensation arrangements.

This chapter:

- Discusses special rules applicable to, and key approaches used for, compensating top executives at companies in Chapter 11 bankruptcy reorganization proceedings. Well-designed compensation packages can help retain and motivate the executives to support a successful emergence from bankruptcy and future business improvement.

- Examines approaches commonly used to retain talent to manage the business, including strategies to address one-off situations. The success of the programs increase greatly when an organization proactively identifies the issues, addresses them within the context of business and compensation strategy and strives to strike the balance between executive and shareholder expectations.

- Addresses executive signing bonuses and awards as a tool for boards to use to attract and retain the top executives, after consideration of the board's objectives, the executive's expectations and shareholder concerns.
- Discusses the private equity (PE) pay model for portfolio companies that aligns the interests of the investors with those of the management team and creates a wealth accumulation opportunity that is a powerful motivator and influencer.

Bankruptcy

Corporate bankruptcies, which wax and wane with the performance of the overall economy, require tailored compensation designs to help struggling companies retain, and in some cases attract, talent to preserve value while also trying to reverse course and achieve profitability. As a company enters this strained time, it also faces the often conflicting demands of creditors, employees and shareholders.

The inherent struggle is to balance the need for a unique, retentive-based compensation program, which historically has meant emphasizing fixed compensation over performance-based variable compensation, in line with the expectations of creditors and other stakeholders who want performance to preserve their value and ultimately support growth and value creation. The challenge is to create a program that discourages the needed talent from exiting a rocking ship and a performance orientation that may restore the ship's course.

Further challenging the compensation design objectives are various legal and regulatory strictures. And ultimately, the compensation arrangements have to be approved by the bankruptcy court. With all of these parties and requirements to satisfy, often with contradictory interests, compensating executives in bankruptcy situations can present a real challenge as it tries to address the people challenges to help restore and create value.

Key objectives in designing executive compensation programs in bankruptcy situations include:

- Motivate and retain essential employees during the reorganization and after emergence.

- Demonstrate to affected parties that the proposed compensation programs are reasonable and appropriate.
- Develop a plan to obtain approval for the compensation arrangements in bankruptcy court.

Bankruptcies take distinct forms that impact compensation design differently. Most notably, a Chapter 11 bankruptcy addresses restructuring (under which key employees will be needed to turn around the business), while a Chapter 7 filing is a liquidating bankruptcy (under which the bankruptcy trustee may only need a small group of employees to help wind down and liquidate the business).

Our focus is on Chapter 11 filings where the company is attempting to reorganize under the protection of the bankruptcy court.

Chapter 11 Executive Pay Packages

Executives in turbulent business circumstances typically seek security — in the form of fixed compensation — via salaries and deferred/retention payments. While retention awards previously were common practice, the Bankruptcy Abuse Prevention and Consumer Act of 2005 (Act) completely overhauled the Bankruptcy Code and pay practices. The Act largely eliminated key employee retention plans (KERPs), which were intended to replace equity grants or other forms of LTIs that would have been awarded in normal course if not for the bankruptcy. KERPs were not performance-related but rather were designed to be retentive in nature.

The Act barred retention payments except when:

- Essential to retain an individual because he/she has a bona fide job offer from another business at the same or greater salary; and
- The individual's service is essential to the survival of the business; and
- The payment is less than 10 times the average amount paid to similar non-management employees in the current year or, if none, no more than 25 percent of any similar benefit provided the insider in the preceding year.

In addition, the Act limited severance payments, except for situations in which the severance is:

- Part of a program applicable generally to all full-time employees; and

■ Limited to 10 times the average of amount of severance payments made to all the employees.

Because KERPs or fixed retention payment styled programs are generally no longer permitted for insiders (officers and directors), it has become critical to focus on the incentive design for executives — to invest the executives in the turnaround of the company.

The Act did not completely eliminate payments to executives; rather, the focus moved from retention payments to incentive-based payments. Companies replaced KERPs with key employee incentive plans (KEIPs), which add a performance-based element to the awards. While retaining some design characteristics of the KERPs (e.g., cash awards with a value typically based on a percentage or multiple of salary), the awards have relevant performance goals attached to the payout of the award.

The performance criteria under a KEIP vary by business, but often relate to financial statement measures (e.g., operating income, cash flow), key strategic milestones in the form of successful sales of assets at predetermined prices or consummating other transactions, emergence from bankruptcy, and other key operational objectives. Program participation and performance goals are key to the design of an effective KEIP. The bankruptcy court generally will not support a KEIP that is too broadly based, does not identify the key executives and their role in the turnaround, and does not require "challenging" performance goals that support real value-add contributions.

In addition to the KEIPs, employees most often continue to receive the same level of salary and benefits as before the bankruptcy filing. However, due to the nature of Chapter 11 bankruptcy, LTIs and severance benefits are usually not available.

Retention Awards

Even well-performing companies can be challenged in retaining talent — often because the company is successful and has a reputation for developing talent. There is a premium placed on top talent; in a competitive market, it is prudent to regularly monitor pay and, when necessary, to structure a program to address competitive gaps to support and enhance executive retention. Public company disclosure, say-on-pay voting, third-party advisory groups and the media have all impacted the frequency and design of these programs; they have amplified the need for sound objectives, rationale and design to support the successful implementation of these special forms of compensation.

Retention strategies vary and range from the short-term (e.g., one to two years) to long-term (e.g., 10 years and/or retirement); the time frames depend on the company's particular requirements. Some organizations may need to emphasize critical short-term objectives (e.g., work toward a successful management transition, address a competitive pay gap). Others have a longer-term focus for retention periods (e.g., supporting succession planning for top leadership positions, launch of a new business).

While fixed awards or payments over time may have been the norm, shareholders have become much more vocal that the awards need to be more performance-based. Accordingly, restricted stock units with time-based vesting as the primary retention vehicle have come under scrutiny. Even though these awards have long been perceived as strong retention tools, external support for these programs is lacking and the usage is being re-evaluated, especially in companies that have a misalignment between pay and performance. In particular, retention awards have been viewed unfavorably by proxy advisory firms in cases where outstanding grants are underwater and/or annual bonuses have not been earned. Retention awards that appear to replace unearned pay may indicate a lack of commitment toward pay-for-performance.

The increased focus on pay-for-performance has complicated the balance of risk and retention in executive compensation programs. As the magnitude of the awards is evaluated quantitatively in conjunction with all other forms of pay (e.g. salary, bonuses, etc.), shareholders and proxy advisory firms now are paying attention to design of retention-oriented awards.

Portfolio Approach to Retention Awards

As a result, a change in practice from RSUs as the sole retention vehicle has evolved; retention awards in the form of time-vested RSUs are now more commonly granted in a portfolio approach (similar to LTI practices observed in ongoing annual grants), delivered in smaller amounts annually rather than in larger up-front grants, and in combination with stock options and performance shares.

While the inclusion of stock options and performance shares respectively require stock price appreciation and the achievement of goals (and are not traditionally considered retention awards), the remainder granted using the time-vested RSUs can support the delicate balance between executive retention and shareholder expectations. The increased leverage and wealth accumulation opportunities created by the stock options and performance shares can create perceived value for the executive while developing a level of external support. The retention award along with additional annual grants of LTIs and overlapping vesting cycles can be an effective way to retain and motivate management.

Alignment With Shareholders

Cash awards were often used to support shorter-term retention goals, but that practice is also evolving. Shareholders want improved alignment with long-term organizational performance, and equity awards accomplish that objective better than short-term cash payments. As such, equity-based awards earned over the short-term are more common, but with extended or delayed sale provisions to reinforce the long-term implications of short-term decision-making. Improved alignment with shareholders through equity can make larger payments more palatable since the ultimate value of the award is dependent on stock performance. In addition, equity-based awards can preserve company cash by funding payment of the grant through an open-market sale of the underlying shares.

Signing Bonuses and Other Signing Awards

Attracting the board's top candidate for CEO or other executive position often requires significant investment, which may include a signing bonus. Signing bonuses are commonly used to compensate the executive for awards and benefits forfeited upon termination of employment with the former employer or as an inducement award that further enhances the value of the pay package.

Signing awards may consist of special equity-based incentives provided to key employees who have a special expertise to entice them to leave their current jobs to join another company. Often the new employer may be in a situation where it is struggling or otherwise in transition, such as in Chapter 11 reorganization or undergoing a merger or acquisition. A new CEO may have been brought in to run the company during a period of uncertainty.

When an executive leaves his/her current employer, a typical result is a forfeiture of bonuses, unvested stock option gains and the value of unvested restricted stock grants and unearned performance awards. To convince the targeted executive to sign-on, a company typically will factor the value of those lost benefits into its offer in the form of signing awards.

Even where no special circumstances exist, many companies provide a new CEO (or other top executives) with signing awards, such as stock options, restricted stock and other LTI awards. Technology companies, in particular, tend to provide stock options as part or all of the signing award package. In the past, key employees left to join start-up companies where they received stock options, often taking a significant risk for a potentially huge payday. However, if the acquiring firm fails, the executive may be left with nothing if a portion is not provided in a cash award. Accordingly, there are situations, although in the minority, when cash incentives are included in the signing bonus in combination with equity-based awards.

Signing awards generally have vesting provisions to facilitate retention and to prevent any short-term gains in the event of voluntary termination. Further, companies often include clawback language in the grant document that allows the company to require the executive repay the bonus if he/she leaves prior to a certain date.

Similar to ongoing LTI programs, some executive signing bonuses utilize a portfolio approach and consist of two to three different incentive vehicles with RSUs and performance shares commonly used, often accompanied by stock options or cash. The goal is to provide retention (via the RSUs and/or cash) along with shareholder-focused, performance-based compensation (performance shares or, in the view of many, stock options).

Shareholder Views

It is important to consider the views of third-party advisers and significant shareholders when contemplating a CEO (or other top executive) signing bonus so that the award does not inadvertently run afoul of their say-on-pay voting guidelines.

The compensation committee's (or board's) objectives and the process used to determine the signing award should be carefully described in the public filings to present a sound rationale to the marketplace.

Private Equity Firms: Compensating the Executives of Portfolio Companies

Industry investment teams at PE firms operate in an environment of high valuations, with constant and intense competition for deals. As these teams may have hundreds of billions of dollars to put to use on behalf of their investors, they continuously search for opportunities to evaluate potential transactions and to operate their portfolio companies more efficiently and effectively. Increased emphasis is being placed on the human capital side of deals to address a key question: how can we align the interests of management and investors more quickly so that the process of value creation can begin sooner and enable us to hit our investors' performance expectations?

In recent years, there has been a greater appreciation of the talent side of the business in driving investor returns: namely, having the right talent that can execute the strategy, supported by a compelling compensation program, to expedite the process of creating value and delivering returns to fund investors. The compensation program is a critical management tool to help shape and motivate executive behaviors.

Although executive compensation arrangements at investment (or portfolio) companies have similar overarching philosophies and structures, each company has unique characteristics and opportunities that should be aligned and reinforced with focused pay programs. The make-up and quality of compensation designs can vary by deal, at times resulting in situations where management and investors are not fully aligned. This can create a need to formulate or leverage the PE firm's best practices to improve the effectiveness of the compensation arrangements.

Overarching Pay Structure

Private equity-backed buyout deals are wealth-creation opportunities where the combination of variable compensation and ownership creates a powerful compensation model that drives management team behaviors and reinforces the alignment of interests among the team, the business and the investors. The pay design typically includes three elements: base salary, an annual incentive opportunity and an LTI opportunity. This compensation structure is widely supported by the marketplace and institutional shareholders.

A fourth (and critical) element of compensation programs is an expectation that management co-invests in the portfolio company along with investors. Such use of personal funds creates real "skin in the game," reinforcing management's commitment to the success of the business and strengthening its alignment with investors. Investment team professionals also are expected to invest in their deals to reinforce their alignment. The commitment of personal proceeds unifies the interests of the fund investor, the deal team and the portfolio company executive team.

Compensation Elements
Annual Cash Compensation (Base Salary, Annual Incentives)
Base salary is de-emphasized in the overall pay program and tends not to fluctuate when a company is acquired unless there is something unique about the existing pay structure. The goal is to provide a competitive salary within a pay framework that emphasizes variable, performance-based compensation.

While many portfolio company annual incentive programs are discretionary (which is also common in the financial services model), we favor the more structured annual incentive programs utilized by public companies: predetermined performance goals that align with a leveraged incentive opportunity. These arrangements typically consist of a target bonus (expressed as a percentage of salary), combined with a threshold payout for near achievement of goals and an upside (or maximum) opportunity that aligns with superior levels of performance. This common model helps limit short-term decision-making and reinforces the long-term upside of the LTI and ownership elements of the pay model.

Long-Term Incentives

The LTI program, along with the co-investment, are the primary drivers of shareholder alignment and the wealth-creation opportunity.

Types of Awards

Historically, the LTIs were in the form of appreciation-only awards (e.g., stock options) that were consistent with a growth strategy and with the PE carried interest model, which, broadly stated, is equal to 20 percent of the appreciation over a performance hurdle. More recently we have seen full-value shares (e.g., restricted stock) being implemented in the LTI program for the same reasons observed in public companies: retention-focused, more akin to ownership, and with fewer shares/less dilution required.

There are also LTI vehicles used in PE-backed deals that mirror the economics of stock options or restricted stock (e.g., profits interests) but with the potential for preferential tax treatment. Operationally, these awards are similar to stock options or restricted stock, but require very specific structuring and coordination with legal counsel.

Grant Frequency

A significant difference in the grant strategies between a portfolio company and a publicly traded company is the frequency of the LTI grant. Given the expected short-term ownership of the portfolio company (four to six years), the LTI is usually granted at one time at the close of the transaction. This approach provides the executives with an opportunity to maximize their returns by receiving their entire grants upfront, allowing for the full awards to participate in the value created.

A challenge to this strategy can occur when a company may be in the portfolio for a longer term than originally anticipated. As the value creation and exit time frames take longer, they begin to impact the perceived value of the LTI award (e.g., with an assumed five-year horizon). In such cases, management teams may seek "refresh grants" and/or opportunities to monetize portions of their investment prior to an exit event; these variations run counter to the PE model.

Participation

Portfolio company LTI plans typically are limited to the senior executives who are most directly aligned with value creation. While programs at public companies commonly go much deeper into the organization, the structure at PE firms reflects their limited share reserves, complexity of arrangements and a philosophy that stresses putting ownership into the hands of the executives who are most directly accountable for delivering returns. Organizations that need to provide LTI to a broader set of employees may use multi-year cash plans, but the emphasis of the wealth-creation opportunities still is focused on the senior management team.

Vesting

The LTI program typically follows public company practice: a combination of time and performance-vested awards. Practices vary, but a common approach is 25 to 50 percent of the award being time-vested, with vesting on the balance (50 to 75 percent) of the award contingent on satisfying performance criteria.

The performance standards generally consist of one or two return-based criteria: return on capital invested (usually 2X and higher) and an internal rate of return requirement (typically 20 percent and higher), which considers the amount of time required to generate the return on capital invested. The performance-vested awards typically have multiple tranches with increasing performance requirements (e.g., 25 percent vests at 2X return, 25 percent vests at a 2.5X return).

Monetization

The ability to monetize, or convert the awards to cash, is aligned with the investors, and occurs when the portfolio company investment is sold (i.e., the exit event) and the investors receive their return.

Co-Investment Opportunities

The alignment of interests is further strengthened when management co-invests in the portfolio company along-side the PE investors. This is a powerful element of PE strategy as it creates a unified ownership model among the fund investors, investment team and management team that ultimately aligns all stakeholders toward a successful exit event (and subsequent monetization) in the future.

The management team's proceeds are often funded by transaction-related payments triggered by the sale to the PE firm: payouts from LTI programs, retention awards, or severance or CIC payments are all potential sources of funds for investment in the portfolio company.

CHAPTER 25

Executive Compensation in Tax-Exempt Organizations

By James Otto

Although their funding comes from private or public donors, membership fees, tuition, grants, and the provision of services, tax-exempt organizations mimic compensation practices of their for-profit competitors. In the field of health care, for example, tax-exempt organizations are important players whose major competitors can include large, publicly held health-care companies and a variety of life-science firms. Like the for-profit companies with whom they often compete for board and executive talent, tax-exempt organizations must attract and retain talented management and provide sufficiently competitive levels of pay and benefits.

Tax-exempt organizations are the focus of considerable external scrutiny, especially regarding governance issues relating to executive compensation. Much like the heightened sensitivities within audit committees that increased their workloads, tax-exempt boards and their compensation committees must now devote considerably more time justifying their executive compensation decisions than they did not too long ago. The tax law's requirement to pay no more than reasonable compensation (now enforced primarily by the "intermediate sanctions" rules) and governance reforms and changes in the private sector have prompted many tax-exempt boards to go beyond mere compliance and adopt best practice models of governance found in successful public-traded companies. Today, the issues and concerns surrounding executive pay and benefits in many tax-exempt organizations are largely the same as those in for-profit enterprises.

This chapter:

- Discusses how the current climate of accountability and transparency in the private sector has challenged tax-exempt organizations to develop governance practices beyond the mandated disclosure requirements.

- Reviews the intermediate sanctions provisions of the IRC and outlines the key elements of good governance practice and related issues such as the need for a precisely articulated compensation philosophy. A total remuneration ("Total R") approach that unites all pay elements in one coherent philosophy and compensation program is presented.

- Describes the use and design of LTIs and SERPs in tax-exempt organizations as part of a comprehensive approach to compensation.

- Answers the question, "Should we pay our board?" The factors that go into determining board pay as well as how and what to pay directors are discussed.

Current Influences on Executive Compensation in the Tax-Exempt Sector

From small associations operating in local communities to well-recognized international charities, educational institutions, private foundations, museums and health-care organizations, tax-exempt organizations span a broad organizational spectrum. Guided in their operations by core missions and values, these organizations have been established and are operated to satisfy the rules that exempt them from federal and state income taxes. Retaining this tax-exempt status is a vital concern, and oversight of executive compensation plays a crucial role.

While the rules that affect this oversight responsibility have been in place for many years, the importance of paying executives based on the outcomes of good governance practice has never been more important. The influence of stakeholders of tax-exempt organizations has increased significantly and shapes how board members and senior leaders conduct the affairs of the organization. These groups include donors, employees, bond holders, local communities, service recipients, labor unions, state legislatures, the media and the IRS, each of which finds the incendiary aspect of executive compensation an avenue to exert influence in one way or another.

The call for increased accountability and transparency that pervades all aspects of corporate governance today in public companies is also being felt in tax-exempt organizations. This phenomenon was first apparent with the passage of the Sarbanes-Oxley Act of 2002, and the specific provisions of the act that affected executive compensation at publicly traded companies (e.g., the ban on loans from corporations to officers). Tax-exempt organizations, many of which include prominent for-profit executives on their boards, were encouraged to adopt some or all of the governance and accountability standards imposed by this legislation and the governance and disclosure practices utilized within their own companies. (See "Influences from Sarbanes-Oxley.")

This impact was heightened by the passage of Dodd-Frank. That statute included provisions that affect executive compensation at publicly traded companies (e.g., independence of compensation

Influences from Sarbanes-Oxley

Loans to Executives

One of the most publicized aspects of Sarbanes-Oxley is its prohibition of most personal loans by a covered company to a director or an executive officer. In the past, tax-exempt organizations occasionally made loans to executive officers, often to enable them to purchase a house upon hire or transfer into a more expensive real estate market. Although such loans still are possible in tax-exempts that have not instituted a policy barring their use, current best practices would require an especially strong reason for using this much-criticized practice.

Codes of Ethics

Under Sarbanes-Oxley a public company must disclose whether it has adopted a code of ethics for its senior financial officers. In the event there is no such code, reasons for this failure also must be disclosed. The basic concept of a code of ethics is readily transferable to tax-exempts, as is the developing view that such codes should also be extended to other officers and board members.

committee members and recoupment of incentive payments in certain instances) that are considered and often adapted by tax-exempt organizations to augment and improve the oversight of executive compensation. (See "Influences from Dodd-Frank.")

Good Governance Practice

The income tax requirement that tax-exempt organizations oversee the compensation of their executives and not pay excessive compensation to its key executives has been in place for decades. However, the 1996 enactment of the "intermediate sanctions" provisions (IRC section 4958) and the IRS' subsequent promulgation of detailed regulations complicated the decision-making process on executive compensation at tax-exempts. (See "Intermediate Sanctions.")

As detailed in the intermediate sanctions regulations, the requirements that need to be satisfied to obtain a presumption

Influences from Dodd-Frank

Clawbacks

A key component of Dodd-Frank's executive compensation provisions requires most public companies to have (and disclose) a policy regarding the recovery (clawback) of certain types and amounts of incentive compensation paid to identified executives if the incentive compensation was based on results in financial statements that must be restated for certain reasons. The interpretation and implementation of the Dodd-Frank clawback rules were conditioned on the adoption by the SEC rules followed by their inclusion in listing standards of the applicable securities exchange. While SEC rulemaking does not apply to tax-exempt entities, these organizations consider SEC rules when developing their own policies.

CEO "Pay Ratio" Disclosure

The Dodd-Frank provision requiring disclosure of the median of the annual total compensation of all employees of a public company (other than the CEO), the CEO's annual total compensation, and the ratio of these two sets of numbers, has generated heated debate and discussion as to the usefulness of the outcome in understanding the executive compensation program at public companies. Even though tax-exempt organizations are not subject to this rule, the disclosure of these numbers by public companies likely will prompt its boards and compensation committees to consider the nature and level of executive compensation in relation to the pay of other employees of the organization and will likely influence the "how" and "how much" discussions that these bodies already are having. The SEC rulemaking also may generate internal discussions regarding the fairness of pay at all levels, "living wage" demands, and other social justice issues that can impact how the organization's mission should influence the executive compensation program.

that compensation is reasonable are now considered to be part of a good governance practice. These requirements, coupled with the increased scrutiny of executive compensation and the fact that boards of tax-exempts can be held accountable for unreasonable compensation, have improved governance practices and the oversight of executive compensation at tax-exempt organizations.

Independence of Board or Committee Members Overseeing Executive Compensation

The income tax regulations on intermediate sanctions (discussed below) describe independence in a way that is fairly narrow in scope: is each member of the board or committee free of any conflict of interest when deciding on compensation for a particular executive who is covered by the regulations? An example of a conflict is when a physician is on the board that determines

Not only has legislation affected how tax-exempt organizations oversee executive compensation, but the regulations that have been developed by the IRS (discussed later in the chapter) and the rules issued by the SEC that operationalize relevant laws have been a major influence. For example, committees that oversee executive compensation in tax-exempt organizations are much more aware of the need to answer the "how" and "why" questions about the levels of compensation provided and the modes used to deliver it. These questions reflect the intent of the CD&A, which is part of the proxy statement for most publicly traded companies. In essence, the CD&A must describe material actions of compensation committees and the reasoning behind their decisions.

Finally, the IRS overhaul of Form 990, which now includes much more detailed disclosure of compensation for senior executives and detailed description of how executive compensation is determined, also has influenced the oversight of executive compensation in tax-exempt organizations.

At the same time that today's regulatory and governance concerns are increasing the focus on (and affecting the oversight of) executive compensation, tax-exempts must attract and retain talented management and provide compensation programs that enable them to deliver upon their core mission. This often requires competing for talent with for-profit entities. For example, in the field of health care, most major providers are tax-exempt organizations whose talent pool can include large, publicly held health care, managed care and life science companies.

These two dynamics — increased scrutiny of executive compensation and the need to attract and keep management teams — provide challenges to any organization. A well-considered oversight process is the bridge to addressing both of these and maximizing the benefits for the organization at the same time.

Intermediate Sanctions

To maintain their tax-exempt status, organizations have been required for decades to pay no more than reasonable compensation to executives and avoid private inurement (net earnings of the organization cannot "inure" to individuals or shareholders) and private benefit (activities must serve public rather than private-benefit interests) when determining the level and method of compensating executives and other identified employees.

IRC section 4958, popularly known as "intermediate sanctions," is a more recent provision affecting executive compensation at tax-exempt organizations. Statutory language is supplemented by extensive regulations that give the IRS the ability to assess financial penalties on both executives and board members of section 501(c)(3) and 501(c)(4) organizations for any "excess benefit transaction" involving a "disqualified person." (Prior to intermediate sanctions, the IRS could either revoke the organization's tax exemption or overlook the violation when it determined that an executive was paid an unreasonable amount; the excise tax under IRC section 4958 provides an "intermediate" result between these two extremes.) Although the intermediate sanctions legislation was enacted in 1996, it was not until the regulations were finalized in early 2002 that active enforcement began.

Paying unreasonable compensation to a disqualified person is an "excess benefit transaction." A "disqualified person" is a person in a position that currently can exert substantial influence over the affairs of a tax-exempt organization or could do so during a five-year "look back" period. Top executive officers and board members generally are disqualified persons. The value of all consideration and benefits received by a disqualified person in a year is examined in determining whether there has been an excess benefit transaction for that year. Both the individual receiving the unreasonable

the compensation of a CEO of Health System, and that CEO is involved in negotiating the compensation of that physician, who is an employee of Health System. Tax-exempt organizations are taking into consideration an expansive definition in determining whether a committee member is independent, which often includes using relevant portions of the "independence" definitions that exist in the national securities exchanges' standards. The objective is to ensure that the organization can take the position that the committee overseeing executive compensation is independent of the organization in making these decisions (and not just free of conflict with respect to a particular compensation arrangement).

Defining the "Market" for Comparability of Data

Two IRS projects examined whether organizations satisfy the requirements to establish the presumption that compensation is compensation and the board members who authorized payment of the unreasonable compensation may be subject to the financial penalties under IRC section 4958.

To minimize concerns with intermediate sanctions, tax-exempt organizations must be able to demonstrate that a covered executive's total executive compensation is reasonable. The regulations provide three basic requirements that, if met, establish a "rebuttable presumption" that compensation is reasonable, which shifts the burden of proof to the IRS to show that the compensation is unreasonable. The three requirements are:

> Executive compensation arrangements must be approved by an independent body with no conflict of interest.

> An independent comparability study that considers all elements of compensation should be conducted and the results used to assist the independent body in determining compensation levels. This data may be obtained through compensation surveys, an examination of compensation of similar individuals in similar organizations and/or an expert compensation study. (See "Defining the 'Market' for Comparability of Data.")

> Approval of executive compensation arrangements should be documented before the latter of the next meeting or 60 days after the final actions of the decision-making body; this documentation should include:

   – The specific terms and conditions of the approved transaction and the date approved;

   – The members of the decision-making body who were present during debate on the transaction that was approved and their votes; and

   – The comparability data that was relied on by the decision-making body and how the data was obtained.

reasonable: in a review of tax-exempt health-care organizations and more recently in a review of private colleges and universities. In the study of the educational institutions, the IRS noted that some failed to satisfy the requirement that they used data of comparable organizations; this was based on the group of organizations that were used to develop compensation data for context in making compensation decisions. The IRS identified a number of factors to be considered, but most importantly, focused on educational institutions as the starting point for determining which of these types of organizations should be in the group. (The IRS also indicated that some organizations used as "comparables" were in entirely different industries.)

Tax-exempt organizations should consider this guidance as they review, update and rationalize their group of comparable organizations when developing comparability data, in particular when tax-exempt health-care providers expand their operating model to include non-traditional business lines such as commercial health insurance offerings. Business lines that are outside the scope of traditional health-care service providers raise the issue of what is the appropriate peer group for these new lines.

Why Are We Making the Decision That We Are?

The use of comparability data provides the compensation committee and board with context for making decisions that are specific to and support the particular needs of the organization. In the past, committees and boards were prone to following the market (i.e., doing what the market says other organizations are doing because other organizations are doing it). Committees and boards are now being asked, and are demanding of themselves, to articulate why they are making any decision that affects any executive's compensation arrangement. For example, "why should the organization adopt a supplemental executive retirement plan?" By asking and answering this type of question, committees are expressing the business rationale for the decision and how their decision makes sense for the organization. Committees also are requiring greater insight from their consultants and HR departments, particularly with respect to the relevance of a comparator group and data that is developed based on that group.

Process and Roles

The intermediate sanctions regulations imply a process that culminates in documenting the decisions made. Organizations are expanding this documentation requirement to formalize the process by which executive compensation is reviewed and modified. This codification can take the form of items such as:

- Compensation philosophy
- Compensation program documents (e.g., annual incentive plan, LTI plan, severance policy)
- Committee charter (number of members, "independence" definition, scope of authority, reporting responsibility, succession)
- Committee calendar (number of meetings, typical agenda items)

- Role of compensation adviser, legal counsel and staff support
- Maintenance of meeting minutes
- Attendance at each meeting by outside counsel.

This level of detail provides the foundation on which organizations can complete the information required on Form 990 and develop the manner in which the organization wants to respond to any stakeholder inquiry on executive compensation.

To evaluate the degree to which the board is driving the process and the decisions, the IRS can access the board's documentation to understand how decisions are made, including compensation committee and board minutes, documentation of decision-making, rationale for the market positioning of specific executives and the board's executive compensation philosophy.

Compensation Philosophy and Components of the Compensation Program: Critical Sub-Elements

A compensation philosophy is the touch point when making compensation decisions. A philosophy can furnish critical guidance for the board, the compensation committee and executive leadership in making consistent pay decisions, and is a key document for the IRS to review in an audit. A philosophy articulates:

- **The "market."** Which organizations are to be compared with the organization? From where does the organization recruit executive talent and to where does the organization lose executive talent?
- **Job match.** How should the organization's jobs be compared to jobs at these comparable organizations?
- **Compensation elements.** What are the components of the compensation program (e.g., base salary, annual incentive, LTI, benefits)? Why are they being used? How does the component play a role in facilitating performance, retention or recruitment?
- **Compensation mix.** How do the components interrelate? For example, how much of cash compensation should be based on performance (incentives) and how much is to be based on service or the job (base salary)? How should benefits be taken into account, in particular any executive-level benefits?

- Compensation positioning relative to the market. What is the target market level for the various components of pay and the various combinations of pay? What is the desired pay positioning with the competitive market for talent and the rationale of that positioning?
- Pay administration. How are the CEO and committee to interact when determining pay levels? For example, does the committee approve all pay changes based on CEO recommendations?

The discussion involved in developing an organization's compensation philosophy provides a timely opportunity for the board or compensation committee and management to agree on how compensation is linked to the organization's mission, and what messages the organization wants to send to its external and internal constituents. The philosophy needs to be approved by the committee or board and

Total R

Link Total R to Performance

Total Remuneration, or "Total R," is the resulting combination of all of the compensatory components of the compensation program. Total R should reinforce priorities and focus employees on the desired behaviors and outcomes for the organization. Hay Group research with Fortune magazine's "Most Admired" companies shows that these organizations differentiate rewards based on performance. Top performers are rewarded highly, while pay is limited for poor performance. In our experience, tax-exempt organizations that successfully link Total R to performance:

> Take the time to discuss what performance is and what success looks like. For many organizations, what constitutes real performance is often not obvious.

> Look at relative performance, understanding how the organization compares with similar ones.

> Examine and negotiate performance measures rigorously.

> May not always pay out incentives. Boards can now look back over some prior period and see how performance compared with payout. What was the payout each year? Was there variability? Did the payouts align with the perception of success?

> Reinforce the importance of the top team by linking a substantial amount of pay to achieving organizational goals.

Broaden Total R to Promote Succession

Organizations that recognize the need to develop and retain experienced, innovative executives are establishing succession strategies based on intrinsic Total R components as well as extrinsic components (base salary, incentives, benefits and perquisites). Executives identify quality of work, development opportunities, work-life balance, satisfying work environments, reputation and values, and leadership effectiveness referenced as a check when executive compensation is established and annually assessed. (See "Total R.")

The IRS has made clear that a compensation philosophy is the foundation on which compensation decisions should be made and is an indicator of good governance practice; it believes that organizations are less likely to pay unreasonable compensation if good governance practices are followed.

A compensation program captures the compensatory components identified in the compensation philosophy and the documents related to these components. Therefore, the program includes such items as base salary, incentives, specific benefits and the manner in which each of these is documented (e.g., for an incentive component, through the combination of a plan document and specific

---

as the top factors that influence their desire to stay with an organization and assume bigger positions. Organizations that focus on those variables show measurable results in attracting and retaining talented executives and achieving business objectives.

Communicate Total R to Participants

Communication translates leadership decisions about Total R into clear messages for executives. Organizations that are most successful in communicating Total R emphasize the integration with mission, strategy, performance and desire to raise employee satisfaction. One approach provides executives with online access to the value of their individual total remuneration arrangements. This approach helps executives understand the true value and employer cost associated with each pay component.

Assess and Update Total R Annually

This process can be conducted internally or through the use of independent advisers. Most organizations prefer outside advisers for their expertise, objectivity and access to benchmarks. The process must involve compensation committee deliberation and use relevant market data as a basis for setting executive pay.

Engage a Third Party to Confirm Reasonableness of Compensation

An independent third party that is qualified to professionally assess compensation can help demonstrate the reasonableness of compensation. A third party can conduct an analysis of total remuneration levels and assist in determining that compensation levels are within a reasonable range. The third party also can issue an opinion letter to confirm the use of comparable data as part of the effort to establish a rebuttable presumption of reasonableness (and shift the burden onto the IRS to overcome this showing) and minimize the risk to the committee members that they would be subject to financial penalties under the intermediate sanctions provision if the IRS were to prevail in a determination that compensation was unreasonable.

actions taken by the committee that are memorialized in committee minutes). The continuous review of the philosophy and the resulting compensation program are a key part of the ongoing oversight of executive compensation.

SERPs and LTIs: Components of the Compensation Program and Design Issues to Consider

One element that committees consider including in the organization's compensation programs is a SERP, a nonqualified plan that long has been and continues to be a key component in compensation programs at tax-exempt organizations. Boards and compensation committees at tax-exempt organizations continue to use this type of plan in a variety of situations, in large part because of the design flexibility afforded.

Organizations must take into account the specific income tax rules that apply to these plans when sponsored by tax-exempt organizations. SERP benefits are taxable when no longer subject to a "substantial risk of forfeiture," which essentially means upon vesting. An executive no longer risks forfeiture that is substantial when he/she does not have to provide any future "substantial services" to the employer to receive the benefit. (In general, this is not the same way that the IRC addresses SERP benefits sponsored by taxable organizations — those plans can be structured so that benefits vest and are taxed later, when they are paid).

Compensation committees or boards have flexibility in designing the vesting schedule within a plan; for example, the same vesting schedule does not have to apply to all participants in the plan, so the vesting schedule for a mid-career hire who becomes a participant in the plan at age 55 may be different from a newly promoted 40-year-old executive who has always worked at the organization.

LTI arrangements are an increasingly common element in compensation programs at tax-exempt organizations. These plans typically are designed to complement the goals of the annual incentive plan and focus a select group of executives on achieving specific, multi-year, organizationwide goals based on the organization's strategy. The plan allows the organization to identify, pursue and measure progress toward performance objectives that further the mission and strategic goals over a sustained period of time and help balance each participating executive's focus between annual and long-term objectives.

In constructing an LTI arrangement, the committee and senior management must address issues similar to those in an annual incentive arrangement, including:

- Purpose
- Eligibility and participation
- Administration
- Performance period
- Plan circuit breaker (i.e., below what performance level will the plan shut down?)
- Incentive opportunity
- Performance measures, goals and weighting
- Funding and distribution.

Note, however, that these plans are almost always paid in cash because the use of equity and the transfer of tax-exempt assets are governed by strict state and federal laws, and typically there is no equity of the organization that is available for awards. Of course, with any compensation element, how an LTI is to "fit" with the other compensation elements is part of the design process.

Considerations for Board Pay

As the accountabilities and liabilities of public company board members have increased, a director's job has become considerably more difficult and time-consuming. This has made the recruitment and retention of directors a much more important and challenging task, often resulting in greater compensation of these directors. Increased board responsibilities, however, are not unique to directors of public companies. Tax-exempt board members also are finding themselves with significantly more responsibility.

While many (typically smaller) tax-exempt organizations historically have not paid their directors, more are asking whether board pay is not only appropriate but necessary. In the increasingly stringent environment of tax-exempt board governance, director roles are getting harder and carrying more weight.

In consulting with numerous tax-exempt organizations, three related issues affecting the compensation of tax-exempt board members have been examined: whether to pay, how to pay and what to pay.

A Changing Environment

In recent years, tax-exempt board membership has shifted from risk-free public service to time-consuming stakeholder accountability. These directors now have much greater responsibilities that include the same types of tasks that directors of publicly traded companies face, including those related to audit, fiduciary matters and executive compensation. Clearly, tax-exempt board governance has changed. As responsibilities and accountabilities have grown, a debate has emerged whether it is appropriate to pay directors at tax-exempt organizations for their services.

There often is a perception that paying board members at tax-exempt organizations is inappropriate and that the practice runs counter to the missions of such organizations. In fact, some tax-exempts still look for guidance to a now-dated independent sector report commissioned by the U.S. Senate Finance Committee that discouraged any compensation for tax-exempt board members unless the complexity, time commitment or skill requirements of the board so warranted. In practice, board pay has been infrequent across the tax-exempt universe.

However, for over a decade, there has been a growing sense that as the role of the tax-exempt board evolves, board pay may not only be appropriate but also necessary to attract and retain the high-caliber directors needed. In general, board compensation is permissible as long as the organization's bylaws allow it and the payment does not result in private inurement or private benefit, and is considered reasonable for the services rendered. Essentially, this requires that pay not exceed the amount that ordinarily would be paid for like services by like enterprises under like circumstances. Also, many tax-exempt directors have opportunities to serve on for-profit boards that pay significant director fees. If particular tax-exempt organizations are competing with their for-profit brethren for top talent, paying directors may be a necessity.

There can be a rationale for compensating tax-exempt directors, and payment can be appropriate when the specific situation of the organization warrants.

Whether to Pay: Five Factors to Consider

The decisions on whether to pay and what to pay tax-exempt directors should be considered very carefully and driven by factors unique to each organization. Based on review of existing research and consulting expertise, the decision to pay the board should be guided primarily by five considerations:

- **Complexity of the organization.** Does the organization have various moving parts or particularly difficult issues, whether strategic, regulatory or optical? If so, the added complexity may furnish support for paying directors.
- **Time commitment required.** Are directors spending significant amounts of time either in the boardroom or otherwise performing board duties and responsibilities? If so, it may be appropriate for directors to be paid for their time.
- **Level of direct operational involvement and special skills required.** Do directors have any direct operational involvement in the organization? Is the organization involved in a situation that requires a specialized skill set? If so, then this is an indication that the director talent may have a substantial effect on the organization's success, and there may be greater justification for paying them.
- **Competitive market for director talent.** With what types of organizations does the board compete for director talent? Are these organizations compensating their directors? If so, these organizations may provide a reasonable benchmark for pay practices. In particular, tax-exempts that directly compete with for-profit companies may determine they need to compensate their directors or lose out on certain candidates.
- **Affordability.** Can the organization afford to pay its directors? Would director pay limit the programmatic offerings of the organization

in any way? Simply put, directors should only be paid if the organization can afford to do so.

Two types of organizations that tend to meet these criteria are health-care providers and large foundations. These employers typically are complex tax-exempt organizations; they are highly regulated, publicly and legally accountable, and require specific skill sets. Also, in the health-care field, tax-exempt providers may compete with large for-profit health-care systems for board talent. As a result, many such organizations may be strong candidates for director pay. Conversely, organizations that do not meet the bulk of these criteria may not appear to be suitable for director pay.

How to Pay: The Components of Director Pay Packages

If an organization, after evaluating itself against these factors, decides to pay its directors, it has various options for delivering that pay. The typical components of director pay include:

- **Annual retainers.** Similar to base pay, a retainer normally is a guaranteed cash amount.
- **Meeting fees.** These are fees for every board and/or committee meeting attended. Some committees, like audit, pay a premium relative to other committees to acknowledge increased importance and accountability.
- **Chairperson fees.** A member who chairs a committee may receive a special retainer for his/her services in the form of an additional retainer or additional meeting fees.
- **Committee membership fees.** Those who serve on a committee may receive an additional retainer for membership.

While these forms of director compensation are typical in the for-profit world, not all may be appropriate for a tax-exempt setting. Given the optics of compensating tax-exempt board members, the structure of pay packages and the vehicles used should be carefully examined.

In keeping with the pay-for-performance philosophy that organizations almost uniformly are adopting in their executive compensation philosophies, tax-exempt organizations may decide to structure their pay packages heavily toward a time commitment orientation. While it is common in general industry to maintain a significant portion of the overall pay package in the form of a guaranteed retainer, at some tax-exempts it may be more appropriate to limit the guaranteed component in favor of meeting fees, which only pay members for the time they spend in the boardroom.

What to Pay: Benchmarking Against Comparable Organizations

Evaluating what target level of compensation is appropriate for a board can be a bit tricky. As discussed, tax-exempt board pay has not been a prevalent practice and, as a result, there are few survey sources available that collect this information.

Given these constraints, an organization should customize its data collection to the specific director talent market of that organization through the development of two "peer groups" — one tax-exempt and one public — that the organization may compete with for board members. These groups could include organizations that are involved in comparable activities, are similar in size and scope, and/or share a geographic area. Some tax-exempt organizations recruit directors locally and may be competing for directors with the publicly traded company across the street, regardless of the business focus of that company. A good peer group may be a blend of these factors, but at the end of the day, it should fairly represent the competitive market for director talent.

Tax-Exempt Peer Groups

Within the tax-exempt peer group, data can be collected from public Form 990 filings, which have board compensation information. While improvements were made to this form, information can be spotty and incomplete and may not be sufficiently current. This time lag may present data that does not capture recent increases in tax-exempt board compensation. For this reason, a custom survey of similar tax-exempt organizations can be helpful when there is adequate time and budget to undertake this approach.

Public Company Comparisons

Use of a for-profit peer group can provide another appropriate benchmark, although it should not be the sole source of comparison. Within a for-profit peer group, data can be collected from public proxy filings, which provide more complete and up-to-date information on all forms of director compensation than on Form 990. However, in most circumstances, tax-exempt organizations should not look to fully replicate for-profit director pay packages. On average, the job of a director at a publicly traded company is subject to greater scrutiny and has more accountability and liability than that of a tax-exempt organization's director. This means that the pay data provided by these for-profit companies generally should be discounted when being used as context for developing board compensation in tax-exempt organizations.

One way to provide an appropriate discount is to eliminate from consideration any equity or LTI grants. In other instances, referencing only the 25th percentile of pay practices in the peer group may be appropriate. The right target-market positioning will depend on the organization itself and the degree to which it competes with these for-profit organizations.

Preparing for Scrutiny

In the end, any tax-exempt organization that chooses to compensate its directors should be prepared for scrutiny of the practice. While we believe tax-exempt board pay will continue to increase in prevalence as board accountabilities grow, some constituencies will continue to see board service as a public service and will understandably be opposed to the practice.

Consistent with the documentation on executive compensation decisions, tax-exempt organizations should maintain transparency of the process for and full documentation of all pay decisions related to an organization's directors. In particular, the written rationale — either in the form of a policy or a formal philosophy — regarding the decision on payment of directors (taking into account the factors stressed in this chapter) is a key part of this documentation.

CHAPTER 26

Executive Compensation Litigation

By Brian Holmen

Executive officers and directors are under increased scrutiny by shareholders, regulators, elected officials, proxy advisory firms and the general public regarding compensation and governance within their organizations. Regardless of whether an organization is private or public, for-profit or tax-exempt, stakeholders have raised the bar on their expectations of organizational performance, transparency and engagement. Plaintiffs' compensation-related claims against organizations continue to increase, although the underlying bases for the claims often evolve and change from year to year.

Good governance is the first line of defense as it more likely results in a sound and defensible process related to compensation; that is, compensation decisions are made in the context of an established and transparent process in compliance with applicable laws, rules and regulations. For public companies, a sound process also includes robust and transparent disclosure.

In essence, an organization's board of directors mitigates the risk of litigation if it identifies a decision-making process that involves the proper governing body; maintains an accurate record of decisions; properly allocates responsibility across departments, including HR, legal, finance, stock administration, accounting and external advisers; regularly reviews incentive plans and total compensation programs; and accurately discloses information about compensation programs and relevant comparator entities used in setting compensation. However, even the most well-intentioned and studied decisions may be subject to legal scrutiny as key stakeholders become more active in challenging compensation programs.

Once a claim is filed, it often will be expensive for the organization both monetarily and in potential reputational harm. Accordingly, organizations help themselves through following best practices in governance, engaging with shareholders and conducting reasonableness studies related to pay.

This chapter:

- Outlines common shareholder claims alleging excessive executive and director compensation and approaches to mitigate the risk of those claims.
- Describes distinct claims that have been filed against public companies and steps that companies can take to reduce the risk of these claims.
- Discusses claims that can arise with respect to family-owned businesses and nonprofit organizations.
- Briefly summarizes compensation-related claims made in special circumstances (wrongful death, divorce and bankruptcy cases).

Claims Alleging Excessive Executive and Director Compensation

The reasons for increasing legal claims related to executive and director compensation are varied and multiple. Although they are most common in publicly traded companies, excessive compensation claims are brought against privately held companies, including family-owned businesses, and nonprofit corporations.

Excessive Executive Compensation

A common claim filed against directors is one for breach of fiduciary duty and/or corporate waste for approving the payment of excessive compensation to executives. Many claims of excessive compensation are dismissed for failure to satisfy the special "demand requirement" related to shareholder derivative actions (i.e., claims brought by a shareholder on behalf of the company). The demand requirement is a procedural step that a shareholder must "demand" that a company's board bring a claim before the shareholder may file a claim. However, if shareholder plaintiffs overcome applicable procedural hurdles, they may bring claims against directors on behalf of the company.

Much of the increased scrutiny (and litigation) surrounding executive compensation paid by public companies followed the 2010 adoption of Dodd-Frank, which mandated non-binding shareholder votes and new compensation-related disclosures by public companies. One of the early requirements adopted by the SEC was the say-on-pay vote in which shareholders are given the opportunity to voice their approval (or disapproval) of a company's compensation practices in a non-binding vote. Some of the companies that received negative say-on-pay results in the first years after the SEC mandated the vote became the subject of shareholder litigation.

Although these early cases were unsuccessful, claims of excessive executive compensation continue. Claims vary in identifying which element of compensation, or combination thereof, results in allegedly excessive total direct compensation, but they often relate to short-term and long-term incentive structures that plaintiffs assert result in excessive bonuses or other payments. For example, claims often state that executive pay is not appropriately linked to organizational performance; i.e., regardless of whether the organization does extremely well, extremely poorly, or somewhere in-between, the CEO and/or other executives are paid largely the same.

A primary defense is to rely on the process employed by the board in approving the allegedly excessive compensation. Boards that demonstrate a reasoned process and absence of self-interest typically will not have their decisions second-guessed by a court. This judicial deference under common law is referred to as the "business judgment rule." In essence, a court generally will defer to the judgment of the board if the board acts in good faith, exercises ordinary prudence in making its decisions, and acts in a manner it believes to be in the best interests of the corporation.

In some instances in which the board's process is called into question, a company will settle these claims by agreeing to non-monetary relief such as changes to the company's governance structure. Even when settlement terms do not involve the payment of monetary compensation, the cost to the company of retaining legal counsel to defend against the claims and paying fees to plaintiffs' counsel may be significant. Therefore, organizations protect themselves by implementing processes and sound methodologies that the board or properly formed committee may use to review, approve and document compensation decisions.

Excessive Director Compensation

Similar to claims of excessive executive compensation, non-employee director compensation is subject to increased scrutiny and vulnerability to lawsuits. Most lawsuits claiming excessive director compensation allege that directors breached their fiduciary duties, wasted corporate assets and benefitted from unjust enrichment by approving total compensation that is excessive as compared to market and/or company size or performance.

Another category of claims is that public-company directors who approve their equity grants under a shareholder-approved plan that does not include meaningful limits on those grants are conflicted in making that decision, and must therefore satisfy the "entire fairness standard" under corporate law in making those grants (instead of the deferential review of the directors' decisions under the business judgment rule described above). If the entire fairness standard applies, the burden of proof shifts from the plaintiffs to the defendant-directors to prove that the compensation was entirely fair to the organization and its shareholders. "Entire fairness" requires "fair dealing" and "fair price," which mean that both the process and price must be entirely fair to shareholders.

Some companies address claims regarding director equity awards by establishing shareholder-approved limits on the equity grants that may be made to individual directors under a plan. Such limits are generally much lower than the applicable limit for employees. Another approach is to establish a separate director equity plan that includes formulaic grants that are approved by shareholders. While this latter approach has the benefit of avoiding any director discretion in granting equity to the board, the downside of this approach is that it lacks the flexibility that is inherent in plans that provide some discretion.

Like claims of excessive executive compensation that survive a motion to dismiss, lawsuits alleging excessive director compensation that prevail against a motion to dismiss also substantially increase in the cost of litigation, including attorneys' fees. Accordingly, care should be taken to provide any opening through unclear or careless processes that could provide plaintiffs with an ability to survive a motion to dismiss; this is especially important regarding director compensation as the entire fairness standard would apply.

Claims Specific to Public Companies

Stakeholders review proxy statements with a critical eye. Media outlets routinely report on, and are critical of companies, regarding these issues. Coupled with the additional scrutiny implemented by the SEC following the enactment in 2002 of the Sarbanes-Oxley Act and then 2010 Dodd-Frank, and the environment is ripe for litigation.

Excessive Director and Executive Compensation

Public companies risk being sued by shareholders for excessive director and executive compensation. A general discussion of these claims is set forth in the previous section of this chapter.

Disclosures and Section 162(m)

IRC section 162(m) generally limits the federal tax deduction that a public company may take for compensation paid to specified senior executives subject to certain exceptions, including performance-based compensation. One of the requirements to qualify as performance-based compensation is that shareholders must approve the performance criteria that may apply under the plan. A category of claims brought by shareholders challenges the sufficiency of proxy disclosures relating to IRC section 162(m). For example, plaintiffs commonly claim that a company represented in its proxy filings seeking shareholder approval of section 162(m) performance criteria that it would avail itself of the applicable deduction, but then subsequently failed to do so.

Another category of claims assert that a company failed to meet the technical requirements to comply with IRC section 162(m), such as the requirement for shareholder approval. A robust process to satisfy the technical requirements under section 162(m) and careful drafting of shareholder communications can help mitigate the threat of these claims. A common approach in section 162(m) disclosures is for the company seeking shareholder approval to state expressly that it is not obligating itself to use the 162(m) deduction, even if approved by shareholders.

Equity Plan Disclosures

Companies disclose a lot of information in their annual proxy statements related to equity plans that they are submitting for shareholder approval. One category of actions brought by shareholders against companies seeking approval for an equity plan (or an increase in shares reserved under an existing plan) is the adequacy of the disclosures made to shareholders. Examples of information that shareholders sometimes claim should be disclosed, but that are not required under applicable law, are shareholder dilution represented by an equity plan, the company's historic "burn rate" under its equity plan (the rate at which the company grants stock under its existing equity plan), and the information obtained from outside consultants in evaluating the equity plan proposal. While these claims have had limited success, some companies mitigate the threat of these claims by expanding their proxy proposals to provide robust information to shareholders addressing dilution, burn rate, overhang (the dilution represented by outstanding awards plus shares reserved for issuance under equity plans), and other data regarding the requested shares.

Governance Claims

Another category of claims relates to a board's alleged failure to comply with applicable law in granting compensation. One such claim is that a company's board impermissibly granted equity awards to one or more individuals (often an executive) that exceeded the shareholder-approved limits under the plan. This type of error sometimes occurs following a corporate stock split, which impacts the equity plan share pool. The problem arises if the plan administrator fails to account for the revised capitalization. These types of claims can be among the most expensive to litigate; a sound governance process that includes stock plan administrators is a good prophylactic to avoid this type of error. While these claims also are made with respect to non-public companies, exchange listing requirements that mandate shareholder approval of most equity plans and proxy disclosure requirements relating to those plans provide shareholders with more information to use in pursuing such actions against public companies.

SEC-Filed Actions

Shareholders are not the only plaintiffs filing suit against companies based on issues related to their executive compensation programs. The SEC often makes claims against companies for alleged violations of its rules and regulations. For example, the SEC has sued individual executives for manipulating expenses to hide what would otherwise be perquisites that should have been disclosed in the proxy. These types of lawsuits generally allege that the executive caused the company to violate the law by filing false and misleading proxy disclosures. In other matters, the SEC has sought to recover (clawback) certain executive compensation pursuant to its authority under Sarbanes-Oxley in instances where financial restatements were required.

Claims Specific to Family Businesses

Family-owned businesses take many forms depending on such factors as the number of shareholders and relative ownership, the size of the company and the industry, whether executive officers are members of the family, and the number of family members who are inactive shareholders of the company. Because of these dynamics, the methods of determining how much jobs are worth and who should hold executive positions in family-owned businesses can differ greatly from other privately held companies. In essence, they are not always "arms-length" transactions. In addition, depending on the relative ownership of shares, certain family members may have greater decision-making authority and exercise that discretion in a manner that the executive officers deem unfair. Consequently, family-owned businesses are not immune from litigation.

Who Should Hold the Executive Officer Positions?

Family-owned businesses are no different than other companies in the sense that they require the right talent for the right positions; particularly, the executive positions. However, the determination of who should hold those positions is often more subjective than it would be in a non-family business, and may result in the incumbent lacking the qualifications to perform effectively. Similar problems may arise in succession planning for executive positions in family-owned businesses.

When an incumbent is determined unfit for an executive officer position, he/she is often forced out by the majority shareholders. If the incumbent feels unfairly treated, he/she may sue the company for wrongful termination, the majority shareholders' breach of fiduciary duties, and/or breach of the duty of good faith and fair dealing. To mitigate this risk, family-owned businesses should strive toward the same governance guidelines that non family-owned businesses generally adopt and implement. To the extent that a family-owned business can act objectively in matters that relate to family member executives, and document decisions in accordance with good governance practices, it further limits its exposure to claims.

How Much Compensation Should the Board Approve for Incumbents?

In family-owned businesses, some family members may sit on the board of directors, some may be executive officers, some may serve in both capacities, and some are inactive investors. These roles may create tensions among different members of the family (and with outside investors, as well), often resulting in litigation.

Lawsuits sometimes are filed against directors of family-owned businesses who approve excessive compensation to executive officers. These cases tend to be more complicated than those in non family-owned businesses because the decisions related to compensation are often made without use of an objective methodology for determining the appropriate amount of total compensation and proper metrics for awarding incentive compensation. Additionally, the perception of excessive compensation being paid to an incumbent, especially when buttressed by allegations that the incumbent is unfit to effectively perform his/her position, exposes the company to a higher risk of litigation. In these cases, the status of family quickly becomes irrelevant.

To avoid claims of excessive compensation, family-owned businesses should follow governance guidelines similar to those applicable to publicly held firms. In addition, standard methodologies should be used to determine compensation, and a family-owned business' board of directors should ensure that incentive compensation of a family-member incumbent is based on metrics that further the company's business strategy, viewed in terms of both short-term goals and long-term objectives.

Claims Specific to Nonprofit Organizations

Nonprofit organizations have different stakeholders than their for-profit counterparts and they compensate their executives differently. The most visible examples of these differences are that nonprofits do not have shareholders and do not issue equity as part of total compensation. However, they are highly regulated with regard to the compensation they pay their executives, in particular; are subject to media scrutiny; often have unions with which they have to negotiate; and must satisfy members and donors that the compensation that they pay executives is reasonable. Complicating the nonprofit landscape is that directors are often unpaid volunteers, and may not have the expertise to understand the reasons for and methodologies used to properly determine compensation, unwittingly exposing themselves to litigation. Nonprofit organizations commonly (but not always) are tax-exempt, which adds requirements under the tax code.

IRS as Plaintiff

Tax-exempt organizations must not pay excessive compensation to executives. As discussed in Chapter 25, they risk intermediate sanctions under IRC 4958, which include the requirement to return to the organization the amount that is deemed excessive and the payment of excise taxes. They also risk loss of tax-exempt status, which may happen in especially egregious cases. Additional penalties apply to managers and directors who approve excessive compensation.

Establishing a rebuttable presumption of reasonable compensation mitigates the risk of intermediate sanctions. To establish the presumption, the organization must take the following steps:

- The transaction must be approved in advance by disinterested members of an authorized body of the organization, i.e., the board of directors or a compensation committee lawfully established by the board. Disinterested members and their family members must not derive any economic benefit from the transaction or otherwise have a material financial interest in the transaction. In addition, employees working for a person who will derive an economic benefit or have a material financial interest in the transaction are not considered disinterested nor is any individual whose compensation would be determined by such person.

- The governing body must obtain and rely on valid comparability data in approving the transaction. Comparable data includes similarly situated organizations measured by such metrics as size, location, services, receipts and budget. Such comparisons often include an independent third-party compensation study to compare market data among members of an appropriate compensation peer group, which may include taxable organizations.

- The governing body must contemporaneously document its decision and the reason for its decision. Such documentation must include information such as the date of the approval of compensation, the methodology used to determine the compensation, who the governing body was that made the decision, and that the governing body was made up of disinterested individuals.

Establishing the rebuttable presumption of reasonableness is an important step that a tax-exempt organization in positioning itself against potential disputes with the IRS. A failure to show that an organization has established the rebuttable presumption may result in the IRS bringing suit and using its own comparability data to measure the reasonableness of compensation.

Unions as Plaintiffs

Tax-exempt organizations are not insulated from the activities of unions. They have been particularly vocal regarding health-care organizations, such as petitioning for caps on the total compensation of their CEO. Such activities put tax-exempt organizations in the media spotlight and require them to engage in extensive negotiations and PR activity. However, if an organization has taken the steps to establish the rebuttable presumption of reasonableness discussed above, it is better situated to argue its case to the union, the public and the media.

Conflict of Interest Policies are Critical

Conflict of interest policies prevent board members from making decisions that financially impact their family members or themselves or generate an economic benefit to them. An effective conflict of interest policy, coupled with compliance with the policy, significantly mitigates risk of lawsuit for alleged violation of the "private inurement" doctrine applicable to nonprofit organizations. Accordingly, boards of directors should prioritize ensuring that effective conflict of interest policies are adopted.

Executive Compensation in Wrongful Death Claims

In most wrongful death claims, the question of compensation that would have been earned by the decedent but for the alleged wrongful death caused by the defendant(s) becomes an issue in calculating damages. Essentially, potential net income, based on income on the date of death and average work-life expectancies, is awarded to survivors. This "valuation by human capital" determines the amount that survivors need to allow them the same standard of living that they would have had if the decedent were still alive.

Executive Compensation in Divorce

Property division and support are central issues in divorce proceedings. The spouses must determine what property is separate versus what property is marital. Compensation becomes an issue complicated by the fact that executives generally are paid a mix of cash and equity. While base salary is easily attributable to income, questions arise regarding when and if the non-executive spouse is entitled to all or a portion of the stock acquired by the executive as current or future compensation. In addition, the ultimate payment of deferred compensation and unvested incentive compensation (especially performance-based incentive compensation) can be unpredictable.

Measuring compensation in divorce proceedings can be further complicated if one spouse was the founder of a successful business during the marriage. A determination may be needed as to the extent to which the company is an asset that must be divided and how much income to attribute to the executive's spouse for purposes of spousal support.

Determining current total compensation, potential future compensation and the value of marital property associated with executive compensation may require expert opinions and valuations. Experts also advise parties in divorce proceedings regarding plan administrators' responsibilities, and the timing of and manner in which equity can be delivered.

Executive Compensation in Bankruptcy

Executive compensation is subjected to special rules if the employer-company files bankruptcy. For example, regardless of the terms of an employment agreement, the Bankruptcy Code limits the amount and timing of severance benefits that executives may receive. Priority of payment of severance benefits also may be unfavorable to the executives, particularly if rank-and-file employees are given little to no severance. If severance is paid to an executive in violation of the Bankruptcy Code, the executive will be forced to disgorge the excess payments. Similarly, base salaries that are increased within a year of filing bankruptcy will be subjected to heightened scrutiny and may be clawed back by the court.

In many instances, though, a bankrupt company remains in business and needs to retain its key talent or attract new talent. As discussed in the bankruptcy section of Chapter 24, companies reorganizing in bankruptcy that need to retain their talent struggle with the limitations placed on them regarding how to compensate their executives. During bankruptcy proceedings, incentive-based compensation must be linked to measurable performance goals and issued pursuant to a KEIP. Such programs may differ greatly from the annual and long-term incentive plans to which executives are accustomed, which can jeopardize retention.

Lastly, in a plan of reorganization, the company may petition the court for new executive employment agreements. To do so, it would have to meet certain procedural requirements such as notice of proposed payments of executive compensation to all parties-in-interest. It would also have to satisfy the court on the reasonableness of the proposed compensation.

Expert assistance in structuring incentive compensation and other payments that will satisfy the Bankruptcy Code is often required. In addition, committees formed to represent the interests of creditors commonly seek a third-party analysis on the reasonableness of compensation-related proposals.

Wrapping Up

Good governance and supportable analyses related to director and executive compensation help organizations avoid litigation, but they are no guarantee. It is important for organizations to understand who their stakeholders are, how they are regulated, and the best methods for providing transparency without disclosing proprietary information. At the end of the day, organizations should compensate executives in compliance with applicable laws, rules and regulations, but determine how to achieve short-term goals and long-term objectives through incentivizing their key talent. The best defense against litigation is articulation of a deliberately determined, studied and reasonable executive compensation program.

CHAPTER 27

International Compensation

INTRODUCTION

By Bill Gerek

Companies cross borders, and talented individuals cross borders — making the understanding of international practices essential for anyone who wants to grasp the subject of executive compensation. Pay practices differ from country to country, driven by economics, culture, legislation and innovation. But equally, practices cross-pollinate where markets for the people that can truly affect the fortunes of an organization sweep through borders without regard for barriers and traditions. And it is not only where people are based that matters but also the context of the industry, the company and the company's stakeholders. This chapter seeks to give some of these flavors to the diversity of executive compensation practices, looking at such different corners of the world as Australia, Europe, Singapore, Brazil, Mexico and Canada, as well as the settings of family-owned businesses, non-capitalist countries and corporate governance debates.

When one looks at differences between geographies one can often generalize, for example:

- CEO packages tend to be the highest in the United States for total compensation, in particular the LTI portion.

- Companies in North and South American countries tend broadly to follow U.S. approaches, though with somewhat lower levels and with local variations.
- European companies tend to have more significant pension benefits.
- Executive pay tends to be significantly lower in Japan and in Northern European countries than in most other highly developed economies with more fixed than variable compensation.
- In most companies in Europe, the pay differential between the CEO, the CEO's direct reports and other top executives in the same company is much less than is typical in the United States.

However, comparing the compensation packages of executives in different countries is fraught with difficulty. Compensation levels vary greatly and the differences are rarely explainable by just taxation or living standards — some of the developed countries with the lowest levels of executive pay, such as in Northern Europe, have high living costs and tax rates. These quirks are evidence of the importance of understanding the cultural differences within which executive compensation exists. A Dutch executive accepts lower compensation and a higher tax rate than a Swiss executive, at least partly because of the cultural difficulty of paying Swiss levels in the Netherlands. That does not mean that the same executive would accept lower compensation in Switzerland.

There also are large differences between countries in the provision of retirement benefits for executives. A Swedish executive, for example, may agree to a lower salary than a British executive but expect twice as high a pension contribution. An Asian executive may not have a pension provision at all in the traditional sense, while the retirement benefit provisions of Australian or European executives could form one of a company's largest liabilities.

Faced with significant differences in compensation practices from country to country, and in many cases within countries, most international corporations base the compensation for top executives primarily on practices and levels in the market where the executive is based. However, it is not unusual to see exceptions to this in short- and long-term incentive plans as a result of corporate innovation in combination with home country legislation driving more global practices. Such innovation and legislation often are a result of the corporate governance debate of the country where an organization has its headquarters.

The topics of executive compensation in corporate governance have evolved swiftly together throughout the world and are now on the agenda of virtually all large company boards as well as those of most investors and legislators. There are several factors that have driven this increased attention. The first, and perhaps most significant, factor has been the increasing institutionalization of ownership creating sharp contrasts between, for example, the practices of quoted companies and those of family-owned businesses.

Most companies begin their days under the ownership of a single individual, family or organization. Increasingly, however, with the search for economies of scale and other synergies, companies around the world have gone in search of capital. At the same time, individuals have sought cost and return economies on their savings by using institutional investments (e.g., insurance, pensions) that seek to reduce risk and increase returns through a diversified portfolio of investments. One consequence has been the emergence of a small number of institutional investors that hold hundreds of investments in every fund. A second consequence is that, in effect, all the individual investors have subcontracted to institutional investment managers not only investment decisions, but also corporate governance decisions.

The investment managers have in turn realized that they cannot consider each and every ownership issue that arises at every investment so have had to find cost-effective ways of casting votes and influencing investments, if doing so at all. Thus the "corporate governance industry" has evolved and through it a set of "truths" and practices that come more out of need for institutional investors to expedite the decisions on thousands of requests for votes every annual meeting season. These institutional views have led to the widespread development by investors and their umbrella organizations and proxy advisers of guidelines on corporate governance. And the most prominent place among all the guidance has been given to the subject of executive compensation.

The UK was in most aspects the first out in the 1990s and has now had a string of codes of corporate governance that have been copied and tailored by country after country across Europe and the rest of the world. Questionable incentive design practices, such as the retesting of performance conditions, have come under close scrutiny and many have been effectively eradicated. Other practices have been noted as undesirable, but to accommodate the understanding that there will be different needs for different situations, many codes ask companies to either comply with the guidance or explain the reasons for deviation.

Where concerns of investors spill into the more public debate (e.g., where votes are cast without one party having understood the arguments of another), the media, the wider public and, eventually, the legislators can begin to lose trust in the quality of corporate governance. This second factor of political interference in executive compensation has two further drivers — scandals and emotions.

Since the beginning of time, mankind has been hit by scandal on a regular basis, in particular where money and power are featured. With plenty of examples in recent times of mismanagement of shareholders' and, in some cases, public resources, politicians throughout the world have pointed to executive pay as a driving force behind poor judgment and occasional criminality. Many commentators thus see the way a company pays its senior executives as not only information needed to assess these often significant costs but, more importantly, as an indicator of the moral compass and effectiveness of the board's decision-making process.

Thus, legislators have introduced increased reporting and conduct codes and regulations affecting compensation decisions in the wake of the financial turbulence of the past decade. The financial services sector has been the hardest hit, but most large quoted companies have been affected in one way or another. For some societies where the interests of other stakeholders besides shareholders play a large part in the determination of strategy and operations, this has been less traumatic than for more pure-capitalist environments.

The key message is that companies can no longer expect to create compensation arrangements for their senior executives according to commercial logic alone, but the views of other stakeholders play an ever-increasing role throughout the world. This in turn has several consequences:

- There is a risk that a single focus on compliance with rules and regulations leads to a failure to create the right compensation structure for the organization. Decisions are made first and foremost to align with processes and tests rather than with strategy and culture.

- A fear of not complying tends to lead to a pursuit of being in the middle of the pack and a subsequent over-reliance on benchmarking rather than the business case of rewards. This often results in the upward ratcheting of pay even when performance may not justify it; competitors chase a median point that automatically moves up as there are only increases with no matching decreases in the market.

- Finally, much of the regulatory interference is focused around risk associated with levels of pay and performance conditions; however, companies often forget to take the risk built into the design of compensation elements into account. One incentive or benefit may deliver the same target value as another but the range of possible outcomes may vary dramatically, hence the "how" matters more than the "how much."

KEY EXECUTIVE PAY TOPICS OUTSIDE OF THE UNITED STATES

By Bill Gerek

The balance of this chapter provides overviews of executive compensation in 10 diverse international settings: Australia, Brazil, Canada, France, Germany, Italy, Mexico, the Netherlands, Singapore, and the UK. The sections describe not just pay practices but important aspects of compensation in these geographies.

The first section, "Executive Compensation Design in Australia," describes the fixed-reward approach whereby employees can choose to take some benefits as part of pay, particularly cars and retirement savings, with the balance provided as base salary. The section also discusses short- and long-term incentives, performance measures and governance issues that distinguish executive pay in Australia, in particular the potentially huge impact of ongoing negative shareholder votes on executive pay.

- In the second section, we discuss the use of short- and long-term incentive pay in the context of Brazil's economic and political environment. We address how, in connection with the vicious economic cycle that started in the early 2000s, the executive compensation model in Brazil shifted very rapidly, moving from a base salary and benefit-driven approach (1980s and 1990s) to a much more leveraged model. We also discuss recent efforts to regulate equity compensation, the need to provide for senior executive safety, and corporate governance developments (including the current state of executive pay disclosure).

- The third section, "Executive Incentives in Canada: Linked to more than Total Shareholder Return", examines the use of performance metrics for share-based incentives in publicly traded companies, including various methods of measuring relative TSR measures.

- In the fourth section, we examine the status of, and likely future for, defined benefit pension schemes in France. We found that an important objective will be for companies to propose new, effective compensation schemes to continue to attract and retain a new generation of executives without indulging in a costly compensation bidding race due to the typical inclusion of the defined benefit scheme in the executive package.

- In Germany, executive compensation has changed dramatically since the 2008–2009 financial crisis. Good corporate governance has become the main driver for the compensation of executive boards. In addition to standards for executive compensation developed by the European Union, Germany has its own rules affecting executive pay. In particular, the Act on Appropriateness (VorstAG), introduced in 2009, and the German Corporate Governance Commission outline the main rules for board compensation standards. VorstAG applies to listed and non-listed legal entities and has a considerable impact on the practice of executive directors' compensation as well as its determination by the supervisory board.

- In the sixth section we examine the implications of the growing presence of foreign institutional investors in Italian listed companies. Along with their activism at shareholders' meetings, these investors have inevitably brought about important changes in the way the top management of Italian listed corporations is paid. Another result has been a progressive alignment of domestic pay practices to those of other Western European countries.

- Turning to México, we discuss the prominence of private or family-owned businesses in the country, a feature that has largely shaped executive pay practices. We examine the changes in executive compensation strategies in México and discuss companies' particular focus on short-term incentives. LTIs are discussed as growing in recent years among large listed Mexican companies and the local Mexican operations of international firms.

- In the Netherlands we studied current thinking on two areas affecting executive pay: (1) how to restore legitimacy in executive remuneration and (2) trends regarding executive remuneration policies and practices. In the first section, we discuss our finding of a legitimacy crisis in top executive remuneration experiences and then address five subtopics on how to restore support from society. The second section considers the impact of how new pay practices that were adopted in the financial sector are spelling over into other industries, focusing on trends that now are being discussed in the remuneration committees of major Dutch corporations.

- In Singapore, we outline some of the key findings of a recent study of top executive compensation at listed companies. We separately examine top executive pay at large, medium and small surveyed companies as well as companies' mix of pay between fixed and variable components. After mentioning new corporate governance guidelines, we address pay for performance in Singapore, including the performance metrics commonly utilized.

- Turning lastly to the UK, we examine how regulators in Europe and the UK in recent years have, through a series of actions limiting variable compensation, attempted to reduce perceived risks to the financial sector posed by banks' compensation arrangements. The impact of the most recent set of limitations are discussed, including how many UK banks and other similar institutions have repeatedly had to modify their executive compensation arrangements. We conclude with views on how the resulting fixed compensation costs faced by UK and other European banks will put them at a competitive disadvantage with respect to non-European financial institutions.

EXECUTIVE COMPENSATION DESIGN IN AUSTRALIA

By Trevor Warden

Although geographically positioned at the southern end of Asia, Australia is culturally more closely aligned to Western economies. The government, legal and social frameworks were derived primarily from the United States and UK, so executive rewards in Australia have many similarities to the models used in those countries.

The geographic separation from Northern Hemisphere ancestors has, however, led to the emergence of some features that are quite different. While these variations are not as extreme as those seen in some of the country's unique animal species (e.g., kangaroo, wombat, platypus), they do have some endearing aspects that sit well within the Australian business environment.

Fixed-Reward Approach

In the 1970s, Australian tax regulations allowed a number of non-cash benefits to be taken with little or no tax payable. This encouraged companies to provide significant levels of perquisites to middle and senior management. The most common perquisite was a company-provided (and fully maintained) car. Other common items included travel, club fees, entertainment expenses and housing or low-interest housing loans. The use of perquisites became a gray area; the "tax-free" position of many was based on assertions that the activity (e.g., travel or entertainment) was for business purposes.

Fringe Benefits Tax

In 1986, the Australian federal government introduced a fringe benefits tax (FBT) that was levied on employers for any benefits provided to employees. The FBT was designed so that the cost to the company of providing $100 in after-tax cash to the employee was the same as the cost of providing $100 in benefits. While this legitimized the provision of benefits by companies provided the FBT was paid, it also removed the financial incentive to use perquisites instead of cash. A few benefits, such as employer-provided cars, received concessional FBT costing, and "superannuation" (pension plan) contributions were fully exempted from FBT to encourage saving for retirement.

The compensation response to the FBT was for companies to define the value of fixed reward they were prepared to pay for each individual. This fixed package or fixed annual reward could be taken by the employee in whatever form he/she chose. Each benefits item is valued at the cost to the company, and the balance is provided as cash salary. Some executives elect to take most or all of the package as cash, while others take a portion in benefits.

The most common forms of benefits are cars, car parking and superannuation contributions.

Effect on Reward Comparisons

A consequence of the above approach is that relatively few Australian companies make external reward comparisons based on base salary. Many organizations are not tracking the cash salary component at all and are providing fixed-pay figures as the base salary for Australian pay surveys. Some companies with overseas parents still use a defined salary and specified benefits because they may have trouble explaining the Australian approach to the parent organization. Nonetheless they are urged to undertake comparisons at the full fixed package aggregate.

Superannuation

At roughly the same time that the government introduced the FBT, it also supported a move to require employers to contribute to retirement savings. The government was concerned that the aging Baby Boomer population was approaching retirement with insufficient resources and would expect the social security system to fill the gap. The government decided to shift the focus of responsibility to employers and employees. The initial requirement was for 6 percent of pay, and this has been progressively increased to 9.5 percent, offset partly by union-agreed reduced salary increases originally. The contributions are fully vested and must remain in approved funds until retirement even if the employee leaves the employer.

At the same time, Australia saw a major movement from DB funds to DC plans, with now only a tiny minority of companies still having active DB plans.

Most companies now allow executives to elect how much they want to contribute to superannuation provided they choose the regulatory minimum (9.5 percent in 2015 but potentially changing in future years, of normal pay up to a maximum required contribution, which is regulated and changes annually). Contributions are very tax efficient up to a certain amount annually, at which point they become tax inefficient.

Cars

Before fixed-reward packaging, company-provided cars were common, but now the most common mechanism for providing cars is through a fully maintained lease. The leasing company handles all the administration and maintenance costs, with fixed monthly costs deducted from the fixed-reward package. A common variation is known as a novated lease, which keeps the primary lease between the lease company and the executive. The company pays the monthly costs while the executive is employed, but the lease obligations stay with the executive on cessation of employment.

Other Benefits

While there are other benefits that may be provided by a few companies, the value is usually small in relation to the executive package.

Short-Term Incentives

The use of executive short-term incentives (with a performance test and payment period of up to 12 months) is common in Australia.

Historically, there was some variation in the type of STI, whether the plan was a target-based incentive with a defined opportunity size or a bonus paid retrospectively. Hay Group estimated that a vast majority of companies use a target-based STI plan. The amount of the incentive payment varies from year to year based on the achievement of specific targets set at a corporate, business-unit and/or individual level. Targets are determined and agreed upon in advance, as are the rewards for achieving and exceeding those targets.

The most frequent performance measure used in target-based STI plans is profit, with a significant majority of companies using this measure. Other performance measures used (not always exclusively), in decreasing order of prevalence, are health and safety, customer service ratings, and then to a lesser extent key management behaviors, return on capital employed, cost control and cash flow.

Recent Trends

Until recently, years of economic growth and the positive effect of strong commodity prices on many companies in Australia had resulted in a war for talent and strong corporate performance for many companies. Impacts to executive STIs were:

- While STI opportunities usually are presented as a percentage of fixed reward, most plans now provide for extra payments if stretch performance targets are achieved. Much of the recent increase in STI payments appears to be attributable to the provision of these additional upside opportunities.

- There is a growing trend of deferring the payout of executive STIs, especially with larger companies (40 percent of the Australian Securities Exchange (ASX300) and those in the financial services sector. This is designed primarily to support the retention of critical executives in the tight talent market. Some companies use a timing deferral — paying the cash over longer periods — and others pay the incentives in restricted shares.

■ Since the GFC clawback provisions have also been put in place for STIs.

Long-Term Incentives

LTIs in the Australian market have been characterized by the use of time and performance hurdles. Shareholder groups have made rigorous performance hurdles virtually compulsory with the intent of increasing the alignment between executives and shareholders.

The typical plan design has a performance period of three years, with a few companies using five years. The combination of the performance and time hurdles means that approximately 50 percent of all allocations do not vest.

The design of LTIs for Australian residents needs to be considered to structure them appropriately for Australian corporate accounting, corporate taxation and individual taxation regulations. This can affect the suitability of overseas-based equity schemes to Australian residents.

Performance Measures

The majority of plans use a relative TSR measure — the combination of share price growth and dividends paid compared to a comparator group of companies. While there has been some movement away from using relative TSR as the only performance measure to the use of combining it with other measures, often EPS, TSR remains the most common measure overall.

The biggest change in executive LTI approach in recent years has been the shift from share-option plans to performance-share plans. The change is striking: stock options declined from a substantial majority of senior executive awards to a significant minority, while the results were the reverse for performance shares, which now account for a significant majority of these awards. The change had been partly driven by tax changes in 2009 that made options less tax effective than other plans. In July 2015 the tax changes have been reversed and we will no doubt see a re-emergence of option based plans in the future.

Governance Issues

Australian governance requirements are fairly similar to those in the United States and the UK. In Australia the decision making for CEOs, NEOs and other key management personnel is the remit of the board. There is an obligation for listed companies to include a remuneration report as part of the annual report. This must disclose all director compensation for the past year plus detailed pay information for key management personnel; companies generally disclose five or more executives. The report also must furnish details of the company's reward philosophy and policies including incentive plans and performance criteria. Share-based equity must be disclosed in line with the international accounting standards, and details of past awards not yet exercised must be shown.

There is a requirement for a non-binding shareholder vote on acceptance of the Remuneration Report at each annual general meeting. Most boards have been very reluctant to proceed with remuneration items that are likely to receive a significant number of negative votes.

Since July 2011 there has been a legal obligation for companies that receive a negative vote of 25 percent or more on the Remuneration Report at two consecutive annual general meetings to have an immediate vote to spill all board positions and have a new election within three months. This has resulted in boards taking action to avoid high negative votes on the Remuneration Report for two or more years in a row.

There is a prohibition on listed companies making any termination payments that are linked to change in control, preventing CIC payments from being used by existing management and directors as a poison pill to discourage takeovers. Payments can be made following a change in control, but only if triggered by factors that would apply in other situations (e.g., the termination of the executive).

Legislation limits the maximum termination payment for executives, under any circumstances, to 12 months base salary unless there is specific shareholder approval for the greater payment.

While the concept of having formal share ownership guidelines for executives and directors has been a topic of late, there are still relatively few companies with formal guidelines in this regard.

Gender representation is becoming a larger issue with regulatory pushes on quotas coming into play. As an indication of the amount of work that needs to be done, only 3 percent of ASX300 CEOS were female in 2014.

Executive Reward Mix

Reward mix differs between the CEO and other executives (KMPs) as well as between executives/CEOs in different size organizations. Data from the ASX 100 and ASX 300 groupings are shown in the table below:

Key Differences Between Australia and the United States

While strong similarities exist between the approaches to executive reward in Australia and the United States, there are a number of important differences:

- The different structure of fixed-pay practice makes the use of base salary and total cash for market comparisons in Australia potentially misleading.
- The Australian regulations on company contributions for retirement income savings make it a very tax-effective form of income.

TABLE 27-1

	Fixed Pay	STI	LTI
CEO — ASX300	58%	22%	20%
CEO — ASX100	46%	27%	27%
KMPs — ASX300	67%	16%	17%
KMPs — ASX100	58%	19%	23%

- There is generally a somewhat smaller proportion of overall pay provided as STI and LTI in Australia.
- The Australian shareholder requirements for strong performance hurdles that result in a high risk of LTIs not vesting may not be necessary for subsidiaries of U.S. companies.
- Basic reward philosophies of U.S. organizations can be applied in Australia, but some adjustments to the mechanics of pay structures and comparisons may be needed to ensure desired market competitiveness.

EXECUTIVE COMPENSATION IN BRAZIL

By Henri Barochel

An understanding of executive compensation in Brazil requires a review of the economic and political developments in the country that have impacted the pay of executives. After experiencing almost a decade of economic and social progress, a promising long-term scenario for the Brazilian economy recently has been offset by a severe recession.

First Boom

Brazil, the seventh-largest economy in the world, after achieving GDP growth of staggering 7.6 percent in 2010 (see Table 27-2), has seen

TABLE 27-2

Brazil Economic Data

Item	2010	2011	2012	2013	2014
Population (million)	195	197	199	201	203
GDP per capita (USD)	11,306	13,240	12,104	11,878	11,567
GDP (USD bn)	2,210	2,614	2,412	2,388	2,345
Economic Growth (GDP, annual variation in %)	7.6	3.9	1.8	2.7	0.1

Source: Focus Economics

its economic growth fall sharply in recent years. Historically Brazil has seen sharp highs and lows in the last quarter century. In 1994 an economic stabilization plan — "Plano Real" — put an end to inflation that rose above 1000 percent. Following the plan's implementation for more than six years, a large sequence of structural reforms were implemented to sustain economic stability, including privatization of several state sectors, the creation of regulatory agencies, the Fiscal Responsibility Law and more open trade with other countries.

Between 2002 and 2008, Brazil's economy had high growth rates expanding at 4 percent per year. The ruling Workers Party, which took power in 2003 under then President Luiz Inácio Lula da Silva, lifted more than 40 million Brazilians up to the middle class, partly through a cash-transfer program known as "Bolsa Familia." Commodities exports and increasing domestic consumption contributed to a booming economy. This fast-growing economy has been able to attract large foreign investments mainly used to improve the country's infrastructure. This enormous progress brought a recognition from the international community that can be symbolically expressed by Brazil being awarded the 2014 World Cup and the 2016 Olympics.

Then Bust

Nevertheless, the boom turned out to be a bubble that has now burst. A sum of factors created a perfect storm of economic disasters. The strong dependence on exports of natural resources (soy, iron, sugar, etc.) was hit by the economies of the trading players such as China and Germany and by the drop of the commodities prices. Unemployment has risen rapidly, while inflation has been running above 9 percent — twice the government's target.

TABLE 27-3

Inflation

Year	2000	2001	2002	2003	2004	2005	2006	
Annual Inflation	5.97%	7.67%	12.,53%	9.30%	7.60%	5.69%	3.14%	

*Estimate

In order to mitigate and control the inflation effects, the interest rates have climbed past 14 percent, making it too expensive to borrow additional money to stimulate the economy. A corruption scandal has also hurt state oil giant Petrobrás, responsible for a huge chunk of public investment.

Brazilian authorities have been trying to fix the economy with austerity measures, but the government faces a political crisis and a rebellion of allied MPs who want to increase spending, rather than reform the economy. More worryingly, analysts believe growth might not return until 2017.

According to the World Bank, Brazil's medium-term outlook will depend on the success of the current adjustment and the adoption of further growth-enhancing reforms. To achieve higher growth in the medium-term, raising productivity and competitiveness is the crucial challenge for Brazil. With the growth drivers over the past decade — credit-fueled consumption, labor expansion and the commodity boom — receding, growth will need to be based on higher investment and gains in productivity.

Executive Market Place

Following the economic vicious cycle that started in the early 2000s, the executive compensation model in Brazil shifted very rapidly, moving from a base salary and benefit-driven approach (1980s and 1990s) to a much more leveraged model. Compensation programs became more bonus-driven. The above-mentioned privatization of state-owned companies and the booming capital markets in Brazil stimulated many companies to go public. This brought a new shift

2007	2008	2009	2010	2011	2012	2013	2014	2015*
4.45%	5.90%	4.31%	5.90%	6.50%	5.83%	5.91%	6.40%	9.50%

broadening LTI programs that are now an important component of executive compensation strategy.

Although inflation has been under control for several years, the memory of the hyperinflation times (the early 1990s) still lives on, and some pay practices are still linked to that heritage. Table 27-3 shows the evolution of inflation over 15 recent years in Brazil.

The most direct effect on pay is that typically Brazilian companies extended their union agreement salary increases to all executives instead of driving pay through market competitiveness. This practice has been reduced, but is still followed by multinational companies. Despite this fact, the hot market, plus a demand for seasoned executives with greater and more sophisticated management skills, contributed to salary growth (above the inflation rate).

Most recently, a recession combined with rising inflation produced a market growth below inflation. Moreover, due to poor company results, actual bonuses were paid below targets. In this difficult scenario (which is projected for the next few years), a combination of inflation affecting people's paychecks and lower bonus payments could apply pressure to resume the old practices regarding salary increases.

Another unique effect of this heritage affects stock option plans. It is not unusual to find local companies opting for premium price stock options, where the price is indexed to inflation as a "safety net," just in case inflation rises again in the long term. This approach leads to a higher dilution to fund the plans and increases the risk of the awards going underwater, as the stock prices have almost no correlation to inflation indexes.

High Cost of Pay

In Brazil, the basic labor obligations, taxes and social charges on base salary are relatively high as shown in Table 27-4. The result is that every time there is a salary increase of R$1,000, it will cost the company approximately R$1,511. Therefore, over the years, companies have struggled to provide a fair pay structure to executives while avoiding, to some extent, direct salary increases.

TABLE 27-4

Impact of Special Items on Total Pay

Item	Brief Description	Effect on Pay
13th salary	One additional monthly salary paid at the end of the year	8.33%
Vacation premium	One-third of a monthly salary due when the employee leaves on vacation	2.78%
Termination fund (FGTS)	Compulsory monthly contribution to build a fund to be paid upon termination of employment	8%
Social charges (INSS)	Public social security contribution	20%
Other social charges	FGTS and INSS contributions on 13th salary and vacation premium	12%
Total		**51.11%**

The high labor cost ultimately led to government action in the form of "profit-sharing" legislation in an effort to reduce overall labor costs and enable the Brazilian economy to compete in a global economy.

Profit- and Results-Sharing Legislation

In December 1994, just after the launch of the economic stabilization plan (Plano Real), the Brazilian government drafted a bill stating that all companies could implement a profit- or results-sharing program (PPLR) that, if done according to some basic guidelines, would not be considered as salary so that all labor costs would not apply.

The intention was to reduce overall labor costs and enhance productivity of all industries and sectors. To fall under this special category, a PPLR program must:

- Extend to all employees of the company;
- Have clear metrics and predefined goals;
- Not have more than two payments per annum, with a minimum of one semester between payments; and

- Contain plan conditions negotiated directly with the unions or through an internal employee commission together with a delegate of the applicable union.

The PPLR bill became law in December 2000, and companies subsequently have systematically shifted their compensation emphasis and now drive their STI programs toward PPLR programs.

The effect on executive pay came very quickly. Bonus arrangements partially or fully migrated to this model; base salary increases were reduced as bonus targets increased significantly over the years. Annual variable pay became a very significant portion of the total compensation package and plan design grew more sophisticated as companies focused on the year-end results.

Brazilian companies were able to respond faster to the new environment than their global competitors whose subsidiaries still struggled to obtain approval from their headquarters of some degree of flexibility on global bonus arrangements for the local executives. This factor enabled local companies to gain competitiveness in compensation and consequently became capable of attracting high-level executives from global organizations. The market in Brazil became "all about the short term," so multinational firms now have a hard time competing at the same level with the Brazilian companies.

Regulation of Equity Compensation

The regulation of executive pay is a recent topic in the Brazilian market. According to a Hay Group executive survey, 35 percent of the companies in 2006 granted some kind of LTI to their top local management. The vast majority were multinational companies granting equity through their global programs. These figures changed significantly, as Hay Group's 2011 survey found that 70 percent of the companies are currently granting LTIs and, of those, approximately one-half are Brazilian-based companies with local programs. This percentage of granting companies is now stable but there are still controversies about the tax treatment for LTI plans, bringing legal uncertainty for both companies and executives.

Recently the Brazilian government introduced legislation that sets tax guidelines on LTIs in the employer perspective. As the main innovation related to equity-based payments, the law (Law No. 12,973/14 regulated in Article 33) set forth the tax treatment applicable to such payments, defining them expressly as remuneration subjected to the same labor obligations, taxes and social charges than salary, i.e., full labor cost (51 percent), (See Table 27-4.)

As a practical consequence of this legislative change, there may be a reduced chance of the Brazilian revenue service agreeing to the non-compensatory nature of stock option plans. Indeed, the new law, although making more explicit the implications for companies, brought some legal uncertainty about future stock option plans. Before the new law, stock option plans were the most tax effective vehicles for both employer and employees (who only paid capital gains upon stock exercise). Now looking to the employee perspective, there is no consensus among lawyers on whether a withholding tax rate higher than the capital gains tax could be applied at the moment of the grant or after the vesting.

Several companies, even listed firms, are reviewing their LTI plans and choosing to grant cash-based plans as a proxy for the actual equity programs, typically through phantom options or phantom restricted plans to avoid any taxation risks.

Those companies that award actual equity manage their tax risk through assumptions such as "the higher the risk of a plan not paying out, the lower the risk of it being considered as compensation." It is advisable to obtain legal advice before implementing any equity-based plan to obtain a thorough risk assessment of each modality.

Roughly assessing the labor risk (and not the inherent risk) involved of the major types of equity plans, it would be fair to state:

- Stock options, if interpreted as non-compensatory plans, are now viewed as at a higher labor risk because of the legal treatment in the new law.
- Performance shares would be considered as at an intermediate risk level as the performance condition would bring a risk element into the plan.

- Restricted share awards could be considered at a lower labor risk level, as there is no additional condition other than the time vesting; thus the tax treatment would be the same as salary.

To summarize, it is clear that to be competitive now in the Brazilian market, having a LTI program is no longer a differentiation from the market place; rather LTI pay has become a regular piece of the compensation package in Brazil and it tends to increase in size and perceived value by executives. Nevertheless, the implementation process for local plans is still complex and a better understanding of the taxation environment, especially regarding the labor perspective, is needed.

LTI Linked to STI

A characteristic of Brazil LTI plans is their connection to STI. This concept created by the Brazilian founders of 3G Capital Fund (with notable interests in AB Inbev, Kraft Heinz, Burger King) in the early 1990s is now widely prevalent among Brazilian companies. Under this design, to be eligible to receive LTIs, a company must voluntarily invest a significant part of his/her bonus in restricted shares of the company. Such voluntary investment can lead to a discount to the market price of the shares (up to 10 percent). This investment can go up to 100 percent of the bonus depending on the executive position. The company will match such voluntary investment by granting matching shares for each bonus share invested, up to a limited total percentage of each participant's bonus.

Under these programs, the liquidity of STI is reduced but the compensation package is leveraged by a high LTI opportunity. Additionally the holders of the RSUs may be entitled to receive from the company additional RSUs equal to the dividends declared, creating a matching upside. Variations of these programs can involve the matching in stock options or combining stock options and restricted shares.

Although these plans provide a high alignment between shareholders and executives, creating a partnership plan during difficult periods can result in lower levels of (or no) bonus payout, which then can mean no LTI.

Urban Violence

Unfortunately, questions on the topic of urban violence are common from people outside of Brazil. It is sadly true that in Brazil's major cities there is an intrinsic risk of urban violence, and it is a market practice to provide armored cars to senior executives. As these problems are far from over, the continued use of this kind of benefit is expected.

Corporate Governance

The issues around corporate governance and disclosure are developing quickly in Brazil. Since 2010, all publicly traded companies have to disclose annually details of their compensation strategy regarding all elements of pay for the board of directors and group administrators (top executives that represent the owners of the company).

Although there is not yet full disclosure (because companies do not provide individual figures for each executive), companies now must report the average compensation packages for each group as well as both the highest and the lowest individual compensation packages. This is a major step in terms of transparency and we expect that, in the coming years, the level of details regarding executive compensation likely will increase, leading to a full disclosure.

In 2012, Resolution 3921 became effective, applicable to financial institutions subjected to the Brazil Central Bank's regulatory supervision. Under this resolution, banks had to adopt stricter compensation rules for statutory officers and members of the boards of directors, such as mandatory bonus deferral into employer stock or stock-based instruments compatible with the creation of value and with risk management over the long term implementation of remuneration committees.

Another improvement in the corporate governance of Brazilian companies was the determination made, in common agreement between the regulatory authority and the companies, to segregate the roles of CEO and chairman of the board of directors, when the same person held both positions.

In 2011, BM&F Bovespa, the Brazil Stock Exchange, introduced this new regulation to the market, giving to the listed companies a three-year term to implement the new requirements. Since May 2014, those companies listed in the "Novo Mercado" Level, in Levels 1 and 2, approved the change to the bylaws, and chose a new CEO to conduct businesses or a new chairman for the board of directors. In the coming years, the expectation regarding executive compensation is that there will be more shareholder activism and more transparency and increased oversight by regulators.

Finally, managing executive compensation in Brazil is very similar to doing it in any other country, with its own issues and complexities. Local operations are not disconnected from the global businesses and should be treated accordingly. Understanding the local environment and what drives compensation in this market allows a better planning process and awareness on how to compete in attracting, retaining and motivating these scarce resource of executives.

EXECUTIVE INCENTIVES IN CANADA: LINKED TO MORE THAN TOTAL SHAREHOLDER RETURN

By Wiclif Ma

For many Canadian publicly traded companies, there are very good reasons to align shareholders' interests with share-based compensation using medium/long term-incentive programs. In our study of S&P/

TABLE 27-5

Use of Equity Vehicles in the S&P/TSX 60

-	% of S&P / TSX 60
Stock Options (SO)	95%
Performance Share Units (PSU)	77%
Restricted Share Units (RSU)	43%
SO + PSU	48%
SO + PSU + RSU	25%

Toronto Stock Exchange 60 (S&P/TSX60) organizations, all companies currently have at least one medium-term or long-term incentive program for their senior executives. As expected, the use of stock options remains the most prevalent and PSUs have become highly popular.

The use of multiple share-based incentives clearly is a common approach, with about half of S&P/TSX60 organizations having both stock options and PSUs.

Performance Share Unit Plan

PSU plans typically grant notional share units at the beginning of the performance cycle. The median term of PSU plans for Canadian companies has been three years, as influenced by the Canadian tax rules (salary deferral arrangement rules under subsection 248(1) of the Income Tax Act).

The share units vest upon meeting certain performance conditions at the completion of the performance cycle. Potential performance considerations in the design of these plans include:

- What are the performance criteria?
- Should the criteria be market-driven or internally driven?

TABLE 27-6

Performance Criteria Used in PSU Plans

PSU Performance Criteria	% of PSU Plans
Internal Metric(s) Only	43%
Relative TSR Only	33%
Relative TSR + Internal Metric(s)	24%

TABLE 27-7

Internal Metrics Used in PSU Plans

Common Internal Metric(s)	% of PSU Plans
EPS / EPS Growth	17%
ROCE / ROIC	13%
ROE	11%

■ Should the criteria only reflect shareholders' gains or the company's strategic achievement?

Of particular interest is the use of TSR, where TSR equals share price appreciation plus dividends. With respect to performance criteria, relative TSR continues to be popular among PSU plans of S&P/TSX60 organizations.

As compared to the common practice in Canada five years ago, relative TSR is currently no longer the dominant/single measure. The use of other metrics, either exclusively or in combination with relative TSR, has become a definite trend:

Measuring Relative Total Shareholder Return

The majority of S&P/TSX 60 PSU plans adopt a relative TSR approach that compares the firm's return achievements to a performance peer group. TSR often plays a significant part in the incentive plans and is most relevant for mature and/or cyclical companies in the mining, energy and financial sectors. Relative TSR is a reasonable method for these organizations to assess the industry performance as a whole within a similar capital, operating, economic, market, risk and regulatory context.

Conversely, relative TSR is of limited validity for the following types of organizations:

■ Businesses targeting substantial growth;
■ Businesses in a turnaround situation; and
■ Businesses that are not competing with other businesses for direct customers to any meaningful extent (biotech for example) "Infant" businesses (e.g., start-ups, upstream oil exploration, mining exploration).

When developing a performance peer group for TSR comparison, the usual approach is to base the peer group on the most obvious alternative investments for a shareholder. This often means simply using the broader market composite or comparators.

However, hindsight and experience have exposed some weakness in this type of thinking, as broad comparator groups may include a high degree of randomness due to the very dissimilar degrees of volatility and cyclical exposure faced by different sectors and businesses. Accordingly, it becomes useful to think about relative TSR in an alternative way by examining:

- **Correlation** — how well does the historical TSR of the overall market correlate to your company and sector?

- **Volatility** — how does the historical share price volatility of the overall market compare to your company and sector?

The great majority of S&P/TSX 60 PSU plans use peer groups that focus on the same industry or a common client market, as opposed to the broader market. In this way, the subject company aims to reward a true out-performance among the competitors sharing the similar business environments.

When assessing relative TSR performance against a peer group, there are three potential alternatives:

- **Simple ranking** — It is the simplest and a fairly common approach. Incentive payments are sensitive to the performance zone (e.g., 50th to 75th percentile). Therefore incremental improvements to TSR may have a large or a small impact on the vesting amount, depending on how widely the performance zone is defined.

- **Smooth ranking** — The payment size is calculated based on the interpolation between the two TSR anchors in the pay-and-performance schedule (e.g. median TSR value and maximum TSR). As compared to the simple ranking method, the smooth ranking approach recognizes any size of TSR increment.

- **Percentage out-performance** — Vesting is typically determined by the TSR gap against the peer group median TSR value or a selected index. If an index is used, should the index be un-weighted or weighted? Weighting an index means that it can reflect the relative size (e.g., market capitalization) with the larger peers having a heavier impact on the index result. The weighted approach could produce an unfair result for management and could attract criticism from shareholders.

To further calibrate the baseline requirement, some companies add a premium spread on top. The out-performance gap over the premium requirement will determine the size of the incentive payment, which is often calculated using interpolation. This method is still rare in the Canadian marketplace.

When calculating the relative TSR, should the subject company be included in the group for ranking purposes? Despite the mixed practices in Canada, "including the subject company" tends to be slightly more prevalent. Interestingly, "excluding the subject company" is much more prevalent in the UK. Also, many Canadian plans still do not impose any cap or restriction on the incentive payments in the case of a negative TSR.

Currently, the simple ranking method is widely adopted among S&P/TSX 60 organizations. In our view, simple ranking works best for a very large comparator group. If the peer group is very small, the percentage out-performance approach may be more appropriate. When facing a small peer group within Canada, organizations might consider expanding the group by including international companies.

Measuring Internal Metric(s)

For various S&P/TSX60 organizations, internal metric(s) are adopted in approximately 80 percent of PSU plans. In general, these organizations believe that relative TSR does not fully capture the performance of the company due to macro-economic factors and is not sufficiently meaningful to management. The high prevalence of internal metric(s) also reflects the importance of certain strategic priorities unique to each organization; for example:

- Net earnings target and sustainable cash flow requirement over the longer term
- Return on capital consisting of relevant debt and equity over the longer horizon
- Operational and production efficiency in manufacturing/resource-based organizations.

PSU Payment Upon Change in Control and Retirement

When encountering a CIC, we see four basic alternatives in Canada, as listed below, for determining the PSU payment. We have not seen a particular alternative that is more prevalent.

- Payout at target; or

- Payout at target, and pro-rated upon service from grant to CIC; or
- Final measurement of payout at CIC; or
- Final measurement of payout, and pro-rated upon service from grant to CIC.

As in the case of retirement, a common provision for outstanding PSUs will continue the normal cycle until the end of the performance period, but the payout is pro-rated based on the service at the separation date.

The Future of PSU Plan

Should the eligibility of PSUs be extended to lower-level executives or managers? In the past, the idea was generally to ensure that "we are all in this together." However, this perspective undermined the value of LTIs for many executives below the top team level.

Current thinking in Canada is to consider the extent to which the LTI plan design can and should vary. Variation allows a more tailored approach to designing plans under a consistent compensation philosophy, supporting the business strategy, and enabling line-of-sight for various employee groups.

DEFINED BENEFIT PENSION SCHEMES IN FRANCE: CONTINUATION OR CONCLUSION?

By Jérôme Rambaldi

France operates two compulsory pension schemes: ARRCO ("Association des régimes de retraites complémentaires") for blue-collar workers and AGIRC ("Association générale des institutions de retraites des cadres") for white-collar workers and management staff. The ARRCO and AGIRC acronyms designate both the pension schemes and the national federations that oversee them. Both are the products of collective bargaining agreements and cover nearly all workers under the general public pension plan. Equally, both are specific types of defined contribution plans, financed on a pay-as-you-go basis and administrated through pension institutions.

The efficiency of pension schemes differs greatly depending on the career path, the level of compensation and the age of the person concerned (because benefits reduce over time), but projections show that statutory schemes will represent around a quarter of compensation at the end of a senior corporate executive's career and a third of the pay of a senior manager. This considerably modifies the standard pattern where compulsory, statutory schemes constitute the majority of an employee's retirement pension.

Use of Defined Benefit Pension Schemes

A DB scheme is a type of retirement program in which the level of the pension is set by the rules of the contract and paid upon retirement provided that the beneficiary remains with the company until his/her retirement. This system is funded by the employer contributions and is generally built to provide an additional pension paid on top of the mandatory and other supplementary retirement schemes. The scheme has long been attractive for many companies that have used it in their compensation package to attract and retain executives.

DB pension schemes have been implemented in France to provide senior managers and senior corporate executives with supplementary pensions against the estimated replacement rate of statutory schemes. The goal was to compensate the deficiencies of the other schemes and to obtain a uniform replacement rate for all employees.

A supplementary pension using the collective mechanisms set up by a company is a very common solution, even if it is only possible using a limited number of supports and within in relatively limited tax and social optimization budgets:

- Optimization using the tax and social deductible budget limits for DC schemes (article 83);
- Constitution of random pension rights subject to a condition of presence at retirement DB schemes (article 39);

■ Voluntary constitution of a pension savings scheme provisioned by the company inside deductible tax and social charge budget limits (Perco).

Developments Affecting Defined Benefit Pension Schemes

The amounts contributed by companies to cover retirement commitments confirms the stabilization or even the return of companies to DB schemes. There are two basic reasons for this somewhat hesitant return to DB pension schemes:

■ **A change in the legislation.** A change in the legislation on objective categories has forced companies that had set up an "article 83" mechanism for their senior corporate executives to extend this benefit. The rate of subscriptions has varied only slightly over the same period (with the companies absorbing the increase of the in the number of beneficiaries).

■ **Relatively low efficiency for senior corporate executives.** Given the ceilings on tax deductibility or social charges exemption, a company is restricted in the allowances it wishes to provide for its senior executives. The alternative is to improve the pension for senior executives either by conserving the "article 39" mechanisms (with the constraints of corporate liabilities and the condition of the employee remaining employed by the company through retirement, along with a reduced tax and social efficiency) or organizing the possibility, through the "article 83" scheme for senior executives to make voluntary payments to reduce their income tax base.

These two reasons have resulted in two market trends regarding DB pension schemes:

■ The maintenance of existing mechanisms (by restrictions on charges and beneficiaries); and

■ The set-up and coordination of mechanisms to enable senior executives to individually create supplementary pensions within an optimized framework.

However, if we analyze the situation of the DB schemes in more detail, we find that a company's maintenance of existing DB schemes probably would not continue for many years.

Defined Benefit Pensions in Jeopardy

The existence of the DB pension schemes is now in jeopardy due to developments resulting in adverse tax treatment and an inability to evolve with market practices:

- In a more and more international environment and a very competitive market for management talent, it is now unusual to see a top executive performing all of his/her career in the same company without any change or any international mobility.
- Although it has been required by the European Union, there is still no portability of retirement rights in France.
- The tax treatment of the pensions is discouraging: 32 percent on the benefit paid plus an additional 45 percent of the amount exceeding eight times the annual social security ceiling (i.e., exceeding €304,320 for 2015).
- The only way for companies to compensate is to buy back the executive's years of work and bear this important cost.

In 2013 the French draft law on governance was abandoned and replaced by the reform of the AFEP-MEDEF code. However, the pressure on the DB schemes increased. The debate on this question is (still) active.

On Aug. 6, 2015, the Macron law ("for supporting growth, activity and equal economic chances") finally increased the legal regulation of DB pension schemes in order to try to reduce the abuses and misuses of this scheme:

- The DB pension scheme became legally governed by the regulated agreement rules;
- The definitive acquisition of these rights should be subject to performance conditions;
- Annual pension rights are now capped at 3 percent of the annual reference compensation of the incumbent; and
- The requirements for the provision of information to shareholders on these pension schemes were reinforced by this new law.

Recent controversies on the amounts of pension considered as excessive have not reversed the current trend: the DB pension schemes are a tax and an administrative burden even if the majority of the scheme's beneficiaries only receive an average of €5,000 per year.

A Search for Alternatives

In this context, the major companies are searching for alternatives. First of all, a decrease in the tax pressure and a portability of the rights (which would lead to a split of the costs between companies) would have given a new life for this system. However, this did not happen.

One must think about the objectives governing the implementation of the DB pension schemes in order to determine alternative programs that could have similar goals. Certain obstacles should be managed by the company:

- Since the DB scheme is part of the work contract, no significant amendment can be made without the approval of the employee, and solutions should be found to compensate this change for the individual.

- As the scheme is a collective program, any change in the plan rules or in the mechanism will lead to various consequences and degrees of satisfaction depending on the situations, levels of income and ages of the existing population covered by the regime.

A first solution could be to replace the DB retirement scheme with a long-term deferred compensation plan that would have the same mechanism (acquisition of the rights upon retirement date). Another possibility is to structure this deferred compensation plan as a bonus plan where the rights would be acquired yearly but payments deferred until the retirement date. A preliminary study would provide simulations and comparisons of the costs for the company and individual "net in pocket" income. Again, even if this would not be efficient for certain beneficiaries, it could lead to a general optimization.

Another alternative, linked to the previous one, is the use of an investment structure like a foreign pension scheme or a French or foreign life insurance contract. These plans can be funded entirely by the company based on time and performance conditions and the event triggering the pension payment would be the soonest of the vesting date, the date of departure from the company or the retirement date. A part of the funding of this investment plans could be made by the top executives with matching amounts or additional payments made by the employer.

Funding of the plan(s) and the event triggering social security assessment are the major issues in the structuring of these alternatives.

Another solution could be to grant free shares with performance conditions. The Macron law increased significantly the legal flexibility and the tax efficiency for both the company and the beneficiary. The legal framework of such a structure would be a major advantage, but the use of the shares to provide the executive with an additional payment linked to his departure of the company may be an impediment.

The long-term vesting period would be structured as a progressive one, with yearly performance conditions determining the acquisition/forfeiture of the rights until the earlier between the last vesting date, the date of departure from the company and the retirement date of the beneficiary. Shares acquired during the entire career of the top executive in the group would be then transferred at the payment date (a form of cliff vesting). Put and call agreements can be signed to organize the liquidity and manage the share portfolio of the group.

Next Steps

An in-depth analysis of the above-mentioned (and other) alternatives would be necessary to best match the needs of the company and the expectations of the executives currently covered by the DB scheme.

A key objective is for companies to be able to propose new effective compensation schemes to continue to attract and retain this new generation of executives without indulging in a costly compensation bidding race due to the systematic inclusion of the DB scheme in the executive package due to the market practice.

GERMANY: EXECUTIVE COMPENSATION

By William Eggers

Since the 2008–2009 financial crisis, the rules in Germany for executive pay have changed dramatically and good corporate governance has become the main driver for the compensation of executive boards. In addition to the European Commission's development of new standards for executive compensation, Germany has its own regulatory system. The Act on Appropriateness (VorstAG) (introduced in 2009) and the German Corporate Governance Commission (GCGC) outline the main rules for current board compensation standards.

VorstAG applies both to listed and non-listed legal entities (of types AG, SE and KGaAa) and has considerable impact on the practices in executive directors' compensation as well as its determination by the supervisory board. Further, listed stock corporations must implement compensation that is sustainable and aligned with long-term company development. VorstAG also applies to foreign-owned companies in Germany. In addition, there is an increasing influence from the European Union on corporate governance related items and from the finance industry.

Overview of the Act on Appropriateness of Executive Compensation

VorstAG sets out rules for determining the compensation of management board/executive directors and additional standards regarding incentives for sustainable (value) management at corporations listed on a stock exchange. Overall, the law was intended to correct undesirable developments; board management compensation should be internally consistent and internally appropriate. At the same time, the responsibility of the supervisory board (non-executive directors) over the management board's compensation is emphasized and transparency to shareholders and the public is improved.

Competence for determining management board compensation

Under VorstAG, the supervisory board as plenum must determine the details of the management board's compensation. Thus, the supervisory board must decide (for each member of the management board) on the base salary, any component of variable pay, allowances, pensions, insurance premiums and any other pay component.

This entails a major change to the previous practice, in which the plenum decided only on the management board compensation policy and not on its details. Now, VorstAG assigns only a preparatory function to the compensation committee. The mandatory role of the supervisory board plenum also applies to a possible reduction of compensation under the German Stock Corporation Act. Besides, the supervisory board is personally liable for any kind of inappropriate pay.

Appropriateness of management board compensation

The supervisory board must not only ensure that compensation is appropriate in relation to the performance of the respective management board member and to the position of the company, but it must also make sure that the "customary/common" compensation is not exceeded without a particular reason. This leaves necessary flexibility to react to special circumstances as, for instance, international board members and special industries.

According to the legislative material, the supervisory board must consider the industry, size and country to determine what compensation would be customary or common (so-called horizontal comparability). According to the prevailing legal opinion, this includes a look at the German "market." International peer groups also can be chosen.

Furthermore, the compensation paid within the company must be considered (so-called vertical comparability). The supervisory board has to make sure that the compensation of the management board members remains in proportion to the compensation system within the company. This approach supports internal consistency and replaced the preliminary intention of the government to introduce a general cap or multiple for the compensation of the board relative to the staff. The vertical comparison takes into account the diversity of company size, industries and organizational structures of the German economy that cannot be reflected by general caps or multiples.

Alignment of incentives with sustainable company development — for listed companies only

The supervisory board is obliged to implement a compensation structure that supports sustainable company development. This is a reaction to the fact that listed German companies focus their pay mix on annual performance and less on longer-term performance.

However, the law does not state what sustainability means, in detail. The long-term effects of variable pay must be kept in mind.

According to the legal reasoning, a mix of short- and long-term incentives is possible if, as a result, an LTI is created.

This means that common annual royalties or annual bonuses remain permissible in conjunction with other parts of compensation applied in the mid- or long-term. Also bonus deferrals and bonus/malus-banks are supported.

Variable components are based on results for several years (a multi-year perspective).

In line with this perspective, stock options can be exercised no earlier than four years after the grant date. Although other stock vehicles are not mentioned explicitly, four years became the standard term for any LTI plan in Germany.

The GCCG also recommends that the compensation may not incentivize management board members to take unsuitable risks. With respect to variable pay, the supervisory board is to include a cap as a limitation for potential extraordinary developments.

Reduction of management board compensation in a crisis

If the company's situation deteriorates, the supervisory board is to reduce the compensation to an adequate amount. This is a soft regulation, as it encourages such reduction but does not provide for enforcement. However, it includes even pensions, although a reduction is possible only in the first three years after the management board member retired.

Liability of the supervisory board

Before VorstAG, the members of the supervisory board were already personally liable for culpable determination of unsuitably high compensation. Now, this liability is expressly emphasized.

D&O (directors and officers) liability insurance deductible

If the company takes out insurance to cover a member of the management board against risks arising from his/her professional activities, then the insurance policy must provide for a deductible of at least 10 percent of the individual damage and at least 150 percent of the fixed annual compensation of the management board member. Management board members may take out additional insurance that covers the deductible, as long as the company does not pay the premium for it. In addition, the GCGC recommends including a corresponding deductible for the D&O insurance of supervisory board members.

Say-on-pay: voluntary vote on the compensation system at the annual shareholders' meeting

In listed companies, shareholders may vote on the approval of the compensation system for the management board at the annual meeting of shareholders. However, the resolution is non-binding.

Extended disclosure rules

The existing disclosure rules regarding management board members' compensation (policy and individual disclosure) in the annual financial statements and group accounts were amplified by VorstAG, especially for benefits accruing after the termination of employment (e.g., pensions and severance payments).

The German Corporate Governance Commission

The GCGC presents essential statutory regulations for the management and supervision (governance) of German listed companies and contains recommendations for good and responsible governance.

While companies may deviate from these practices and features, they then are obliged to disclose this annually and to justify the deviations ("comply or explain").

The main changes from prior practice were:

- Recommending a cap on both the total amount of individual compensation and its separate components, which is determined by each company (thereby strengthening internal appropriateness).
- Calling for a consideration by the supervisory board of the relationship between how it pays the management board, senior management and total staff, as well as monitoring how it develops over time.
- Improving disclosure on pay policy and pay actually realized, using standardized tables (taking effect for fiscal years starting in 2014).

Some subsequent refinements were made to clarify which information concerning remuneration in the tables was recommended, and how this is to be understood and presented. The GCGC in the future will focus less on developing new recommendations and suggestions, and instead will seek to analyze and comment on new third-party regulatory initiatives.

As recent developments show that many regulatory initiatives are defined on a European level, the GCGC will not have a direct influence on those items. In the future, the GCGC aims to counteract negative or excessive regulatory developments in corporate governance which lead to negative consequences for the GCGC.

Key Effects on Current Practices

Concerning management board compensation, we see four areas of major importance:

- **Process:** The general approval of the policy and of the individual compensation of the management board by the supervisory (plenum) is enforced by the personal liability of each supervisory board member. This raises their awareness on management board compensation. In fact, compensation-related items appear on many meeting agendas. The say-on-pay for listed companies also supports this: a negative vote at the shareholders' meeting may harm company and personal reputations.

- **Change in variable pay mix:** In listed companies the variable mix has moved from an annual focus to long-term performance measurement. As a trend, non-listed companies have adopted the same procedure.

- **Benchmarking and external appropriateness:** There is increasing pressure on job pricings and pay benchmarks by focusing on adequate peer groups and on reliable, robust methodologies. In particular, peer group selection for global players is a challenging exercise. In the light of liability, documentation of ratios and assumptions to perform the benchmarks have become more

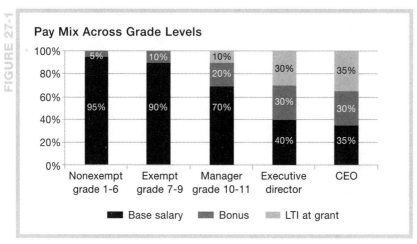

FIGURE 27-1

Pay Mix Across Grade Levels

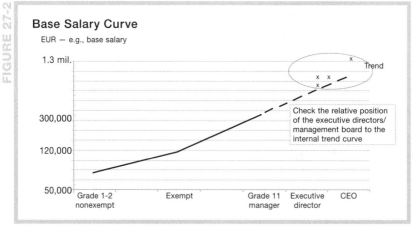

FIGURE 27-2

Base Salary Curve

important. Up to now, we have seen a trend toward establishing benchmarks rather than using external consultants. However, supervisory boards still only have a moderate understanding of robust and solid benchmarks; this especially applies to the impact of peer groups and values of variable pay. Nevertheless, we see an increasing awareness of investors and shareholders.

- **Internal consistency and internal appropriateness:** This item is less popular than others and can be difficult to handle. The employee representatives in the supervisory board have an eye on this check as they use it as an indicator for salary raises of the nonexempt and exempt, non-managerial jobs. A pragmatic approach to check the internal appropriateness can be seen in the graph below:

Questions to consider here include:

- Does the variable percentage (target and actual) rise by increasing job size?
- Does the long-term variable part rise with increasing managerial impact on results and strategy?
- If the answer is no, are there any good reasons for such a result?

- Our general experience shows that base salaries for all employees, including the board management, can be cross-checked by a linear line based on the company grading scheme.
- German companies often use very similar (or the same) plans and base their grants on their grading schemes.
- As for pensions, the service costs cannot always be presented by a continuous curve — especially when there are different pension plans for the management board. There is a room for discussion on internal appropriateness.

Summary

Executive pay is debated openly in the public and the media and has been a hot topic in Germany since the 2008–2009 financial crisis led to taxpayer bail-outs of banks and governments. It was one of the issues in the 2013 election, with Angela Merkel elected for a third term as Chancellor of Germany. She stated, "Exorbitance cannot be allowed in a free and socially minded society."

Furthermore, social inequality is back on the agenda in Germany, and, with this, executive compensation is a tempting target for attack. In that respect, the current regulations for executive board and supervisory board compensation have become rather complex. Governance rules combined with public pressure on executive compensation have led to a strict set of regulations that listed companies especially must follow.

FOREIGN INSTITUTIONAL INVESTORS IN ITALIAN LISTED COMPANIES: EXECUTIVE PAY IMPLICATIONS

By Katia Riva

According to the latest annual report of the Italian security exchange commission (Consob), investment of foreign institutional investors in Italian listed corporations increased steadily over the past years and it is now up to 18 percent of the share capital of mid- to large-cap Italian corporations. Investment in such companies of domestic institutional investors remains stable at about 1 percent.

Despite the so-called "Italian country risk," investments from abroad into the Italian economy continue to grow thanks to, among other factors:

- The evolution of several family-owned businesses (many of which have strong global brands) into international corporations that opened up their capital to fund further growth;
- The slow but constant privatization process of state-owned companies; and
- The ongoing improvement of corporate governance rules.

The years when in Italy "shares had to be weighed, not counted," meaning that a limited number of stakeholders with key political and networking influence could drive all core decisions in the business environment, are now definitely gone.

The growing presence of foreign institutional investors and their activism in shareholders' meetings has inevitably brought several changes in the way the top management of Italian listed corporations is paid and resulted in a progressive alignment of domestic pay practices to those of other Western European countries. In particular, the weight of variable compensation increased, the balance between short- and longer-term compensation improved, the use of equity-based compensation grew materially, and disclosure on pay improved significantly.

IPOs Attracting Foreign Investors

The market is experiencing a positive trend of IPOs with an increase in the number and value on the Italian stock exchange since 2013. In 2014 there were 26 new offerings for a total value of 470 billion € (7.3 percent higher than in 2013), and there is a robust pipeline of IPOs planned for 2015 and 2016, among which the privatization of the Italian postal service that is expected to be the largest IPO of the past 15 years. Due to the volatility of financial markets, Italy is experiencing a "stop & go" dynamic of IPOs with some companies giving up or postponing the listing at the very last minute if the market outlook is not reassuring.

Many of the recent IPOs originated from privatization of state-owned assets while in several other cases the IPO was the exit strategy for private equity investors. In both cases, the target buyers were mainly foreign institutional investors.

Implications on Executive Pay Structure and Governance

Going public has significant implications for any company, including on the people side.

- **Leadership Team:** Quality and credibility of the top management is an important decision-making factor for investors. Companies undertaking an IPO strive to have in place a strong management team with strategic and international vision, replacing often a "local" or even family management culture.

■ **Governance:** A listed company must ensure a high level of transparency and independence in representing the interests of all shareholders. Its governance system needs to mirror international best practices. Independent board members play a role of growing importance in listed companies as they impact several topics — executive remuneration being one on the top of the list.

■ **Transition:** Getting ready to be a public company requires a change process of the organization involving some degree of risk and uncertainty: communication and education at all levels in the organization is critical.

■ **Compensation:** Executive pay needs to align to new metrics such as shareholder's value creation, short- and longer-term performance need to be balanced in the pay package, link between result and pay has to be crystal clear, and disclosure on pay — a sensitive cultural topic in Italy — has to increase.

Privatization of State-Owned Companies

IPOs are seen by the Italian government as good way to accomplish the privatization of state-owned assets while keeping the control or a majority stake of such companies.

Structuring the remuneration package of the executive team and the governance of remuneration systems is typically a hot topic because the reward strategy of state-owned companies is usually completely different from what market and investors would like to see.

In order to be "market proof," these companies must perform a profound rethinking of their approach to compensation, including:

■ Set up of a pay governance framework ensuring that interests of all stakeholders are represented, decisions are taken in a sound and transparent way and disclosure is appropriate.

■ Shift from an inward-looking reward approach (focus on fairness) to a market-based reward approach (focus on competitiveness).

■ Higher focus on connecting rewards to results and balance between short-term results and longer-term sustainability of such results, also in light of the company's risk profile — all with the paramount goal of creating value for shareholders. This is a challenging topic as the executive pay package is often made up largely by fixed compensation.

■ Definition of formal rules and policies such as shareholding policies, clawback and malus provisions, non-compete agreements and severance provisions. Such policies often aren't clearly defined by state-owned companies prior to an IPO, but have high relevance for investors and therefore need to be addressed.

■ Redesign of short-term incentives — the market requires executives to be paid on the basis of the results they bring to the organization and companies are often lacking a STI system with straightforward connections between bonus opportunity and clear KPIs deriving from the business strategy and goals. During the IPO process, Italian state-owned companies have to put a strong effort in strategy decoding and target setting process to define the company balance scorecard and to assign goals ensuring business sustainability.

■ Use of equity compensation: state-owned companies typically do not have in place LTI programs and the concept of paying a portion of executive's compensation in equity is brand new to them. Executives are often adverse to the idea of being paid in shares as they see they have a limited impact on share price performance.

Transitioning From Private Equity Investors to Institutional Investors

The IPO has been adopted as an "exit strategy" by a number of private equity and venture capitalists wishing to exit investments in their portfolio.

PE and venture capital tend to use a fairly different approach to pay compared to publicly traded firms. The main principles guiding PE investors are:

■ Alignment of top management rewards with the return targets of the PE fund (time horizon of 3–5 years; focus on cash-on-cash return of investment, management investment required).

■ Focus on the top team only (CEO and few senior executive are eligible for incentives).

The company: fashion retail company, which designs, produces and distributes clothing and accessories for men, women and children. The company completed successfully a turnaround and it seeks further profitable growth through and aggressive program of new store opening across the country.

Equity story for investors: to fund its next growth cycle, the company needs to raise capital. Track record of positive results is appealing for investors despite the difficulties that the industry sector is experience (the company out-performed systematically its direct competitors).

Reward challenges: need for a remuneration framework that aligns interests of key stakeholders: management, current PE investor, future investors.

Changes made to the remuneration approach pre-IPO:

> Set-up of an overall compensation policy for the organization addressing key elements of total rewards.

> Implemented new "market-like" LTI program transitioning from a co-investment to a stock option program.

■ Highly leveraged LTI plans paying out upon exit and use of unconventional financial instruments such as warrants.

Transitioning from the highly-leveraged reward approach of private equity/venture capital (PE/VP) firms to a more "market like" approach proved to be challenging, especially as it raises:

■ The need to comply with corporate governance rules, where decisions are taken on the basis of the interests of many stakeholders and guidelines, are stringent.

■ The concept of creating value for all shareholders — including minority shareholders and longer-term investors who have a different view as compared to PE/VP investors on executive compensation (less risk appetite, longer-term business sustainability, more ongoing reward programs versus one-time big bonuses, more policies and rules rather than individually tailor-made pay packages).

■ The need to onboard the broader management group — often PE/VP investors focus rewards on a few top people. With the IPO the company needs to think about rewarding all roles with impact on successfully becoming a public company and delivering results in a continued and sustainable way.

Evolution of Pay Governance With a Growing Share Ownership From Foreign Institutional Investors

Many of the largest Italian corporations were state-owned, and in several cases the state continues to own a material minority stake even after privatization. The compensation culture in Italian state-owned or controlled companies is hardly comparable with the one in the private sector.

State-owned companies are generally not required to make profits, but to manage services at the best within a budget much more dependent on political decisions than business factors. Key elements like cost structure, investments and pricing, just to name a few, are usually at least partially beyond the power of management. Compensation packages of top management are under public scrutiny and, as the performance of many of those companies looks unimpressive to the average citizen, a strong pressure to contain remuneration exists. The entrance of new investors, often foreign, into their capital requires a modernization of the compensation culture, which has to be aligned to the new stakeholders' needs, and to be compliant with the regulatory framework.

A similar situation is found in privately owned company that went public and, although starting from a much more "market-like" approach to executive remuneration, was required to quickly understand and meet new investor's expectations. The opening of the capital of state-owned and private companies to foreign investors is fostering a quick evolution of executive compensation systems.

A shift from a bureaucratic approach to a businesslike one is unavoidable by the same rules of the "discipline code of listed companies." The adoption of variable pay arrangements, of equity compensation instead than cash, of a long-term approach to sustainable and measurable business targets are becoming the norm.

The presence of independent board members on compensation committees is facilitating the change process especially as it concerns the soundness of the decision-making process about pay, including avoiding conflict of interests.

As pressure on disclosure on pay levels and structure of reward programs is becoming more and more stringent, opaque practices around topics such as severance (too often extremely generous termination packages even in case of evident business failure) are now not acceptable anymore. For example, discretionary and performance unrelated payments are disappearing, clawback and malus provisions are becoming more and more common, and termination packages are defined ex ante and generally reduced in value as compared to the past.

The need to tie reward to sustainable value creation is generating a broader use of market measures such as total shareholder return along with internal budget-based measures such as EBITDA that continues to be widely used. Along the same lines, the use of equity based compensation for executive grown materially.

EXECUTIVE COMPENSATION IN MEXICO

By Enrique Perez

While executive compensation practices have existed in Mexico for more than 30 years, it was not until the last decade that some local companies began to view executive pay design as part of their general strategies. Previously, compensation practices were implemented more as a way to differentiate executives from the rest of a company's employees, with benefits like company cars and medical check-ups. Linking the executives' remuneration with the business strategy was not part of the program.

This situation arose for several reasons; one, of course, is the small number of publicly traded companies compared to private ones in Mexico. Many of the largest Mexican companies previously were part of a family conglomerate. The purpose of the executive compensation plans was largely hygienic, such as status or working conditions. Nevertheless, some of the components of the executive package were based on international market trends like STIs, although the link with performance did not appear until the late 1990s.

Finally, with few exceptions, private or family-owned business in Mexico are not willing to dilute their capital. The number of organizations that become public or at least listed on the Mexican Stock Exchange in a year, on average, typically fluctuates between five and eight. In that regard, while those companies could eventually implement some type of long-term compensation plans, they tend to be discretionary.

Market for Executive Talent

Looking at the market in Mexico, a fight for executive talent between family-owned companies and multinational firms has not occurred often. It was not until the past few years that an executive would make a career move from a multinational, publicly traded company to a family-owned business (or the other way around).

As a consequence, executive compensation strategies in Mexico have developed slowly. Most changes have been in reaction to the executive compensation practices of the multinational companies that either established operations in Mexico or recently made STI and LTI awards in their subsidiaries. To the extent that global corporate governance standards have been implemented in Mexico, it generally has been because local companies tend to align their governance practices with the global firms. The growth of executive pay arrangements in Mexico also has resulted from decisions of some of the largest Mexican companies that became regional or global and are now competing at that level.

Short-Term vs. Long-Term Compensation Perspectives

Although business plans have been put in place practically in all major Mexican companies, the relationship with long-term variable compensation of executives is much less common in comparison to global market practices. According to our research, between 25 and 30 percent of the Mexican market has an LTI plan, while STIs are part of the compensation package in more than 90 percent of organizations.

That said, it is also important to understand that the use of STIs linked to performance is a common practice in Mexico. The use of STIs has grown over the last decade as shown in Table 27-8.

TABLE 27-8

STI Prevalence

Year	STI Prevalence
2005	74%
2006	78%
2008	77%
2010	90%
2011	90%
2012	95%
2013	92%
2014	95%

Besides an STI, the compensation package for an executive in Mexico is affected by several small pieces that are provided regularly. Table 27-9 shows what a typical compensation package includes. As Table 27-9 shows, Mexico is different from many other countries in that an executive receives more than three months of salary in guaranteed, short-term cash compensation. With this practice, combined with years of high inflation rates in Mexico, the mindset of many executives is focused on the short-term. As part of the same trend, the vehicle preferred by both companies and executives is the STI.

In addition to cash plans, the benefit that is considered key in competing for talent is a company car. While the benefit is provided by practically all Mexican companies, the type of car and the associated benefits (such as frequency of replacement) play an important role in retaining executives.

Long-Term Incentive Plans

About 15 years ago, large, publicly traded Mexican companies started using LTI vehicles such as stock grants and stock options mainly for employee retention purposes. Also, local operations of multinational companies typically offer stock options. A common practice involves granting LTIs to the CEO and the next one or two levels of the organization.

TABLE 27-9

Typical One-Year Compensation Package

Item	Description	Percentage of salary (rounded)
Christmas bonus	One additional month of salary	8.33%
Vacation bonus	An extra payment for vacation days paid at 75% or 100% of salary	5.5%
Saving fund	13% of the annual salary (capped up to 10 times minimum salary)	5.0%
Food coupons	10% of annual salary (capped to 1 year of minimum salary)	4.5 %
Mandatory profit sharing	10% of the profits are shared to the employees capped by a maximum blue collar salary CEO is not considered	5.0%
Total		**28.33**

While companies currently use LTI to retain employees, the focus on LTI as a way to drive performance is rapidly growing. In order to compete against multinational firms, an increasing number of companies are implementing LTIs as a reward vehicle to be more competitive in the talent market. The characteristics of the plans include:

- LTI plans typically are designed on a three-year basis and provide an opportunity to exercise stock options upon the second year anniversary of the grant. In several cases, the options then are 100 percent exercisable.
- Besides stock options, common vehicles include restricted stock and cash.
- At almost all of the companies, only one type of award is used. A few more sophisticated plans might include two or more vehicles in the same plan and the introduction of stock ownership guidelines.
- Companies typically prefer to use awards that are simple to implement, communicate and administer.

- Going forward, the use of non-stock based awards likely will grow, since the Mexican exchange market is not likely to expand significantly.
- Privately owned, fast-growing, small and medium-sized family-owned businesses seeking institutionalization are introducing aggressive LTI plans to attract and retain executives. The LTIs are mainly at large multinational firms with a strong performance drive in the design and using cash-based vehicles.

TOP EXECUTIVE PAY IN THE NETHERLANDS

By Eric Engesaeth

Focusing on top executive pay, this section discusses two perspectives regarding current thinking prevailing in the Netherlands: how to restore legitimacy in executive remuneration; and 10 executive remuneration trends in the Netherlands.

How to Restore Legitimacy in Executive Remuneration

In the Netherlands, executive pay has long been a subject of heated debate. Dutch stakeholders are more and more questioning of whether non-executive directors are able to ensure appropriate remuneration policies and outcomes that are considered as "legitimate" by society.

We conducted interviews with 60 of the most influential business leaders, non-executive directors, professors and media heads. These showed that there indeed is a perceived legitimacy issue regarding top executive pay. Although all companies need support from society, for some this is more crucial than for others (e.g., utilities, retail banking, consumer-oriented businesses). In this section, we discuss some possible ways to enhance the legitimacy of executive rewards.

We define legitimacy as the perception or assumption that the actions of an organization are considered socially desirable or appropriate within the social construct of norms, values, beliefs and definitions. Companies in the Netherlands are increasingly pressured to conform to what is considered to be appropriate and desirable by Dutch society. Organizations search for legitimacy for the sake of credibility, reputation and continuity. Basically, legitimacy ensures that investors are likely to invest, customers want to buy products and employees are willing to invest human capital.

In this regard, there is a force toward uniformity. Companies often prefer to have similar policies as a means to ensure legitimacy. However, these similarities could be disturbed by fundamental technological changes, environmental issues or a financial crisis. When one of these events occurs, the level of legitimacy could decrease and both internal and external stakeholders may reevaluate their investments. Companies then may try to find ways to restore legitimacy.

Our interviewees confirmed the existence of legitimacy problems concerning the remuneration of top executives and five topics were discussed in light of obtaining legitimacy: remuneration level; remuneration design — simplification; performance measurement — sustainability; incentive strength — risk assessment; and communication.

Remuneration Level

Given that a uniform relationship between supply and demand in the market for top executives is not present and that significant deviations exist compared to the competitive market model, a substantially identical way of setting pay levels is not attainable.

Over the past few decades, executive pay in the Netherlands has increased more rapidly than wages under the Dutch collective labor agreements (CLA). This widened the gap between the top and the bottom of the organization, which sometimes puts pressure on internal legitimacy. Also, we have observed a wider gap within the top of the organization than before. In Western Europe, the difference between the CEO and direct reports to the executive board has increased by 65 percent in the decade since the financial crisis.

Discussions are currently focused on the sustainability of this development and whether there should be smaller differences at the top of the organization in order to emphasize that leading a large corporation is a team effort. Furthermore, there is pressure from governance bodies (e.g., the Dutch Corporate Governance Code) to determine internal relativities for different layers in the organization and to see top executive rewards as the result of the internal pay pyramid. Changes in top executive base salaries, in years in which there is no formal policy review, are more and more tied to the CLA increases within the organization or important society indicators, such as a rise in minimum wages.

Remuneration Design — Simplification

In terms of remuneration design, our interviewees expressed a resistance against the complexity of executive remuneration programs and a desire to create more simplified structures for rewards. Being able to easily understand executive pay programs is actually one of the catalysts of legitimacy. Simplicity can be created by eliminating or combining some of the reward elements. In the Netherlands, this is particularly the case for pension arrangements. As a result of changes in tax regulations which have restricted tax efficient build-up of retirement savings, pension schemes have become relatively simple and easy to understand.

Another driver of legitimacy is the introduction of "stock ownership guidelines." These guidelines are a trend among large corporations headquartered in the Netherlands. The CEO is asked to build up typically between 200 and 400 percent of his/her base salary (note the typical LTI level is around 100 percent of base salary). The interviewees believe that when executives purchase some shares from personal funds, this would likely increase the legitimacy to society, as a result of sharing both "pain and pleasure" of company performance.

Performance Measurement — Sustainability

More emphasis on sustainable performance measurement has been mentioned as one of the drivers to restore legitimacy. This can involve broadening the way performance is measured and giving sustainability a central place. From a social perspective, driving shareholder value as the core of the corporate strategy has been scrutinized. This is particularly the case for companies with an important social role such as retail banks. Businesses in other sectors are increasingly expected to contribute to society as well. In this case, it is important to reward top executives for actions that increase "sustainable legitimacy."

Currently, approximately 85 percent of the largest listed financial and non-financial companies in the Netherlands include sustainability-related performance measures in their STI reward program with a typical weight of 25–40 percent. Examples are health and safety, employee engagement, customer satisfaction, reputation, and green criteria such as reduction of greenhouse gas emissions. Sustainability can also be defined as investing in new technology. Regarding LTIs, sustainability measures are observed in approximately half of these companies, typically at the expense of (relative) TSR.

Incentive Strength — Risk Assessment

The increasing relevance of legitimacy emphasizes the dark side of variable remuneration, which in the past could consist of very strong and asymmetric incentives, sometimes associated with lying, cooking the books and fraud. Accordingly, the movement has been to focus more and more attention on the measurement of incentive strength. This is partly related to the size of the incentive but more importantly related to the design. Overly risky packages with "big wins" and "big losses" may drive the behavior of betting with corporate assets and generally would not be considered legitimate within the context of public companies. As such, these companies may feel pressure from stakeholders to rebalance as a means of avoiding unwanted volatility and unsustainable results.

Communication

In order to avoid losing legitimacy, companies have two basic choices regarding communication about executive rewards. The first one is to rationalize and substantiate the remuneration package and provide a clear explanation of the components and their rationale; the second route involves camouflage and symbolism. If pay is difficult to explain, the second route is possible. After all, if stakeholders would not notice the potentially outrageous remuneration, there is no current problem. Although the rational for both strategies can be strong, today's level of required transparency makes the first the long-term winner. Transparency (including explanations of programs and their rationales) coupled with clear communication can contribute to legitimacy by increasing the trust of stakeholders and society in the corporate governance of the company.

10 Executive Remuneration Trends in the Netherlands

After the start of the most recent financial crisis, remuneration policies were redesigned in the Dutch financial sector. The first new policies were developed in 2009 and tabled at the annual general meeting in 2010, primarily based on industry reforms. Following European rules and regulations, remuneration policies were further fine-tuned in 2010 and tabled at the annual meeting in 2011.

Apart from mandatory deferrals and partial payment in company instruments (such as shares or convertible instruments), an important feature was a maximum variable compensation of 100 percent of base salary (with the possibility of 200 percent if adopted by shareholders). The largest Dutch-headquartered financial companies reduced their variable pay from typically 200 percent at the target level and between 300–400 percent at the maximum level (combination of STIs and LTIs) to 100 percent. The Dutch government further restricted maximum variable compensation to 20 percent and companies adopted this for the top of the organization from 2015 onward. This resulted in increases in fixed compensation, typically in the range of 20–30 percent. Apart from the more traditional financial metrics, companies also are required to measure half of performance in terms of non-financial metrics such as customer satisfaction and reputation.

After the reforms in the financial sector, other companies now are expecting some form of spill-over of the new remuneration policies and practices that were adopted in financial organizations.

In this regard, we see 10 trends in the upcoming years. These trends are being discussed in the remuneration committee of most major corporations.

1. Increased robustness of external benchmarking: two reference groups (instead of one) with a higher minimum number of companies. Robustness is increased by using two reference groups instead of one for benchmarking purposes. The first group typically contains (international) sector-specific peer companies that are related to the particular scope or activities of the company. The second group consists of cross-industry companies, like Dutch-headquartered multinationals, based on comparability in the listing environment.

2. Taking into account internal pay differentials. Questions to answer are to what extent pay at the top of the organization follows logically from the broader remuneration construct, to what extent pay differentials within the top of the organization are taken into account, and what should be disclosed in terms of internal pay differentials.

3. Increasing level of transparency and disclosure. There is increasing (external) pressure (e.g., from Institutional Shareholder Services and various investors) on disclosure of process, approach, benchmark results and so on.

4. "Special bonuses" are heavily scrutinized. "Sign-on bonuses" (especially bonuses rewarded in cash or shares without performance conditions) and "deal bonuses" (mostly associated with mergers and acquisitions, split, etc.) face heavy scrutiny by stakeholders and the general public.

5. Increased focus on the longer-term. Companies are increasingly focusing on rewards for longer-term sustainable performance. Especially at the board of management level, this is combined with decreased focus on the STI (annual bonus). Best practice shows a shift from the typical ratio in the past between short-term and longer-term incentives from 50–50 to 40–60.

6. In some cases, increasing pressure to decrease total variable incentives (e.g., to 100 percent of fixed pay).

7. Focus on share ownership: incentives increasingly paid in shares. Examples of incentives being paid in shares are STIs partly paid out in shares, investment of net bonus proceeds in company shares, possibly combined with a share match, the use of shares only for LTIs (no options) and the use of share ownership guidelines.

8. Introduction of risk in performance measurement (e.g., risk adjusted measures).

9. Increased focus on leading non-financial indicators. Instead of using financial performance measures only, non-financial measures are becoming more prevalent (e.g., a business health test).

10. Increasing fee distance between chairman and member supervisory board. Within the Dutch two-tier board system, the non-executive chairman is typically rewarded at 1.5 times the fee level of the non-executive member. This fee is shifting toward 1.6–1.7 (the Dutch law even implies a factor of 2 given the fact that a member counts for 1 point and a chairman role for 2 points within a maximum number of 5 points). In addition, attendance fees for extraordinary meetings (outside the annual agenda) are increasingly observed.

REVIEW OF SINGAPORE TOP EXECUTIVE REMUNERATION

By Pamela Shee

The challenges that remuneration committees are facing in Singapore today remain heavily focused on top executives' pay levels and the design of the incentives. Companies now must demonstrate how the compensation plans align with financial performance and share price to support all business objectives that create shareholder value. Discussed below are key findings from Hay Group's 2015 Singapore Top Executive Remuneration Report.

Level and Mix of Remuneration

The first question to consider is how much a company should pay for its top executives. In 2014, the median total remuneration for the CEO in a listed company was S$1,101,000 per annum. A further breakdown analysis by company size shows that the median total remuneration for the most senior executives in large-sized companies was S$3.88 million per annum, followed by S$1.63 million in medium-sized companies, and S$713,000 in small-sized companies.

Meanwhile, executive directors (excluding the most senior executive) took home a median total remuneration of S$375,000 per annum. In large-sized companies, the figure was S$ 2.89 million, followed by S$742,000 and S$375,000 in medium- and small-sized companies respectively.

Other functional key executives in Singapore listed companies, including COOs, CEOs of subsidiary companies, top finance executives, top HR executives, top marketing executives, etc., on average had a median total remuneration package of S$250,000 per annum. The key executives earned S$905,000 per annum in large-sized companies, S$375,000 in medium-sized companies and S$250,000 in small-sized companies.

Total Median Remuneration of Top Executives by Company Size

A closer examination of the data in the report reveals that the highest paid key functional executives in the listed companies are the deputy CEOs or COOs. The median total remuneration for these

TABLE 27-10

Composition of Executive Pay in Singapore

	Fixed Pay	STI	LTI
CEO - ASX300	58%	22%	20%
CEO – ASX100	46%	27%	27%
KMPs - ASX300	67%	16%	17%
KMPs – ASX100	58%	19%	23%

key executives was S$613,000 per annum, followed by S$375,000 for CEOs of subsidiary companies, top finance executive and divisional/regional operation head. Comparatively, the median total remuneration for technology/design/product development executives, HR/administrative executives and marketing/sales/business development executives is lower, ranging from S$250,000–325,000.

In large-sized companies, the median total remuneration for the second most senior executive is around S$1.88 million per annum. The total remuneration for other functional top executives is typically within the range of S$625,000 to S$1.54 million. Among medium-sized companies, the median total remuneration for other functional top executives is typically within the range of S$375,000–875,000. For small-sized companies, the median total remuneration for the second most senior executive is S$399,000.

The total remuneration for other functional top executives is typically within the range of S$250,000 to $375,000.

Internal Equity

Another key consideration for remuneration committees and top HR executives in recommending executive compensation is internal equity. The data show that, in general market practice, the executive chairman or CEO in a listed company is paid approximately three times the remuneration of the executive directors, and four to five times the remuneration of other key executives. In addition, the market practice shows that about 66 percent of executive chairmen or CEOs' total remuneration account for 0 to less than 10 percent of their companies' net profit and 21 percent of the companies spent 10 percent or more of the net profit on the remuneration of executive chairmen or CEOs and 13 percent of the companies have negative net profit.

Further, as executives gain seniority in a company, the balance of the mix between the fixed components (base salary and allowances) and the variable components (variable bonus, share-based compensation) moves to a higher proportion of variable components, as opposed to fixed components.

TABLE 27-11

Three-Year Pay-for-Performance Ratio

2-Year Average Ratio	Illustrative Description	% Of Companies	3 yr TSR (%) Median
<0.6	Significantly lower bonus for higher profitability	3%	-19.0
0.6 - <0.9	Lower bonus for higher profitability	19%	34.3
0.9 - 1.1	Similar bonus for similar profitability	40%	43.3
>1.1 - 2.0	Higher bonus for higher profitability	26%	30.4
>2.0	Significantly higher bonus for lower profitability	13%	-9.7

Note: TSR data is extracted from Bloomberg. Analysis is based on the companies that have three years data. Exclude those that have missing data and those with negative profit in one the three years.

Our pay mix analysis reveals a general consistent pattern. In companies that did not reward their key executives with LTIs, 38 percent of the total remuneration of executive chairmen or CEOs is attributed to variable bonus, whereas 24 percent of the total remuneration of other key executives is attributed to variable components. In companies that rewarded their key executives with LTIs, 61 percent of the total remuneration of the executive chairmen or CEOs is attributed to variable component, with 39 percent in the form of bonus, and 22 percent in the form of share-based compensation. In comparison, 46 percent of the total remuneration of other key executives is variable, with 29 percent of bonus and 17 percent of LTIs.

Low Utilization of LTIs

According to the report, 57 percent of the sample companies established some form of LTI schemes. Share options comprise the most popular scheme (used by 42 percent of the companies) while 35 percent of the companies have either a restricted share plan or performance share plan. In contrast to the high prevalence rate, only 23 percent of the companies utilized their schemes to award their executives with LTIs in 2014, with 11 percent of the companies awarding share options and 14 percent awarding shares.

LTIs are most popular in large-sized companies, with 73 percent of them awarding their key executives with LTIs in 2014. 20 percent of the medium-sized companies awarded their key executives with the scheme. Less than 15 percent of the small-sized companies used LTIs to award their key executives.

Pay for Performance in Singapore

A new guideline was introduced in the revised Code of Corporate Governance to stress "the link between remuneration paid to the executive directors and key management personnel and performance." Remuneration committees are expected to articulate the performance conditions of both the short-term and long-term incentive schemes, explaining why they are chosen and if they are met.

The practices in choosing performance conditions in Singapore vary from company to company but the common themes are: (1) profitability metrics are the most common measures; and (2) multiple measures are commonly used, including strategic objectives, non-financial metrics (e.g., customer satisfaction, employee engagement, etc.).

An analysis of the TSR — share price appreciation plus dividend payout — of the sample companies showed that companies that have better pay-for-performance alignment tend to have higher TSR, with 40 percent of companies having similar CEO bonuses for similar company profitability (achieving a three-year TSR of 43.3 percent).

In addition, 13 percent of the sample companies had significantly higher CEO bonuses for lower company profitability, indicating a significant misalignment between CEO bonus payout and company profitability. These companies achieved a three-year TSR of -9.7 percent.

There are ongoing debates on whether better pay for performance translates to better shareholder returns. While our analysis shows that companies with a better pay for performance alignment have higher TSR historically, it will be interesting to observe if the pattern continues in the longer term.

Looking Ahead

Listed companies in Singapore now are required to "fully disclose the remuneration of each individual director and the CEO on a named basis," instead of "bands of S$250,000." In addition, the companies must disclose, in aggregate, the total remuneration paid to the top five key executives.

Following more transparent disclosure, we expect increased scrutiny on executive compensation from shareholders, regulators and the media in Singapore. Remuneration committees need to understand that the corporate governance paradigm has dramatically changed after the global financial crisis, and this is not just a Western phenomenon.

MANAGING THE FINANCIAL RISKS OF EXECUTIVE PAY: THE UK'S APPROACH

By Simon Garrett

Since 2008 the world's banking sector and its regulators have wrestled with the consequences of the global financial crisis and its causes. The consensus view is that many banks got their priorities badly wrong by focusing too much on annual profit maximization and not enough on effective risk management and good customer service.

Excessive bankers' bonuses in particular were held to be a significant negative influence on how these priorities developed and how they were communicated. Indeed, so the argument goes, banks' compensation arrangements meant that too high a proportion of profit was taken by employees (including senior executives) and not enough flowed through to shareholders or to provide better deals for customers. Shareholders tolerated this imbalance before 2008 when profits and shareholder returns were good, but not anymore.

Management of Risk Posed by Executive Pay

For their part, regulators around the world responded by adopting rules designed to:

- Manage systemic risk to avoid, where possible (or, if not, quarantine), major banking failures and mitigate the resulting need for taxpayer-funded rescues in future; and
- Rebalance the priorities communicated by banking processes, pay structures and their cultures generally to place more emphasis on the interests of customers, shareholders and other stakeholders and less on those of the banks' employees and its senior executives.

In Europe as a whole, efforts on this front have evolved as a body of regulation governing banking and other similar institutions. These regulations have been issued as a series of pan-European directives called the Capital Requirements Directives (CRDs).

Pan-European Regulation

In the UK the Financial Services Authority (FSA) and its successors, the Prudential Regulation Authority (PRA) and Financial Conduct Authority (FCA), have introduced UK-specific regulations to comply with these CRDs. These include an evolving framework governing the compensation of firms' senior executives. Initially this framework was principles-based, but, as tougher directives were introduced by the European Banking Authority (EBA) — encouraged by the European Parliament — they have become much more prescriptive and the framework is now effectively rules-based.

CRD III

In 2009 CRD III (enacted in the UK by regulations introduced by the then FSA) introduced the requirement for banks and other similar institutions to defer high proportions of variable executive compensation for at least three years and for at least half of such compensation to be paid in the bank's stock or some equivalent form. The main objectives were two-fold:

- To reduce the focus on short-term performance and place more emphasis on longer-term outcomes; and

- To create much stronger alignment between the senior executives and their bank's shareholders through the medium of longer-term stock ownership.

In addition, the regulator required that the performance conditions attached to such variable compensation should specifically take risk into account.

These requirements were complex and operated at different levels depending on the individual's role, his/her overall compensation, how much of it was variable, etc. Broadly speaking, however, the most senior executives were required to defer at least 60 percent of any variable compensation and less senior executives at least 40 percent. In both cases an obligation applied to pay at least half in stock or some equivalent form at each payment point.

At the same time the regulator introduced the requirement for banks to implement clawbacks. This meant that deferred compensation could be substantially reduced if certain negative factors later came to light, even if the performance conditions governing the amount payable had originally been satisfied.

All of these regulations were subject to the principle of "proportionality" so larger firms had to operate the requirements in full whereas smaller ones typically escaped the worst of their complexity. Subject to the application of this proportionality principle, however, all banks or equivalent institutions operating in the UK were required to comply with these rules, regardless of the ultimate parent organization's location — an important factor for overseas banks operating through a branch or subsidiary in London, for example.

The Impact of CRD III

Fortunately for some banks, their existing pay structures could be modified to comply with CRD III, rather than requiring a complete redesign (e.g., annual bonuses and LTI plans could sometimes be viewed together, with the LTI plan forming the deferred element of variable compensation). In such cases, top executive compensation was not radically changed by the new regulations — perhaps just the balance between the variable compensation elements, the proportion delivered in stock, the performance conditions used and the adoption of a clawback provision would need to be revised.

That said, however, many banks had to adopt extensive new internal governance structures and processes. In addition, the FSA imposed a new system of annual monitoring and bonus payment approval to ensure compliance. Although the outcome in terms of compensation design may not have looked radically different, many firms still found the road a hard one. Their experience was made worse by the fact that the FSA had to develop a knowledge of compensation arrangements from scratch at the same time as it was developing the new regulations — it had next-to-no prior experience in regulating compensation to draw upon.

Some banks did take the initiative and sought to drive a change in their culture and amended their executive compensation arrangements to suit their particular businesses: for example, reducing package risk to reflect lower levels of desired business risk or extending deferral periods to emphasise the importance of long-term performance. In any event, other elements of the regulations imposed from London and Brussels meant that many pre-2008 banking practices had to change. Not least of these was the impact of the extended bank capital requirements and the desire by regulators to protect retail banking from the risks of so-called "casino" or investment banking. Executive compensation at banks therefore tended to change to match these lower-risk business models.

CRD IV

In 2013 CRD III was followed by CRD IV (implemented in the UK by both the PRA and the FCA and effective from the start of 2014). Its main provision on executive compensation was disarmingly simple but caused a radical shift in compensation practices at banks and other similar institutions. In some respects, CRD IV undid much of the work that banks in conjunction with the FSA and its successors (the PRA and FCA) did in connection with CRD III.

The main provision, included at the insistence of the European Parliament and now adopted with enthusiasm by the EBA, was imposition of a maximum limit for variable compensation of no more than 100 percent of fixed compensation. This limit can be increased to 200 percent (but no more) if the bank's shareholders formally approve. Individual country regulators can adopt lower limits (the Netherlands has done so) but not higher ones. The UK has kept these maximum limits.

Unlike CRD III, the limits imposed by CRD IV appear to be universal — that is, they do not just apply to senior executives or only at systemically important firms, they apply to all UK employees at all UK banks and other similar institutions, regardless compensation levels or the firm's size.

The Impact of CRD IV

The UK government originally intended to challenge CRD IV's variable compensation limits in the European Court in early 2015 but withdrew its objection in late 2014 when legal advice indicated that the basis of its case was insufficiently strong. Many UK firms had hoped that such a challenge would be forthcoming and would be successful as they had adopted executive compensation structures designed to circumnavigate the new limits by observing the letter of the rules and ignoring their spirit.

The mechanisms used by affected firms took the form of non-contractual allowances (some of which were partly paid in the form of the firm's stock). These would be fixed for a period but could be changed or withdrawn altogether at the employer's sole discretion. They were nevertheless counted by these firms as part of fixed compensation for the purposes of determining how much variable would be allowed.

In discussions with the banks and other similar affected institutions, the UK's PRA and the FCA accepted that such allowances should be treated as fixed. In late 2014, however, the EBA challenged this conclusion and set out a list of parameters required in order for the EBA to agree that such allowances could avoid being treated as variable. This list included features such as the allowances being job- rather than person-related and pensionable; many of these features had specifically been avoided by the firms adopting the practice.

The consequences of the EBA's position has been that many UK banks and other similar institutions had, yet again, to change their executive compensation arrangements. They had to accept that they either substantially reduced the potential earnings of many of their key executives or increased their fixed compensation in a manner acceptable to the EBA and thereby significantly increase their fixed costs; there really was only one choice.

Impact on Long-Term Incentives

The reduction in the overall opportunity to earn variable compensation seems likely to weaken the impact of any long-term elements. Although some firms have compensated by completely abandoning annual bonuses for some senior executives, the messages delivered by increases in fixed compensation will be make any variable compensation very much secondary in importance.

It remains to be seen whether banks and other similar institutions based outside Europe take advantage of the difficulties faced by UK and other European firms or whether European firms will relocate to avoid the variable compensation limits and other regulatory burdens imposed there. HSBC was one of the major banks that publicly stated that it keeps this question under review, but, as of this publication, there has been no general exodus.

Wrapping Up

The European market is a large and sophisticated one, requiring complex banking and other financial services. Any bank operating in Europe will have to apply these rules to be able to carry on its business there, and locating its head office outside of Europe will not remove the obligation to do so. It therefore seems unlikely that many firms will actually relocate.

However, the increased fixed costs faced by European banks will put them at a competitive disadvantage to others outside Europe. Furthermore, any future economic downturn will result in senior executive lay-offs sooner in Europe than would be the case elsewhere. European firms will not be able to cut costs by cutting variable compensation to the same extent as they did in the last downturn, or as will be possible for non-European competitors using higher proportions of variable pay. The only way of significantly cutting cost will be to cut staffing. Not a comforting thought for those in the UK.

About the Editors

Irving (Irv) S. Becker is the North American Leader — Executive Pay & Governance, at Korn Ferry Hay Group. Over the course of his career, Becker has worked with boards and senior management at major public and private corporations across multiple industries to design and develop rewards programs that align executive efforts and results with the success of the company. His financial background provides him with a grounded perspective on performance measurement and management. Becker's clients have included Fortune 100 industrial companies, major financial services firms, global consumer products companies, large professional service organizations, national chain retailers, small pre-IPO companies, and large private businesses. He also has worked with companies in distressed or turnaround situations.

Prior to joining Hay Group, Becker was the National Practice Leader for Executive Compensation Consulting at a Big 4 accounting and tax firm. During his combined 10 years at this firm, over two time periods, he worked with numerous clients to assist them with developing overall reward philosophies, as well as more specific executive compensation programs.

Becker also has 10 years of in-house corporate experience heading up the compensation and benefits functions at Goldman Sachs, First USA Bank, The Home Depot and Young & Rubicam.

He is a frequent speaker on executive compensation topics, and has been quoted in numerous notable publications, including *The Wall Street Journal, The New York Times, The Financial Times, The Economist, workspan, Compensation Focus, Agenda* and *Human Resources Executive*. Some of the organizations for which he has presented include: The Conference Board, National Association of Stock Plan Professionals (NASPP), NACD Directorship Forum, Outstanding Directors Exchange (ODX), The Directors Roundtable, RiskMetrics (ISS) Governance Exchange, Society of Corporate Securities and Governance Professionals, National Foreign Trade Council (NFTC), Financial Executives International and WorldatWork.

Becker has been named to the Directorship 100 for each year from 2008 through 2015, a list published by Directorship magazine, recognizing the most influential people who are shaping agendas and corporate governance issues in boardrooms across America.

Becker received his master's of business administration in finance from Columbia Business School and has a bachelor's degree of business administration in accounting from the University of Massachusetts. He is a licensed CPA in New York State and also earned a Certified Executive Compensation Professional (CECP) designation from WorldatWork.

William (Bill) M. Gerek is the U.S. Regulatory Expertise Leader — Executive Pay & Governance, at Korn Ferry Hay Group where he assists organizations on all aspects of executive compensation, with a particular focus on tax, corporate, securities, accounting and other regulatory matters that can affect executive compensation.

Gerek helps employers and executives obtain a clear understanding of the relevant issues involved in design and implementation of executive pay programs, including base pay, annual incentives, long-term incentive programs (especially those based on or settled in equity), deferred compensation, severance and change-in-control arrangements, executive benefits and perquisites. Gerek also designs executive compensation packages, works on employment agreements, incentive plans and deferral programs, and critiques both existing and proposed executive pay arrangements. In recent years, Gerek frequently has been retained to consider and address the reasonableness of compensation of executives across various litigation perspectives, including income taxes, shareholder derivative suits, disputes among shareholders, securities law disclosures, and other instances where the reasonableness of pay is a core issue. Gerek's experience spans taxable and tax-exempt organizations, corporate and noncorporate entities, and public and private companies.

Gerek is the long-time editor and publisher of The Executive Edition, Hay Group's quarterly newsletter on executive compensation. In addition to this book and his authorship of numerous Hay Group and Korn Ferry publications and alerts, Gerek has written over two dozen articles on executive compensation, deferred compensation and benefits topics that have been published in a wide variety of professional journals and books. Gerek is active in numerous professional organizations, including the National Association of Stock Plan Professionals and bar association committees that address executive pay issues. He also is a frequent speaker at executive compensation, benefits and tax forums.

Immediately prior to joining Hay Group, Gerek was a partner in the executive compensation and employee benefits practice of the Chicago-headquartered national law firm of Ungaretti & Harris (which subsequently merged into Nixon Peabody LLP). He also was a partner for many years in the executive compensation and employee benefits department of the 600-plus lawyer international law firm now known as Katten Muchin Rosenman.

Gerek earned his Juris Doctor degree from the University of Michigan Law School after graduating magna cum laude and Phi Beta Kappa from Dartmouth College with a bachelor of arts degree in psychology. In addition, his post-graduate studies earned him a master of laws in taxation degree from the DePaul University School of Law. He also earned a Certified Executive Compensation Professional (CECP) designation from WorldatWork.